PHYLLIS PELLETIER
11 LINNELL CIRCLE
BRUNSWICK, ME. 04011

W9-AUS-168

WE ARE ALL PART OF ONE ANOTHER

"Learning from Barbara Deming—
First: She's a listener. So you can learn something about paying attention.
Second: She's stubborn. So you can learn how to stand, look into the other's face and not run.
Third: She's just. So you can learn something about patience.
Fourth: She loves us—women I mean - and speaks to the world, so you can learn how to love women and men."

—Grace Paley

"Barbara Deming's life and work have been constantly germane to my own growth and process, weaving together—as she does—the necessary elements of lesbianism, feminism, and nonviolence."

—Judith McDaniel

"Barbara Deming reminds me that 'you can't throw truths away.' She shows me that I can use each part of my messy complex identity—my anger at men who harm us; my love for my sons; my power to harm as a white person; my losses and strengths as a woman, a lesbian. She shows me that creative, imaginative change can emerge from the conflict between the truths of our real lives."

—Minnie Bruce Pratt

We Are All Part of One Another

A Barbara Deming Reader

Edited by Jane Meyerding with
a foreword by Barbara Smith

© 1984 by Barbara Deming and Jane Meyerding for their respective writing in *We Are All Part of One Another: A Barbara Deming Reader*. All rights reserved.

Inquiries regarding requests to republish all or part of *We Are All Part of One Another: A Barbara Deming Reader* should be addressed to New Society Publishers, 4722 Baltimore Ave, Philadelphia, PA 19143.

ISBN: 0-86571-037-6 Hardbound
       0-86571-038-4 Paperbound
Printed in the United States.

Cover design, book design, and layout by Nina Huizinga and Dion Lerman
Cover photograph by Diana J. Davies

This book is made possible, in part, by a grant from the A.J. Muste Memorial Institute.

New Society Publishers is a project of New Society Educational Foundation, a founding member of Coop America, and a collective of Movement for a New Society. The opinions expressed in this book do not necessarily represent agreed-upon positions of any of the organizations mentioned above.

New Society Educational Foundation is a nonprofit, tax-exempt corporation. Tax deductible contributions can be made to any of their projects. Coop America is a National Marketing Cooperative. For more information write: P.O. Box 753, New Haven, CT 06503. Movement for a New Society is a network of small groups and individuals working for fundamental social change through nonviolent action. To learn more about MNS, write: Movement for a New Society, 4722 Baltimore Avenue, Philadelphia, PA 19143.

Acknowledgements

In every aspect of my work on this book, I received tremendous help and support from Barbara Deming and from Nina Huizinga of New Society Publishers. Their suggestions and their comments on my work as it was in progress have become an integral part of the final product you hold in your hands. As the three of us had agreed from the beginning, however, the final responsibility for the choices and editing of the book's contents, and for the additional material I wrote myself, is mine alone—a responsibility I feel privileged to accept.

Others who have contributed to this work include Stanley Marcus, who copy edited the manuscript; Donna Warnock, who made several insightful comments on the manuscript of the Introduction and suggested the book's title; Betty Johanna, who gives me courage by trusting me more than I often do myself; Esther Meyerding, who made me and who patiently put up with acres of manuscript spread all over the house; Leslie Redtree and the other women of my Puget Sound Women's Peace Camp affinity group, who brought nonviolent action alive for me again during the preparation of this book; and all the members and supporters of the New Society Publishers collective. (JM)

Permissions

All of the written material by Barbara Deming included in *We Are All Part of One Another: A Barbara Deming Reader* is reprinted with the permission of the author. For the interest of the reader here are the sources for the essays included in this book. Note that Grossman Publishers is now a part of Viking Press of New York City.

"A Portrait of Ourselves" and "Success Boy" were originally published in *Running Away From Myself: A Dream Portrait of America Drawn from the Films of the '40s* (New York: Grossman, 1969).

"Death and the Old Woman" was originally published in *Wash Us and Comb Us: Stories by Barbara Deming* (New York: Grossman, 1972).

"The World of Hamlet" was originally published in *The Tulane Drama Review,* December, 1959.

"The Peacemakers," "Southern Peace Walk: Two Issues or One?," "Letter to WISP," "In the Birmingham Jail," "Notes After Birmingham," "The Temptations of Power—Report of a Visit to North Vietnam," "We Are All Part of One Another," "On Revolution and Equilibrium," "Mud City," and "On the Necessity to Liberate Minds," were originally published in *Revolution and Equilibrium* (New York: Grossman, 1971).

"Excerpts from Prison Notes" was originally chapters one, two, three and seven of *Prison Notes,* which was published as a hardback by Grossman and as a paperback by Beacon Press in 1966.

"On Anger," "Two Perspectives on Women's Struggle," and "Confronting One's Own Oppression: An Exchange of Letters" were originally published in *We Cannot Live Without Our Lives* (New York: Grossman/Viking, 1974).

"The Purpose of Sexuality: A Dialogue with Bradford Lyttle," "Love Has Been Exploited Labor," "To Fear Jane Alpert Is To Fear Ourselves," and "Remembering Who We Are" were originally published in *Remembering Who We Are* (Pagoda Publications, 1981).

"On Revolution and Equilibrium" was reprinted as a pamphlet in the A.J. Muste Memorial Institute Essay Series and is available from the A.J. Muste Institute, 339 Lafayette St., New York, NY 10012.

"Two Essays: On Anger and New Men, New Women" is available from New Society Publishers, 4722 Baltimore Avenue, Philadelphia, PA 19143 and "On Anger" is available from Frog in the Well, 430 Oakdale Road, East Palo Alto, CA 94303.

Editor's Note

In putting together a collection of this kind, spanning more than 25 years of the author's life (more than 40 years, counting the poems), it is very tempting to edit the older material according to current standards of "correct" thought. The book's very raison d'etre, however, is to show the growth, the change, the development of Barbara's thinking, and thus any attempt to edit out evidence of outmoded perspectives would be directly contradictory. As Barbara wrote about her editing (for length) of an early essay: "I've with great restraint *not* changed my generic use of the word 'man'—for that would certainly mislead the reader as to the state of my consciousness back then."

I believe we all can learn a great deal from seeing Barbara's consciousness developing over time, as that process is reflected in this book. As editor, part of my responsibility is to see that the book communicates Barbara's values clearly. The "generic male" which Barbara used in her earlier work, for example, is not something she or I recommend to readers; but the book as a whole clearly shows both how Barbara was liberated from this usage and how this grammatical liberation influenced her thinking and writing in other ways. So I can feel comfortable with reprinting essays from her "generic male" years in their original form. There were two pieces of language—two metaphors—in the essays I selected for this book with which I could not feel comfortable. If these metaphors appeared without comment, I feared they might perpetuate oppressive stereotypes held (consciously or unconsciously) by many, many people in this society.

The first of these metaphors appears in the excerpts from *Running Away From Myself,* a book Barbara finished writing in 1950: a character in a film, she wrote, "displays an almost epileptic bewilderment." Whether or not some or all people with epilepsy do occasionally feel bewildered is not the point here. My concern, which Barbara shares, is with the still-pervasive stereotyping of people as "epileptics." For some readers, the implied image of "bewildered epileptic" may reinforce assumptions about people with epilepsy as disordered, confused, nonfunctional, subnormal, crazy, etc. In other words, the description may be seen, by some readers, not as one aspect or moment of a person's life, but as an inclusive and limiting description (definition) of the whole class of people with epilepsy: an epileptic is a person who is bewildered, who typifies bewilderment.

It certainly is not Barbara's wish or intention to convey or support such an oppressive and destructive stereotype, and I deal with it here at some length because I do not want this book to support that stereotype either, by even one word.

The second metaphor Barbara and I agree should not appear unchallenged is the use of "blind" to mean ignorant, a usage which often has overtones of stupidity and inability or unwillingness to learn, to function, to be responsible. All too often, this metaphor is carried over into the daily lives of blind people in the form of antagonistic and/or paternalistic behavior (oppressive behavior) by sighted people. Several selections in this book—including Chapter 1 of *Running Away From Myself,* "The World of Hamlet," and "The Temptations of Power"—use this metaphor. Again, we chose not to alter Barbara's original language, but instead use this opportunity to educate readers who have not yet recognized the oppressive effects built into this common figure of speech.

Metaphors of sight and seeing (e.g., "We begin to dare...to trust our own eyes") can be found throughout this book. Although these metaphors could function for some readers as the flip side of the "blind" metaphor *if the latter were presented unchallenged,* I believe that the long-term goal of all well-intentioned people must be to increase our culture's range of language and metaphor so it becomes inclusive of all people's realities, and that we won't progress towards that goal by disallowing the use of the best language we have found so far. It is important to recognize, however, and to state explicitly, that these sight metaphors *are metaphors* (for, as Nina commented, "our inner sight, our understanding and intuition") and are meant to include us all.

In that spirit, it is my hope that this selection of Barbara Deming's writings will encourage many readers to explore more deeply and more concretely the philosophy, strategies, and tactics of radical feminist nonviolent action in relation to work against (hetero)sexism, racism, capitalism, ablism, and all the other blatant and insidious hierarchies which oppress us from without and within.

Foreword

December 20, 1983

The first time I saw Barbara Deming was in 1967. I was in college and she came to speak at a neighboring campus. I didn't know anything about her, but one of my best friends said that we should go and hear her because we were involved in the movement—working for civil rights and against the war in Vietnam, and in my case doing black student organizing. We valued the chance to hear somebody speak about this work—someone older, someone who had experienced much more than we had firsthand.

That night Barbara undoubtedly talked about going to jail, about nonviolence, about the escalating war, in short about her total commitment to the radical politics of those times. I cannot remember details of what she said, but I do remember having a rare feeling being in that room, because she made what we were trying to do seem essential and possible, and she gave me hope. The next day I went and bought *Prison Notes*.

This was well before the women's movement, long before I had acknowledged to myself that I was a lesbian, and before Barbara had publicly declared that she was a lesbian. Back then I was trying as much as possible to avoid the terrifying question of my sexuality, felt that it was absolutely impossible to survive being black and queer at the same time. Yet I'm sure one of the reasons why Barbara made such an impression on me was that, without a word being spoken, I sensed that she was "different" too. I never forgot her.

The second time I saw Barbara was in 1981 at the National Women's Studies Association conference on racism. Someone introduced us at a lesbian poetry reading. I was thrilled to meet this woman whose life had inspired me for so long. I thought about the years between that first and second meeting, about the political struggle that had made it possible for us finally to say everything we were out loud.

This collection of Barbara's work is essential to me for many reasons, but most significantly because it shows what it is possible to do in the name of activism and writing. Barbara's writing provides the kind of history, teaching, analysis, and poetry that can only come from actually being there. *We Are All Part of One Another* demonstrates how activism and the act of writing

xi

undeniably connect and can result, not in rhetoric or impenetrable theory, but in the clear and accessible telling of a life. What this book provides most vividly is a directly personal history of the major progressive movements of the second half of the twentieth century.* So much has been forgotten about that time—especially about the sixties, which have so shaped the time we live in now. Our conditions today are so similar to those of the sixties. This government is again at war—against Grenada, against Nicaragua, against El Salvador, against Lebanon, against the black people of South Africa, and against the female, the colored, and the poor right here. Nothing has been solved, but we are a little further along in understanding what needs to be done. It excites me that everyone who reads this book, and particularly those feminists who may know little or nothing of the movements and history that have shaped our current work, can learn so much in these pages about the earlier struggles.

For me, the material that is most compelling is Barbara's writing about the Civil Rights movement and about racism as it has been and still is being lived by black and other people of color in this country. She makes absolutely clear that racism is ingrained in the fabric of North American life, that it affects men as well as women, that it is something that does not only happen in the confines of the women's movement, nor will it be eradicated by working only within the women's movement or on traditional, that is white-defined, women's issues. Barbara writes how, in the early sixties, peace activists were debating whether they should get involved in the nonviolent organizing against racism that was then being done primarily by black people. In "Southern Peace Walk: Two Issues or One?" Barbara states that the initial decision not to link the two movements "depressed" her and that it soon became obvious that dividing them was a grave mistake. She offers here and in many other essays the rudiments for understanding coalition politics, a supposedly "new" approach to bringing about political change. Indeed, the very title of this book, Barbara's own words, "we are all part of one another," challenges us to consider that our oppressions and chances for freedom are inextricably connected.

This book also conveys the basic truth that activism often requires putting your body on the line. Barbara writes the following about her first encounter with people committed to nonviolent theory and practice: "What soon became apparent about these people was that they were above all *people ready to act.*" (Italics mine.) So often, contemporary politicas prefer talk to action, prefer to conceptualize ideas of liberation without ever facing the dull, terrifying, passionate day-to-day reality of organizing, of being there. It is obvious from her writing how ready Barbara has always been to act. Whether

*Because this anthology functions as a chronicle, I strongly suggest that it be read in sequence and in its entirety.

xii

she writes about being jailed in Albany, Georgia, demonstrating in the streets of Birmingham, going to North and South Vietnam during the war, living in Resurrection City, or coming out to straight comrades with whom she had worked for many years, it is obvious that she has always put herself in the most difficult and dangerous situations and done so with great humility.

One aspect of this humility is Barbara's unsparing honesty about herself, her not being afraid to admit what she does not know and even that she has made mistakes. In 1960 she wrote: ". . . I suddenly asked myself—for I am the daughter of a well-to-do Republican lawyer—'What am I doing here? This is talk of revolution.'" In "Notes After Birmingham" she titles a section, "Having Entered This World That Is Theirs, I Live in It Too Now. But I Am Able to Leave." She goes on to explain:

> I have begun, even before this day, to feel a sudden unpleasant catch in my stomach every time I step out onto the street and see a white man. What is he going to do? So now I know what it is like. Now I am a Negro. Except that I can drive away from it.

She writes to Ray Robinson, who criticizes her for leaving Resurrection City, that he is right, that she never should have left—even though the leaders said that everybody should go, even though she was being called away to another important political task.

This same quality of humility characterizes Barbara's disagreements and criticisms of others. I myself do not agree with everything she expresses here, especially in some of her later writing on women's oppression. Yet it feels very possible to disagree with her respectfully, because Barbara's own convictions do not require the obliteration of those who differ with her. As she writes in "On Revolution and Equilibrium": "Vengeance is not the point: change is." In the last piece in this collection, "Remembering Who We Are," she writes specifically about how very different women might work with each other:

> But the longer we listen to one another—with real attention—the more commonality we will find in all our lives. That is, if we are careful to exchange with one another life stories and not simply opinions. If we adopt the mode that is now traditional for consciousness-raising: take turns speaking, speak from experience, don't interrupt, and don't deliver judgements upon one another. This mode of relating can work a kind of magic. . . . But—very simply—I think no woman should be judged unfit to be seeking her freedom.

I'm sure this desire to differ lovingly is connected to Barbara's commitment to nonviolence. Many contemporary activists dismiss nonviolence as an outmoded and unworkable strategy (though some are beginning to understand that it is a logical position from which to oppose militarism, nuclear proliferation, and global violence.) Barbara, on the other hand, believes that nonviolence works, explains here its basic principles, and provides example after example of exactly why and how it is effective. I believe, of course, that oppressed people have the right to defend themselves, to fight for their homes, their land, their freedom, but I can also verify from experience the capacity of nonviolence, militantly practiced, to make freedom possible. It feels appropriate to state in this context that my own opposition to current warfare, poverty, racism, and sexual oppression is, like Barbara's, informed by a basic belief that the use of violence to combat all of these is not a final solution, but a wretched last resort. Without violence we could live on this planet like human beings. Barbara writes that the reason why nonviolence has seemingly not "succeeded" is because too few people have been brave enough to commit themselves to seeing that its success becomes inevitable.

In her essay "Coalition Politics: Turning the Century,"* Bernice Johnson Reagon, another veteran of the movement, describes the kind of activist who has continued to grow during these years. She writes:

> Now, there were a few people who kept up with many of those issues. *They are very rare.* Anytime you find a person showing up at all of those struggles, and they have some sense of sanity by your definition, not theirs (cause almost everybody thinks they're sane), one, study with them, and two, protect them. They're gonna be in trouble shortly because they are the most visible ones. They hold the key to turning the century with our principles and ideals intact. They can teach you how to cross cultures and not kill yourself. And you need to begin to make a checklist—it's not long, you can probably count on your two hands. When it comes to political organizing, and when it comes to your basic survival, there are a few people who took the sweep from the 60's to the 80's and they didn't miss a step. They could stand it all.... So all of these people who hit every issue did not get it right, but if they took a stand, at least you know where their shit is.

I don't think Barbara has missed a step. You and I are lucky to have the chance to know her.

Barbara Smith

Barbara Smith is a writer and activist who lives in Brooklyn, New York. Her most recent book is *Home Girls: A Black Feminist Anthology* (Kitchen Table: Women of Color Press). *Home Girls* includes the essay, "Coalition Politics: Turning the Century," by Bernice Johnson Reagon.

Contents

Contents

Section 4: The Late Sixties

Section 5: The Seventies

Section 6: Full Circle

Introduction

This is a book about one woman's journey towards truth. In a sense, then, it is also the chronicle of a woman's liberation. There can be no freedom where truth is not recognized and affirmed, because the liberation of any group or individual begins with the process of discovering, claiming, and *acting on* the deepest truths of our experience.

With the recent welling up of interest in the conjunctions of feminism and nonviolence, knowledge of Barbara Deming's work has begun to spread—from feminist to feminist, across the United States and abroad. Best known, of course, are her later essays, many of which deal specifically with feminism and nonviolence, and which tend to be more accessible because the books in which they first appeared are still available. It is a major premise of feminism, however, that the process of development is just as important as the product developed, and this book is meant to be an expression and illustration of that premise. Although the discovery of an isolated Deming essay—e.g., a photocopy, passed from hand to hand, of the 1977 essay "Remembering Who We Are"—can be an exciting and even revelatory experience, we, the editor and publishers of this book, believe the value of Barbara's work can best be appreciated when it is seen in the context of its development.

Where did these truths come from, these insights into feminism and nonviolence, women and men, black and white? Where are their roots? How did they grow? This book is a partial answer to these questions, a glimpse into the "natural history" of the pacifist-feminist phenomenon, and an opportunity to participate—albeit at second hand—in one of the most rewarding philosophical explorations undertaken by one individual in these waning decades of the twentieth century.

The Early Years

Let me be really here, here in this place and this time where I am.

Barbara Deming began her truthward journey from the relative security and privilege of a white, middle-class American family. Born in New York City in 1917, she went to a Friends (Quaker) school from kindergarten through high school. She was sixteen when she fell in love for the first time, became lovers with her love—a woman her mother's age—and began writing poetry.

From these beginnings came her dedication to seeking for truth. About her experience of love—her lesbian experience—she wrote in 1939: "This is not the devil. It is the devil who / says this is the devil." And she vowed,

"Will look at everything, will not turn eyes down or / sidewise." She would look her truth in the face.

Until 1960, Barbara's journey was primarily an individual one, despite two long-lasting relationships with lovers. She worked as an editorial assistant to writer Bessie Breuer, studied literature and theatre at Bennington College and drawing with George Grosz, directed stock company plays, taught dramatic literature, and held a variety of "pink collar" jobs in New York City. In 1942, she was hired as a film analyst for a Library of Congress national film library project based at New York's Museum of Modern Art; this work led to the writing of her first book, *Running Away From Myself—A Dream Portrait of America Drawn from the Films of the '40s,* which was not published until 1969.

The selections from *Running Away* which are included here reveal both Barbara's instinctive method for seeking after truth and her increasing understanding that running away from the truths of one's own experience is not only useless but also self-defeating and disempowering. "If one stares long enough at film after film," she wrote in 1950, "the distracting individual aspects of each film begin to fade and certain obsessive patterns that underlie them all take on definition." The underlying pattern in the chapter called "Success Boy," most of which is included in this book, is "of one who, when he casts himself into the race, succumbs to a sort of amnesia, in which he loses the original dream that he had, loses the knowledge of where home is." And "the faster he runs, the more and more lost to himself he becomes"—lost to the realization of his own truth.

Barbara finished writing *Running Away* in 1950, at the beginning of a decade which was to bring many more rejection slips than acceptances of her work. Only two short stories, two essays on theater, and a few poems were published during these years. Stubbornly, however, she continued her search for truth, finding clues even in such a seemingly academic subject as an analysis of Shakespeare's *Hamlet.* "The central situation in the Hamlet story," she wrote, revolves around the fact that "the impulse to reject unpleasant truths is present in every man born."* Moreover, she found in the play an exploration of *choice:* if we can find the courage, we can choose not to "turn eyes down or sidewise" from the truth. Hamlet, for example, "is unable to accept those truths that confront him; but he will not allow himself to disregard them. He turns his eyes to them, although in anguish, over and over again."

A year of travel in Europe, June 1950 to July 1951, provided the material for *A Book of Travail—and of a Humming Under My Feet,* an autobiographical narrative begun in 1952, set aside, and recently completed.

---

* Barbara did not liberate her writing from the then-ubiquitous falsity of the "generic male" until many years later; See the Editor's Note, p.ix

And there were other, briefer trips to Mexico, Japan, and India during the 1950s. "It was after the visit to India," Barbara recalls, "that I began to read Gandhi. Realized that I was in the deepest part of myself a pacifist. Read more and more by him and about him. Became at once deeply committed to nonviolent struggle."

And thus, in 1959-60, Barbara quickly moved from being "vaguely liberal—I voted Democratic, knew I was for civil liberties, against loyalty oaths, for unions, against racism, etc."—to being "an instant radical." The loneliest part of Barbara's journey was over: discovering the Committee for Non-Violent Action "felt like finding a long-lost family. With nonviolent politics"—unlike any other sort of politics, she says, "I felt very much at ease." In an early poem, Barbara had written, "To fight / is almost the easiest part. / It is the search for the battlefield / that tries me." Nonviolent activism is the battlefield Barbara found in 1960, and she has been at work upon it ever since.

The Early Sixties

People may find it more comfortable to listen to us if we equivocate, but in the long run only words that discomfort them are going to change our situation.

Beginning with "The Peacemakers," originally published in *The Nation* in December of 1960, the selections in this book constitute a partial history of Barbara's next dozen years. A three-week visit to Cuba earlier in 1960 had initiated Barbara into the role of journalist, and she continued in that role throughout the decade—until serious injuries sustained in a 1971 car accident caused her to restrict her travels and her activities. All of Barbara's writings could not be included here, of course, but I have tried, with Barbara's help, to select essays which most clearly reflect the movement of her search for truth in these very active years.

There is a sense in which the major change for Barbara between the 1950s and the 1960s was a change from a personal to a political focus—from a private search for her personal, individual truth to a public effort to find and implement the political truths of large-scale social interactions. For those who lived through the sixties, a list of the decade's major names and incidents easily recalls the force which drew so many of us together in political action. I have constructed a chart showing some of these milestones (beginning, of necessity, a bit before the beginning of the decade) together with the concomitant public events in Barbara's life and the resulting essays appearing in this book.

<u>1954-59</u>   **History:**   McCarthy hearings on TV; Rosa Parks refuses to move to the back of the bus; bus boycott in Montgomery, led by Dr. King.   **Barbara's Activities:**   Barbara travels from San Francisco to Mexico, then to a new home in Massachusetts: writes short stories; trip to India; begins reading Gandhi.   **Selections:**   "Death and the Old Woman;" "The World of Hamlet"

<u>1960</u>   **History:**   U-2 spy plane incident—Gary Powers; Nixon debates J.F. Kennedy on TV.   **Barbara's activities:**   Barbara visits Cuba and talks with Castro; meets the folks of the Committee for Nonviolent Action; joins demonstrations against Polaris submarines.   **Selections:**   "The Peacemakers"

<u>1961</u>   **History:**   Bay of Pigs (The CIA tries to overthrow Castro).   **Barbara's activities:**   Barbara walks with the San Francisco to Moscow Walk for Peace; attends international peace brigade conference in Europe; joins fast calling for abolition of CIA.

<u>1962</u>   **History:**   Cuban missile crisis.   **Barbara's activities:**   Barbara is arrested in a protest against atomic bomb tests; publicly advocates unilateral disarmament; joins Nashville to D.C. bi-racial walk for peace.   **Selections:**   "Southern Peace Walk: Two Issues or One?"

<u>1963</u>   **History:**   Nuclear test ban treaty; George Wallace fights integration; bombs in Birmingham; massive civil rights march in D.C.; JFK killed.   **Barbara's activities:**   Barbara attends HUAC hearings; jailed (May) in anti-racism protest; jailed (Nov.) during "peace and freedom" walk.   **Selections:**   "Letter to WISP;" "In the Birmingham Jail;" "Notes After Birmingham"

<u>1964</u>   **History:**   "Freedom Summer" in Mississippi; Gulf of Tonkin incident; war in Vietnam heats up.   **Barbara's activities:**   Barabara jailed in Albany, Georgia, during "Québec-Guantanamo Walk for Peace And Freedom"   **Selections:**   chapters 1,2,3 & 7 of *Prison Notes*

<u>1965-67</u>   **History:**   Malcolm X killed; Selma, Watts; cultural revolution in China; Che Guevara killed.   **Barbara's activities:**   Barbara travels to North and South Vietnam; jailed during 1967 Pentagon action.   **Selections:**   "Temptations of Power;" "We Are All Part of One Another"

<u>1968-70</u>   **History:**   Dr. King and Robert Kennedy killed; invasion of Czechoslovakia; police riot at Democratic convention in Chicago; 250,000 march against the war; Kent State; Jackson State.   **Barbara's activities:**   Barbara travels with group to Resurrection City and lives there for three weeks.   **Selections:**   "On Revolution And Equilibrium;" "Mud City;" "On the Necessity to Liberate Minds"

4

This chart, despite its superficiality, makes clear the historical importance of Barbara's writing. Her work gives us an honest, firsthand account of places and people we must not forget—not, primarily, the famous people, but those masses of other women and men from whose commitment to struggle against racism and war we need to learn.

For the purposes of this book, however, there is another, equally important thread of history running through these essays: the continuing history of Barbara's search for truth. We find the themes of the previous years recurring throughout the decade, becoming intertwined with new insights and discoveries. For example, in "The Peacemakers" the "heroes" of "Success Boy" appear again in the persons of some workers at Electric Boat (makers of Polaris submarines), while Barbara herself feels she is "entering a new world"—the community of nonviolent activists—of people who choose to act on the truths they refuse to run away from or ignore.

The next two selections—"Southern Peace Walk" and "Letter to WISP"—reflect both Barbara's past and her future ideas. In community now with others who trust the truth to be stronger than "pragmatic" compromises with the falsity of oppression (racism), Barbara begins in "Southern Peace Walk" to develop her major theme of nonviolent struggle as a powerful, dual-natured strategy for change. And the joyful flash of "pre-feminist" insight in "Letter to WISP"—that women's truths lie in the here-and-now of our culturally trivialized daily lives—does not divert Barbara from insisting upon her own first-found truth: that we must not allow ourselves to look away from the radical implications of each truth we find. Although this essay reveals an as yet superficial (and thus, by definition, unradical) analysis of Woman-as-Mom, the radical challenge the essay makes to the women of WISP (in relation to unilateral disarmament) is at heart the same challenge Barbara would later sound to the entire left, and especially the nonviolent left, in relation to sexism and feminism. Her challenge: dig deep for the truth; when you have found it, and the courage to acknowledge it, then *act* truthfully upon it.

The Mid Sixties

Another world still catches at me. I live both here and there—until the two worlds can be one.

In the preface to her 1971 book *Revolution and Equilibrium,* which contains most of her published writings of the sixties, Barbara recognized some perspectives she already had rejected by the end of that decade. About the essay "In the Birmingham Jail", for example, she said,

> I [wrote] of the women with whom I was in jail (poor white women): "They did, in truth, belong out in the streets with the Negroes, petitioning those in power for the right to be treated like human beings." The habit of mind of identifying one's own being with the state under which one lives, and giving it awed respect even when it is reckless of the general welfare it supposedly exists to secure, dies slowly; so does the habit of looking to that state to change itself. . . .

This flaw, this anachronism—like Barbara's use of the "generic male" in much of her life's work, and the use of now out-moded words such as "Negro"—becomes an advantage rather than a drawback for readers who approach these essays as a process rather than a disjointed series of products. Because she is too honest to deny her own past, Barbara's writing invites us to share in her growth, her self-education and the lessons she learns from others. She does not hesitate to look at her own history, nor to offer it up for our critical examination. In learning from her lessons, we can begin to learn from our own. We can learn both how to change and how to be true to our selves, how to claim our *own* power rather than seeking to assume the power of others.

"In those days," Barbara wrote in a discussion of her early poetry,

> I was a ghost to myself—as all women were, not yet quarreling (consciously) with the use of the word "man" as generic. In several poems which were poems about myself, I wrote "man," "him"— because I wanted to place myself clearly within humanity. My use of those words now seems to me absurd.

Perhaps this is the ability most essential to maintaining a truly radical, truly nonviolent perspective: the ability to recognize the absurd. To many would-be revolutionaries, of course, nonviolent struggle itself seems absurdly naive and impractical. But Barbara's truth-seeking vision continually recognizes the absurdity of violence—whether it is violence against the self, as in the internalized sexism of the "generic male," or the violence of the state's court system, as described in *Prison Notes:*

Can the truth really be manipulated as simply as this? The actors themselves appear a little self-conscious. The cops seem almost to be playing at cops. During recess, a reporter steps up to one of them to congratulate him on a promotion and the officer blushes, laughs, points at his shiny black books: "Yes, I'm the big Gestapo now!" While the trial is in process, they sit sometimes, hands on billysticks, chins jutting—pictures of "the law." Then all at once they abandon this posture to give one another boyish punches in the stomach or to set each other's caps wrong side forward over their eyes. I half expect everyone to break out suddenly into loud guffaws and cry, "All right, all right, now let's be serious. Order in this courtroom!"

No one cries out any such thing. The absurd drama plays itself out. The absurd verdict is rendered. The prisoners are marched down to their cells, to the reality of steel walls, hard bunks, foul air, groans, curses.

The tragic absurdity of violence is revealed most clearly, perhaps, in Barbara's portraits of racist white people she encountered in the South during the sixties. Some, like Claudius in *Hamlet,* as Barbara had described him earlier, were "deeply perverse." Although it was the demonstrators' behavior which these white folks claimed to find outrageous, as Claudius claimed to be outraged by Hamlet's, "...in fact what is outrageous to him [to Claudius, and to many of the southern racists] is that he is not to be allowed to enjoy the fruits of his crime"—in this case, racism—nor to pretend the crime never happened, to pretend that the status quo is a product of some impersonal "natural order" for which he, and they, are in no way responsible. Not all of the people with whom Barbara demonstrated against racism in the South could truly be described as coming from the "outside" but they certainly *were* all "agitators," stirring up uncomfortable truths.

Other racist southern white people were more like Ophelia than Claudius. I think especially of the middle-aged woman with the trembling voice and crumpled face whom we meet in chapter 3 of *Prison Notes.* As Barbara wrote of Ophelia, "...she has, with childish stubbornness, expected the various people she loves to dispel the need for choice on her part—to somehow bring everything into harmony for her, make all well." And, of course, Barbara recognized also the ridiculous, mournful absurdity of the racist attitudes expressed by the poor white women she met in the southern jails. Perhaps it was the racism among these poor whites which nourished the early growth of Barbara's pacifist-feminist analysis, based on "the complicated truth...that many oppressors are also oppressed," as she would write in 1977.

All of Barbara's reports on her jail experiences in the South—represented here by "In the Birmingham Jail," "Notes After Birmingham," and four chapters from *Prison Notes*—are, first of all, incredible writing. In addition, they present a firsthand account of a confrontation between bigoted whites who refused to see and admit the truth of their own violence, their own violation, and nonviolent activists, both black and white, who insisted on acting out the truths of their lives. It is interesting to note two of the section heads in "Notes After Birmingham": "One Part of the Truth is Out" and "Another Part of the Truth"—again, "the complicated truth." By the end of *Prison Notes'* seventh chapter, Barbara can say to black lawyer C.B. King, "Now I dare look at you, too." She has become able to face the truth of what racism is and does to us all, including what it makes us do to each other and how it had distorted her own vision of the truth.

Another major insight Barbara gained during her jail experiences of the sixties was her recognition of the jail as an institution dedicated to hiding, and thus temporarily disposing of, the uncomfortable truths of people's lives. A jail is a tool by which society tries to "wish away" those whose poverty—or resistance to poverty—is too forceful a reminder of institutionalized injustice. In "We Are All Part of One Another," written some ten years later, Barbara would remind us that we, too, as individuals, can be guilty of "wishing away" those whose behavior discomforts us, whose truths we would rather ignore. ". . . I have to acknowledge," she would write in the 1971 essay "On Anger," "that in many moments of anger I have, in effect, wished a man dead— wished him not there for me to cope with." We are all part of one another, indeed; even the jailers and the jailed have many truths in common.

The Late Sixties

Surely all of us are nerved by one another, catch courage from one another.

It was the war in Indochina which brought to its final end Barbara's— and many other people's—"habit . . . of identifying one's own being with the state under which one lives." In her essay "The Temptations of Power— Report of a Visit to North Vietnam", she wrote of the many Americans who were unwilling to believe that normal, decent American men would burn children alive with napalm or use antipersonnel weapons indiscriminately against a civilian population. "I sympathize" with those doubting Americans, Barbara wrote: "There were many times in Vietnam, seeing the things we saw, when everything in me wanted to cry out: this is not so! But there it was, in front of my eyes. . . ." The Barbara of 1967, no less than the Barbara of 1939, would not allow herself to "turn eyes down or sidewise." Like

Hamlet, she turned her eyes to the truth, "although in anguish, over and over again." And she challenged anyone who would listen to her to recognize the radical implications of these horrible truths:

> I would...ask you if our loyalty is not due primarily to the people of our country, and don't we owe loyalty to government only in so far as it serves the interests of the people?...I would ask you: Don't we owe loyalty not only to the people of our own country but to people everywhere...?

But the America of the 1960s had not changed deeply from the America Barbara perceived in the films of the 1940s. Consider, for example, the following excerpts. The first, from "The Temptations of Power" refers to American attitudes towards the war in Vietnam:

> I find this unwillingness to look at what we are doing particularly frightening because I find it again and again in conjunction with another mental block. That is the refusal to believe that we could possibly withdraw from this war. I am sure that you have all talked to people who say, "You're right, we never should have gone into Vietnam, but now that we are there, how could the powerful United States possibly withdraw?" So look what you have: in one and the same person you have the refusal to believe that we could be playing the part of the bully, and the refusal to believe...we shouldn't really be able to expect to have our way. These two visions of ourselves, of course, are deeply contradictory...but few Americans are able to recognize the contradiction. And I beg Americans at this point to begin to try to look at themselves, to know themselves.

We Americans wanted to be both innocent and "successful"—with "success" measured in terms of military power and capitalist wealth; but most of all, we wanted to avoid recognizing the contradiction inherent in our aspirations.

Twenty years earlier, Barbara recognized similar contradictions in the American character, revealed through the popular films of the day. The heroes of the films described in the "Success Boy" chapter of *Running Away From Myself* attain the sort of success so dear to Americans (wealth, primarily). And yet,

> Listen...to the hero's cry when he is faced by his harsh accusers. Over and over, to clear himself, he cites his helpless commitment to the deeds for which they account him responsible. Here is nothing *he* intended, he cries....Events quite out of his control intervene....Here is always none of *his* doing.

Even in films where the "hero" is overtly a villain, the same contradictions appear:

> Here is the same sick figure I have been sketching all along—his sickness merely graver now. In this character, in fact, the kinship of the other...figures I have been describing in this chapter is confirmed, for their pitiful cries are interwoven here—the cry of the first: "I am homeless!" and the cry of the other: "I am doubted! Do not doubt me!" This latest figure adds the desperate cry: "Believe in me or I will have to destroy you!"

In Vietnam, it was called "winning the hearts and minds of the people." We had to "destroy the village in order to save it"—in order to save ourselves from their refusal to believe in us and in the righteousness of our imperialist mission. No wonder, then, that Barbara wrote, in the 1969 foreword to *Running Away From Myself,* "I began to recall these figures [from the "Success Boy" chapter] sharply as I studied this country's involvement in Vietnam."

"On Revolution and Equilibrium," perhaps Barbara's best-known essay, explores the source of all these "heroic" contradictions in the context of explicitly revolutionary struggles. Why do those who work for radical change become trapped, again and again, in patterns over which we feel we have no control? Why does revolution after revolution around the world fail to achieve the thorough, lasting, and *liberating* change of its early dreams? We lose control—we "become dizzy," as Frantz Fanon acknowledges—and the more violently we struggle, the faster we run, the more lost to ourselves, to our ideals, we become. At the root of this condition, Barbara asserts, is the awful contradiction inherent in the use of violence. "It is my stubborn faith," this essay tells us, "that if, as revolutionaries, we will wage battle without violence, we can remain very much more in control—of our selves...and of the future we hope will issue from" our struggle. Violence is now seen to be not only tragic and absurd, but also incompatible with sustained and coherent work for radical change: it makes us dizzy, and, like innumerable other would-be heroes, we lose our "original dream," we lose "the knowledge of where home is."

"On Revolution and Equilibrium" is invaluable for its clear-eyed, meticulous examination of strategies and tactics, challenging old assumptions about the true nature—and thus, the effects—of both violent and nonviolent struggle. Drawing on new insights as well as lessons learned from the civil rights movement, Barbara restates the dual force of nonviolence:

> We put upon [the adversary] two pressures—the pressure of our defiance of him and the pressure of our respect for his life—and it happens that in combination these two pressures are uniquely effective.

And Barbara also presages in this essay an important later development of feminist analysis of nonviolence in her discussion of the difference between aggression and assertion, recognizing the need to achieve equilibrium between respect for one's self and respect for one's adversaries. From today's perspective, however, "On Revolution and Equilibrium" is remarkable for not distinguishing between "manhood" and humanity. We can see very clearly here how the then-unchallenged use of the "generic male" functioned to hide the truth about culturally constructed masculinity and its role in perpetuating violence on all levels. In her challenge to advocates of nonviolence which concludes this essay, along with an equally strong challenge to those who disparage nonviolence, Barbara wrote prophetically: "May those who say that they believe in nonviolence learn to challenge more boldly those institutions of violence that constrict and cripple our humanity."

"Mud City," like Barbara's reports from the southern jails, is simply wonderful writing. In addition, it is an attempt to preserve on a human scale—the scale of individual experience—the complicated truths of an important historical event: the Poor People's Campaign and, especially, its creation of Resurrection City, a muddy, makeshift collection of huts and tents in Washington, D.C., inhabited during the summer of 1968 by poor people of every color. Barbara's belief in the urgency and vitality of truth must have been reconfirmed a thousandfold at Resurrection City. In many ways, the experience was proof of the feminist idea that "the personal is political." The enormous diversity of people gathered in the City, living very closely together in circumstances which made privacy and nonengagement impossible, created a situation where many truths were virtually unavoidable. Daily life—"the personal"—became fully politicized. As one young woman told Barbara, "I've never learned so much about myself or about other people in such a short time. Here you can't run away from confrontations and what your responses to other people really are; you finally have to look at them."

"On the Necessity to Liberate Minds" is the last essay in the collection *Revolution and Equilibrium*. Although the essay was written in 1970, it seems in several ways to belong to the sixties—or, more precisely, to be a transition between the decades. The central question of the essay is a very feminist one: "How do we set all of us free to trust our own experiences of the truth?" (The question also has anarchistic implications, reverberating, perhaps, from some of Barbara's conclusions about leadership, as reported in "Mud City.") But there are ways in which this essay, from today's perspective, seems superficial due to its lack of an integrated feminist analysis. Besides the use—the *last* use—of the "generic male," the essay's need for a more developed feminist analysis is shown most clearly in its failure to push the analysis past a certain point (the point where some of us—those who are in a position to oppress as well as be oppressed—cannot simply trust the truth of our own limited experience).

This anachronistic flaw is minor in the context of this brief essay, however, because the purpose of "On the Necessity to Liberate Minds" is more directly practical than philosophical. As an argument for and explanation of nonviolent direct actions involving selective property destruction, the essay is invaluable. It brings those important actions firmly within the tactical boundaries of nonviolence and also clarifies, for nonviolent activists who participate in such actions, both the philosophy behind them and the methods which will communicate that philosophy most clearly.

The Seventies

So much has been taken from us.
But we will take it back...
Woman, woman.
We take it back.

If, as I have suggested, Barbara's focus shifted during the sixties from a personal to a political search for truth, the seventies was the decade in which she chronicled the deeper, feminist understanding that the familiar personal/political dichotomy is itself a lie. We can see this understanding reflected in each of the remaining selections in this book, and we can see it in the form of the selections as well as in their content. In an interview with *Kalliope,** Barbara said, "One of the struggles writers have to make—*I* have certainly had to make—is the struggle to dare to trust the form that feels right." Her readers are fortunate indeed that Barbara found the courage to trust her feelings in this regard, because it was at this point in her life that physical fragility interrupted Barbara's activism, and thus, her journalism. "Illness holds me by the ankle," she wrote in 1972, a year after being seriously injured in a car accident; and, in another poem,

> ...*I can look into the woods of Death.*
> *My friends are gathering there...*
> *How near they are!*
> *A few steps and I could be among them.*
> *Would be now if, waking in a hospital last Fall,*
> *Battered, appalled, I had not fought for breath,*
> *Fought to hold this remaining ground.*

Barred by her physical condition from travel and physical activism, Barbara turned—on "this remaining ground"—to new forms of written activism: the letters and open letters of the seventies in which she brought her personal

*In an interview by Ruthann Robson, soon to be published in *Kalliope: A Journal of Women's Art (Jacksonville, FL: Florida Junior College).*

and political analyses together in a sharper focus than ever before. Their synthesis, of course, is the philosophy of feminist nonviolence.

We begin this portion of this book, however, with "On Anger," the last essay Barbara wrote before the accident. Like "On Revolution and Equilibrium," this essay has been reprinted, and thus has received somewhat wider distribution than most of Barbara's other works. It would make little sense to judge the two essays against one another; they were written for very different purposes—"On Revolution and Equilibrium" as an exposition of theory for publication, and "On Anger" as a talk to a group of people many of whom were friends, acquaintances, or co-workers in nonviolent activism. But despite these major differences in form and style, an even greater contrast is evident in the later essay's vastly more conscious woman-identification. Suddenly, it seems, Barbara's feminism has broken through the barriers of socialization, training, and habit so that the feminist attitudes and assumptions we glimpsed in her earlier writing now shine forth openly.

The contrast between the given topic of the talk—"the relation between war resistance and resistance to injustice," a subject fitting nicely into the mainstream of traditional nonviolence theory—and the method Barbara chose to approach this topic is particularly striking. "I'm going to talk particularly about our relation to anger," she says. Although she speaks here of a destructive kind of anger identical to that she described in "Success Boy," she locates the anger in herself now, as well as in others: ". . . when I study myself I have to acknowledge that in my moments of anger I have, in effect, wished a man dead. . . ." Barbara had for years been struggling to trust her own feelings, but in "On Anger" it becomes clear how much of her own experience and emotion—as a woman, as a lesbian—had been set aside from consideration, or had been recognized and expressed only (as she put it) "by analogy" in the struggle against racism. Simply by drawing many of her examples in this talk from her own and other women's experiences *as women,* Barbara challenged her anti-war comrades to reject the traditional trivialization both of women and of personal experience as such: ". . . for what seems deeply personal is in truth deeply political."

The next selection, which was also prepared as a talk, repeats the methodology of *Running Away From Myself:* "If one stares long enough at film after film [here, book after book]. . . certain obsessive patterns that underlie them all take on definition." And like the film makers whose films were reviewed in that earlier work, the authors of the books discussed in "Two Perspectives on Women's Struggle" reveal their deepest truths, Barbara believes, unconscious of their meaning and their implications. She quotes Charlotte Brontë: ". . . the writer who possesses the creative gift owns something of which he is not always master—something that, at times, strangely wills and works for itself." Despite the similarity in method, however, the focus of this essay is far changed from that of *Running Away*. Instead of looking outside herself to the broad abstraction of "America" and then seeking to apply general observations to the individual experience, Barbara here begins with her own intuitions and then uses the intimate insights of other women writers in an attempt to identify some general truths about how the nature of our culture is revealed in individual experiences. The first section of "Two Perspectives" is a powerful evocation of women's central dilemma in this culture: how can we live without our lives, without the Selves which it is the purpose of our culturally ordained sex role to seek out and destroy?

In the second half of "Two Perspectives," Barbara brings the power of her nonviolence to bear on this dilemma, refusing to let even legitimate personal anger and need stand in the way—and thus block out the light—of truth. She makes the essentially feminist nature of nonviolence explicit here, calling its dual nature "androgynous," but that vital theoretical insight is not the main emphasis. Instead, she remains focused on the cultural function of sex roles and the violence they inflict on women and men. "It is the truth that frees us," she writes, and the truth is that we, who are all part of one another, cannot live without the whole lives to which our nature calls us.

With the publication of "Confronting One's Own Oppression" in the 1974 book *We Cannot Live Without Our Lives,* Barbara took a major step towards the creation of her own freedom as a writer and a lesbian. The decision to publish this private correspondence with Ray Robinson freed her from the traditional separation between "real" literature—"important," public, usually masculine-identified forms—and the forms of writing traditionally trivialized as belonging particularly to women—personal letters and journals. As I mentioned earlier, her increasing acceptance of less traditional forms for her writing was vital for Barbara, because of her diminished physical capacity for the activities which sustained her earlier, more journalistic style. These letters also represent an even more important move towards freedom, however. Previously, Barbara had written nothing which focused directly on "the struggle that is particularly my own—the struggle of lesbian women," because, she stated, with the courage of her honesty, "I had not felt free enough to do so."

Barbara's letters to Ray Robinson are very strongly feminist; they are about the owning and acting out of our own truths: "My efforts have to be, first of all, to find my proper pride for this struggle" against (hetero)sexism, she writes, and

> I learned. . .to trust my own deep sense of what I should do, and not
> just obediently trust the judgment of others—even others better than
> I am. I can't just come where you call me, Ray. I have to find my own

bearings....I have to continue to analyze and to face up to my own oppression. As you have done to yours. *This* will make us true comrades—not my running off meekly to jump aboard a ship you're captain of.

As a feminist and lesbian, I am thrilled by the strong, honest commitment to lesbian liberation and women's liberation in these letters. As a lifelong "fellow traveler" of nonviolent activists, I am moved by this correspondence with a rush of hope: hope that if we lesbians, we feminists, we women can draw upon our nonviolent skills as personally and as carefully as Barbara did in these letters, we may yet be able to articulate our truths so clearly and powerfully that our male co-advocates of nonviolent revolution could honestly say, as Barbara said to Ray, "I think, very truly: I do understand your anger."

Full Circle

I must undress down to the bone, take all the
pictures off the wall
and remember who I am.

In the four final selections in this book—all of them in the form of letters—Barbara uses feminist truths to illuminate many aspects of traditional nonviolent and/or leftist analyses. This process, of course, changes them all, waking up sleeping truths and forcing us to look at them anew, never allowing the truth—and especially the truths of women's lives—to be hidden or distorted by rhetoric. Although each of these letters has a different central subject, the four have in common their permeation by both the radical visions of feminism and, though less explicitly in the first three, the powerful values of nonviolence. A major expression of the nonviolent attitude in all of them is Barbara's use of questions directed toward the recipient of each letter. "Here is a question for you," she writes to Brad Lyttle; and to Arthur Kinoy, "That is what we are both talking about, isn't it?" In her letter to Susan Sherman she says, "I write to ask you..."; and in her letter to Susan Saxe, "May I converse with you again?" These letters are exercises in truth seeking, not declarations of a static position or "line." As such, they both give the reader valuable insights and convey Barbara's openness to receiving contrasting insights in return; they both accept and refuse—from Marxist writers, for example; and they show respect for others and respect for self. They are profoundly nonviolent in spirit—and, more specifically, they are profound expressions of nonviolent *activism*. As carefully structured as any arguments I have ever read, they are nevertheless *in action,* acting upon us as we read them and sparking us into action of our own.

"Love Has Been Exploited Labor," the second of these four letters, asks the question, "Into what new territory can it lead a Marxist if he begins to open himself to feminist insights?" In the course of her detailed search in response to that question, Barbara remarks:

> ...my impression is that in their study of history Marxists have concentrated much too much upon the ownership and upon the production of *things* as "the means of subsistence" and have scanted a study of the ways in which people try to subsist upon one another. I more and more realize that this is why I never was able to become a Marxist myself. The realities that Marxists scanted were the realities with which I was most concerned.

The realities, in other words, of women's lives as we live them in capitalist patriarchy. Giving credit—and respect—where it is due, Barbara recounts the truths about women's lives which Marx did in fact discover—and then ignored, because he could not integrate them successfully into his androcentric analysis. Women, she says, are now discovering those truths which Marx found and lost again; but women are able to "look steadily at the truth" upon which Marx was unable to focus. Even as she turns the whole structure of orthodox Marxism on its head, Barbara recognizes the cultural forces which make it harder for men to accept these truths, and thus (as she wrote in "On Anger") "the need to reassure them at the same time that we stubbornly refuse" to allow them the comfort of familiar falsities.

But no one—no man, no woman—can "look steadily" at every truth without discomfort and confusion—and anger, sometimes, at those who speak the truths that disturb the fragile equilibrium in which we struggle for social change. For me, the letter to Susan Sherman ("To Fear Jane Alpert Is to Fear Ourselves") is, above all, an attempt to share with feminists unfamiliar with nonviolence the perspective from which we can simultaneously reject a person's oppressive behavior and accept—validate— that person's self. This perspective is absolutely vital if feminists are ever to forge meaningful coalitions with our natural allies among the classes of people targeted by other oppressions, many of whom are men and therefore also often oppressors, or are potential oppressors also (including many feminists) because of economic, color, age, or other class identities. Of all feminist truths, the truth that *all* classes of women are oppressed by *all* classes of men is perhaps the hardest for many radical women to accept. "We are daring to look at this now," Barbara writes, meaning: we are daring to acknowledge the truth that patriarchy "splits each one of us, away from each other and away from our true selves." In the midst of such complexity, she continues,

> I think the only choice that will enable us to hold to our vision without being scared into wanting to retreat [from feminism] is one that...adopts a concept familiar to the nonviolent tradition: naming behavior that is oppressive, naming abuse of power that is held unfairly and must be destroyed, but naming no *person* one whom we are willing to destroy.

In the final selection of this book, "Remembering Who We Are," all of Barbara's themes reappear and are renewed. "Let me be really here, here in this place and this time where I am," she wrote in the fifties; and now, in the seventies, she recognizes that our feminist analysis must be grounded here, where we are, in our selves: our bodies, our lives, our experiences of truth. Her nonviolent commitment insists that the truths of feminism must live in more than words, and that we are all—all women, all people—finally part of one another. In order to see the truth, she writes, we have to be willing to "look at everything differently;" we have to *look*, and we have to refuse to deny or simplify truth's complexity. Through feminism, "we begin to dare to presume to trust our own eyes." And for the first time she regains fully the knowledge the "success boys" lost by running away from themselves: "the knowledge of where home is." She feels, at last, she is "allowed to be openly just the person I really [am]...and to act upon this," here where she really is, here in her whole self, at home in the truth of her own life.

And yet, happily, there is no ending here. "Even today," Barbara has written in her autobiographical narrative *A Book Of Travail,* "I take up again each morning the labor of learning to know what it is that I really do know." We each can continue that labor, that journey, with her; and we travel more clearly, more courageously, because of her work.

Jane Meyerding

Section 1: The Early Years

Let me be really here, here in this place and this time where I am.

—from the short story in "An Illness" in *Wash Us and Comb Us*

Have been not admitting it all to be present, and given.
Dreaming.
If love, love. Possible or impossible because of other
person. But actual, not dreamt.
And I no more the victim of than anyone of any
love. This is not the devil. It is the devil who
says this is the devil.
Will look at everything, will not turn eyes down or
sidewise. For it is not for me to say where the hope
lies, where death is made life.

This stiff shroud of ice, this mock of bloom,
this weight, this glittering load with the appearance
of feather, is promise given of spring, this anything
but green, this load from above, most icy, most harsh,
yet there it is—spring.

1940

Excerpts from *Running Away From Myself*

Barbara worked as a film analyst for a Library of Congress national film library project between 1942 and 1944. In that capacity, she saw one-quarter of all the Hollywood feature films released during those years. Running Away From Myself: A Dream Portrait of America Drawn from the Films of the '40s *is based on that experience and on her more selective viewing of Hollywood films released between 1945 and 1948. She finished writing the book in 1950, but it was not published until 1969 [Grossman]; the foreword (excerpted below) was written in 1969. As Barbara recognized by the time the book was published, its fourth chapter—"Success Boy"—has particular relevance to the development of her pacifist/feminist philosophy. An edited version of that chapter is presented here, along with an edited version of the introductory first chapter. As with all selections in this book, I have edited only for length, to avoid repetition where two essays cover very similar material, and to delete references to work not included here, never to alter the original substance or tone of Barbara's writing. (JM)**

---

* Introductory comments and footnotes which conclude with the initials JM were added by editor Jane Meyerding during preparation of this book. Barbara's original introductory notes and footnotes are indicated by the initials BD.

From the Foreword:

The original version of this book was finished in 1950—entitled then *A Long Way from Home: Some Film Nightmares of the Forties.* No one was ready to publish it—except for the magazine *City Lights,* which began to serialize it, but shortly went out of existence for lack of funds—and I put it aside and turned to other writing. Then in the 1960's I became active in the nonviolent movement, and as the struggle in which this engaged me brought me a new kind of knowledge of the country, I began more and more to recall certain images with which the book had dealt. When I wrote it, I knew that it could be read as a psychological study of America, but my own experience of America was so limited still that writing it was a curiously abstract though fascinating labor. When I finally took out the manuscript and reread it, I found that it was very much more alive for me than it had been when I put it away.

This was especially so, perhaps, of chapter 4, in which I deal with the distracted heroes and heroines of various "success stories." Some of these heroes exhibit a strange split in consciousness. They boast openly of being out for what they can get and of not caring what means they use. At the same time they utter piteous cries claiming to be misunderstood—to be innocent of the cruel charge that they are out for what they can get. I began to recall these figures sharply as I studied this country's involvement in Vietnam—reading, on the one hand, bald statement's like Eisenhower's explanation of our support of the French war to keep Vietnam a colony ("When the U.S. votes 400 million dollars to help that war, we are not voting a give-away program. We are voting for...our power and ability to get certain things we need from the riches of...South East Asia"); reading also pronouncements made by Eisenhower and others about our selfless fight to help the South Vietnamese preserve their freedom—the same men making the one kind of statement and the other, and in some strange fashion able to believe both.

All the characters I trace in *Running Away From Myself* can be seen to be products of a deep crisis of faith. It is striking to me that the period in which this country is most aggressively trying to impose its will upon the rest of the world follows a period of suffering from this deep uncertainty. And again a particular character in chapter 4 holds a new interest for me: the one who in effect declares, "Believe in me or I will have to destroy you!"

from Chapter One:
A Portrait of Ourselves

"Abandon all hope, you who enter here!" Dante found these words written above the entrance to Hell. I should give the same warning to anyone about to enter the world through which this book will lead him—a world that has been shaped upon our movie screens. That world is the image of ourselves, and the image is discouraging. The reader can comfort himself with the thought that the portrait is incomplete. I am not speaking of any direct likeness that Hollywood films offer. It is not as mirrors reflect us but, rather, as our dreams do, that movies most truly reveal the times. If the dreams we have been dreaming provide a sad picture of us, it should be remembered that—like that first book of Dante's *Comedy*—they show forth only one region of the psyche. Through them we can read with a peculiar accuracy the fears and confusions that assail us—we can read, in caricature, the Hell in which we are bound. But we cannot read the best hopes of the time.

If our films reveal only this hapless side of us, it is because of the role most film makers choose—that of giving the public "what it wants." Most films made in Hollywood offer—as certain dreams do—wish fulfillment. In wishful dreams one can discern quite clearly the condition from which a man wants to escape, but never the more difficult, the *real* hope he might have of escaping from it—never, that is, his real strength.

As in wishful dreams, Hollywood films offer an escape that is disguised. The fact is less obvious than with dreams, which often, if taken literally, make no sense at all (some films, to be sure, make almost as little sense), but the drama here, too, is secret. The thrill that movies hold for us is usually thought to be that of identifying with persons unlike ourselves—of imagining ourselves Ingrid Bergman (or one loved by her), Humphrey Bogart (or one loved by him), or of imagining ourselves a millionaire or a musical genius or some equally remote figure. The truth is that the spectator always knows very well—in essence—the dramatic situations in which these screen figures are placed. The heroes and heroines who are most popular at any particular period are precisely those who, with a certain distinction, act out the predicament in which we all find ourselves—a predicament from which the movie-dream then cunningly extricates us. But the moviegoer need never admit to himself the real nature of the identification—never admit what that condition really is from which he is being vicariously relieved. Virgil describes Hell to Dante as that blind world in which the good of the intellect has been surrendered. His words could also be used to describe the darkened world of the movie theater.

If the dreamers are unaware of what it is they dream, the men who contrive these dreams know little more than they do. They consciously enough indulge the public—because it pays. But their cunning at providing blind comfort is, itself, largely blind.* I have remarked that the plight from which these dreams extricate hero or heroine is disguised for us. The film makers might very well deny having intended this. But no art is involved here. Rather, it takes art to be always aware of what the actual subject is with which one is dealing. One may be shrewd at spotting a subject of general appeal and at the same time quite ignorant of the true nature of that appeal. Often in these films, the hero's extrication from his difficulties is effected by sleight of hand. The film makers could again protest that they were unaware of executing any such feats. Cunning of that sort need not be plotted; it is instinct. The least knowing among us cunningly enough delude ourselves. It takes again precisely art to avoid these motions which, even when one attempts an honest representation of life, have a way of intruding themselves spontaneously.

The film medium lends itself especially to sleight of hand. The spectator, in the first place, plays a more passive role than he does in relation to any other art and so is in a more suggestive state. He is seated in darkness. The screen, the only source of light in this darkness, easily usurps his attention. This is so of the lit stage at a play, of course, but at a play, at least, the eye of the spectator must move to take in the scene. At a movie, the camera performs the work *for* the eye. We need not even turn our heads to follow the action; the camera does that for us. It squints for us, to note details. It is alert; we need not be.

As a movie communicates both at the visual level and at the level of the word, it is easy for it to distract us with words spoken, with a name given an event, while the underlying sensuous appeal it makes remains unacknowledged—and may have very little to do with those words. This is possible in the theater also; and something comparable is possible on the printed page; but in the movies it is so to a new degree, because of the freedom the camera has to range through the physical world—quite casually, it would seem. (To those who make the film, it can seem casual too; here is always much that is involuntary.) It is very possible for a person in the audience to ridicule the film he has seen, to point out glaring absurdities of plot—and

*See Editor's Note, page ix.

still, in spite of himself, to have responded to it very actively, at a less obvious level. A man can wake from a dream too and say, "I have just had the most absurd dream"; yet he has dreamed it.

Even if he laughs at his dream, the dreamer often carries the taste of it with him through the day—troubled by his memory of it, unless he can decipher it. This book attempts to decipher the dreams that all of us have been buying at the box office, to cut through to the real nature of the identification we have experienced there—to that image of our condition that haunts us, unrecognized by most of us, unacknowledged, yet troubling our days.

Because it is a blind comfort they offer, our movies are hard to read in this way individually. But in unison they yield up their secrets. If one stares long enough at film after film, the distracting individual aspects of each film begin to fade and certain obsessive patterns that underlie them all take on definition. Film after film can be seen to place its hero in what is, by analogy, the identical plight—the dream then moving forward carefully to extricate him. From such a series of instances one can deduce a plight more general, sensed by the public (and by the public-minded film makers)—a condition that transcends the literal situation dramatized in any single film.

The heart of this study has been the juxtaposition of many texts, and the number of films that I have studied in this way is a substantial one. But the number of films to which I will actually refer is small. This is so because I felt that I should tell each film story in some detail. One who writes about the movies can never assume that the text he is discussing is common both to him and to the reader. With the exception of certain favorites which do tend to be revived fitfully from year to year, films make their sudden appearances upon the nation's screens and as suddenly disappear. No comprehensive film library exists. The reader cannot turn to a certain text at will....

In writing this book, I felt that I should provide the reader with some sort of substitute for the text to which he cannot turn—should try my best to evoke it for him, so that he could judge for himself whether or not the pattern I trace is there in fact. I could not do this with very many films, without entangling the reader in plot after plot. Nor could I examine certain films in detail but refer to many more in passing. The real substance of a film never lies on the surface, and so cannot be "noted briefly." If by the end of this book those analyses I do make seem legitimate to the reader, if the images I trace in films representative of a variety of genres seem together to compose a world that is consistent with itself, perhaps the reader will be willing to assume that any other films chosen from these years would contribute to the same portrait of ourselves.

I offer no interpretation of that dream portrait. My feeling is that it stands by itself; that if it is presented—as I try to present it—not in fragments but all of a piece, it will wake in the consciousness of the reader echoes more resonant than any special reading I might give it.

from Chapter Four:
"Success Boy"

"Part of me is lost"

One figure is supposed to dominate the American myth: the success boy, the self-made man. By definition, he has overcome hesitations, found a place for himself....Here are four spectacular careers:

Rhapsody in Blue—The Jubilant Story of George Gershwin (1945): A struggling musician from the Bronx has "ideas that are different," doesn't want to be "just a concert pianist." "When I get started, nothing will ever stop me," he declares. And nothing does. "Up like an elevator" he goes, "looking for new buttons to push." Up he goes to penthouses and fame, the idol simultaneously of Broadway and Carnegie Hall. "How does it feel to be sitting on top of the world?" they ask him. He stands in his expensive new apartment, across whose spaces the camera seems able to travel forever, stands in front of a self-portrait he is trying to paint—and here is his jubilant cry: *"I keep running away from myself!...Part of me is lost somewhere!...I don't want to hurt anybody!"*

Incendiary Blonde—"The skyrocket story of Texas Guinan" (1945): A little tomboy of humble origin (Betty Hutton) wins a contest in a rodeo, which gives her the chance she's "been waiting for all her life": the owner invites her to join. Once in, she rapidly makes herself its star. Silver pistols she's wanted and she gets them. One day she decides to "have a look at" Broadway. "Have a look at it? You could *be* Broadway!" her agent tells her. And soon she is just that. She decides to open a night club and soon she is "Queen of the night clubs." "One of the immortals," they name her. She set the town "on fire." "My little girl!" crows her poppa.

And *her* cry? "Sure, I got everything I ever wanted—except the one thing I wanted more than anything. There's a black curse on me! I'm scared!"

Humoresque (1947): Another struggling musician, like Gershwin a poor boy living over his father's grocery store—but this time the name fictitious as well as the history, Paul Boray (John Garfield), violinist—again has ideas: "Nobody's going to sit on my head....Nobody's going to step on me, not me!" And nobody does. He becomes the protégé of wealthy Mrs. Wright: she manages his debut and he's "in." Soon the camera is traveling lengths of concert hall lobby, hung with one life-size poster portrait of him after another; soon his picture is on the cover of "Today" and his proud poppa, visiting his penthouse, exclaims in wonder, "It's an eagle's nest!"

And he? His eyes turn wistfully to the little photo on his mantle, photo of himself as a kid, holding the first fiddle his mother gave him: "All my life I've tried to do the right thing and it's never worked out!...*I keep feeling I'm far from home, and where home is I don't know. I can't get back to that simple carefree kid I used to be!*"

Or here is an earlier film, set this time in England, *Random Harvest* (1942): A victim of the First World War, an amnesiac (Ronald Colman), yearns to "be someone again," and with the aid of a noble-hearted show girl who believes in him, very soon is. The show girl (Greer Garson) helps him to escape from the rest home where he feels like a prisoner, flees with him to the country; and there soon encourages him to start upon a writer's career; there too encourages him to propose, and sets him up in a humble little cottage (comfortable poverty, MGM style). Nor has he long to struggle along. A bump on the head restores him to his real identity and he discovers that he belongs to an aristocratic family. (The ladder could hardly be ascended more swiftly.) The family fortunes are in a bad way and to recoup them he enters industry. Soon he is a great success in this role; soon he is a Prince of Industry. Then he is elected to Parliament. He is even mentioned as material for the cabinet!

But he? He fingers wistfully, obsessively, the little key that dangles on his watch chain—key to the humble dwelling...where he lived as a struggling young writer: *"I keep feeling that there are people I have hurt!...I keep feeling that there is something I have lost!"*

Here they stand: success girl, success boy, Queen of Broadway, Prince of Industry, Man of the Year....Among their riches, these heroes utter cries of loss, of lack, a wrong road helplessly taken.

I have not described these four films in detail, of course. Nor have I told their stories as anyone would who had seen the movies casually. For the movie audience at large, the dream is safely veiled: in each case, it *seems,* what spoils the happiness of the one who climbs the ladder of success is the fact that he is never united with the one he loves.

Gershwin's father sums it all up in *Rhapsody in Blue*: "Success is not enough—it should've been Julie." Gershwin has met Julie early in his career. It is to her that he blurts out his eager dreams. When his first shows are produced, she stars in them.... But then he goes off on a trip to Paris, where he meets Christine; and when he returns to America, Julie sees that she has been forgotten. "Don't be a naughty baby, come to momma, come to momma, do!" she sings at his coming home party; but he is not listening. Christine has watched this, and one day she walks out on Gershwin. She leaves a brave little note: "You think of yourself first," she writes. "That is as it should be.... You don't need anyone or anything.... Your destiny lies straight ahead." She will travel in Mexico for a while. Gershwin goes back to Julie. "I've been all mixed up," he tells her. But he has shown her Christine's letter; and if he doesn't need anyone or anything, he doesn't need her either, she tells him. "With you it's different," a friend assures her, but she is not to be dissuaded; she rushes off to Florida.... But Gershwin does need Julie. He goes driving ahead in his work.... more and more successful, more and more lost to himself. "What are you trying to forget?" his friend Max Dreyfus asks him. "Julie?" And Gershwin with an anguished cry confirms this guess: "Way down deep I'm a family man without a family!" He drives himself at last to the verge of a breakdown. And now Julie hears of it and she calls. "Oh, Julie!" he cries. "Oh, Julie!...Meet me!...Make up for all the lost years.... Hurry, darling, hurry!" She is coming at last, and he sits at the piano and he can play again, and he plays, "Love walked right in and drove the shadows away"....But it is too late. He is a very sick man.

In *Incendiary Blonde* again, "it just wasn't in the cards for (Tex and Bill, the rodeo owner) to get together." "It had to be you...had to be you," the music throughout the film reiterates. But first Bill is married already. His wife has been in an asylum for years, but he doesn't tell Tex this, just that he's married—"Better run along, kid." And she runs along, not knowing that he cares. A couple of years later a friend tells her what "the angle" really is; and she goes running off to Bill, to say now listen to her, she is willing to wait, no matter how long. And suddenly, then, news comes that his wife has died. But to Bill comes news too that Tex and her father are due to land in jail, because of some phony theater stocks for which her father is responsible. To save Tex, Bill buys them both out, keeping his real motive from Tex, bravely bluffing that he's out "to make a killing" at her expense. "I guess I'm lucky at that!" she cries. "You'd be too much for a little country girl like me!"; and once again, not knowing how he cares, she "runs along." A year later her father spills to her what the angle has been this time. "Bill! Oh, you big lug! That's another year of my life wasted!" she cries. But at last they are going to be married. The justice of the peace is waiting, the wedding cake is baked, with a diamond bracelet baked right into it, and then—some gangsters make a raid. Bill must kill one of them in self-defense. The sentence is five years. And—the doctor has just informed Tex that she has only two more years to live. Bravely she does not tell Bill this and he, bravely, will not marry her before setting off to jail, for fear of hurting her career. No, it just hasn't been "in the cards" for them to get together. Of course this poor girl cries of wasted years.

In *Humoresque,* it is the same story. This time it should have been Gina. Gina is a girl rather like Gershwin's Julie—Garfield's childhood sweetheart, and again the girl to whom he blurts out his early dream. But when he becomes Mrs. Wright's protégé he forgets Gina. Mrs. Wright (Joan Crawford) is a married woman. And besides, the two of them seem able only to torture each other with their love—"What is this thing, this funny thing called love?" the music asks. "Let me alone," she tells him. "You're a hangman's noose to me!" Then comes the news that Mr. Wright will grant a divorce. And "I want to marry you," and "Don't try to fight it," Garfield tells her; and "I can't fight it," she tells him. So they are going to be married. But "You don't want me, not really!" she has cried; and one night, out at her place by the shore, as the music from his distant concert swells on the radio, she walks out on him, father this time than to Mexico or Florida or jail—walks into the ocean. No wonder this hero feels confused.

In *Random Harvest,* when the bump on the head restores his early memories to Ronald Colman, it simultaneously robs him of his most recent ones. He is away at the time from the little cottage and Greer and the son she has borne to him; and he never returns. Greer after years of searching (during which their little son dies) catches up with him—but he doesn't know her. She becomes his secretary and waits...patiently for recognition—but it does not come. (Nevertheless, when he is about to be married to a nice young girl who has wooed him, and at the wedding rehearsal the organ plays "Oh perfect love," the girl can see, from the suddenly vague and gently troubled look that comes over him, that there has been someone else in his life whom she could never replace, and she makes *her* brave exit.) After a while Ronald makes Greer his wife again, but it is on a strictly social secretary basis. Still—though he sometimes stares oddly at her red hair in the sunlight and she holds her breath—recognition does not break. And the years wear on. This hero might well have the sense that there is something he has missed.

At the very end of this, the earliest film of the four, just when Greer is ready to walk out on it all, Ronald comes by chance to the scene of their early meeting and, memory stirring at last, finds his way back to to that cottage. Greer, getting word of it, is there before him; and when he pushes open the creaky gate, walks down the little path, pushes aside the blossomy branch—all just the way it once was, as in a fairly tale—the door opens and

there she stands, calling out to him the old name she had for him—
"Smittie!"—and he remembers his lost love, and falls into her arms.

Yes, viewing any one of these films by itself, one could say: Here is one
who mounts the ladder of success, who also just happens to be unlucky in
love. But viewing them in conjuction, the question one has to ask is: why
is this note always added, and always fatally—the one film granting us a
a happy ending granting it, in effect, at the foot of the ladder again: it is
as "Smittie" that he embraces her. Why is it added even in two biographies,
where it has little to do with the facts—and not just easily added but strained
for, far-fetched?

If these frustrations in love are carefully examined, at those points especially
where the credibility of the story is most strained, one sees how closely they
are interwoven with the stories of success. The pattern that is strained for
is apt to be worth study. The fact that, labored as it is, an audience accepts
it time after time, is indication that it veils some deeper pattern of experience
they feel in their bones to be true.

In both *Humoresque* and *Rhapsody in Blue,* the drama becomes most
forced when the hero's second love walks out on him. The various
explanations the two films offer here are. . .inconsistent. Each of the ladies
remarks to the hero at some point that she is leaving him because he is the
"ideal bachelor." "You're married already—to your work," says Joan
Crawford. . . .And Christine: "You don't need anyone. . .your destiny lies
straight ahead." Here the suggestion is that she walks out on him, nobly,
so that she will not distract him. But neither woman really seems the self-
sacrificing type, and at other moments we are given reason to suppose that
she is jealous of his career and walks out because she feels that she cannot
sufficiently possess him. At still other moments, each of the women seems
to hunger to possess him precisely through his work. Christine eagerly plays
the part of Gershwin's press agent; Joan Crawford even more eagerly takes
John Garfield's career under her management. In *Humoresque,* the most
intense love scenes are the concert sequences: as Garfield plays his violin,
the camera moves up on Crawford in her box, lips pouting wetly, then
parting in little gasps—while his mother stares up at her from her seat below,
deeply shocked. It would hardly seem that a woman *could* possess a man
more utterly through his work. Grant this woman her jealousy of his work,
however (or, if you prefer, her noble decision not to stand between him and
that work), the films offer us a further reason why she walks out on him.
In the very speech in which Crawford declares to Garfield that he doesn't
want her because he has his career, she declares to him, "You need the home
maker type!". . .Gershwin's friends offer this diagnosis too, and he agrees:
"Way down deep I'm a family man without a family!"

They cannot be happy together, then, first: because he is married to his work, and second: because he is at heart a family man. The two reasons do not add up—at the literal level on which I have been presenting them. They add up only in terms abstracted from the context of the doomed love affair— into the clumsily labored picture of one who loses much that he needs from life in the process of making a way for himself. In both films, note, it is when the hero finds himself definitely on the way up that he becomes estranged from the girl he really needs, the girl with whom, as Garfield puts it to Gina, he can "be himself." This point of timing is not obtrusive; it is then simply, it seems, that he meets the other woman. In *Random Harvest*, it is most distinctly when he starts his upward climb in earnest that the hero becomes estranged—not just from a "home maker type" but from an "ideal home." The estrangement is marked literally with the neatness of a bump on the head.... "A start in life!" he declares, leaving for a new job in the city. "A career!" And the stroke descends; he wakes to fortune—and loss.

As usual, it is when several films are examined together that the pattern with which the film makers are really concerned (whether or not they know it) stands out clearly. Ronald's amnesia in *Random Harvest* is the strained-for, the far-fetched element. Set this film next to *Rhapsody in Blue* and *Humoresque* and the hero's amnesia drops its literal character, appears as a transparent symbol. Note how closely, really, Ronald's story matches the stories of those other two heroes. Greer Garson plays a role equivalent to the separate roles played by two women in each of the other films....

If the story of *Random Harvest* opens out for us when it is set in conjunction with *Humoresque* and *Rhapsody in Blue*, the hero's amnesia suddenly taking on a less literal character, conversely that image brings into a clearer focus the plight of the other two heroes. *Humoresque* and *Rhapsody in Blue* suggest that the women involved make themselves unattainable. *Random Harvest* clearly names the hero's own "illness" as the root of the trouble. If *Rhapsody in Blue* is unconvincing when Christine walks out on Gershwin, it is even more unconvincing when Julie walks out on him too after he has realized that he needs her. His failure to find in her arms a "world completely new" makes real sense only in terms of his own distraction, his not knowing what it is that he is missing. *Humoresque* is more persuasive here at least. This hero admits that he doesn't know "where home is." Perhaps one reason that the women are made to take the decisive steps in *Humoresque* and *Rhapsody in Blue* is that these two films too strain to present a picture of estrangement *helplessly* suffered. From the three films a common pattern emerges—of one who, when he casts himself into the race, succumbs to a sort of amnesia, in which he loses the original dream that he had, loses the knowledge of where home is. To dull the sense of his loss, he engages himself even more frantically. But the faster he runs, the more and more lost to himself he becomes.

The innocent

I have been slighting mention of the fourth film of this group, *Incendiary Blonde*, because it does not quite parallel the other three. The crucial estrangement here, recall, results from Bill's apparent decision to make a "killing" at poor Tex's expense. Tex herself is not responsible. It also turns out that Bill never really did abandon her: his was an act of loyalty, really— misunderstood. In this film, at least, it might seem that one could call the story of success and the story of frustrated love coincidental and nothing more.

But if *Incendiary Blonde* fails to display the exact pattern of forgetfulness that I traced in those other three films, it displays another pattern not at all irrelevant to that one. It offers us on the one hand the pathos of innocence misunderstood: this hero is unjustly suspected of not *caring* if "there is someone (he has) hurt" along the road to success. It offers us at the same time a zestful exhibition of hero and heroine boasting about the unscrupulous methods they use to make their way. "Hello, sucker!" is Tex's battle cry.... What is the special attraction between the two lovers? Here is their first meeting: Tex enters a bucking broncho contest, disguised as a man; is bucked off but charges that the girth was loose; demands another try and this time carries off the prize; then barges in on the owner of the show, the hero. Was he responsible for that loosened girth? No, he says, "but it's an idea." He offers her a job. They bargain in lively fashion. When they have reached a compromise, "Put that in writing!" one cries; and this becomes a sort of byword between them throughout the film. Clearly the very ground from which their love springs is an exciting mutual wariness: they keep each other on their toes, teach each other new tricks.

A funny lapse is evidenced here on the part of the film makers, who flaunt for our pleasure the enjoyment these two take in pulling off tricks, and simultaneously offer us the pathos of innocence wronged—the hero in effect crying, "I never really did it!" the heroine, "You'd be too much for a little country girl like me!" Here, one could say, is another case of amnesia—and it is worth examining at greater length, for it gives further definition to the vague pattern of distraction observed in those first three films.

It can be examined in a whole series of other films, and in a form more pronounced, because in these films the one misunderstood *is* the one whose career we follow.... Over and over, in a series of for the most part "Grade B" musicals, the hero suffers estrangement from one who is dear to him when he is charged with advancing his career at this loved one's expense. Over and over, time proves him to have been misunderstood; and here, for a change, the lovers do finally come together. But over and over, too, the happy acquittal of the hero of the charges against him is curiously inconsistent with certain other general impressions the film has given us.

In a number of these films the hero is shown to be clearly innocent at least of the particular offense with which he is charged. For example, in *My Best Gal* (1944), a young playwright is accused by his friends and by his best gal of having sold them out, by giving his musical to a producer without holding out for an agreement that they will be cast in it. "He got his bank account!" they sneer. The hero *has* sold the script without them, but he has refused first many times and sold it only upon learning that his girl's father is gravely ill and has no money to pay for a doctor—has sold it on any terms he could get so that he can take care of the old man—anonymously, of course, silently suffering their scorn. The incongruity here, as in *Incendiary Blonde,* is simply the manner in which the film quite shows off in *other* instances how this hero, and his friends too, stop at nothing to sell their wares, gayly *disdain* innocence.

But in many films it is even a question whether the hero is innocent of the particular act with which—we are made to feel—he is so unjustly charged. Here, for example, is a film called *Hi Beautiful* (again 1944). This hero suffers most pitifully when accused by his sweetheart of cheaply exploiting their love by submitting an intimate photograph to the Brisbee Patent Pills "Happiest G.I. Couple" Contest. A telegram arrives, informing them that they are the winners. "It's horrible to get money that way!" she explodes; and she walks out on him. It's been a "screwy mistake." He never submitted the photograph at all. The maid did it, without his knowledge. But—we *have* seen him wistfully yearning to submit it, murmuring, "A guy has to work so hard and long . . ." Nor when he learns what the maid has done does he tell the Brisbee Pills people that it's been a screwy mistake—and a fraud as well, since he and his girl are not married. Instead, he quickly fakes a happy home, so that he can claim the prize when it is delivered. And he tricks his girl into playing along with him. She has a job with a real estate firm, tending a . . . model house, and pretends for the occasion that this is their home—borrowing some neighbors' children and animals for a finishing touch. When the real estate man walks in on the game, which has begun to get out of hand (but "I can't let anything happen to him until I get that check!" the hero cries in an aside), a little bribery and blackmail save the day. The hero suggests to the irate real estate man that if he wins his prize his first purchase may be this very house; and he scares Brisbee with the suggestion that he may lose face with the public if he announces that his winners are phonies. "There's no end to his lies" and his tricks, the girl exclaims in distress. But the maid steps in now and explains everything; explains that it was she who submitted that photograph—the hero, as she puts (as we happily accept it), merely tried to "fix up" what she had started. The two lovers fall into each other's arms. "Happiness is good for you," chirrups the maid, turning to face us from the screen and recommend, "You too!"

Other films show us the hero caught in even more precisely the act of which he is so cruelly accused.... Here is *Once Upon a Time* (1944). The hero, Flynn (Cary Grant), is a Broadway producer who's just had three flops and is about to lose his theater—until he runs into Pinky, the urchin, and Curly, his dancing caterpiller. When Pinky plays "Yessir, she's my baby" on his mouth organ, Curly stands on end and wiggles, "dances!" "Caterpillers come and go, but that one has talent. A miracle!" Flynn exclaims; "I'm going to hold on to my theater!" He promptly forms a "partnership" with Pinky and is soon giving the caterpiller nationwide publicity. Pinky joined the partnership, of course, only after making Flynn promise that he'll never sell Curly, for the two mean everything to each other. And Flynn has given his solemn word. But the first chance he gets to sell (Disney will give him $100,000), he says bluntly, "I can't worry about that kid." "You liar!" cries the heartbroken boy; "We were wrong about you!" For Pinky, who's an orphan, has looked up to Flynn as to a father. "Once I thought I wanted to be like you; but now I never want to be like you. You're a mean man, Mr. Flynn!"

And it would certainly seem so.... Yet this film, too manages to acquit its hero of all harsh charges. The way in which it does this is flagrant. It begins by gayly flaunting Flynn's ability to sell anything. The banker who comes to tell him he is losing his theater almost succumbs to backing another super production—then catches himself: "No! That's the way you sold me the last time!" When Flynn exults to his sidekick, Moke, that the dancing caterpiller will save his theater, "Wait till I tell the public what he means," he cries. "What does he mean?" asks Moke. To which Flynn replies, "I don't know yet, but I'll think of something." When he very soon does think of something, the film continues to treat as a source of fun his gift for putting it over on the public. He sells the little worm as a symbol of "the Spirit of Man:" "The worm was crawling around in the dirt, and suddenly it heard music; it raised its head! It brings us all a message!" The public buys. Flynn's office is soon mobbed with people begging permission to make Curly cookies, Curly toys. And Flynn's justification to us in the end? Chided with trying to take the little worm from Pinky, he cries, "You can't understand what the caterpiller has begun to mean to the world!"

The film adds a final twist. When Pinky cries out his accusation, Flynn, very hurt, sets Curly right down (in the little shoebox in which he lives) and walks out. But when Pinky goes to talk to Curly, he isn't in the box! Pinky thinks Flynn has taken him—here really does misjudge him. Though Flynn and Pinky miss each other sorely, neither will approach the other now. But one day some of Pinky's friends march Flynn to Pinky's house. And as Flynn sits there at the upright, sadly picking out on the keys Curly's old tune, a butterfly emerges and begins to flutter about in time to the notes. Pinky comes running in, and of course the butterfly is Curly: that's where he had gone, to spin himself a cocoon! "And he's never going to leave us again, is he?" cries the ecstatic boy. But Flynn gently counsels him now: they cannot really keep him. How could they? And Pinky begins at last to understand. No one's been trying to rob him of anything. One just can't hold onto these things for oneself. As the butterfly flutters out the open window, the two, arms around each other, wave happily: "Thanks for everything!" (Flynn may well wave his thanks, for though the deal with Disney fell through, the banker has announced that he's going to back him again—he's been so impressed with what he made of that bug.)

Unlike the heroes of *Rhapsody in Blue, Humoresque,* and *Random Harvest,* the successful one in this type of film utters no pitiful cries toward the end—anxious about something he has missed, someone he has hurt. This hero always regains the love from which he has been estranged, and always stands at last acquitted of all trespasses against others. But, as I have noted, in the process of giving us this happy ending—sparing us the portrait of the poor amnesiac—the film makers themselves display strange lapses of memory. And we in the audience, dreaming the dream we are offered, succumb to a kind of amnesia ourselves—disavowing at one moment feelings that have engaged us just a moment before.

There is a more direct sense too in which these films reinforce the image of one helplessly lost to himself. Listen, in each of them, to the hero's cry when he is faced by his harsh accusers. Over and over, to clear himself, he cites his helpless commitment to the deeds for which they account him responsible. Here is nothing *he* has intended, he cries. The maid did this; or his agent was to blame. Tyrannical agents abound in the genre, and publicity departments "set loose" on the hapless hero; or meddling friends or meddling parents. Events quite out of his control intervene—like the fact that caterpillers have to turn into butterflies and flutter away.... This hero may stand there at last securely at the top, and cleared of all charges against him; but what has become of the familiar myth—the youth striking out boldly after his dream, the self-made man proudly surveying the fruits of his own enterprise? That myth has been overturned.

In the films of Preston Sturges—in *Hail the Conquering Hero* (1944), for example—this overturn of the old myth can be seen very clearly. For Sturges, refining in a comic vein upon this dream, managing more nimbly than all the rest to move his hero unsullied to the top of the heap, borrows for his purpose a familiar figure from early films—one brought to life in the twenties by Buster Keaton and Harry Langdon: the clown figure of the Innocent, the unworldly one, pure of heart. The contrast between his version of this conquering hero and the original is a telling one.

Sturges's hero never reaches out his hands to seize what he finally gains, and one does not need to listen to his wild cries about it, one can see that he is not responsible for the path he takes. There is no room for argument at all as to the nature of this hero's intentions. He is a little guy who loves his mother very much, and his girl, and his home town, and yearns to make a place for himself in that town, however humble—he'd proudly be dog catcher. But as the film opens, he sits in gloomy self-imposed exile: he has tried to join the Marines and he has been rejected because of hay fever. Son of a Marine hero, he is ashamed to return home. He has written his mother that he has been sent overseas, has written his girl not to wait for him, and as we meet him he is moping over his beer in a tavern in the big city, far from home, trying hard not to hear the four singing waiters, for "Home to the arms of mother!" they wail. He need not grieve. Home to the arms of mother, to the arms of his girl, to a hero's welcome, to election as mayor of the town, the film brings Woodrow LaFayette Pershing Truesmith (Eddie Bracken). But it brings him home protesting all the way.

Six Marines on leave, treated to beers by Woodrow, impulsively give him his start. Learning his sad story, they decide that his exile is not fair to his mother; they cannot have her thinking that he is over there in danger; so one of them...gets Mrs. Truesmith on the phone and tells her that her son is headed home, honorably discharged after heroism at Guadalcanal. Woodrow, dragged to the phone, wildly stammers out his denials, but the lie has been told; his protestations sound like a hero's modesty. They march him to the train. Among their firmly stepping feet his two feet balk and drag, but in vain. They hoist him aboard; there, though he struggles and squirms, force onto him a corporal's uniform hung with medals. And they decide to stick right along with him so that he cannot thwart their plan. That mother of his mustn't "worry no more." When Woodrow spots the welcoming committee drawn up at the station, he cries, "let me outta here!" and tries to hide in the lavatory; but the six deliver him into the arms of the crowd. If he wanted to cry out his denials now, he couldn't, for his words would be lost in the din of the competing brass bands. And besides, he cannot even speak, for a little girl has thrust a great bouquet of goldenrod into his face and he is sneezing helplessly.

From here on, the town itself takes over and events sweep him along. A statue is being erected in his honor. At a special ceremony, his mother's mortgage is torn up. Woodrow writhes, stammers, doesn't know what to do. The six Marines keep careful watch to prevent him from doing anything. ("See that look in your mother's eye?" they gloat.) A crowd of citizens moves on his house. "Here it comes," says Woodrow. "I'm ready." He assumes that the hoax has been discovered. But this turns out to be a committee to draft him as a candidate for mayor. He tries to protest. He loves his mother very much, he stammers, and he loves this town, and the very dogs and cats in the streets; but he isn't worthy, and he's no hero, he protests. "He could be president!" the crowd murmurs. "He has a natural flair for politics!" "Why, you couldn't stop from being mayor," they tell him. "A miracle couldn't stop you." So he tries to leave town, but the six prevent him. At last from the platform of Town Hall, where he is swept in a tumultuous parade, he flatly names himself a phony, gives them the whole history of the lie (absolving the six of all complicity, though); and now he quickly heads for the railroad station, to leave forever. Again a mob moves down upon him. He thinks this time that they have come to lynch him. But they have come to *insist* that he be their mayor; for, they cry, he has given them proof of his courage and honesty. "No! No!" he stammers, unbelieving. And there he stands his very heart's desire his—and swept to victory without ever trying for it....

In those earlier films of Keaton and Langdon, the hero too is wondrously innocent of half that goes on about him. He too is carried to victory by a sort of preposterous good luck. At a glance, these heroes might seem to be identical. But it is not so. In the original, the old myth...still precariously stands.

At the beginning of *The General,* a Buster Keaton film (1927), the hero sits in sad exile too. He too has tried to enlist (in the Civil War) and has been rejected—on the grounds that he is more useful at his job: he is an engineer; "the General" is his beloved engine. He is unaware of the reason for his rejection. Furthermore, his girl, believing he has not tried to enlist, has turned him from her door. We see him sitting dejected on the side of the big engine, so rapt in his grief that when another engineer starts up the train, he doesn't even notice—still sits, listlessly riding the slow-galloping piston-rod. But the two exiles with which the films commence are not the same. When this hero steps out onto the street, after the Army has turned him down, he turns solemnly to address them: "If you lose this war, don't blame me!" Disdained by his girl, he walks off in a grief profound but haughty. It is no self-imposed exile he suffers, meekly convinced of his own ineffectualness.

Nor does this hero wait for others to launch him upon the way. One day some enemy soldiers make off with his "General" while he and the passengers are having lunch at a station—make off with it up the track back toward their own lines, taking with them, too, the hero's girl, who has stepped into the baggage car to look for something. Open-mouthed, everybody watches the train vanish, our hero's mouth open wider than all the rest. But gesturing for others to follow him, he promptly starts running after it. Those others who join him as promptly give up the chase, for it is obviously mad to try to catch the train on foot. But our hero, glancing back and finding that he runs on alone, runs on still, doggedly. This is the stamp of *his* innocence: to persist even when the race seems impossible.

Those more sensible who have stayed behind think to wire ahead to the next station, but the enemy has already stopped to cut all the wires. On the hero, in crazy pursuit, everything now depends. A little hand car that he finds and boards...is soon derailed. Abandoning it in a huff, he runs on to grab up a bicycle, pedals headlong until this spills him; on foot again reaches another train finally and commandeering it, gives more effective chase. This train is full of soldiers and he thinks he proceeds in force now; but the engine has not been coupled to the rest, and glancing back, again—blinking—he finds himself alone. But again he keeps on.

Superficially this could be the Sturges hero. Amazement drops his jaw as continually as it does Woodrow's. And he too is the beneficiary of crazy chance. The enemy uncouples a rear car to impede him. With it in front of him he must proceed quite blindly. He manages to switch it off onto a side track, but this—unknown to him—rejoins the main track; agape, he finds the car right there ahead of him again. Then while he is busy at something else, a log thrown onto the track by the enemy to further hinder him manages instead merely to derail this one car. When he looks again, it is no longer there....Meanwhile the two trains enter enemy territory. He is unaware of this. He is busy chopping wood for his fire, first with a hatchet, then patiently with the head of the hatchet after it flies off the handle. Beyond him we see, in panorama, streaming by, one army retreating, another, the enemy, advancing—horsemen, wagons, foot soldiers. He chops on, unaware—until suddenly he puts his head up and his jaw drops again. But luck goes with him all the way—enables him, after he hops from his train, to find the cabin where the enemy proceeds; there to rescue his girl; there too to overhear the enemy plans; then steal off, in a borrowed uniform, with the girl in a sack over his shoulder to board his "General"—under their noses—and drive off back toward his own lines. And every time the enemy soldier who is on the train, unknown to him, starts to creep up on him, some random hunk of wood that he tosses as he stokes the fire knocks the man senseless. The news of the enemy plan he brings back helps his side to win the ensuing battle. And that dazed enemy soldier, noticed at last by the hero and led into camp, turns out to be an important commander.

Of either success, Woodrow's or this hero's, one could declare: magic. Yet it is a very different magic in the two films. Woodrow's success is gratuitous and ironic, one of life's pranks: his protests of unworthiness gain him the heights—turn out to equal a flair for politics. Whereas in the case of this earlier hero the impression is that by special persistence, the intensity of his belief that he will succeed, he magically does—this luck generated, as it were, by his faith itself.

The innocence of these two heroes is of a very different sort. They are oblivious in quite a different way to what goes on about them. Woodrow displays an almost epileptic bewilderment, but Keaton has, still, the air of one distracted by a compelling vision.*

The endings of the two films sum up the contrast. "Where did you get that?" the commander of the armies demands of Buster Keaton who has dressed in a second borrowed uniform. "Take it off!" And Keaton does so, expecting to be punished. "Put this on!" comes the next order, and he is climbing into the clothes he is handed before he recognizes them as a lieutenant's uniform. The commander next hands him the sword of the enemy officer he has captured—to be his own. "No! No!" Woodrow sputtered, when presented with *his* heart's desire. But Keaton assumes his new rank gravely, even haughtily—as one who knows his due. And it is in the spirit of the deserving knight that he then walks off with his girl; whereas Woodrow continued to the end to cry to his girl, "You are well rid of me!"

There is a further sense in which the myth, still alive in these earlier films, is overturned in the films of Sturges. Swept home to the arms of sweetheart and mother, the status of hero, election as mayor of his town, Woodrow Truesmith does gain his heart's desire.... Though accidental, his victory might seem at least tangible. But even as Woodrow stands there, his dreams all come true, laughter can be said to explode those dreams. Where the innocence of Keaton proved to be inspired, that of this other dreamer stands revealed as the innocence of the dupe. All that Woodrow Truesmith adores so faithfully is winked away for us in the course of the film. His love for his mother is slyly spoofed by including in the cast a Marine with a mother complex. His worship of the Marines is spoofed in the staging of the solemn visits the boys pay to the portrait of Woodrow's bemedaled father, which hangs in the parlor as in a shrine. And his home town is savagely caricatured, the elaborate welcome home it offers Woodrow revealed as obscene, each citizen shown to be looking simply to his own advantage. "There's something rotten in this town," someone says right out. And even Woodrow declares to them that they are attracted to him because he is a big phony. Supposedly at the very end he accomplishes the spiritual reform of the town, a reform the town itself has been yearning for. But a kind of sly laughter envelops even this event. Sturges in this film cunningly crowns his hero a victor—and then, as it were, winks at us over his shoulder.

*See Editor's Note, page ix.

"Believe in me!"

One hero, then, stands at the top of the ladder of success uttering piteous cries—part of him lost, his belief in himself and in all his youthful dreams lost. A second figure of success is tortured by the fact that others refuse to believe in him. A third stands there, all he has yearned for safely clasped; but if one looks again, his dream too dissolves, although in comic innocence he clasps it still. There is yet another figure in the films of these years, superficially like none of these, superficially the very opposite of the Innocent, cast indeed as a villain, but again, if one looks, really the same figure— shown us in extremity.

In the films that feature him in this darker guise—for example, in *Dragonwyck, Undercurrent, The Strange Love of Martha Ivers* (each 1946)— it is ostensibly some other figure with whom we sympathize; but he remains the central figure of the piece. For in each film the story is of one who has fallen helplessly in love with him or with her. This villain has charms.

Dragonwyck and *Undercurrent* start out brightly. In each, a restless girl, still living at home, yearns to leave that home. The villain appears and carries her off as if to the happiest of endings. In *Dragonwyck*, set in the past century, she is a girl on a small Connecticut Yankee farm, the villain a wealthy patroon, a distant cousin, who writes one day to engage her as a governess to his daughter. "Golly Moses!" she cries in ecstasy when her poppa allows her to go, and again when she sees her new home on the Hudson.... When the grand visitors at the manor look down their noses at her, the patroon takes her by the hand and waltzes with her at the ball before them all. "Golly Moses!" is all she can exclaim again. When his wife dies and he asks her hand in marriage, she is too breathless even to utter that exclamation. It is a dream come true for her.

In *Undercurrent,* she is a chemistry professor's daughter in a small college town, the villain a young millionaire captain of industry who visits the father to ask him for a new formula he has perfected and promptly returns to ask him for his daughter—because the meeting of these two has constituted a very special chemical event too.... "Judas!" this heroine exclaims when she sees *her* new home, Washington, spread out below their plane. "You've led me by the hand," she tells him, "into a strange and wonderful world"—she too breathing that it is "like a dream!"

Each of these heroines wakes from this dream—not merely to a sense of loss but to recognition that death lies all about her in the world into which she has been led. But she wakes slowly and incredulously.

In *The Strange Love of Martha Ivers,* the protagonist is not a wide-eyed young girl but a tough young man. As a kid he had hopped a circus train and run off from his home town.... Now, passing through the town by chance, he discovers that his childhood sweetheart—who almost ran away *with* him that day—has become the reigning power there. The town has even been renamed for her. "Welcome to Iverstown," he reads on a sign, and "Maybe this time they mean it," he breathes. He is soon adding, "Yes, now I've got luck!" because Martha Ivers, though a married woman, is still in love with him, and if he wants to, it's clear, he can share that power with her. This hero too wakes to the fact that there is only death to be gained here, and pulls out—just in time. Each one of these protagonists is very nearly killed at the hands of the beloved.

In the first film I described in this chapter, the figure of success uttered vague cries about having perhaps injured other people. Here there is nothing vague about the fact that he has. Nor is his guilt ever wished away, as in the second group of films I described. And the estrangement that grows between him and his beloved as she learns of his guilt is never healed.

In *Dragonwyck*, the patroon (Vincent Price) is trying to keep his enormous land grant intact, but to do this he has to break the anti-rent movement spreading among his tenant farmers. In this fight he is gradually defined as altogether ruthless. He lacks an heir to whom he can leave Dragonwyck, and he is defined here even more clearly as a villain: we see him poison his first wife when she fails to bear him a son; we see him try to poison his second wife, the heroine. The captain of industry in *Undercurrent* (Robert Taylor) owes his fortune too to ruthlessness. It rests on a certain remarkable invention of "his"—which turns out not to be his at all but that of a little refugee whom he has murdered for it. Taylor has also robbed his own brother of his proper share in the business, rigging the books to make it appear that his brother was the crooked one. And this man too tries to take the life of the heroine. In *The Strange Love of Martha Ivers* too, the fortunes of Martha Ivers (Barbara Stanwyck) are founded on murder. Martha, we learn, never ran off with the hero because in a last-minute quarrel with her aunt she struck her and accidentally killed her—the aunt toppling down a steep flight of stairs. Through this accidental killing she came into her aunt's fortune. She secured that fortune through a willful second killing. For she took her tutor's advice and lied about her aunt's death—pretending to have seen a stranger run off from the scene. And some years later she coolly "identified" as that stranger and sent to the chair an innocent man. Her husband, the tutor's son, acted as prosecutor, and this gave him his start on a political career. He is D.A. now; soon, it's predicted, he will be governor—"whatever his wife wants him to be." We see Martha try to take the life of this husband, when he stands in her way. And we see her try to take the life of the hero.

This figure of success is carefully defined as a twisted character. Vincent Price in *Dragonwyck* takes dope; Robert Taylor in *Undercurrent* beats his horse; Barbara Stanwyck—Martha Ivers—all but beats her...husband. Each of them, we are told, is "sick." Look closely, however, and the special case, here as always, becomes the familiar case. Here is the same sick figure I have been sketching all along—his sickness merely graver now. In this character, in fact, the kinship of the two other figures I have been describing...is confirmed, for their pitiful cries are interwoven here—the cry of the first: "I am homeless!" and the cry of the other: "I am doubted! Do not doubt me!" This latest figure adds the desperate cry: "Believe in me or I will have to destroy you!"

As all is told, as usual, in terms of boy meets girl, look closely at the gesture with which this villain approaches his victim. Here, for example, is the scene in which Vincent Price proposes to Miranda in *Dragonwyck:* Down the hallway his wife has just died—poisoned by an exotic plant he has had placed in her room. Wasting no time, he hurries to Miranda. He utters no villainish laughter, however, as he approaches. Here is the familiar pathos. Face dark with suffering, he comes to her—a suppliant. His line is dying out, his authority is no longer believed in, Dragonwyck is threatened. Perhaps Miranda can give him a son. And she believes in him, believes in his dream. As Gershwin, toward the end, came to Julie, asking her to restore his lost life to him, the patroon comes to Miranda. Dressed in a dark robe, the crest of Dragonwyck embroidered over his heart, he approaches—and pours out to her all his anguish. "I wish I knew something I could say to help you," she tells him. "I want to so much!" "Do you, Miranda?" he cries. "You must have faith!" she tells him. And he? "As long as you are with me!" He knows, he says, that he has no right to speak at this time, but he cannot help himself....When they are married soon after, "You will be with me wherever I am, always!" he cries. But Miranda in her turn fails to give him a son. And then as he begins to lose the fight against the anti-rent movement and as he grows more violent in his ways, she begins, too, to look upon him with a difference—to judge him. Frantic again—for "You shall not destroy Dragonwyck!" he has cried to them all—he feels driven to destroy Miranda too. She is rescued by a doctor, a leader in the anti-rent movement, who loves her. And the patroon commits suicide. The film keeps him a touching figure even at the end. As the shot rings out, as he gives one last look toward Miranda, who has been his hope and his loss, then slumps forward, all who stand there silently remove their hats.

In *Undercurrent* too, the villain approaches the heroine as a frantic suppliant, his appeal the same: he too wants her to restore to him a life that has somehow eluded him, a belief in himself that fails. Soon after their marriage, Robert Taylor pours out all *his* anguish to Katherine Hepburn. The story he tells is one of cruel injuries suffered at the hands of his brother, Robert Mitchum. Clinging to her like a child, he cries, "He can't hurt us if we hold on to each other!...We'll never let him come between us!" The heroine decides that she must learn more about this man who shadows her husband's life; and so his nature is gradually revealed to us. He turns out to be the very opposite of the person Taylor has pictured. Unlike Taylor, he has never had much money, "never cared about it"; but when Hepburn at last finds her way to his house, in contrast to the house to which Taylor has brought her (which is strangely "unused"...), *Mitchum's* house is "like someone's home." (Taylor, in a jealous frenzy when he finds her in this place, starts throwing about the books, the records, the pipes, the various tokens of a life really lived.) And Taylor's sick hatred of his brother turns out to be more, too, than a matter of jealousy. His brother is the one who knows his guilt—who has guessed about the murder of the little refugee. Throughout most of the film, no one knows where Mitchum is. He has run away to avoid facing his brother with what he knows about him. He has joined the Army, hoping to be killed. But he comes out alive. And after he meets Hepburn (she doesn't recognize him—takes him to be the caretaker at the place), he goes at last to Taylor and confronts him; for she's "a fine woman," he tells Taylor, and mustn't be hurt. Taylor must tell her all the truth about himself.

"I can't give her up!" Taylor cries. "I'll give it all back—but not her!" "I can be all right!" he cries. "She loves me!" And as the brother still faces him, he promises that he will tell her the truth. But give him a little time—until he's sure of her. "To whom do you belong?" he has cried frantically to Hepburn. Then, as estrangement has grown between them, because of his weird behavior..."Please," he has begged her, "try a little old-fashioned trust, a little blind faith." And she has tried. But for Taylor too, as for the patroon, everything suddenly fails—here in a most ironical fashion. "Forgive me!" she cries to him one day. "I almost destroyed our happiness by doubting!" She confesses that someone had planted in her heart the suspicion that he had murdered his brother; but she has evidence now that he is very much alive. "I am deeply ashamed," she tells him. "I was going to go away and never see you again!" He asks her softly, "You couldn't have endured living with a murderer?" Unknowing, she has spoken fatal words. *"I'm going to see,"* he tells her, *"that you never have the chance to doubt me again."* So Taylor in his turn tries to destroy the woman who was once all his hope but has become instead a judgement upon him. This heroine escapes death even more narrowly than the heroine of *Dragonwyck*—escapes only because Taylor is trampled to death by his horse (the horse that was once his brother's and that he has tried in vain to master). And from the wheelchair in which she will have to stay for a while, the heroine comes at last to meet Robert Mitchum. Some day, we gather, when it becomes fitting to hold out his hands to her, he will lead her among humbler but happier ways.

Behind the figure of Martha Ivers there range themselves even more clearly in kinship those other lost figures I have sketched—their gestures the same, here simply exaggerated, the malady turned acute. When Sam after the lapse of many years meets his childhood sweetheart again, now virtual sovereign of "America's fastest growing industrial city," he asks her, "Aren't you glad that you missed that circus train?" But staring at him she mumbles, "I don't know"—thrown quite off balance, her husband notes in amazement. He has never seen her lose her poise like that before. Martha drives Sam to the top of a high hill from which all her kingdom can be surveyed—Iverstown. (Martha's name had been Smith, but her proud aunt had insisted that she take *her* name, Ivers, if she wished to inherit her money; for her aunt had scorned Martha's father, who was a millhand.) Yes, her father had been a millhand here, Martha boasts to Sam, and now she owns the town. Now she employs thirty thousand workers at the mill, instead of the mere three thousand who had been employed in her father's day. "And I've done it all myself!" she boasts. Nor does she intend to have it taken from her. When Sam appears on the scene, she suspects at first that he has come to blackmail her—for she assumes that he was a witness long ago to the death of her aunt. Yet as she gazes down upon her conquest spread out before her, "it doesn't even look real," she breathes. "If anyone asked me, I would say that my name was still Martha Smith." Martha takes Sam to her house. And in this mansion that was once her aunt's and that she's completely redecorated, one room remains untouched, "nothing changed since that night" when she almost ran off with Sam. "I come here often," she confesses (as Ronald Colman often fingered that little key dangling from his watch chain, while his spirit groped to remember the home he had lost). One thing that Martha craves from Sam is release from Walter—weakling, drunkard, "scared little boy," who is helplessly in love with her and whom she bullies as she likes, but who does "know her" and knows the history of her ascent to power. His inability to forget her guilt, which he shares, has *made* him a drunkard, and the daily spectacle of his distraction serves to keep her too from forgetting. Walter assures Martha that Sam too has come to remind her of that guilt—come with "blackmail in his eye." Actually, Sam had slipped away that evening just before everything happened, and never knew why Martha did not follow him. But now, his curiosity aroused by Martha's strange behavior (just as Hepburn's curiosity was aroused by Taylor's), he consults newspaper files, pieces together what he learns there with Martha's own remarks, and soon does know what happened and knows about the conviction, years later, of an innocent man. He faces Martha with his knowledge.

And now Martha must "be sure of him." The way in which she tries to win him is familiar, recalls Taylor's protestations as he paints himself the helpless victim of his brother, recalls too the protestations of the other heroes sketched in this chapter—the cruelly misunderstood heroes of all those Grade B musicals. She was helplessly swept along, Martha insists. Walter's father,

her tutor, was the one responsible. Seeing the power he could gain for himself, he persuaded her not to confess; assumed the role of her mentor from then on; married her off to his son; arranged the trial of that innocent man; manipulated everything, right up to the day of his death—she quite helpless all this time and longing so for Sam to be there. And Sam lets himself succumb to this argument, as we have seen others succumb. The kingdom to be found in Martha's arms is a tempting one. On the hill above Iverstown, these two cling together in a frantic embrace. Sam has met a young girl in the town—a wanderer like himself, who has thought he might be moving on with her. She is now distraught.

Happily, Sam is not lost. He too wakes; is able at last to say, "You're sick, Martha," to tell her that he is leaving. When Walter speaks *his* mind about all those years and Martha then begs Sam to kill Walter ("You believe *me*, don't you?"), Sam suddenly hangs back. Martha bursts into further frantic self-justification. "I've put thousands to work!" she cries; whole families owe their livelihood to her. "Look what I've done!" (Her words match those spoken by Ronald Colman in *Random Harvest* explaining why he has stayed on in industry longer than he had intended.) When she sees that Sam is no longer bound to her, "We can't let him go, can we?" Martha cries to Walter. And now she begs Walter to help her kill Sam. But Walter, so recently the proposed victim himself, hesitates, and Sam slips away.

If Sam has broken free of her, Walter is bound to Martha still. "You're insane," he too has told her—but has added, smiling, "and me too." He turns to her now: "Don't cry. He'll never tell." She tells him, "For the first time in my life I was afraid; I felt you were no longer standing by me!" He puts his arms around her and says, "It's not your fault." "It isn't, is it, Walter?" she begs. "It's not anyone's fault," he assures her. "It's just the way things are!" (the precise comfort, recall, offered by the musicals I described). "And you'll see," he continues, "things will be different now between you and me—just like nothing ever happened." "*You* believe me!" she cries. And Walter, who has always been rebuffed by her before, asks, "Will you kiss me?" And she kisses him; and in a kind of bliss the two commit suicide together. As she falls dying, Martha cries out, "Ivers Ivers Ivers!" but then, "No—Martha Smith!" And here too is an echo of *Random Harvest*. In that final embrace, too, things were to be as though nothing had ever happened. The same magic name, even, summoned bliss: "Smittie!"— two worlds here joined at last, and the amnesiac relieved of all his agony.

Death and the Old Woman

from Wash Us and Comb Us, *a collection of Barbara's short stories, published by Grossman in 1972. The story originally appeared in* Charm, *November 1954, under the title "The Siege." (JM)*

The old woman was dying. This was the doctor's opinion; it was not the old woman's opinion. Nor were her family able to believe in it. She had been declared dying before, and she had already accomplished ninety-seven years. Let it be gently said that her family could not believe in it because for too many years they had been looking forward to it. For all these years she had lived not merely her own life but, without restraint, as many other lives as possible, and those of her family, of course, had most tempted her. So they had hungered for the day when their lives would be their own at last. Obsessed with that day, they had long since ceased to be able to imagine it.

Florence Rouse lay in the local hospital eyeing her nurse from one of those beds with sides that look like cages. Back at the house she had left, her son and his wife waited, immobile as she; unable to stir or to think. Her son lay with his leg in a cast. He had fallen on an icy street the week before. "A slip in time," his mother had remarked. "Now he doesn't have to visit me." His wife could not visit easily, either. She was having the terrible migraine headaches that often plagued her. "And that's just as well," said Mrs. Rouse. "She has never been able to address me directly. So what would she have done? Propped up his photograph between us, I suppose. 'Dear, is your mother feeling any better today?' "

It was Caroline, her granddaughter, who visited. For this too Mrs. Rouse had tart words: "Might as well have sent the cat." For her granddaughter had been ignoring her latest advice and so she had been elaborately ignoring her granddaughter. The young woman had been afraid, even, that her grandmother might have the nurse turn her away. But she did let her visit. Caroline moved between home and hospital in agitation.

She too had wished for the old woman's death. It was difficult for her not to wish it when her parents wished it so much. As a child, she had wished it for their sakes; older, she often found herself wishing it for her

47

grandmother's sake—the life she led was such a bitter one. But the thought of it now filled her also with terror. A passage from the Bible ran through her head, distorted to a new sense for her: "If a man abide not in [the vine], he is cast forth as a branch, and is withered...." Her terror was lest her grandmother, in dying, be cast forth out of life utterly. Before this time, death had never seemed to her dismaying. Those whom she had known to die had seemed to her to live on after death, as vivid sometimes in memory as in life. "Abide in me and I in you...." The generations formed together one vine. Of course by the vine the Bible meant Christ and his church; but the words had come to hold for her an unorthodox meaning. Now it was hardly that her grandmother, after death, might be forgotten. Her presence among them had been, as far back as she could remember, the central fact of that household. But the manner in which she had lived among them had been a peculiar one. A visitor to the house had once asked, "Do you live here with your son?" "No, I don't live here," she had stated sourly, and when her son had exploded, "Mother, how absurd! You've been living here with us some fifteen years," "No, I don't live here," she had repeated. There was a more than literal sense in which her statement was quite accurate, for in their hearts both she and they furiously denied the arrangement. She could never really live where she did not reign absolutely; and they, for their part, had cultivated over the years a careful amnesia where she was concerned: there were times, when she wasn't actually speaking—indeed there were times when she was—when her son and her daughter-in-law seemed almost successfully to be pretending that she wasn't there. And so it wasn't that she might be forgotten; but her memory would be resisted as her presence had been. Caroline would make her memory welcome; for she had come, over the years, to love her—that is, to hate her and to love her at the same time; and she had come to cherish the fact that she was descended from her. But would her grandmother accept this particular welcome? Or might she not declare of this too: "No, I do not live here"?

The two of them had always been at odds. And the more Caroline had come to love her, the truer this had become. For she was a greedy old woman and she asked all or nothing. She would if she could make Caroline her creature. If you love me, you will do my will. Caroline had learned to be elusive. Her grandmother had set this fact to rhyme:

> There is a young lady named Carrie
> Who is so very wary
> She never sits down
> But fidgets around
> Ready to leave at my query.

Caroline could hear now, in imagination, the old woman's challenge: "Here I lie. And you want to stroll in and, standing first on one leg, then on another—no time to sit down—give me your blessing: Then off again about your business. I don't need it."

Nevertheless Caroline was obsessed with one purpose: to prevent her grandmother from dying in loneliness. The old woman would seek, probably, to disdain her love—any love not given on her own terms. But somehow she must be persuaded to accept it.

This war of love could not have reached its crisis at a less auspicious time. For Caroline and her grandmother had just had a quarrel. Caroline needed a job and Mrs. Rouse had urged her to try for one in radio. "You say you want to be a poet. There's your audience! Get your foot in that door!" She had an old friend she wanted her to see at a local radio station. But Caroline had applied instead for a teaching fellowship on the West Coast. Her grandmother had argued with her that her parents needed her at home, but Caroline, disagreeing, had sent the application in anyway. Since then the old woman had not been speaking with her or acknowledging her presence when she entered the room.

For the past three nights, before the ambulance was ordered, Caroline had been her nurse. Her grandmother had refused to acknowledge her presence even through those hours. She had let her needs be known to her by signs, without speaking to her—her long finger pointing or her eyes flashing at what it was she wanted: the red pill or the yellow pill, milk, more ice in the milk, more whiskey (a medicine she had prescribed for herself), or the pillows banked up behind her (for by now she must sleep upright or wake in a coughing fit)—she had given her haughty signals in the air as though it were the objects themselves she summoned, and her granddaughter did not exist. Caroline meanwhile had played a role as stubborn. She had tried to keep up the pretense that her grandmother's wrath did not exist—replying to her always as though she had made a courteous request. Each had sustained her own part without breaking, though by the time the ambulance came, the morning after the third night, each showed the strain.

By the third night, the struggle between them had become outlandish. The old woman had often to get into the bathroom that opened off her room. The first nights she had staggered a little, in danger of falling; but by the third night she was too weak to rise from the bed by herself; and still she would not allow her granddaughter to put hands upon her to help her. With blazing eye and palms upraised she forbade her to interfere. She sat on the edge of the bed, her puffed old feet swung round to the floor, but not quite able to get herself up onto them, her breast heaving, her face flushed with the effort, and her eyes wild, as she flopped back each time helpless. But as Caroline put out her hands simply to be ready to catch her if she should start to fall, she commanded, "Keep your hands by your sides!"

It took her twenty minutes to heave herself up and then to inch the short distance to the toilet—onto which she fell awkwardly; but she accomplished it by herself—Caroline standing there, marvelling and exasperated, her hands by her sides. And she attempted a second trip on her own, wavering this time in the middle of the floor, so sick that she no longer even knew quite how to begin to move her feet—or which foot was which—but from the springs of her being summoning up the will. And she managed again to flop herself down on the toilet, and managed again to rise. But on her way back this time she had to grab hold of Caroline. They stood there, clasped, in the middle of the room, her granddaughter holding her up and she half swooning, but even now not acknowledging that Caroline helped her, her flesh simply not acknowledging the contact. And Caroline, exerting all her strength—for her grandmother was a big woman—eased her to the bed and down upon it. Propped there on the bed's edge, her grandmother looked up at her and then—in helplessness or in vengefulness?—began to slip, eyeing Caroline, who hung on, straining to somehow fling her back onto the bed, the old woman with her eye fixed on her speaking at last a second time as she settled on the floor: "Well done!"

Caroline had run for her mother and then—the two of them could not lift her—had run for a neighbor just up the hill. For him Mrs. Rouse had a crooked smile and a quip: "Quietly now. My poor son needs his sleep."

At the first sight of her grandmother caged in the hospital bed, Caroline halted in the doorway. Stripped down to the hospital smock, her blackrimmed glasses removed and the yellowing switch which she stacked on top of her own now meagre hair, the mask of powder and rouge gone, and gone from about her the camouflage of her own room—lying there quite like an animal in a trap, snatched abruptly from its daily life—she looked both more sick and more potent, more pitiful and more impregnable. There she is! thought Caroline, There she is!—staring as one does at an animal behind bars; in grief that he should be caught so, and on guard, not really believing that he can be held.

Mrs. Rouse, when she sighted her granddaughter standing in the doorway, awestruck, her arms full of flowers, cast one cold look in her direction and turned her head away. Caroline gave her flowers to the nurse ("I am Miss Kelly," said the young nurse). Then she approached the bed—drawing on patience in a motion almost visible, the carefully calm face, calm voice, of the past three nights. She delivered her messages of love from home. (These were invented. Her parents had watched her leave for the hospital, as though in a trance, wordless.) Her grandmother did not look at her. "Dad feels so badly that he can't visit," Caroline repeated herself. The nurse, returning with the flowers in a vase, held them out for her patient to see. Staring past them, the old woman inquired of the air, "Your father—does the doctor hold out a little hope for him?" Miss Kelly looked from her to Caroline in surprise. She was a sweet-faced young woman, with a small turned-up nose. The old woman informed her, "He slipped on the ice. I wasn't there to hold him up." The nurse's look of wonder provoked her to further animation. "His students will all be in to scribble on his cast, I suppose. Carry him over here to me," she demanded with sudden ferocity; "I'll sign my name to him. What a piece of work is my son." The young nurse, embarrassed, turned to put the vase of flowers on the bureau. She stepped back to take her patient's pulse. "Now," said the old woman, "my granddaughter will have somewhere to appear. She's a poet but the world doesn't know it." Caroline, embarrassed in her turn, moved to the bureau to ease the roses in the vase a little. "Which way is North, which way is South?" cried the old woman. She still addressed the bewildered nurse, but it was Caroline for whom her words were chosen. She was quoting now from one of her granddaughter's poems. This was a pastime with her. "What are the words that blow out of my mouth?" she chanted.

She began to cough. "Hush, you're trying to talk too much, gran!" Miss Kelly told her, holding her up. Caroline had started toward her, but her grandmother had stopped her with one glance. The fit subsided. The nurse wiped her forehead, shiny with sweat. "My Park Avenue cough," whispered the old woman.

Caroline decided she had better not take a seat. She was still half expecting her grandmother to dismiss her. She drew near the bedside again. "Is there anything I forgot to pack for you that you'd like me to bring?" With this question she did at last gain the old woman's direct attention.

"You may bring me a bottle of whiskey," she said. "What I have isn't going to last very long." The little vial of whiskey she always carried with her stood on the bedside table.

Caroline hesitated, looking toward the nurse. "Will the doctor let her have it?" she asked.

"I'll see him . . ." the nurse began.

But the old woman's voice cut hers down. Miss Kelly stared, for this was a voice she had not heard from the patient. It was the voice Mrs. Rouse summoned for the telephone (half believing still that it was the voice by itself which must pierce the distances), it was the voice she used on servants, the voice by which she made her wishes known and clear—each syllable given an accent, e-nun-ci-at-ed: "You may bring me a bottle of whiskey," she told her granddaughter. "*Get it?*" The last two words were spat.

The nurse stared again. Caroline turned her head aside—anger against her grandmother suddenly flooding her. On her way out, she whispered, "I'll be back tomorrow."

Back home, her parents asked no questions, but greeted her with asking, non-asking eyes. "Did you have any trouble on the road?" her father wondered; "it must have been slippery down near the river."

"No, it wasn't bad," she answered. "She's comfortable now," she told them. "The hospital bed makes all the difference. They can keep it jacked up high for her. She seemed quite peppy, really." Their eyes. expressed, in spite of themselves, alarm.

As soon as she could, she sought out her grandmother's room. She was restless to approach her again, and to enter this room was to do so. She felt quite hopeless. It used to be the sport of emperors, she mused, to watch two gladiators who had been given mismatched weapons—one a sword and shield, one a trident and a net. She and her grandmother were contestants as unevenly matched. Her grandmother held sword and shield and trident too, she thought; and she simply a many-times-mended net. Too often her own anger tore it. How ever could she catch the old woman? How could she avoid entangling merely her own self in love's knots? She stood there, wary as in her grandmother's presence, and cast her eyes about the room.

In ancient Egypt, when a member of royalty was buried, there would be buried with him the likenesses of food, drink, servants, pets, jewels—all that the deceased had enjoyed while living, so that they could continue to serve his will. The excavation of one of these tombs would reveal to the digger an image of the royal state. So it was here. For Mrs. Rouse, taking up her residence in this room fifteen years back, and entering it as though she entered her tomb, had dragged in with her the memories of *her* pleasure.

Above the door, over Caroline's head, heavy-hung the great Conte-Galli hors d'oeuvres plate. "Many famous hands have plucked olives out of my Conte-Galli." Mrs. Rouse's list of these great tended to extend back even into days it was not likely she had seen. "It's not everyone can say that she has had an interesting conversation with Disraeli." "Ha, the parties I have given!" Her nostrils would flare as though breathing again that finer air, the incense of days that were her own. "Before I lived in a cupboard. Like old Mother Hubbard."

The room was of decent enough dimensions, but it *was* crowded, with the heavy Italian pieces she had dragged in upon the early American ones with which her daughter-in-law had furnished it. Caught in the many-winged mirror of her large dressing table, a piece like great aunt Bissell's maple desk did look a little skimpy, and to accentuate this fact she had poised on its narrow top the giant samovar that had served her "multitudes." Her carved arm chair elbowed other pieces into corners. And her gallery of pictures took up every inch of wall. Looking down into this room from elaborate frames were those who had done her bidding—or those who would have done it if they had not been mad or doomed.

Her husband, Frederick, leaned from his gilt laurel wreath frame, elegant and mild, his fist full of paint brushes. His money had enabled her to give those parties which had then set him on the verge of Artistic Success (or so she declared, to whom success was a matter always of moving in among the right people; from that, all would follow). But death had intruded. Casting about for help now, Caroline's eyes glanced upon him. Should she invoke his name? For *he* had loved her—apparently had done her pleasure readily. Or had he, in dying, fled her the only way he knew how?

From a larger still more elaborate frame looked forth her son, the second Frederick. Staring at the picture of her father, Caroline stopped invoking others in the name of love; for she knew that her father was unable to feel love for his mother any more. She remembered with a pang his remark some years before when he had been about to undergo a serious operation. He had told a friend (who had repeated it to Caroline), "Don't worry about me, please; I am determined to outlive my mother." The picture of her father was a self-portrait, executed in the days when he still faithfully carried out his mother's wishes: he at his easel, smiling out at her, and from the studio wall behind him, the carefully copied self-portrait of his painter father, smiling out at *him*. Caroline could still recall the voices that had been raised, when her grandmother first moved in with them, over whether or not this picture was to hang in their living room. It never had. But of course anyone who entered the house was led by the hand into the old woman's room to view it. "He had a remarkable talent. But one does not light a candle and set it under a Bissell."

Alice Bissell's face—her mother's—was absent from this gallery. Possibly, had he never met her, her father *would* still have been living out the life the portrait imagined—swept round Europe in the wake of his mother's parties. (Portraits would be his fortune! She would surround him with subjects! Now they must return to America, for she had endless connections there to exploit. And she herself would "dabble a little in oil—the Texas kind.") But the return home had brought him face to face with "Miss Bissell-body"; and under her influence he had resigned pretensions as a painter and become the teacher he had long wanted to be. It was at this time that there had occurred those tantrums and those wild connivings on her grandmother's part which neither her father nor mother would ever forget or forgive. Her mother, in her temperate fashion, matched Florence Rouse in energy. She had the advantage, besides, of finding Mrs. Rouse a little vulgar. She had stood up to her. And so, finally, had Frederick. When her grandmother took to tampering with the mails, her mother had been confident enough to know it and to circumvent it. When her grandmother took to falling in swoons upon the floor, her mother had found it in her to step across her prostrate body—at which, of course, the body had revived; and her father too (as her mother told the story) had finally stood up on his feet. Teaching was Frederick Rouse's proper profession, and over the years, his mother had been compelled to note the reputation that he had gained for himself. But his success was not in terms she could understand. Look at the house that they must live in—she must live in (her own income squandered finally on her adventures in oil). They could not even afford a full-time servant. She had had six "in service."

From the walls stared forth those who were to have restored her to fortune, those in her "debt," one of whom, some day, would surely repay that debt in gold, "They'd not have gone far without that push I gave them!" There grinned forth her husband's cousin, the banker—for whom she had found the right house and "furnished it with everything he needed—including the right wife. 'You'll never lack for anything while I'm alive,' he told me. That very week he died in an automobile crash." "But someone may yet repay me," she would muse—year after year.

Caroline's own likeness looked back at her there. She had, at any rate, not been removed from the wall. Her grandmother had hung round the frame the poetry medal she had won at high school. But there had been nothing so shiny to show since. Poor high-stepping old woman, thought her granddaughter—to see her blood, as she must think, thinned down to this.

The room held the scent of her grandmother still. Her mother, she saw, had flung the window wide open, to let in air, but the scent hung there impervious—and summoned her now tangibly before her granddaughter, witty, disdainful. The dominant note was her cologne, one that smelled somehow of incense. She may want that, Caroline thought: I didn't pack it. She stepped to the dressing table to get the bottle.

On the label of the bottle was a bright design showing Eve and the serpent. The picture suddenly recalled to her with a shock a dream her mother had told her about, two years before. Her grandmother had travelled to the hospital then, too, pronounced dying. Two weeks later she had returned. The morning after her return, Caroline's mother had told her, puzzling, "I had the strangest nightmare last night, Carrie. I dreamed that someone had killed a poisonous snake in the garden—cut it in half. But then the two parts of its body joined together again and it crawled into the house." Caroline had not interpreted the dream to her mother.

Dear poisonous but splendid old woman, she thought; dear persisting old woman—do I think that I can contend with you? And she paused, also, to wonder: is she, even now, really dying?

Over her grandmother's bed hung the Rouse coat of arms: a moated castle with a wind-still banner, lettered: "*J'endure pour durer.*"

The next afternoon when she mounted the hospital steps again, she had in her arms a number of bundles for her grandmother. She held them to her gingerly, picking her way from the car across the somewhat icy winter ground.

She was carrying the bottle of whiskey her grandmother had demanded (the doctor had given his O.K.); also the bottle of cologne. And on impulse she had added from her grandmother's desk a small photograph of her grandfather. She had wanted an ally, a charm.

Once inside the door of her grandmother's room, she felt abruptly self-conscious. But she took the photograph to her grandmother's side. "I thought you might like to have this here." The old woman looked at it without comment. She asked, "Did you bring my whiskey?" When Caroline answered, "Yes," "Put some more whiskey in my milk," the old woman told the nurse.

Caroline set the photograph of her grandfather on the bureau, under the flowers, his mild eyes turned upon his widow. How much slighter he was than she, she mused. Her grandmother was not fat and not taller than is ordinary, but she was large of frame. She had a very large head, sunk a little into her shoulders, hunchbacked with age and with coiled up power. She is handsomer down than when up and about, thought Caroline, staring at her as the nurse fed her whiskey in milk through a glass straw. Up and about, with her wig on and her rouge, and hung with beads, and her silvertipped cane flicking before her, she was marvellous to see. No one whom Caroline knew made so complete an effect—and this still, though her dresses tended to be a little shabby, now that she could no longer see to sew, or see not to drop food on herself. (Caroline, hanging things up for her these past days, had been startled to note what rags they were. When she had had them on, she so invested them with her own pride.) Trapped out, she was marvellous. But there was something a little grotesque in the vision, too. She was a figure out of Punch and Judy. (She had just this effect, Caroline noticed, on the man who came round to the house to do odd jobs. She had seen him once, when the old woman appeared at the door, eager for gossip, pick up a broom—without knowing what he was doing—and strum it like a guitar, as though she might go into a zany dance for him. And her grandmother, as a matter of fact, to her amazement, had done a brief jig for him.) Lying there as she was now, out of costume, she was finer looking than one would have supposed; and her face, for all its wicked thrust, was delicately fashioned. But it was a bold face always, with its great arch of nose, its gash of mouth and unusually long upper lip. Her ears were quite large and long. Her chin was stubborn, jutting. Her eyes glanced out, blackbrown, quick, immense, from behind these prominences. Her hands were quick as her eyes and as imperative. Even now, hump-veined and gnarled, they moved above the coverlet, electric.

Caroline had been designed less boldly. On her, the big nose seemed a little out of scale. She had not the ears to match it, or the upper lip. She had also her mother's paler coloration. She was taller than her grandmother but slighter—hunchbacked, a little, not with power but with hesitancy. "Always frowning, always musing, always wondering, always weighing," her grandmother would chant. Still, you could see that she was the old woman's kind. The total effect here, too, was a stubborn one.

The nurse, returning the glass to its tray, reached under the bedclothes to make some check on her patient. Mrs. Rouse reared up, come to life: "Are you mauling me again? Last night," she informed Caroline, "two demons attacked me; but I fought them off."

"The doctor wanted us to catheterize her," Miss Kelly whispered to Caroline.

The old woman swung her glance upon her: "I'll resist you all, little lady— to the end." She informed her granddaughter, "The night nurse left me for two or three hours. They were having a party down the hall. All the birds and the beasts were there. See that it's taken off the bill."

She had another sudden violent coughing fit. Caroline knew better, this time, than to run to her. Miss Kelly held her up. As her choking subsided, she intoned ferociously, "Her sis-is-ter us-est to booses-ter." As Miss Kelly shot Caroline a sidelong look, it suddenly occurred to her: They think she is delirious! Her snatches of limericks and tongue-twisters, bits of Shakespeare and the Bible—this is a speech they have not encountered before. And again it occurred to her: she may not be dying at all; for when they think they know her, they do not.

She sat for a moment, but then stood up. At her gesture of settling down she could feel her grandmother grow restive. She had not been there very long when a neighbor arrived. The neighbor was a great admirer of Mrs. Rouse's and had counted on her often to enliven her teas. Mrs. Rouse tended to make fun of this woman, but when she stepped to the bedside now, she gripped both her hands in her own and chanted loudly for Caroline's ears, "She is the tree upon which the fruit of my heart is growing!" She added, "Now you can go along, Carrie." Caroline, before leaving, stopped by her side and touched her hand. Her grandmother pretended not to notice.

Miss Kelly walked to the stairs with Caroline. "What did the doctor say this morning?" Caroline asked.

Miss Kelly told her, "He doesn't really understand why she is alive."

Ha, thought Caroline. She told the nurse, "She isn't delirious, you know. That's the way she always talks."

Miss Kelly nodded. Then she added, "She's frightened now. When we're alone, she wants to hold my hand. She keeps telling me, over and over, 'I'm so afraid.' "

And Caroline left, shaken. Then she *is* dying, she believed at last—if she herself thinks so. And even so she will not let me draw near; turns, in her terror, not to me but to a complete stranger. She thought: how deeply angry at me she must be,if even the fact of approaching death can not dissolve that anger. To look at this appalled Caroline—and for a moment roused her own anger again, in response. She despises my love, she thought, for I am a failure in her eyes; always turning from her counsel, I turn in that gesture from grace.

Nevertheless, she thought, I must insist on that love. She thought this with an edge of anger still. And conscious, suddenly, that it was an incongruous element in such an impulse, she asked herself: Could the real truth be that her grandmother turned from her simply because she had never made her love for her sufficiently believable? Yes, she loved her, but it had been easy enough to put her out of mind, too. And she had been ready, after all, to leave for California—though it could well have meant that she would never see the old woman alive again. Perhaps when her grandmother had argued that Caroline's parents needed her, she had really meant: *I* need you—and had felt abandoned. Caroline left, this day, despairing and in terror.

Home, her father asked, "Carrie, should you maybe have chains on the car?"

Her mother still lay in her room with the curtains drawn, her face haggard.

When Caroline arrived at the hospital the next afternoon, she stepped to the bed and then stood staring down at her grandmother. She was asleep, her mouth wide open (the nurse had removed her teeth), her head flung back against the pillows and her arms out by her sides, her hands in the gesture of grasping. And her breathing had changed. It sounded like some small gasping engine that is breaking down. This discord was punctuated by a queer note like the note of a whistle under water. And Caroline, staring, heard above these sounds a further sound, quite distinct, as of a fly buzzing in circles. This sound was so precise that for a moment she looked for the insect there in the air above her grandmother's dishevelled head. But there was none. It is Death, she thought, circling above her. But she will not let it settle; she will not let it alight. Her body lay stiffened against it, her brow knotted against it, and with her breath she blew it from her.

Caroline stood there still, staring. If the day before had made real for her her grandmother's fear of dying, now for the first time death itself was real to her.

Miss Kelly edged a chair under her and she sat. How does one pray? Caroline wondered.

Miss Kelly whispered, "Are you all right?"

Caroline whispered, "Yes."

She had leaned her head for a moment against the side bars of her grandmother's bed. How does one pray? she wondered. You are loved! she began to pray, you are loved! But the old woman's rigid sleeping form denied it. She will hold me off as she holds off death, thought Caroline—with her last fierce breath. She recalled as a young girl hearing her father challenge his mother: "Mother, you'll have to give in this once!", but she: "I am what

I am! I am what I am!'' But one cannot stand out in this lonely way throughout eternity, thought Caroline—in terror now at her grandmother's terror. How does one pray? she wondered.

Outside, it began to snow. Caroline, lifting her eyes to the window, saw the quiet flakes falling beyond the glass. She prayed: Fall on her, dissolve her, reconcile her.

Meanwhile, a fly seemed to circle in the air above her grandmother's head, and the droning note to call forth, as it will, summer in all its fullness.

Miss Kelly sat with a copy of the *Reader's Digest* in her lap, sometimes turning the pages surreptitiously, sometimes watching the old woman and Caroline. At one point she got up and tapped Caroline on the shoulder and gave her a glass of water.

The day began to go, and Caroline sat hunched there by the bedside. The snow fell more lightly. Mrs. Rouse stirred but did not wake. Her breast rose and fell more easily, and the discord of her breathing subsided. Her hands released whatever it was she had grasped in her dream. It was as though within her sleep she slept.

"It is the first time she has rested like this," said Miss Kelly in a whisper.

It was dark when the old woman woke. She opened her eyes suddenly and smiled at Caroline. And she spoke in a blurred mild voice, "I just had the sweetest sleep."

Caroline whispered to her, "It's late, but I wanted to wait and say hello. And I'll come again."

Her grandmother stretched out her hands to her. "Yes, come again tomorrow," she said.

Caroline drove the miles home, over the whitened roads, slow-motion, her heart in turmoil, thinking: then love, after all, does find its way.

Home, she found that her mother had staggered up from her bed and made dinner for her. Before sitting down to it, Caroline made an excuse to slip into her grandmother's room. There, in light quick motions, she straightened the pillows on the bed, the jumbled objects on the bureau, her hands performing, without her thinking, any gesture, any gesture of love.

Later, sitting in silence with her parents, she remembered suddenly a look her grandmother had given her across the table one Thanksgiving Day. Some of the Bissells had been there, her mother's brother and his family. The Bissells were always very stiff with Mrs. Rouse, for they knew something of the family history. The three children had contracted the hostility of their parents and were barely polite to her. Watching the conversation pass over and around the old woman, who sat grim and haughty, not even bothering to listen to what was said, Caroline had tried catching her eye at intervals and smiling at her, calling casual remarks across the table to her. Glancing at her toward the end of the meal, she had found the old woman staring at her, and suddenly her grandmother had mouthed, surprisingly, "I-love-you." And I, you.

The next morning the doctor phoned to say that there was no need now for Caroline to visit, unless she wanted to, for Mrs. Rouse was in a coma and could not wake from it. But Caroline went back just to sit by her again.

The doctor was wrong. Mrs. Rouse was awake. When Caroline came in, Miss Kelly had her propped up high and she was having her whiskey in milk. The nurse still wore on her face the look of surprise that had appeared on it when Mrs. Rouse woke. The old woman pushed the glass away and spoke.

The nurse asked her, "What is it, gran?" Though she had broken out of her sleep, she was not disentangled from it. Her speech was confused. "Don't worry about it, gran," said the nurse.

The old woman's eyes flicked from one to the other of them. Her cheeks grew red. And from some terrible depth of her she summoned out of anger enunciation: "This-isn't-cold-enough!"

Miss Kelly stepped quickly for ice.

"You'd better go," the old woman told her granddaughter, getting out the words barely—"I can't talk."

"You don't have to talk," Caroline told her. "I'll just sit here, just to be with you."

Her grandmother shot her a baleful look.

The old woman sank back after her drink and lay there, panting. And sleep seemed to come over her, then, but she shook it from her. Her hands moved upon the coverlet, as though seeking something to which to cling, to keep from going under. Caroline began to try to pray again.

Her grandmother started to hiss like a cat. For as she lay there, Death formed before her eyes. She hissed it off. It formed more clearly. She screamed. Caroline rose to her feet, but her grandmother turned from her to Miss Kelly on the other side of the bed. She grabbed at Miss Kelly's hand. The nurse wiped the sweat from her forehead with a towel: "What's the matter, gran?"

Caroline sat again. She tried to pray, but her spirit trembled too hard. Her grandmother sank into sleep and came up out of it again; sank into sleep and came up out of it, gasping. Her eyes widened as Death, in the air above her, moved in too close. She screamed.

Caroline jumped to her feet and, not thinking, bent and kissed her grandmother's cheek.

The old woman turned round on her, hissing, "Why did you do that?"

Caroline, aghast, whispered back, "I love you."

The old woman turned her head aside. And soon she said to Miss Kelly, "Tell my favorite granddaughter to go. She tires me."

She couldn't go home yet. Mrs. Rouse's nephew and his wife had wired that they were driving over this afternoon to see her. They lived some distance away. She had better wait, to meet them, she thought. She went downstairs, to wait in the entrance hall. A young farmer was sitting on the bench there, waiting for news of his daughter in the operating room. He kept rubbing his eyes, as though to wake in some other place, and raising his nose to sniff at the antiseptic air—bad weather. Down the corridor, two nurses were in a fit of giggles over a whispered exchange of news.

She sat for a while, across from the troubled man, and then got up and paced up and down. She felt: What have I been trying to do? I have just been annoying her, in my own delirium. It is not my prayers she wants, and not my insisted love. She wants, very simply, for as long as possible, not to have to know that she is dying. I have been reminding her of it and that is all that I have accomplished. She knows enough to send me away. She remembered stepping to her grandmother's side with the photograph of her husband—from which she had turned away her eyes. All she really wanted me to bring of course was whiskey—life. She could hear suddenly, loud in her ear, her grandmother's voice chanting a verse that was a favorite of hers:

> Oh what a thing is love
> It cometh from above
> And settleth like a dove
> On some
> But some it never hits
> Except to give them fits
> And take away their wits
> Hohum!

God forgive me, she felt: I have lost my wits, and been impertinent in the word's full sense.

Her relatives arrived. The nephew was an economist, a tall good-natured man with dimples at the corners of his eyes. He and his wife were her grandmother's most cordial relatives. They had always appreciated her as a dramatic figure, and they had never lived very near her for very long.

She tried to prepare them for how their aunt might be; and she stood in the door as they went in. The two of them drew near the bed and the old woman turned and stared at them. They murmured their greetings. From the door, Caroline could see that they were taken aback. Mrs. Rouse held out her hands to them vaguely. "My nephew," she tried to say to the nurse— she gestured in the air—"has often been recommended to the government." Her nephew and his wife strained their heads forward, trying to understand her, but they couldn't decipher her speech. The wife still clutched some flowers they had brought. Miss Kelly took them from her now and she thanked her. The old woman wet her lips with her tongue. She was trying to speak again. She stared at her nephew. "I'm writing a book," she told him. (But he couldn't make out the words.) "It's called 'I'm afraid now, I'm afraid now.' It's going to sell all around Caroline's beautiful literature." The nephew tried to smile at her. He told her, "You'll feel better very soon, Aunt Flo." And they both stood there, awe-struck. "You'd better go now," the old woman mouthed, slowly. They did not understand her. Caroline whispered from the door, this time, what it was that she had said.

The two of them followed her back to the house, to speak a few words with her mother and father, but they turned around soon for home. "They were so good to come," said her mother, "and so good to go." Caroline retired to bed early. She was still shaken. Her grandmother's final words had further humbled her. Such wit, in the middle of terror! And in the middle of terror, such disdain! She was shaken by pride, herself, in her grandmother's pride, however fatal; and by a kind of ribald despair of her own strength, matched against her. She *is* what she is, she thought, and who am I to have thought to succour her? At the end of this day, she had quite resigned her action.

Nevertheless when she woke the next day, her purpose had returned. She discovered it to her own surprise—that she had not actually resigned it.

This morning again the doctor had reported that her grandmother was in a final coma. Again she had broken out of that sleep. But her speech today was quite gone. She could articulate now only the one word, "Whiskey." "It's all she asks for now," Miss Kelly told Caroline. She asked for it incessantly. She pulled at it in long hungering sips, as though it were air and she coming up from under. Sometimes she struggled to speak. But it was no longer the nurse or Caroline whom she addressed—except to call for whiskey. It was Death Himself. Her eyes no longer seemed to hold any other image. Her tongue managed, her lips out-thrusting it: "I-I-I-I-" Can she get no further with the sentence? Caroline wondered. Or is this, in fact, the all of it—her two words, two remaining words, the same: whiskey (life)—I—I live still, am what I am, here I am.

Though she had had from her today no hostile glance, because no glance at all, Caroline drew near warily. She sat not too close, with her chair by the window. She was careful, even, at first, not to gaze at her grandmother too openly, lean out of her eyes too far. And it was in this manner that she prayed—so quietly within herself, at such a shy distance, that the air about her could not be troubled by it.

The next day, too, the doctor told Caroline that her grandmother would not wake again; and the day after that, and the day after that. Each afternoon, she came to sit by her, all the same, and each afternoon she found her wakeful still. Her grandmother lay heavily now, her limbs passively washed by the tides of sleep, but her head still heaved above the flood, sipping life—her nostrils flared with it and her mouth gasping it in, drawing it in, her upper lip desperately out-thrust. It is as though she hangs on by that great lip alone, thought Caroline—a great tortoise, clinging to this floating thing, this life.

Her grandmother no longer shied from her now. Perhaps she no longer recognised her. Her eyes were alight, but what they watched was no longer within that room. As Caroline slowly drew her chair in closer, there shaped before her eyes as well the hovering images of Death. She prayed: Death, she is loved. Put a value on her. But sometimes she simply sat and stared, in awe. Here, she felt, are two adversaries who are matched: Death and my grandmother.

As the old woman no longer sent her away, she sat there now throughout the long afternoons.

Meanwhile, outside the window, the countryside was locked in winter. The snow had turned to ice, and every branch and twig lay in an icy casing. Fretting in that vise, the trees shifted in the winds with the sound of leather creaking. At day's end, when the declining sun caught in its pink shine all this glass, a Springtime was simulated, so brilliant that it hurt the eyes. "Melt away, melt away," her mother tried chanting at it from her window.

The ninth day was Sunday, and Caroline reached the hospital before noon. The morning nurse, Mrs. Beman, was still on. She was an older woman, stout and chatty. Mr. Peters had been in earlier, she reported, but he had stayed only a moment. Mrs. Rouse had told her about Mr. Peters when she could still speak. "He wrote a book, she said. Said she'd lend it to me but that I should burn it when I was finished with it. She wouldn't want it found among her belongings. Said it was filthy." Caroline laughed, amazed. To the end, she thought. Peters was her father's close friend, a young instructor in literature.

"Well, it's a love story," she told Mrs. Beman. "'Filthy' doesn't really describe it. How is she now?" she whispered.

"The same," the nurse answered. "It's a marvel. The doctor says she's full of..."

"Shhh!" mouthed Caroline, gesturing toward her grandmother.

"Ah, she can't hear us, dear," the nurse told her. "She's under. And when she's awake, she's only half awake. She doesn't recognise us."

Caroline insisted, "But you can't be sure, can you?"

"Oh, she can't hear us, dear," the nurse repeated.

But Caroline was thinking: If her familiar senses have faded, perhaps she is aware in some new way.

Mrs. Beman said, "If you're here now, I'll just duck down for a sandwich."

And Caroline told her of course, and sat, relieved to have her go. When Mrs. Beman came back, she avoided her eye, not to have to talk again.

Her grandmother had not roused to ask for whiskey in some time now. The nurse stepped over to take her pulse. She looked over at Caroline: "Her pulse is as strong as mine." She said it with a kind of surprised outrage. Ha, thought Caroline, they do not know her. Her grandmother lay there now, breathing as profoundly as a sleeping baby, mouth open, one hand across her breast. The old woman's words came back to her suddenly from that time two years before when she had visited this hospital. Nurses had been scarce and the first night Caroline had sat up with her—for then, too, everybody had thought that she lay dying. As day broke, her grandmother had whispered to her, "I will remember what you did for me this night as long as I live"—and Caroline had been struck with awe at the accent she gave those word, the vista that had opened out of years unwinding one from another endlessly. Not many weeks ago, she had watched her readying herself to go out for tea, peer into her great mirror, cock her peaked black felt hat at an angle, then wink at her image, "Hello, you old witch!" Staring at her sleeping grandmother, "Hello, you old witch," Caroline breathed. The great lip sucked in the air, drew it in. I think, Caroline mused, that she has found the very Source of life; she lies there like a baby at its very breast, pulling at it, peaceful, and is immortal now, cannot die. And musing this, she felt the pride of the old woman running in her own veins. Then, very suddenly, her grandmother's breathing changed. The nurse stepped to her side again. Suddenly her breathing was rapid, broken—as though she panted above a stream from which she could not drink fast enough.

"Why, I think she's going," said Mrs. Beman. She said to Caroline, "Go to the desk, dear, and ask them to send the house doctor to this room."

Caroline ran down the corridor, to give her message, thinking: I must get back. When she got back, her grandmother was breathing normally again.

The house doctor arrived. She was short and redfaced. She went about her duties rather as though she had been rudely dared to. She did not bother to nod to Caroline. As she pulled the hospital gown down ungently from Mrs. Rouse's old breasts and placed her stethoscope, "Be gentle!" Caroline wanted to cry, "She's alive still"—adding, "She will outlive you all!"

The doctor declared to the nurse, "There's nothing really that's worth doing. Her doctor didn't expect her to pull through?"

"No," said Mrs. Beman.

"Ah well." She left.

Then it began again, the rapid lapping at the stream. Mrs. Beman stepped to one side of her, and Caroline to the other, the old woman's body sitting up now, crouched strangely, the nurse holding her. Caroline saw her grandmother's face wrinkle up, slow-motion, as though to cry. It crinkled up as children's faces crinkle up when something they want is taken from them—and before they have learned to dissemble crying, and stiffen chin, mouth, eyes against it. She saw it crinkle all up from chin to forehead—as it was taken from her.

Mrs. Beman said, "She's dead."

The house doctor returned. Again, without ceremony, she pulled the hospital smock down over the flat old breasts, to place her stethoscope. She looked at her watch, a large one. "Three past three," she said, as the station master might note the arrival of a train. Mrs. Beman jotted it on her chart. The doctor turned on her heel and left. Miss Kelly had entered, and stood near the door, in unbelief. Mrs. Beman patted Caroline's arm. "Are you all right, dear?" She told her, "If you should want me, I'll just be down the hall."

Caroline still stood close to the bed. She felt: I mustn't move yet. She felt: If they come back and try to take her away, I shall bark at them like a dog: Keep off.

Miss Kelly stood watching her, with an inquiring look. Seeing the look, Caroline asked her, "May I stay here a little while?"

"Of course," said Miss Kelly, and she asked her, "Would you like me to pack up her things for you?"

Miss Kelly began gathering up the old woman's things: the bed jackets Caroline had packed for her, but which she had never worn; her cologne; her comb and brush, her hairpins and the yellowing wig; the photograph of Mr. Rouse.

There's a little whiskey left in the bottle," said Miss Kelly. "Shall I pack that?"

"No," Caroline said, "I guess not." Spill that to the ground, she thought. To the Gods.

She drew a chair suddenly close to the bed, and sitting, placed her hand upon her grandmother's shoulder. The shoulder was still living to the touch. She stared at her grandmother shyly. Her face looked very fine in death— bold, beautiful, and without malice now. Her eyes had been shut, and the nurse had closed her mouth, too, but it had fallen open again—more beautiful so, reaching out still for life, the whole thrust of the face toward life. As she sat there now, Caroline's heart slowly stopped its cry of *no no no no,* which had begun at the sight of her grandmother's face wrinkling up as though to cry. Sitting here by her now it slowly occurred to her that she had witnessed an affirmation to marvel at: that her grandmother at ninety-seven should put still such a value on life that she could cry like a baby to have it taken from her. She felt, suddenly, hope again, clear in her: she *will* persist—was sure of it, suddenly, that her grandmother's life would not be snuffed out; feeling: Death must surely value less those who run to him uncombative; and thinking: if she found human love unmanageable, to life, simply, in itself, she did give her heart.

As she stared at her, her grandmother's tongue stirred suddenly in her mouth.

"Her tongue!" she whispered at Miss Kelly. "She's not dead!"

Miss Kelly, starting, whispered back, "No, no! It's just that as she relaxes—"

Miss Kelly looked at her as though she should leave now. But Caroline sat there thinking: I mustn't leave yet. For there are some whom one might leave and no sacrilege, but surely *her* spirit clings still to its flesh. Except that she was not thinking, but only sitting, waiting—as, under her hand, the old woman's life circled to its standstill in her veins.

Miss Kelly shut Mrs. Rouse's suitcase and set it by the door. She said, "I'll say goodbye."

Caroline thanked her and the nurse left. And she sat on.

Her grandmother's shoulder was cold under Caroline's hand. She stood up, gazing down at her. Now, she thought, it does not house you. Now you no longer cling. And she stood there, blank. Still she did not go away. She stood there looking down at her grandmother, her hands by her sides, not knowing what she waited for. Nevertheless, I just stand here for you, she felt, not thought.

Suddenly, out of blankness, it seemed to her that from far off there was a terrible out-reaching to her, a crying out. Without thinking, she held out her arms in the air as though to answer: Yes, yes! Don't be afraid! And you do live in me.

She heard footsteps approaching the door. Quickly—before anyone could come in—she leaned and pressed upon her grandmother's cold cheek the kiss the old woman had not let her give before.

Remember: Descent into my parents' living room.
The lit lamp. Supper. Elbows off the table, eyes
in front! One must be a poet only in one's own
room.

That dream I had once of breaking through ice, through
ice, through ice. Through bands. More than the
muscles can bear. And at the end, half-woke to seem
to see a severed head squatting about where my knees
were in bed.
(Hit at the wall, but my brother in the next room
didn't wake.)

Oh, have been flapping shutters to, flapping shutters.
And now would toss open, bang open windows, look and
look. Have been buried alive and now would, as in the
Poe story, splinter open the box, hurl down the gate,
and stand at the door til the demon fall dead.

1940

The World of Hamlet*

"There is a world in each of Shakespeare's plays" (John Jay Chapman)

It is a strange fact that although *Hamlet* has spoken with unique force to the most diverse audiences for over three centuries, and has been so incorporated into our lives that it is—as the joke goes—a patchwork of quotations, yet the majority of contemporary critics agree with T.S. Eliot that it is essentially incoherent. Eliot says, "Here Shakespeare tackled a problem that was too much for him....Nothing that [he] can do with the plot can express Hamlet for him." Another critic concurs: "The dramatist never succeeded in finding a dramatic form that could completely express his idea"; another: "What is seen is a series of pictures, vivid, brief, isolated"; another: "No play, doubtless, is so ill constructed...and all efforts to reduce it to unity fail." Could it be these critics rather than Shakespeare who have failed to express his "idea," to find the play's unity—while the general public, unconstrained by the necessity to translate its experience of *Hamlet* into judicious words, has year after year somehow apprehended it?

I think *Hamlet* has that almost miraculous coherence that only genius can impart to a work. A key to its integrity is offered by Francis Fergusson, one of the few modern critics who differ with Eliot's verdict. Fergusson writes, in *The Idea of a Theater:* "The elements of Shakespeare's composition are...not abstract concepts...but real people in a real world, related to each other in a vast and intricate web of analogies." Recalling Aristotle's definition of a play, "an imitation of an action," he suggests that the unity of any Shakespeare play is to be sought in terms of one action in which every character is caught up. Adopting just this perspective, I want to offer an alternate reading of *Hamlet* to the one Fergusson offers. He defines the action imitated in *Hamlet* as "the attempt to identify and destroy the hidden 'imposthume' [abscess] which is poisoning the life of Denmark." I think a less rational action is the subject of the play, an action more familiar to every one of us, and I think that this is why the play speaks to us as directly as it does.

* This is a slightly edited version of an article which originally appeared in *The Tulane Drama Review*, December, 1959. *(JM)*

As I read it, Hamlet is one for whom fortune is "outrageous fortune"; if he is incapable of action, it is because he stands hypnotized before what has happened already, and all his energy is spent on wishing it were not so. He is, in a phrase from the play itself, "wonder-wounded." "Would heart of man once think it?" he cries, after the ghost has delivered its horrid message. His own heart refuses, appalled, to think the facts with which it is presented: "a father kill'd, a mother stain'd"; an "uncle popp'd in between the election and [his] hopes"; Ophelia, whom he loves, suddenly refusing to see him; trusted friends betraying that trust—the painful facts accumulate as we watch. But the play is not about one man; it is not only Hamlet who is confronted with "thoughts beyond the reaches of our souls." Character after character is shown with heart refusing to accept the given facts. It is this act of refusal that is Shakespeare's subject in *Hamlet*. From the first characters we meet, the soldiers on the battlements, whom the ghost "horrors...with fear and wonder," and the ghost himself, still unreconciled to the manner of his death, still rehearsing it, appalled: "Oh horrible, O horrible most horrible!"—throughout the play, over and over, the cry is, "Woe is me, to have seen what I have seen, see what I see!" "Do you see this, O God? ...I must call't in question." Every character is shown in the act of calling it in question, of attempting to have "no more on't"—to wish it away.

"Peevish opposition," Claudius names this gesture when he observes it in Hamlet—"unavailing woe"—"For what we know must be...Why should we...take it to heart? Fie! tis...a fault to nature, to reason most absurd." But we see all in the play caught up in this absurdity: Laertes, informed of his father's murder, demanding, "Give me my father!"; Hamlet crying out, "O that this too too solid flesh would melt!"; Claudius himself, struggling to refuse the natural consequences of his crime, trying to insist "my fault is past...Help, angels!...All may be well!"

I am not suggesting that *Hamlet* is a case study of a special group of people unable to face the facts of life. The impulse to reject unpleasant truths is present in every man born. The central situation in the Hamlet story interests Shakespeare because it brings this irrational inclination profoundly into play; and the characters come to life for him as they exhibit it in the widest possible variation. John Jay Chapman wrote of Shakespeare, "These things are much more than plays: to me they are metaphysical treatises." The description is more apt than it might first appear to be. For within his own medium, Shakespeare explores the very reaches of human impulse; he shows just where a certain bent can take one, the multiple shapes it can assume, its potentialities for good and for evil—he investigates almost as a metaphysician would the boundaries of the human spirit and of the human condition. In *Hamlet,* he confronts his various characters with almost every one of the chief facts of life that men find hard to accept.

The protest of each character in the play is of a very different nature. Claudius' protest is deeply perverse. It is Hamlet's behavior, of course, that he claims to find outrageous. But in fact what is outrageous to him is that he is not to be allowed to enjoy the fruits of his crime, nor to think of that crime as now irrelevant. Hamlet prevents him, disrupts the hypocritical show (of all being *right* in the state of Denmark) which Claudius, with some skill, attempts. Here is an instance where Fergusson's definition of the action which is the subject of the play seems to me imperfect; for surely the king is not so much concerned to seek out the infection that endangers Denmark as he is to pretend that there *is* no such infection, to be rid of the man who says there is—to name him diseased for saying so, though Claudius knows well enough where the infection lies. In his scene at prayers, Shakespeare shows him at his depth: what is actually unbearable to him is the knowledge that guilt is guilt, that one cannot both be "pardoned and retain the offence." He attempts to refuse this knowledge.

Here already is one action seen in two aspects that conflict absolutely— one essentially noble, one ignoble. Hamlet stands appalled before the fact that evil exists, and protests its existence. Claudius protests, not the fact of evil, but the fact that he cannot call it by some other name. These two are, as Hamlet himself calls them, "mighty opposites."

Whoever tries to uphold Claudius' regime, of course, finds Hamlet's behavior outrageous. One of these is Polonius. The trend in recent productions of *Hamlet*, happily, runs against the tradition of playing Polonius as an obvious fool, unaware of the general laughter he provokes. Polonius is a man of authority at Claudius' court, a very successful politician. It is Hamlet who penetrates his facade, as he does the king's; and to have the court in general smile at him is to blunt this drama. Polonius is all too sensitive to Hamlet's ridicule. His struggle is to ignore it—to deny it even to himself; for what most concerns Polonius is *never* to "play the fool." When he tells his daughter Ophelia to avoid Hamlet, it is "Tender yourself more dearly or you'll tender me a fool." For Polonius, a situation is outrageous if he feels that it is out of his control. His pompous lectures, his wordy "encompassments" of whatever subject, are attempts to reject any such uncomfortable feeling. The fact that he cannot fully understand or manipulate the next generation is what particularly discomforts him; and so he struggles to make believe that he can.

If Polonius were an obvious fool, of course, Ophelia would not be in her dilemma. The outrageous fact she tries to wish away is that her father demands one thing of her and Hamlet another. Unable simply to disobey her father, all she can do is protest, in her inward being, that a conflict of loyalties exists. In her mad scene, "I hope all will be well, we must be patient," she sighs; and a few phrases later, "and so I thank you for your good counsel''—which contains a painful irony, for she has, with childish stubbornness, expected the various people she loves to dispel the need for choice on her part, to somehow bring everything into harmony for her, make all well. Her scenes with Hamlet are painful as they are because neither is capable of moving toward the other. Each can only demand: Undo what has been done!

The queen, like Ophelia, is unable to accept the fact that opposing loyalties involve one in choices. She "lives almost in Hamlet's eyes," but in marrying Claudius she has lost Hamlet. This is what she refuses to acknowledge. She continues to reach out for the old warm connection with Hamlet, a connection which she has destroyed.

All these protests are in some degree perverse, and all are indeed gestures of "unavailing woe": every one of these characters is destroyed. Hamlet, too, brings about his own destruction; and he assists in the destruction of Ophelia, whom he loves. But in the case of Hamlet, to call his protest unavailing is too simple a statement; and one thing, too, distinguishes his protest from these others: what he protests *is* essentially outrageous. Because this is so, it is even easy to mistake his gesture sometimes for a reasoned one. Actors of the role frequently do so mistake it—in those scenes, especially, in which he "tests" the king with the play-within-the-play and then, going to his mother, chastises her. Hamlet longs to believe his own actions reasonable here. What he attempts is, nevertheless, as irrational in these scenes as it is throughout the play: in setting up the glass wherein evil may see itself, he hopes, as if by magic to have evil in that instant no longer so. When evil still confronts him, he is quite helpless.

In *The Tempest*—where Shakespeare explores an impulse almost the opposite of that in *Hamlet,* the impulse to dare new worlds—Prospero is in control of the scenes he stages, able to predict their results, able to boast: "My spirits obey me, my charms crack not!" But the magic Hamlet attempts is childish magic; and his charms crack, his spirits disobey. He is not aware of the nature of the hope that moves him. He says he is staging the play to test the truth of the ghost's story (which in his soul he does not doubt); he declares, "If [the king] do blench, I know my course"—which we can assume would be to wrest the throne from Claudius and declare himself king. But when Claudius not only blenches but runs headlong from the room, Hamlet can only inquire of Horatio, hysterically: doesn't he agree that this success could get him a job as an actor?

Hamlet sees a course for himself less clearly than before, because he has been confronted all over again, more irrefutably, with the facts he has tried to wish away. When he goes to his mother now, he is beside himself. In this scene, he wants to believe that he is soberly correcting her; but what he is really doing is demanding again, more wildly: Make what's so not so! Don't be what you are! The ghost appropriately enough enters to remind him of the purpose he has quite forgotten. This scene painfully confronts Hamlet with one of the most outrageous of the facts with which fortune presents all men: the fact that we have but slight knowledge or control of our own deepest beings. He is seen here, bewildered, trying not only to dispel his mother's fault by the magic of a tirade, but to wish away the violent feelings toward her that rage in him, to his own amazement.

This is, of course, what constitutes the complexity of Hamlet's situation. He experiences a double outrage. Throughout the play we see him staring appalled, in turn, at the evil in the world around him—the evil that Claudius and his mother have brought about—and at facts about himself that he finds "monstrous." "I could accuse me of such things," he declares to Ophelia, hoping against hope that she can pray away these faults: "Nymph, in thy orisons, be all my sins remembered." He strives to dispel, by cursing himself, the fact of his strange incapacity to take the revenge he has sworn: "Oh what a rogue and peasant slave am I!" In his soliloquy just before he goes to his mother's bedroom, his alarm about himself reaches an extreme:

> ...now could I...
> ...do such bitter business as the day
> Would quake to look on...
> O heart, lose not thy nature, let not ever
> The soul of Nero enter this firm bosom;
> Let me be cruel, not unnatural:
> I will speak daggers to her, but use none.

In *Hamlet and Oedipus,* Dr. Ernest Jones cites this last speech, among others, to prove that Hamlet's trouble is an aggravated Oedipus complex. (Nero is said to have murdered his mother after sleeping with her.) Hamlet, he says, cannot take action against Claudius because his feelings toward him are those of a jealous rival, and if he struck at him, these feelings would confront him too plainly; he is a man "struggling to escape from knowing the horrors of his own heart." This definition of Hamlet's struggle fits easily enough within the large definition I have suggested, though any production of *Hamlet* based solely upon *Hamlet and Oedipus* would grotesquely distort the play. Jones throws a sharp light upon the "central mystery" about Hamlet, and upon some of his wilder utterances, but he throws much else into shadow; and nowhere does he illuminate Hamlet's nobility, or remark the special sense in which, in spite of weakness, Hamlet does ultimately prevail. He reduces Hamlet's gesture in all its wide range to that of a man struggling to be rid of a sense of guilt; and the play for him moves toward a sickly close as Hamlet, by steadily provoking Claudius, invites death as an easy way out of conflict. There at the door of death, he says, Hamlet is free to slay "this other self—his uncle."

In the first place, Hamlet is never simply concerned to rid himself of a disturbing "other self." He is not that sick a man. He is capable of seeing Claudius for what he is—a false king; and throughout the play, he protests him as such. The state of Denmark is quite as real for Hamlet as is his own psychic state. What especially characterizes him is his inquiring glance at the world around him; there are more things in heaven and earth for Hamlet than the state of his own soul. His progress towards death can be described with quite a different stress from that which Jones gives it. Hamlet's dilemma, says Jones, is that if he doesn't want to face the truth about his own feelings, he must try to condone or if possible even to forget his uncle's evil. The precise point he fails to make about Hamlet is that he never does allow himself to condone or forget that evil. If he is incapable of actually striking at his uncle, he continues, still, to protest against him in the only way that is within his strength. The note he sends Claudius when he returns from exile reads, "I am set naked on your kingdom. Tomorrow I shall beg leave to see your kingly eyes." To look into his uncle's eyes, and with that look to protest his reign, is about all he can do. But he persists in this, even though he knows it provokes Claudius to destroy him. One could describe his death as a courageous sacrifice.

Jones sums up Hamlet as one who was unable to "dare the exploration of his inmost soul"—an intellectual coward, he says, like the majority of the human race. Perhaps the only heroism Jones would recognize would be if Hamlet had managed to psychoanalyze himself and discover the Oedipus complex in advance of Freud.

But if Hamlet is incapable of Freud's heroism, he manages, nevertheless, to be the hero of this play; and it is through intellectual courage of an extraordinary sort that he prevails. Hamlet is unable to accept those truths that confront him; but he will not allow himself to disregard them. He turns his eyes to them, although in anguish, over and over again. Hamlet's staging of the play-within-the-play is an attempt at magic, and in that sense childish; but it is more than that, too: it is the stubborn return of his gaze to the realities which outrage him. As a witness to the truth, he *is* bold; unable to initiate on his own a new reign in Denmark, he manages at least, with the strong fires of criticism, to burn the field so that another may plant.

The fact is, too, that Hamlet attains a knowledge of himself that is heroic. He is not, like Ophelia, "pull'd. . .to muddy death. . .incapable of [his] own distress." He dies capable of it—aware of it—in the rarest degree. He may not, by the end of the play, know "his inmost soul," but he has the very clearest sense of just how little he knows, is profoundly aware of his own measure. Throughout the play, Hamlet tries to outstare what he finds painful, to rail it out of existence, to wish it away; but he never tries to call it by any other name than its own. And so his vision steadily widens. He never, like Claudius, tries to call guilt innocence; or like Polonius, to call ignorance wisdom; or like Ophelia, to pretend that the necessity of making choices does not exist. His protest is the protest neither of the hypocrite nor the weakling. He protests, essentially, those facts that do in truth constrict human life: the fact of the power of evil; the fact of our inability fully to know or to control our own selves; the fact of death; the fact of our ignorance of what lies beyond death. More and more, as the play proceeds, he is aware of his own distress in this perspective; more and more he calls in question not simply his own particular ill fortune, but those conditions that humiliate all men— set "naked...alone," each man, on the kingdom of life. In the last act, especially, his gestures take on a more than individual eloquence. In this act, which opens with the grave-digger's scene, Shakespeare confronts Hamlet with the final fact that men find hard to bear: the fact of the inevitability of death. Here, at Ophelia's grave, the scene, no longer within the castle bounds, widens in a more than literal sense. We have watched Hamlet, at Claudius' court, grow more and more dissatisfied with his paltry position there. He has joked, "I lack advancement." But when, at the graveside, in a moment of frustration, he cries out, "This is I, Hamlet, the Dane!" his earlier complaint sounds again in our ears with new import—sounds as the vain cry of every man on earth, eager to assert his identity, but born to die.

But Hamlet has returned to Denmark, after his sea voyage and a near escape from death, with clearer perspective, too, upon the vanity of his own protest. "There's a divinity that shapes our ends, rough hew them how we will." We see his protest gradually transmuted into tragic acceptance—until, finally, he would "take away [fortune's] power" simply by refusing to cry out under it, by accepting it. His opposition to Claudius and his court assumes now a deeper and quieter quality. In the final scene, Hamlet moves with new grace and self-possession—moves almost with ease.

In *Hamlet*, Shakespeare calls into play a world of those motions with which men vainly protest "gainst [fortune's] state." His ranging glance scans what is weak and what is daring in that protest; what is most perverse and what is most noble. In Hamlet, he examines the furthest reaches of that protest. He shows a man at his most helpless, so constricted by circumstances and by his own nature (by "fortune's star" and "nature's livery"), heir to so many "natural shocks" that it has made him almost mad, he can at first only strike out blindly and without control, disastrously, harming those he loves as often as his enemies.* But in the course of the play, that protest grows less blind, less vain. When at the end of the play Fortinbras' captains lift Hamlet to their shoulders in a rite of honor, they lift up before us, in that gesture, our humanity: we may look upon the measure of our frailty and of our force, our bondage and our power—in spite of it—to win a curious kind of liberty.

*See Editor's Note, page ix.

To fight
is almost the easiest part.
It is the search for the battlefield
that tries me.
I feel as though I were fighting in one of those
Shakespearian battles in which
the king protects himself by having a dozen or so warriors
wear his dress.
Which is the real king—whom I must challenge?

1940

Section 2: The Early Sixties

People may find it more comfortable to listen to us if we equivocate, but in the long run only words that discomfort them are going to change our situation.

—from "Letter to WISP"

After my father died, I, one night, in a dream,
Entered the ground in which they had planted him.
I found him, not asleep, but lying at anchor, propped
In a narrow boat, on his elbows, as if rising in bed.
The ribs of the boat were his ribs, old wood,
and his head, toward me, was its figurehead.
A tangle of matted roots, his hair
Had sprouted thickly through the air.
Air, earth, or was it water? All here
Was one dark but transparent matter.
In awe again of parting with him, I dropped
To my knees. Despair of meaning in our lives
Fluttered in me. I groped to touch him. Unreasoning
Hope then thrust my hands
Into the thicket sprung from his brows.
The floating shaggy web embraced me;
I felt my blood race back and forth to me along the vine,
And my breath stop; the sour strong perfume
Of upturned earth choked my lungs;
And in the one harsh stroke
I felt my life renew, and woke.

1959

The Peacemakers

In 1960, when "The Peacemakers" was written, "Negro" was an accepted, nonoffensive word used by people of all colors in referring to a black person; and the "generic male", of course, was unquestioned. The term "colored" was (and still often is) used in regional dialects*. The "beats" Barbara mentions were rebellious individualists—mostly white, mostly young—who developed lifestyles and literature challenging the conformity and lifelessness of white American culture in the 1950s: the hippies of an earlier generation. (JM) Published in The Nation, *December 17, 1960.*

> *"A vast conspiracy of silence has spread all about us, a conspiracy accepted by those who are frightened and who rationalize their fears in order to hide them from themselves. . . . And for all who can live only in an atmosphere of human dialogue and sociability, this silence is the end of the world. . . Among the powerful of today, these are the men without a kingdom. . . nor will they recover their kingdom until they come to know precisely what they want and proclaim it directly and boldly enough to make their words a stimulus to action."*
>
> —Albert Camus

I encountered recently a small number of Americans who seem to me to be headline news, for they answer the call from Camus I have quoted above—for bold words and bold action to rid our world of fear. But the press ignores them. These people are members of two related groups, the Committee for Nonviolent Action and the Peacemakers. It is time that they were noticed at least by those publications that regularly bewail the arms race and the cold war; for they propose a clear alternative: staged unilateral disarmament, and national defense, should it be necessary, through nonviolent resistance— Gandhi's way, with which the Negroes in our own South are now experimenting. They argue with some eloquence that their means of contending with an adversary are not only powerful but the only means consistent with our professed belief in the sanctity of human life. They also believe that if we disarmed, there is a very fair chance that Russia would follow suit.

* *and among radical feminists.*

77

The Committee for Nonviolent Action has been concentrating its activities, since June, in New London, Connecticut—home of the Polaris submarine. The Peacemakers, late in August, chose the same town in which to hold a sixteen-day training program in nonviolent methods. I attended all sixteen days of the program. When I first learned about it through chance, I decided to attend for perhaps a day. I had been reading Gandhi eagerly for the past year. But I expected to be unimpressed by the people I would find in New London. I assumed blandly that if they were, in fact, impressive, I should somehow have heard about them before this.

The first hour or two after my arrival seemed to confirm my skepticism. Peacemaker headquarters were not impressive—or, rather, the impression was a vivid one but disheartening. An abandoned three-story tenement had been rented for the occasion—rooms above and two empty shops on the ground floor. The place had been furnished hastily with rented folding chairs, three long tables, a stove and icebox, and enough army cots for some of us; the rest would sleep on the floor. Plaster dropped from the ceilings in little pellets upon our heads; and now and then drainage water ran down the walls. A plumber's visits were little help. The first evening, as the group sat about in discussion, a sudden crackling report brought us all to our feet. I thought for a moment that a bomb had been thrown in among us; but it turned out that a beam had just given way. Not long after these meetings, the building was condemned.

When I arrived, only about a dozen of the participants had gathered. Attendance would vary, but usually there were anywhere from thirty to fifty people in the place. These first arrivals were assembled in the larger of the empty shops, their chairs pushed up against the room's four walls. They were young men for the most part, and shabby as the old building itself. They wore dirty blue jeans and khakis, T-shirts and rumpled sport shirts. A good number had their shirt tails out. One young man had eased off his shoes and was wriggling his toes energetically. Flies buzzed about the room. An older gray-haired man, mild and grave, dressed in a neat brown business suit, was giving the first lecture. This was Richard Gregg, author of *The Power of Nonviolence*. He was presenting the essentials of nonviolence: respect for the other person, whoever he is; patience—"Patience is the recognition that change takes time." He played with his watch chain as he talked, and seemed not quite to look at his audience—his foot quietly tapping the air. Did the listeners seem to him unpromising? I wondered. One young man passed a paperbound book to another, and I noted the title: *Jesus Was a Beatnik*. Was this, in fact, a Beat gathering?

As more people arrived, however, the group became more various: there were women now, as well as men; old and middle-aged as well as young; a number of couples with children; a range of dress—though no one looked prosperous. Before many hours had passed, I began to look twice, too, at the young men I had met first. My skepticism faded. I began, I might add, to take more seriously the Beat movement itself; for many of these young men, I hazard, are kin to them. That is, their distaste for the *status quo* is similar. But they are Beats raised from limbo by a positive faith.

The reason for the dismal headquarters was clear soon enough. Most of those present had adopted a life of voluntary poverty. (It was announced that nobody would be approached for money: let those who could afford $2.50 a day contribute it, and those who could afford a little more, do so if they were moved to. No one who was hard up should pay anything, and if anyone needed financial help, he should ask for it.) Many in the group had chosen to be poor because of a wish to identify their lives with those of a majority of the world's people. But also they had chosen to be poor to fit themselves for battle—lest anxiety about losing what they had should make them hesitate. What soon became apparent about these people was that they were above all people ready to act. Somewhere in the history of nonviolent resistance, the term "passive resistance" has been picked up. This term should be discarded. The "pacifists" are the only freely active people I have met in a long time. Coming face to face with them was, in fact, like entering a new world.

A large number of those present had already risked and served jail sentences for their stands. The majority, for example, refuse to pay taxes, because the bulk of taxes go for armaments. (Some of them refuse to pay what is due, some of them manage to live on incomes that are below the taxable level.) They all stand, of course, for refusing the draft. Those who have been sent to jail for these "offenses" have usually protested the prison system while they were about it—their battle being with violence wherever it is met. They have engaged in protests against capital punishment; against segregation (many are active in the sit-in movement); against imperialism (some had joined a peace walk across Puerto Rico, calling for the true independence of that country); against Congressional abuse of investigating powers (they had often had to fight for their own lives here and also had picketed for others in trouble). But the most distinctive activity in which they engage is civil disobedience at various war plants. For example, during the summer of 1959, eleven of them trespassed upon the missile plant at Omaha, Nebraska, in symbolic protest—"to reclaim the land for peaceful purposes." One of the eleven to serve a six-months' term for this was a mild-faced mother of four, Marjorie Swann—whose husband meanwhile cared for the children. (Her story has been told in the August, 1960, issue of *Redbook*: "You Are A Bad Mother.") With members of the Fellowship of Reconciliation and the Quakers, they have held continuous vigils of protest at Fort Detrick, the chemical and biological warfare plant; they have organized protests against the absurdity of civil defense; they have demonstrated in various cities on Hiroshima Day; and backed the voyage of *The Golden Rule* into the Eniwetok H-bomb testing area.

In New London this past summer and fall, the act of trespass has consisted of rowing across the Thames and attempting to board a Polaris-missile-carrying submarine. (They protest the Polaris submarine especially because in any effort at achieving a disarmament agreement, it is bound to complicate the problem of inspection). In their first attempts, the activists failed to find a submarine present—so trespassed, instead, upon the property of the Electric Boat Company, manufacturer of the submarine. The authorities decided that there would be less publicity if they made no arrests, but simply dumped the invaders outside the company gates. The publicity *was* less. but the protesters were enabled to return again and again; and the fact that no one had been jailed encouraged others to swell their numbers. After I left New London, members of the group managed at last to board the *George Washington* and the *Patrick Henry* for a few minutes. And at the launching of the *Ethan Allen* on November 23rd, nine people trespassed and two young men managed to swim through the frigid Thames and climb up the sides of the sub. This day all who trespassed were arrested—and these arrests did finally make *The New York Times*.

There is room in the movement, of course, for those who are not prepared to risk jail. A much larger group of volunteers backed up these actions— with vigils at the scene, with peace walks, and with leafleteering. A series of leaflets were passed out among Electric Boat workers at every working shift; lectures were arranged at local churches and clubs; and everybody involved engaged whomsoever he could throughout the town in conversation. ("Polaris Action" was organized by the Committee for Nonviolent Action, but members of the Peacemaker program took time out from the daily discussions they held to assist them.)

I was present at a certain number of these conversations, and some of them were startling to me. Many took place at C.N.V.A. headquarters—a tiny office at 13 Bank Street—where townspeople dropped in either to heckle or to ask questions; most of them were at Electric Boat, where larger and larger crowds of workers, as well as passers-by, would gather after the acts of trespass. Over the months, more and more townspeople expressed sympathy, and a handful of workers volunteered to quit their jobs if the committee could find them other work. (A Committee for Useful Work is a C.N.V.A. project.) But first responses were for the most part violently hostile. That readiness to act which I have noted among the group was viewed as a disposition not admirable but highly questionable. "Why must you make fools of yourselves?" it was asked again and again, with a tone of horror. There was deeper horror still in the other question asked most frequently: "And why must you break the law?'' Several of the leaflets reminded the reader of the many examples of civil disobedience in the history of this democracy; reminded him that the phrase itself—civil disobedience—had been coined by Thoreau. One leaflet quotes Thoreau: "If the law is of such a nature that it requires you to be the agent of injustice to another, then, I say, break the law. Let your life be a counter friction to stop the machine." It continues: "The government of the United States is derived from the consent of the governed. Just as a citizen in a democracy freely obeys all just laws, so, too, he is obligated to protest unjust or immoral laws...resisting them openly and nonviolently." Heads would shake. "But why break the law?" The depth of many Americans' awe of authority astonished me. "Would you have broken the law if you had lived in Germany under Hitler?" I heard one workman questioned. He answered stoutly, "No. I believe in obeying the law." Another was asked, "And when you feel that the law contradicts a higher law?" With stress: "I believe in my country!" Those who viewed with most alarm the act of challenging authority—and who invariably assumed that individual action must be ineffectual: "What can you or I do? It's up to our leaders"—were the same people who with extraordinary heat swore that they would rather die, would rather see mankind itself exterminated, than live "as slaves" under "authoritarian" Communist rule.

The longer I listened to the advocates of nonviolence in conversation with the people of the town, the more I was struck by the difference that marked them off from the majority. One incident, though minor, sticks in my memory as illustrative. The last day I was there, four people trespassed at the submarine base at Groton, and their act was prefaced by a peace walk the five miles from New London. Passing motorists yelled "Ass holes!" "Commies!" "Go back to Cuba!" and a few waved and smiled. A *few* onlookers, indeed, at the sight of our posters, seemed to me to smile with a freshening look of relief—as at the sight of clearing skies, of sanity. A newspaper reporter walked alongside, and a good deal of the time he questioned a woman directly behind me. Like others before him—myself of course included—he was bothered about the sloppy clothes of a few of the marchers. Why couldn't they be more careful of public opinion? Well, some among the marchers, she answered, thought it important not to be concerned about middle-class conventions. For some, this was an important protest, too, though for others it wasn't. Did a few beards and a few shirt tails out really matter? The reporter seemed to think they mattered painfully. There was a note of peevish anxiety in his voice—a curious note, considering the fact that this was not, one gathered, *his* Cause the untidy ones endangered. A C.N.V.A. car came along—a large poster on its roof—and the driver pulled off at the side of the road for a moment; but not quite all the way off—still took up perhaps two inches of the highway. A police car appeared in the stream of traffic, and again the reporter began to fret: "Oh why do they do that? Now they'll get a ticket! *Why* do they have to do that?" His tone was again one of nervous alarm. I turned to observe them both. The young woman looked at him with calm surprise. "I don't think they'll get a ticket. But why be nervous about it?" she asked him. As the police car drove on by, and I turned away, it struck me that here were two people living in quite different worlds, breathing an altogether different air.

The nervous agitation of the reporter was not an agitation at all peculiar to him. By now it was a phenomenon familiar to me. It seemed to me, sometimes, in these encounters with those who opposed us, that Fear was tangible in the air between us—a free-floating creature. Often we ourselves were its object, incongruously. In spite of the fact that one argument used against us was that our acts were ineffectual, people hardly ever passed us by with a pitying or a careless smile. They passed us with eyes averted as though from some obscene or acutely embarrassing sight; or turned on us looks of such venom and such panic that it was hard, at first, to believe; some snatching leaflets from our hands to tear them into shreds—"Get out of here!"; some few getting rougher still. By the end of the summer, a great number of the workers were accepting leaflets with open friendliness: "You get up early, don't you?" But I speak of those who were still unsympathetic. When those in the group who had trespassed were dumped, limp, outside the gates of the plant (they went limp, once officials laid hands upon them, to emphasize both their attitude of disobedience and their rejection of violence), onlookers would sometimes scream with fury: "Smack them down hard!" "Crack their heads on the sidewalk!" I remember one middle-aged woman in a light cotton house dress appealing with desperation to a nearby cop: "You ought to drown them all!" A young naval officer who wandered into the C.N.V.A. office one evening screamed at one of the women volunteers: "When the first Russian soldier rapes you, I hope you remember me!"

The real source of all this panicky fury was clear enough in any prolonged conversation. Most conversations followed a pattern. The man or woman objecting to unilateral disarmament would first declare that the country had nothing to fear if only it would keep itself strong, and not play the coward, "like you lousy pacifists." If we just kept strong, war could be prevented. The risk of war through some accident of miscalculation would be dismissed with a scoff. Didn't we think the people in charge were going to take such possibilities into account? But then at a certain point there would break from their lips some remark revealing the assumption at heart that disaster *must* come, of course, sooner or later; there was just nothing anyone could do about it. Many remarked that it was all in the Bible, after all. "Read *Revelation*." Many remarked "Sometimes I think it's what we deserve." Those who make this latter remark usually assume it to be daringly original.

The uniformity of all these responses is, in fact, striking. The responses of the workers at Electric Boat match almost phrase for phrase—if one censors a few rough words—the responses I have heard from intellectuals. Their source is the same acute suffering: the same infuriating sense of helplessness; of the impossibility any longer of battle that is not self-defeating, of gallant action; and the same deep sense of guilt from which there is, seemingly, no way out—unless perhaps in that almost-wished-for explosion which would be the End of the World.

A lively admission of the paralysis experienced by so many, but rarely made a matter for public discussion, is contained in a statement made by one of the young men who volunteered to try to board a nuclear submarine. (C.N.V.A. always announces beforehand to the public and to all officials involved just what action it plans. Each individual who is about to commit civil disobedience writes his own statement of motives, too. None of these statements, of course, is ever quoted by the press. Here is a portion of a statement by Victor Richman, a student at Columbia:)

> An awesome specter threatens me now, invading the seclusion of the most precious parts of my existence, carelessly flaunting its meaning and visions, identifying itself, terribly, with my being. I try, perhaps, to write a poem, to discuss the specter with others, to think seriously about it, and yet it remains, ever conscious of my movement, always ready to inhibit and restrict. It will be at times a dark, inky mist, blocking my path.... It appears also as a hard steel chain penetrating insidiously far below my skin, to hold the molecules of my body, to make them...cold and uneventful. And I have discovered, eventually, that I am not free.
>
> I have been told that I must not refrain from learning to kill. I have also been told that I must prepare myself in every way for my annihilation. And I have been told that I cannot be present at the places where these conditions are set down.
>
> I have not the right to obey these conditions.

If there is a difference between these people and the majority, this decision has made the difference. In refusing "to obey these conditions" they have found at least a degree of freedom. How much change the actions of these people will bring about in the world at large, remains an open question—how many others, that is, will finally join them. But there is no question that their actions have changed *them*. The people I saw gathered in New London were people of altogether mixed background: Quakers, Catholics, Episcopalians, Methodists, Jews, atheists; Negro and white; men and women from all over the country, of both humble and privileged birth, and drawn from any number of occupations. They were people, also, of strong temperament; the group was hardly monotone. Yet the longer I observed them, the more I was struck by a certain similar air that could be said to mark them all—and most particularly those who had experimented with nonviolence for any length of time. They all share an extraordinary spontaneity—the sense that an individual *can* act, and *has* weight. "If no one else will do it, then do it yourself," a homely, vivid old man said to me lightly—Max Sandin, a house painter, who had staged a one-man memorial protest in Cleveland on Hiroshima Day. (He had been a C.O. in World War I and survived brutal abuse at General Wood's detention camp.) A southern minister described the beginnings of resistance to segregation in his community: "I told them it would be nice if several other people would join me, but I'd decided to do it alone if nobody else would." As a result of their commitment to action, all were conspicuously hardy—fearless in a very special manner. There was an atmosphere among them both grave and lighthearted. The place was full of wit. The more particular quality and cause of their boldness struck me one day as I listened to a group discussion, full of talk of radical changes that should be made in our society. We were sitting in the abandoned store, its windows heavily shrouded (the landlady had insisted on this, for rocks had been thrown through the windows over at C.N.V.A.). The shrouding gave the place rather the air of a gangster's hide-out, and as the talk touched upon one thing after another wrong with things as they were, I suddenly asked myself—for I am the daughter of a well-to-do Republican lawyer: "What am I doing here? This is talk of revolution." Which of course it was. Then I recalled the methods to which they are committed. I recalled their rejection of secrecy; their careful advance notice to their adversary of all their plans. If the windows here were shrouded, the door was open to anyone who cared to wander in. And indeed a number of meetings were attended by curious neighbors—not always sober—who freely injected their own views. I recalled their commitment to the use of persuasion in place of violence—seeing in memory their harmless though stubborn forms dragged by Electric Boat officials from the company cars and dumped on the sidewalk—at which they would rise, brush the dirt from their clothes and tell the flustered officials: "We're sorry to have to put you through this." I suddenly recognized the source of their distinctive boldness: the source is innocence. No ordinary misgivings about injuring another person need dilute their resolution and make them hesitate. Max Sandin, the seventy-one-year-old house painter whom I've quoted already, writes in the Peacemaker bulletin of being carried out of the submarine base after trespassing: "I looked all the time to the clear blue sky, and on the tree tops—how they shaked their heads with approval of what we did." The candor and innocence of their actions gives to these people—for all the very great differences among them—a likeness to each other. The actions themselves leave their mark upon them.

This fact was remarked upon by Reverend Fred Shuttlesworth, the minister I have quoted, who attended the conference for one day—a man active in the integration struggle in Birmingham, Alabama. He was being questioned about whether nonviolence had been adopted by the Negroes in the South as a tactic or as a way of life. For himself, and for many others, he answered, "It is our philosophy—though we don't understand it as fully as we ought or must. . . . 'Love thy neighbor, love thy enemy, do violence to no man'— that's what I preach, you see. . . . Every person who has to say something continually has to try to bring himself into accord with what he teaches. . . . This is our slogan: 'Not one hair on the head of one white person shall be harmed by us in this struggle.' "

For some, nonviolence *was* a tactic. "We couldn't afford to be seen as the oppressors." But, he added, the question actually was not a simple one. "Because the more you try to practice it, the more it becomes a part of you." Asked how he had found the courage to persist as he had, in the face of provocation and terror, mob action, the bombing of his house, he answered, "When you get into it, you discover things about yourself that you didn't understand before you began." Before all this, he related, he had been deadly afraid of airplanes. "You couldn't have given me money to fly. Now I hate to hear a plane go off unless I'm on it." He put out his hands in a gesture of wonder.

Among all those present who had experimented with nonviolence, I encountered the same surprise at the power of the actions they engaged in to bear them up. "I'm not an authority on nonviolence," Reverend Shuttlesworth said of himself; "I've just been exposed to some incidents. . . . There don't have to be big men—just big actions." Many of them had impressive tales to tell of what they had endured and what they had accomplished; but in the telling of these stories they boasted not of themselves but of these new means they had adopted. Shuttlesworth described for us at length an encounter with a Birmingham police captain one evening, when the captain was clearly after his life—trying in every way he could think of to provoke him to some move which would give his men an excuse to shoot him down. "I've never seen so many riot guns. The captain said to me, 'We protect people in our town.' I said, 'I see you do.' " He had refused to be provoked, and at the end of the incident, "The man might hate me," he said, "but he could at least respect what I aspired to. He wouldn't tell me that, of course, but nonviolence had won a victory." The fact that they marvel not at themselves but at the possibilities in a certain mode of action gives to each of them a dramatist's eye upon events, lively, impersonal, frequently humorous. "The captain asked, me 'Are all these men with you?

Why are there so many?' 'Well, I like company.' 'Everywhere you go?' 'Captain, you see, I have more or less someone with me everywhere I go. They like me and I like company.' 'Are you expecting to run into trouble?' 'Well no, Captain, but you know life—one can get into trouble just trying to stay out of trouble.' "

One of the most remarkable tales told at the training program was that of Eroseanna Robinson, the track star. Arrested for refusing to pay taxes, she refused to cooperate with the authorities at all. "In conscience I couldn't be part of this drama. Everyone was playing a role and I was asked to play one, too. Each official was like a man who had learned a script—learned it so well that if you adlibbed, he didn't know what the next line was. What we have to do more and more is teach them that the script is wrong—by adlibbing in the spirit of nonviolence." So she refused to walk into court, and was carried in; she fasted in jail, and was tube fed. In the beginning, officials were very rough with her. She was carried along by the chain of her handcuffs. "But I said, I'll just detach myself." One man couldn't resist jabbing her with his fingernail. They carried her with her feet angled up in immodest fashion. "But I felt: This is not my indignity." They put her in solitary; they threatened her with a mental institution; they promised her that the other prisoners would beat her up. But the other prisoners, who had begun by asking "Who is this silly?," ended by identifying solidly with her resistance. When another inmate was badly hurt and the prison was slow about getting her to a hospital, a large group, for the first time in the history of that prison, went on hunger strike—in imitation of Rose—and the prison got the woman off to the hospital with unusual dispatch. By the time she left, prison officials themselves were talking to her "not as a child but trying to reach courteously across quite a gap." She was released after serving only ninety-three days of a year's sentence. Other Peacemakers were by now picketing outside the prison walls: all the inmates were stirred by this fact; and it was too much for the authorities. Again, it was not herself at which Rose marveled but at these new means that she had adopted. The effect of her resistance upon the other prisoners occasioned her special wonder. When I went up to her some time later and said, "That was a very beautiful story that you told," she answered with simplicity, "I felt that way about it, too."

One constant question, of course, recurring in all the discussions, was how the nonviolent method could gain mass support. No one thought the answer obvious—though one man, Richard Gregg, declared himself "not too troubled about the future of this thing. The idea has been simmering for a couple of thousand years," he said; "I rather feel its time has come....People have been used to trust the past as a guide, but the past has almost ceased to be a guide, the world is so utterly different suddenly." There was much discussion as to whether it was wiser for the group to act on many fronts or to concentrate time and effort on a single action. The executive secretary of C.N.V.A., Bradford Lyttle, argued with passion that it was essential to forget for the moment all other projects and to concentrate on protesting against nuclear armaments. Another man argued just as passionately that "It has always been the folly of pacifism to think of violence and nonviolence as only overt. Resistance to war is impossible without resistance to imperialism, to racism, to violence as an everyday pervasive reality." This was Ralph Templin, now a teacher of sociology at Central State College, for fifteen years a missionary in India. He was recalled by his church when he tried to start a Christian nonviolent movement—at the time when England was our war ally, and Gandhi, of course, an embarrassment to the British government. The majority shared his view: "It is all one picture."

Everyone felt that a considerable impact upon public opinion had been made in New London. When the summer ended, though many had to return to jobs and schools, a few made the decision to pull up roots and actually move to the area. One man gave up a printing business to do so; another man, a builder, left a community where he was well established to risk this move with his entire family. But a variety of other projects were set in motion, too, before the conference closed—with emphasis on concerted support of the sit-in movement.

One of the most dramatic events of the conference was an exchange between Reverend Shuttlesworth and one of the less humble members of the C.N.V.A. Reverend Shuttlesworth had just spoken to the question of whether the Negro in the South had adopted nonviolence as a way of life or simply as a tactic. Speaking of his own faith, he had concluded, "Maybe one day I can meet the man who bombed my house, and we can shake hands and talk about it." A young pacifist suddenly declared bluntly: "The key to whether you have really adopted nonviolence or not is: How many of your men refuse to go into the army?"

There was a moment of surprised silence and I expected the southerner to reply: When you have endured some of the things that I have endured, then I will let you tell me what it is to be nonviolent. This was not his response, however. There were others at the meeting who spoke out angrily for him.... One man jumped in: "Pacifists demand too much of other people and not enough of themselves! To ask the Negro to take this added burden is absurd!" Anne Braden (author of *The Wall Between*) quoted the title of an editorial she had recently seen: "Are Pacifists Willing to be Negroes?"

One of those who spoke was Ralph Templin. He said, "Maybe the larger percentage of learning has to be on *our* part in this thing.... We began," he said, "under the inspiration of Gandhi, trying deliberately to bring nonviolence into the pacifist movement. But in studying Gandhi, it became a matter of amazement to many of us that there never was any real *pacifist* organization in India. The whole picture was one of nonviolence used to end colonialism.... There is violence in the very nature of the southern social structure, and nonviolence is being used to overthrow it.... How can we say that our own use of nonviolence against a particular violence is more legitimate? There is a complex violence in the Western world. We have to think: Where can one take hold? It has to come out of an historical situation, and we have not yet found in the pacifist movement the historical situation that makes it similar to the process in India or here in the South. The day may come. When it comes, if we are ready, it may mean everything to what happens.... But in the meantime what is natural for us is to get into *this* struggle. We mustn't think that we can be against war and not against racism, or against the whole structure of colonialism."

Reverend Shuttlesworth himself said—quite simply and without heat: "I will confess that I don't know very much about pacifism. I'm not an expert on nonviolence. I'm simply a person thrown by the hand of destiny into a position of leadership.... A man has to go according to his degree of understanding and dedication. He can be no more dedicated than he understands. You may be right," he told the young pacifist, "that this is something we must consider.... I think, as you do, that somewhere somehow maybe these various actions are kindred actions. The only way they can be related is by your meeting me, like this—all of us meeting each other—so that we can see and relate the whole situation in a better pattern.... The possibility looms for the future that we may find we are on common ground.... The word 'pacifist' in the South has a bad ring. It has it even here in the North. So you have a job. But you *are* allied with us.... We have to improvise as we go."

Southern Peace Walk: Two Issues or One?

Published in Liberation, *July-August 1962.*

The man took a leaflet and read a few lines. "This is the Nashville, Tennessee to Washington, D.C. Walk for Peace," it began; " 'Since 650 B.C. there have been 1,656 arms races, only sixteen of which have not ended in war. The remainder have ended in economic collapse.' " He looked up. "Are you walking with that nigger?" he asked.

This kind of discussion of our message had been anticipated by the Committee for Nonviolent Action, when it decided that the walk should be integrated. "Token integrated," somebody later commented. Of thirteen young men and women committed to walk the whole distance, Robert Gore was the only Negro, though we hoped others might join before Washington. Whether they did or not, it was assumed that in the many talks about war and peace we would attempt to provoke along the way, we were sure to be asked a good many times whether we would be happy to see Robert married to our sisters. Before we headed south, we discussed the question of just how distracting our obvious attitude to race relations might be, and the proper way to cope with this. Events then proved our tentative conclusions to have been utterly inadequate.

Most of those advising us felt that battle on the two issues simply could not be combined. Of course we ought never to deny our belief in racial brotherhood; but Robert's presence was enough to confirm it. We should try to avoid talking about it; we were there to talk about *peace*. And it would be folly to seek to associate ourselves too closely with the people down there who were struggling for integration. Many people would then shy away from us. And they, the Negroes, could be harmed by it even more than we. They had enough of a burden to bear, already, without our giving their opponents added ammunition—the charge of their being "unpatriotic."

I supposed that the advice was practical, but it depressed me. I think we all left the meeting feeling unsatisfied—wondering a little why, then, the walk *was* to be integrated. We'd talked about the fact that this could lead us into danger. The South was unpredictable, it was stressed: we might not run into

89

any trouble at all; on the other hand, we just might all get killed. In a cause we were not to appear to be battling for?

I had felt for a long time that the two struggles—for disarmament and for Negro rights—were properly parts of the one struggle. The same nonviolent tactic joined us, but more than this: our struggles were fundamentally one—to commit our country in act as well as in word to the extraordinary faith announced in our Declaration of Independence: that all men are endowed with certain rights that must not be denied them. *All* men, including those of darker skin, whom it has been convenient to exploit; including those in other countries, with whose policies we quarrel; among those rights which are not to be questioned, the right to be free to pursue happiness, and among them the right not to be deprived of life. In short, the Christian faith, still revolutionary, that men are brothers and that—no matter what—our actions must respect the fact. The only mode of battle that does, implicitly, respect this fact is that of nonviolence, and I had heard that for more and more of those in the civil rights as well as in the peace movement, the very attempt to practice it had implanted a corresponding faith, however tentative. But of course it is possible to hold a faith and yet not recognize all its implications, to be struggling side by side with others and yet be unaware of them. Perhaps it wasn't realistic to think of joining ranks.

We started out, in Nashville, with only a wistful look in the direction of the integration movement. We marched past a sit-in demonstration at a "Simple Simon's" and "smiled in." We didn't even picket for a few minutes; didn't pause in our marching. "There they are"—we turned our heads. We caught a glimpse of a row of young people at a counter—a glimpse, as in a flash photograph, of young heads held in a certain proud and patient fashion; and then we had marched past. A few steps away, in front of a movie theater, several adolescent toughs loitered—faces furtive, vacant. Did they plan trouble? In a minute, we were out of sight. It felt unnatural, I think, to all of us.

That afternoon we held a small open meeting at Scarritt College for Christian Workers. Two Negro leaders were among those present—James Lawson and Metz Rollins. Members of the group staging the sit-in—the Student Nonviolent Coordinating Committee—had been invited; but none came. Was this because *they* were shy of association with us? Or was it perhaps because, as one walker suggested, they felt that we should have done more to demonstrate solidarity with them? Rollins inclined his head, smiled. "It may well be."

Lawson spoke that afternoon. In the course of his talk, he remarked, "There is a clear-cut relation between the peace walk and what some of us are seeking to do in the emerging nonviolent movement in the South. Some people have tried to classify our effort here as one that is of and for and by the Negro. They have tried to define the struggle for integration as a struggle to gain the Negro more power. I maintain that it is not the case. Go among the common ordinary people . . . for the 'leading Negroes' are not the leaders of this movement. . . . Listen to their prayers and to their speech. They are constantly thinking not in terms of civil rights but in terms of the kingdom of God on earth, the brotherhood of all men. . . . What is behind it is an effort to build a community for all of us . . . 'the beloved community.' I say that this work is related to the work for peace. . . . It might be a prototype to speak to the whole world. . . . And the peace walk is related to the task of building community here. . . . The movements are related to each other, in a sense are one and the same enterprise."

I took down the words he spoke, in my notebook, nodding, "Yes"; and at the same time, disregarding them—perhaps because I was tired from the long drive south, and the process of breaking myself in again to group life, to sleeping on the floor, to packing up and moving each day; or perhaps because the meeting room was very nearly empty: the peace movement and the civil rights movement were certainly not visibly related here.

On Easter afternoon, we walked out of Nashville, heading out along Route 70N toward Knoxville. Two Fisk students, members of S.N.C.C., did appear just before starting time, to walk with us for a little while. Their presence was well noted. The signs we carried were unconventional: "If your conscience demands it, refuse to serve in the armed forces," ". . . refuse to pay taxes for war," "Defend freedom with nonviolence"; but more conspicuous than our signs, quite obviously, were the Negro students—while they remained with us—and after a while the single figure of Robert Gore. Robert carried the "lollipop" sign that simply labeled the walk: NASHVILLE TO WASHINGTON; but he was in himself our most provocative, most instantly legible sign—walking along very quietly; dressed, carefully, not in hiking clothes but sober sports jacket and slacks; head held high, a quiet tension in his bearing.

We encountered a certain amount of southern courtesy—"Well, have a nice walk!"; and now and then an expression of active sympathy—"God go with you!" "You mean you agree with us?" "I sure do!" But less friendly messages were of course more common—"Boo!", "Get out of here!" As we held out our leaflets, car windows were rolled up swiftly; some cars actually backed off from us in a rush; citizens on foot stepped quickly behind shop doors. Approaching a leaflet victim, one tried, by remaining very calm oneself, and looking him quietly in the eye, to prevent his flight, and infect him with corresponding calm; but the exercise was difficult. Soon the "hot rod gang" began to face us in the field. Parking their cars by the roadside, they would line up, leaning against them, waiting our approach, assuming looks that were meant to kill—expressions glowering and at the same time pathetically vacant. We would offer leaflets, walk past; they would hop into their cars, speed past us, line up again by the roadside. And now the first warnings began to be delivered to us. I handed a leaflet to the manager of a garage, and to the Negro employee who stood beside him. "I hear they're going to shoot you a little farther down the line," the white man told me softly. "They don't like niggers there, you see." He turned and smiled fixedly into the eyes of the black man by his side—"That's what I hear." The Negro made no answer, returning the stare but allowing nothing to come to the surface of his look—his shining eyes fathomless. The white man turned back to me. "I just hope you'll be all right," he said—not pretending not to pretend. I told him, as brightly as I could, "Keep hoping."

That first night we slept on the floors of a white church near Old Hickory; the next night our "advance worker" had arranged for us to stay in a Negro church in Lebanon. Lebanon was a small town which had lately seen much violence. Fifteen months before, a young Negro minister, Reverend Cordell Sloan, had been assigned to the town to try to build a Negro Presbyterian church. He had felt called, as well, to try to build a sit-in movement. This was the first small town in the South in which the struggle had been taken up; and it involved not college but high school students. Retaliation had been vigorous. Just recently the headquarters of the group had been demolished with rocks, while the Negroes themselves stood pressed against the walls inside, and the police looked on. This day, as we filed along the highway, a car slowed down in passing, a young man leaned his head out: "You walking into Lebanon?" "That's right." "Good place for you to be walking. We're going to hang you all there." It was a bright beautiful day. Fruit trees were coming into bloom; the purple redbud was out. Horses and goats and litters of many-colored pigs ran in mixed company through the long Tennessee fields. The fields were vivid with flowering mustard. We marched along, trying not to straggle out, but to keep fairly close together. Just before midday a car approaching us suddenly whizzed into a side road and stopped; the doors flew open, and several men leaped out. Well, here it is, I thought; may we all behave well. Then I saw that their faces were dark. They were students from Lebanon, two of them come to walk into town with us. More planned to join us later. They held out their hands for signs to carry.

We stopped by the side of the road and shared a picnic lunch. We bought a carton of milk at a nearby store, and in a shy ritual gesture passed it from hand to hand, each drinking from the spout. On the road again, we walked past an all-Negro primary school, set high on a hill. The entire school stood out in the yard, waving to us. I ran up the hill with leaflets. A sweet-faced teacher asked me—so softly that I could hardly catch the words: "How many colored are with you?" I told her that two of the young men she saw were from Lebanon. "I thought I recognized J.T.," she said; and in her voice, in her face, was a contained, tremulous pride and excitement. A few miles further on, more students waited by the road to join us; a little further on, more; and at the town's edge, still more. As we stepped onto the sidewalks of the town, more of us were black than white.

A car sped by, an arm jerked out of the window and slung an empty coke bottle. The youngest of the team, Henry Wershaw, gave a little cry: he had been hit in the ankle. He was able soon to limp on. We kept close ranks, to be ready for worse than that; but everyone was stepping lightly; the mood among us was almost gay. One small boy, Sam, strode with us, eyes sparkling. A pretty young woman named Avis, in a light-colored summer dress, almost skipped along the street. The citizens of the town, as usual, stepped back from us in dread; withdrew behind their doors and peered out, through the glass panes, in amazement and dread, as the unarmed troop of us passed. There were several among us who bore the marks of violence at the hands of townspeople. The skull of one of the young Negroes showed, beneath his close-cropped hair, an intricate tracery of scars: he had been hit with a wrench during one of the sit-ins. There were others walking, too, who had suffered such blows; and none had ever struck back. They walked along the street now, lighthearted, as if secure, faces extraordinarily bright, while those who had, in one way or another condoned the blows struck, drew back, in the reflex of fear. Before we headed south, the women had been cautioned against walking in public next to a Negro man; it might make things dangerous for him. At any rate, we were told, best to take our cue from the man himself. I had carefully made no move to walk next to any of these students. But now one after another, as we moved through the town, stepped alongside me, to introduce himself, to exchange a few words—free of caution. They had made their choice, had entered a fight, and if one was in it, then one was in it—ready to take what might come. At lunch one of them talked about this a little: "When you see those hoodlums arriving, you just divorce yourself from your body—prepare your body for anything: spit, fists, sticks, anything—"

Police cars had begun to drive past us at frequent intervals; but our friends remarked that we mustn't assume that they were there for our protection. During recent trouble, one woman had asked an officer whether the police intended to protect them from the mob. "We're hired to protect the city, not individuals," had been his reply. We headed for the town square now, preparing ourselves for "anything." We walked through uneventfully. Within our hearing, an officer in a squad car pulled up next to a car full of young toughs and told the driver, "Not today, Hank, not today." We turned the corner and limped the final block to Pickets Chapel Methodist Church.

In the white churches where we had stayed so far, we had had the use of the church kitchen in which to fix our meals, from supplies we carried about with us; once the pastor's wife had kindly fixed us sandwiches and lemonade; and evenings, after supper, as many as five members of the congregation had sometimes dropped in to ask questions. This day, as we sat in the churchyard easing our feet, women began to appear from the four points of the compass, carrying bowls and platters; all who had walked were soon summoned into the room behind the church to a feast: fried chicken, garden peas, turnip greens, two kinds of potato salad, three kinds of pie. After we had sat down together to eat, we were invited into the church itself; word of a meeting had been spread through the community; the door kept opening, and soon the church had filled up.

The shape this meeting took swiftly dissolved any remaining anxieties about the harm we might do to the integrationists and to ourselves if we sought association with them. Reverend Sloan spoke first—a thin, handsome man with gentle but stubborn demeanor, and the luminous wide eyes of a man who is almost blind but who sees what it is that he wants to do. "I hope the town never gets over what it saw today," he began. What the town had seen of course, as we walked through its streets together, was the first integrated gathering that had ever occurred in Lebanon. The white community had seen, and the Negro community had seen, too, the brotherhood of which Sloan preached made visible—turned fact. "I hope it gets into its system, I hope it gets to the bone," said Sloan. It was clear that he meant both white community and Negro. We learned, at the end of the meeting, that this was the largest audience he had ever had there. He had made great headway with students, but adults had been largely apathetic. Because of the drama of our arrival, many adults were present tonight, gazing about them in quiet astonishment, and he was addressing them particularly.

He spoke of the struggles in which he and his followers had been involved; he spoke of the opposition they had encountered—sprayed with insecticides, hit with ketchup bottles, threatened with pistols, run down with lawn mowers, "name it, we've had it." "The proficient, efficient, sufficient police" had been on the scene. He smiled wryly. "We like to get killed." Many had been arrested. He asked those who had been to jail to stand. A large number stood. The leader of the peace walk, Bradford Lyttle, here interrupted to ask those among the peace walkers who had been to jail to stand, too; and an equal number rose. "Let no one be afraid of going to jail," the minister urged; "It has become an honor. . . . It's easy to say, isn't it? But come and try it." They shouldn't be afraid, he repeated; they should be afraid of being slaves any longer. "The only thing I'm afraid of is going back into the old way of living again. We've gone too far." He reminded those in the audience who had not been fighting that when freedom came, they, too, would enjoy it—unless perhaps they'd feel too guilty to enjoy it. They had better begin to get the feeling of it right now. Then he got very specific about the ways in which they could help, and the ways in which they had been doing the movement harm.

After he had spoken, Bradford Lyttle spoke about the work of the C.N.V.A. He spoke at ease, his words briefer than they often were—so much obviously could be assumed to be understood by this audience. He felt very strongly, he told them, that America was in a desperate situation today. Here were the most prosperous and happily situated people who had ever lived, on the verge of giving up their souls—for we were professing ourselves quite willing to murder hundreds of millions of other human beings to try to preserve our own standards of life. Many Americans were beginning to demonstrate in protest—to name themselves *un*willing. He urged them to join the protest. C.N.V.A. believed in disarming unilaterally, and in training for defense through nonviolent resistance. Heads nodded. No one stood up to hurl the familiar challenge: Are we supposed to lie down and let the Russians walk right over us? Of all the signs we carry, the sign that usually remains the most abstract for those who read it is "defend freedom through nonviolent resistance"; but when the students of Lebanon walked through their town carrying that banner, the message could not remain abstract. If our walking beside them had made visible for the community the substance of what Reverend Sloan had been preaching, their walking beside us had made visible the substance of what Bradford Lyttle preached. Forty-five people in that audience came forward to put their names on C.N.V.A.'s mailing list.

Reverend Sloan called for a collection to be taken up for both causes. Many who had little enough to spare opened their purses. Some who had never given before gave this night. We stood and clasped hands and sang the hymn that has become the theme song of the movement in the South: "We shall overcome some day! . . . Black and white together. . . . We shall live in peace!" The words seemed to belong to both our causes.

The next day we were scheduled to walk to the small town of Carthage, set on the bluffs of the Cumberland River. A number of the people who had walked into town with us the day before turned up to see us on our way. Reverend Sloan was among them, and a leader among the students, Bobby, and Sloan's right-hand man, a tall, very homely newspaper reporter, Finley, a man of wit and feeling; and quite a few others. We expected to be escorted to the town's edge and I rather think they had expected to walk only this far, themselves; but most of them ended by walking with us all the way to Carthage. Passing motorists again leaned out of their cars to shout threatening or vile remarks. "Let not your hearts be troubled," Reverend Sloan advised, in his soft, rather lilting voice. He and Finley left for a while to ride up ahead with Bradford and find a place for us to stay that night. They found it at Braden Methodist Church, where Sloan knew the assistant minister, Beulah

Allen. "How could we turn you out?" she said to Bradford; "You can never tell when the stranger will be the Lord."

After we had entered Carthage with our banners, Sloan and Finley and Bobby took a little stroll about its streets. The walk had now linked them dramatically with *that* town; and who knows when their battle may not be taken up there?

Again, this evening, women of the community appeared, arms laden; a feast was spread for us in the church basement. Again, after dinner together, we moved into the "sanctuary"; and again the church filled up. It was the first integrated meeting that had ever taken place here, too. That night, the women in our group slept in the house of Beulah Allen's sister, Dona. As we tiptoed through her room, Dona's old mother woke, and Dona introduced us. "Honey, they look white," Dona's mother whispered to her. "Mama, they are," said Dona. "Lord bless us!" said the old lady.

Braden's Methodist Church was set up on a little rise just above the large town square, and as we gathered noisily first in the basement and then in the church proper, a good many of the white people of the town and of the country round the town gathered in the square and stood glaring up. A few of them had thrown some rotten fruit and vegetables, as we sat outside before dinner; a few had walked past, holding empty coke bottles—but not quite bringing themselves to throw those. During the meeting, the door would open and shut, open and shut, as more and more of the Negro community kept arriving; and one was never quite sure that some of the crowd below might not be arriving at last. But again there were a lot of cops around, and again they had decided to keep order. The crowd just stood, until past midnight, glaring up at the small frame building which resounded with our talk and laughter and singing and prayer. Dona reported to us afterward that she had gone outside once and found several white boys loitering and had asked them in. "They don't understand," she explained to us; "They've never even been outside the county." If the resistance movement had not yet taken root among the Negroes of Carthage, they hardly needed to be introduced to the idea of nonviolence. They had found it long ago in the New Testament.

This meeting was above all an old-fashioned prayer meeting. Bradford Lyttle talked again briefly—drawing a picture of the worldwide nonviolent movement. And he issued a rather shy invitation to them to walk with us the next day. Reverend Sloan then rose and declared that he would be less shy about it: he would simply tell them that they *should* walk with us. Robert Gore asked Beulah Allen if he could say a few words from the pulpit, and he spoke of how the message of Jesus—to love one's enemies—was a strange message, a revolutionary one. "That's right," came from the audience—"Amen!" But it was Beulah Allen who led the meeting, and who spoke the prayers. I think few of us had ever before this evening felt that we were being prayed for. The days we were now approaching on the walk promised to be the most trying. We were about to enter Cumberland County, where—we had been told by both friends and antagonists—no Negro was supposed to remain after nightfall. The last Negro family that had tried to build had been burned out; the last Negro who had tried to walk through the county had been found dead by the side of the road. Beulah Allen had heard these stories too. She stood solidly before the altar rail, spread out her arms, raised up her voice—half in a piercing shout, half in a song—and addressing God as though he were indeed there just above us, just beyond the roof—"Heavenly FATHER! . . . Heavenly FATHER!"—she asked Him to give us courage, and also a good night's sleep that night, asked Him to teach all of us, including the people out there in the square, and the people along the road we were going to walk, how best to behave. The words themselves vanish now in my memory, having entered too deeply that evening into my flesh. I looked about me, and the other walkers, too, were sitting up, stock still. We had all of us heard, before, theatrical versions of such prayer—intended sometimes to be funny or sometimes to be endearing; and Beulah's prayer retained for us of course something of the extravagance of theatre; but now we were in the play; we were at the heart of it, amazed.

Again we sang together. Dona, accompanying us at the upright piano, hit the keys with a heavily pouncing, laboring but joyful, heartfelt emphasis of her own. The rhythm was always almost jazz, and as we nodded our heads, tapped our feet, our weariness and the nudging fears we'd kept down all the past days dissolved. Again, at Reverend Sloan's prompting, we sang the integration hymn—reaching out and taking hands: "We shall overcome some day!" "Now this is difficult," Reverend Sloan said, with a flickering smile, and prompted, "Black and white together some day." He prompted, "We are not afraid *today*." At the end of the meeting, Beulah Allen gave us a blessing, and exclaimed, "It's been so sweet!" At that moment, I recalled the words of James Lawson about "the beloved community." It seemed that we had been living in that community this past hour.

The next morning I learned to my astonishment that our evening's meeting had not caused the breach between us and the white community that might have been supposed. I entered one of the shops on the square to buy some things, expecting to be served with glum hostility. The young woman behind the counter—who clearly knew who I was—was full of both curiosity and warmth. She chattered eagerly about the peculiar weather they had been having this past year, and "It's the times, I think," she ventured. I asked whether she felt that atomic tests were disrupting the weather, and she nodded: "There's One who is more powerful; we forget that." As I left, "I hope you come back and see us again," she said.

In the course of the next few days, we walked into mythical Cumberland County and walked out of it, unharmed. Two Quaker couples who bravely put us up received middle-of-the-night telephone calls, threatening "roast nigger for breakfast"; one night the fire department arrived in the yard, summoned by false alarm; one night local high school students swarmed up to the house—but when invited in, sat and talked until late, quietly enough, their curiosity about us obviously deeper than their hostility. (As they left, they were arrested by the police—as eager to protect them from us as to protect us from them.) It was actually at the edge of the county, the first night after we left Carthage, that we had our nearest brush with violence. Reverend Sloan and Finley and Bobby and others had walked with us again this third day, but had taken their final leave of us at a little one-room Negro church by the side of the road, way out "nowhere," between towns. No one was in the church, but we had been told that we could spend the night there. We had crawled into our sleeping bags, scattered out on the floor between the pews, and were listening sleepily to the small country noises in the air, when abruptly the ruder sound of rocks hitting the building brought us full awake. Two of the men stepped outside and called into the dark, inviting the besiegers to come and talk to us about it. The hail of rocks stopped and the people rustled off into the dark. We could hear the crickets again for a while and then the barrage began again; a rock came crashing through one of the windows. Another two stepped outside, this time carrying flashlights aimed at themselves, to show the strangers where they were and that they were unarmed. We could hear their voices and we could hear the stones still flying and suddenly we heard a small gasping cry. Eric Weinberger had been hit on the side of the head and knocked off his feet. He staggered up, and called to them again, "It's all right. You hit me in the head, but it's all right. But now why don't you come and talk with us?"—and seven or eight young men finally emerged out of the dark and consented to talk. They were young workingmen from around there. They talked for a good while, and finally they said that well, they might perhaps agree with some of the things we said about war and peace, but they couldn't understand our walking around with a nigger, and all sleeping in the same building with him. And then one of them asked the time-worn question: "Would you let a nigger marry your sister?" The question was posed to Sam Savage, who is a southerner himself. When he answered that yes, he would; the decision would, after all, be hers to make—they exclaimed in sudden anger and disgust: well, he was no real southerner then, and there was no use talking about anything further; and they stamped off into the dark. At which point, one might have said that the advice we had been given before starting out on the walk had now been proved to be correct: the two issues of race relations and of war and peace could not be discussed together. However, there is a final chapter to this story. After a short time, the young men returned, wanting to talk further. The talk this time went on until the one who had done the most arguing remarked that they must be up early to work and had better get some sleep. But would we be there the next evening? he wanted to know. (We had of course, unfortunately, to move on.) As they left, he shook hands with Sam, who had said that yes, he'd let his sister marry a black man. It is my own conviction that these men listened to us as they did, on the subject of peace, just *because* Robert Gore was traveling with us. It made it more difficult for them to listen, of course; it made the talk more painful; but it also snatched it from the realm of the merely abstract. For the issue of war and peace remains fundamentally the issue of whether or not one is going to be willing to respect one's fellow man.

Winter holds these woods within its vise.
The cold boughs creak like harness. The ground
Is stiff as stone. At the woods' edge
Jays call. Their repeated cries
Wake the heart, as the flick of a nail
Wakes crystal: locked in winter, summer lies.

1960

Letter to WISP

Published in Liberation, *April 1963.*

Some background: HUAC—the House Un-American Activities Committee—was a committee in the federal House of Representatives which conducted a "witch hunt" for Communists in peace and leftist organizations during the early '60s. Its work was similar to, though less successfully destructive than, that of Sen. Joe McCarthy, et al., during the '50s. In this article, Barbara quotes a WISP member's reference to "strontium 90 and iodine 131;" these are two radioactive by-products of atomic bomb explosions. The U.S. was still testing atomic bombs above ground at the time of these HUAC hearings, and as a result, levels of strontium 90 and iodine 131 were increasing in the food chain—especially in milk. WISP, of course, stands for Women Strike for Peace; the "I" is for pronunciation purposes only. Barbara's pre-feminist view of Woman-as-Mom in this essay is superficial compared with her later understanding—as represented, for example, in "Remembering Who We Are". (JM)

When I returned from the hearings in Washington to which HUAC had called several nonmembers of our unorganization, Women Strike for Peace, my first impulse was to write a colorful report of the victory we won there. The happy fact is, though, that this report has been given in newspapers across the country, and WISP has been clever enough to publish a collection of the clippings. There is no need to go on celebrating. I think it is more to the point to try to take fresh stock of WISP's strength, in anticipation of battles still to be fought.

There is little question that at this moment WISP is stronger than it was before the hearings. A move intended to make us doubt ourselves and each other served in fact to sharpen our sense of why we are acting and to bind us more closely together. There is the special bond between us now of having lived through those three days together. The committee would have been wise to think of this, but then it probably did not anticipate that after it had set the hearings at the most inconvenient time one could name for mothers of young children—shortly before Christmas—hundreds of women would still manage to turn up, in support of those who had been called, boarding buses at two o'clock, four o'clock in the morning, some of them coming from as far away as Michigan, sitting up all night or all day and night to get there.

"It was like an operating room," one woman declared about the hearing room in the Old House Building—"with one woman after another being wheeled in, and the rest of us sitting there and suffering with the patient." As the committee went about its work—its operation so at odds with the democratic faith—one did feel the injury upon one's flesh. Guilt was assumed in this room unless innocence could be proved. In one awkward slip, which he tried later to disavow, Chairman Doyle actually declared that he would assume one woman to be a Communist, there being no evidence to the contrary—unless she'd care to give some. But here were no rights of trial. And here was no serious inquiry. The committeemen certainly didn't want to be given any new information. The rule here was the old-fashioned rule for children—"Speak only when spoken to"—and the occasion, clearly, was that of a lesson for the naughty or foolish children. Now and then the role to which committeemen wished to assign us would become grotesquely clear—when they described patiently how certain former "friendly witnesses" had chosen to behave. These witnesses had turned to them as to wise parents, surrendered their wills to them as children should, and asked humbly for guidance. The committeemen described this with an almost touching faith that a similar course would sound attractive to us. It is an odd fact that the people who see in the existence of the authoritarian Soviet state such a menace that they would like us to risk the world itself to battle it, are the same people who advise us to bow low to authority here. They are quite willing to have our government imitate that other government with which, they say, it is hopeless to think of living in peace. This last phrase of course contains the lesson they want to teach us—the lesson Chairman Doyle elaborated in his opening statement: deluded children, can't you realize that our enemy, Russia, behaves and always will behave in a way that makes the attainment of anything by any of us impossible? So if you are seeking peace you are either a fool or a Communist seeking to fool others.

Sadly enough, we had to sit through this same lesson on our visits to various government officials after the hearings were over for the day. Disarmament was carefully referred to as an "unlikely event" by the President's special assistant, Arthur Schlesinger, Jr. Everywhere it was impressed upon us that, given the nature of the enemy, there was really very little we could hope to do. And though the tone was blander in these offices, it was the parental tone still, the advice implicit in it essentially the same: leave government to government, because you don't really understand.

We lived through together on those three days the experience of being treated like foolish or wicked children, and the chilling vision of that defeatism with which we have above all to contend. And we lived our common refusal to accept either—the role of those without a voice or the lesson of hopelessness. Our response was: *you* don't understand. This particular phrase sounded again and again throughout the hearings, springing irresistably to nearly every witness's lips. Though none was allowed to make a formal statement, though each was cut off time and again in the middle of a sentence, each managed, by a phrase here and a phrase there, in patchwork fashion, to say that the committeemen understood neither the rights of Americans to act to influence the course of government, nor the new facts of the nuclear age which make our particular attempt to influence government a very plain necessity. Nor, each made clear, did they understand anything about women and how they go about getting things done. How little the committeemen understood—under any of these headings—became progressively so obvious that after awhile the most common response evoked by the questioning was uncontrollable laughter, circling the hearing room. Indeed some of the questions—some of the sinister charges—seemed lifted from a Marx Brothers comedy. Counsel takes off his glasses to point them at the witness, portentously demands: "Did you then...have you recently operated a mimeograph machine?"..."This news item reports that a peace group met at the Unitarian Church hall and planned a theatre party at which the film *Grand Illusion*, described as an antiwar film, was to be shown. Did you prepare the press releases and make them available to the press?" One began even to feel a little sorry for the committee. To the end, Mr. Nittle leveled each charge as though sure this time of cutting the laughter short.

Having declared that I think we are stronger now than we were before the hearings, it is appropriate to pause and acknowledge the fact that some of our allies in the peace movement doubt that we are as strong as we think. The source of their worry, I need hardly add, is Dagmar Wilson's flat statement to the committee that she would not discourage Communists from working in WISP. No one in the peace movement, I hope, shares HUAC's view of the threat Communists among us would pose—the simple-minded view of a few women leading the foolish rest of us astray down reckless paths. As various witnesses reiterated during the hearings, "No one leads anyone in WISP"; "Ask our husbands, if you think we can be led." Anyone who has any real contact with WISP—anyone not incapacitated by literal obsession with the Communist Threat—knows how it is that we move. Witness after witness made it clear. If word is passed of a particular idea for action and a woman feels: that's just what I've been thinking we should do—or perhaps: that's just what I was about to think—then she goes to the trouble of making all the complicated arrangements her absence from home requires. Otherwise, she "sits that one out." Nobody gives or takes instructions. WISP is not an organization; it is a great communications system. A plot by Bell Telephone, one woman's husband has named it.

No one in the peace movement with whom I have talked doubts this. Those who are worried are worried, they say, not that WISP will be perverted, but that it will lose its force. We may have no leaders, they argue, but in any communications system there are key people who can determine which proposals for action are put forward promptly and energetically and which somehow get lost. There needn't even be conscious scheming here. A certain instinct operates. And what do the worriers visualize? Some with whom I have talked can imagine a series of statements or demonstrations proposed in which pro-Soviet bias is implicit and which cause more and more women to "sit that one out" and gradually withdraw. Others imagine a situation in which the really strong proposals that are needed are passed over, never presented adequately to the movement as a whole for consideration. Because, they explain, Communists are by nature tacticians; what we have to fear from them is actually exaggerated caution.

Happily, as one of the women wrote to the committee, "We are basically unsuspicious of one another," and that's just why we have been able to move as we have. Would they now introduce suspicion among us—loyalty oaths, some kind of screening process? Those whom I've questioned deny this vigorously. Pressed for their answer to the "problem" they see on our hands, many of them come up with the same recommendation: if we would be clearer about what it is for which we stand, the problem would solve itself; no woman failing to take that full stand could then be influential among us.

The question of whether or not we are going to ask any woman about her politics is now academic. We have given our answer: "Certainly not!" We are not likely to retract it. In an eloquent letter to the committee, Carol Urner wrote, "We who have grown up in a democratic society and who function in democratic families...don't worry about being 'taken over' by other people's ideas....There is nothing to fear...." Our refusal to fear seems to me a very important event in this country's recent history; and I can't help wondering whether a few of those who express anxiety now are not caught up still in the mood of an earlier unhappy time, anxious above all about appearances, hoping to appease those forces of repression which cannot be appeased, which can only be faced down. But though we rightly refuse to be infected by timidity, and the question of whether or not we will welcome any woman who wants to work with us is academic, one question raised in the context of that discussion is not: whether or not the stand we take is clear.

It would be easy—especially after the experience of those three days in Washington—to dismiss the charge as ridiculous. What struck one sharply at the hearings was that these women knew very well why they were in Women

Strike for Peace. They had gathered in Washington from many different parts
of the country: few of them had ever met before; their backgrounds were
diverse; and they were able to communicate with an ease that was astonishing,
to make very rapid decisions together, quite informally, improvising as they
went—precisely because they all knew just why they were there. To put it
in the simplest terms: their children were threatened—or their friends'
children, the world's children; and they were angry, and they wanted to be
heard. It was this clarity of motive that had made it possible for the movement
to spring into being virtually overnight a year ago November, by chain
reaction, once one group of women had spoken—women across the country
moved to announce that they were on strike too. It was this which gave even
the most timid of the women questioned by the committee a certain advantage
over those who were trying to bully her, enabled her to find a voice and face
them stoutly. Not even the insulting and threatening tone of the counsel or
her own stage fright could confuse her and make her forget what had moved
her, because it was nothing abstract or abstruse that could be shaken out
of her head, but certain hard facts of her daily life. The very first witness,
Blanche Posner, put it plainly. "Now witness, now witness!" Chairman Doyle
tried to interrupt her, but she simply raised her voice a little and finished
what she had to say: "You don't understand the nature of this movement.
It was motivated by mothers' love for their children. When they set their
breakfast on the table, they see not wheaties and milk but strontium 90 and
iodine 131 and they fear for their health and lives." It is not only fear for
the physical well-being of their children which has stirred these women. One
woman told me, shaken, that during the Cuban crisis her daughter had
brought her best friend home from school with her because the two of them
had decided they wanted to die together. They see their children's lives
touched and damaged in one way after another.

The struggle between the women and the committeemen was an unequal
one because the women spoke out of their own direct experience—their
concentration upon their children—and the committeemen spoke out of long
acquaintance with certain portentous words and phrases—"excessive desire
for peace" impeding "adequate defense preparations," sapping "national
strength," serving the "aggressive plans of world Communism," to quote
Chairman Doyle's opening statement. It was as though these phrases
themselves had for them some immutable reality. It has not dawned on them
that the rapidly altering nature of the world about us has drained certain
words of all former meaning—that the word "strength," for example, is
meaningless when one speaks of weapons which, if we used them, would
ensure our destruction—the mere testing of which damages us. When they
think of testing—on our part, that is—they just think automatically: necessary
to preserve that "freedom" for which Americans have always been willing

to lay down their lives; and they are hypnotized by these words. Whereas the women see the cold fact that we are now willing to lay down our *children's* lives, and are already doing so. The crime which has always been spoken of as the most craven that man can commit—the slaughter of the innocent—the women are able to recognize as just that. And they are able to recognize it as a form of insanity, the abandonment of all concern for the future—since freedom is not some precious object that can be buried deep underground and after the nuclear storm has raged, dug up again, intact, whatever becomes of our children. In the years ahead it is these very children who must be able to create our freedom anew, as it always must be re-created, not being the peculiar God-given property of any particular people—something that Americans *have,* so that one need only be sure that more Americans would survive a war than Russians and freedom would survive. It has never been grasped once and for all by any people, as it has never been stifled once and for all in any, since with every child born anywhere in the world the appetite for it is born again.

Their concentration upon their children is the source, in these women, of their refusal simply to despair. I heard one woman reasoning with another who was not a participant in WISP. The other woman's attitude was: what would come would come, and we all had to die some day. "When you say that," said the woman striker, "I remember a passage in *Macbeth*—where Macduff hears that his children have been murdered, and a friend tells him to try not to think of it. Macduff turns from his friend, crying, 'He has no children!' You have no children, have you?" she asked the other fiercely. "It is one thing to resign your own life—."

But here I have to pause, and finally weigh the challenge of those who say that we are not clear about what we stand for. I have written that we see the world's children threatened and that we refuse to accept this. But is our refusal as clear as I have been suggesting? In the declaration of principles we adopted at Ann Arbor last June we say: "We represent a resolute stand...against the unprecedented threat to life....We...challenge the right of any nation or group of nations to hold the power of life or death over the world." Everyone would agree, I think, that we take a clear stand against nuclear testing—by any nation. But if a test ban agreement is reached, and the threat from further fallout is removed, how resolute will our stand against the threat of nuclear slaughter remain?

While I was in Washington for those three days I couldn't help but be struck by one discrepancy. Confronted by the committeemen with certain phrases intended to scatter them in alarm, the women stood their ground, laughing outright at the scare phrases. There was a wonderful exchange between one of the witnesses and the committee's counsel, Mr. Nittle. The witness had volunteered, under protest, that she had not been a Communist for some years past. She was hoping to show that no questions about her beliefs before the present period could be pertinent. Only the proper childish obeisance, of course, could stop further questions from this committee. It was necessary to probe her good faith, they informed her. Had she become an anti-Communist? The women uttered a great roar of laughter, and the witness told him calmly that she would be happy to answer the question if he would define the term—for there were many different views as to what either a Communist or an anti-Communist was. "The question is perfectly clear," Nittle insisted; but the witness faced him down, while all the other women applauded. In contrast, here is another exchange I observed—during a visit a small group of us paid to Arthur Schlesinger, Jr. After a few minutes had passed, Schlesinger suddenly inquired, "You women are not for unilateral disarmament, are you?" There was no burst of laughter now. At this scary phrase, at last some of us did flinch. There were quick cries of, "Oh no! People keep trying to assign that belief to us, but certainly not!"

Is it really logical for us to take flight at this question? Might not an appropriate response here, too, have been to ask the questioner what he understood by the term? And should we not ask ourselves what it really means? Could it possibly be, in this case, that people keep trying to assign that belief to us because it would be the only consistent one for us to hold?

Let me pose this question: Suppose an attack upon us by the Soviet Union, war having begun by miscalculation or any one of the various ways which have been listed so many times as possible. Would we be in favor of retaliation? To spell it out: Would we at that point be in favor of slaughtering children? It is hard for me to imagine any woman in our movement—if she were to answer without thought of the political consequences of candor—giving any answer but "No." Yet if that *is* our answer, then we are unilateralists, because that is very simply what unilateralism means: to be unwilling to have mass murder of innocent people committed in our name under any circumstances—to be unwilling to let it be "credible" that we would assent to it. In our Ann Arbor statement, we say only: "We...are dedicated to the achievement of general and complete disarmament under effective international control." Who doesn't want multilateral disarmament? But we can't pretend to answer the question which I asked above by saying that we hope both sides will come to an agreement before war does erupt. Until they do, the question faces us, and the answer must be either that we are willing or that we are unwilling to have the innocent slaughtered in our name. I don't really see how our stand can be: we take a resolute stand against it, but count us as temporarily willing, if it just can't be helped. Isn't that the position of those with whom we have been struggling?

Some of you will argue that it would be unrealistic unequivocally to condemn the willingness to wage war against children, because there is no hope that we could persuade our government to be the first to abjure such wars. My answer is that this is a narrow view of realism. If Women Strike for Peace came out clearly tomorrow for unilateral disarmament, Congress would certainly not vote the next day to have it adopted as national policy. But this is not to say that our taking such a stand would have no political effect. People may find it more comfortable to listen to us if we equivocate, but in the long run only words that discomfit them are going to change our situation. WISP's December *Bulletin* quotes from a *Memorandum* addressed to us by Anatol Rapoport. "Do not spend much time wondering how effective you are.... You are not a political party," he reminds us. "You are our conscience.... Women should condemn war against children unconditionally. Do not ask whether you can. You have no choice."

Some of you will ask a further question: If we abandon reliance upon military force—before international agreements have been signed—upon what alternative power can our country rely? The answer, I would say, is clearly the power of nonviolent resistance. And it seems to me an answer which we, as women, are peculiarly fitted to give. Gandhi once declared that it was his wife who unwittingly taught him the effectiveness of nonviolence. Who better than women should know that battles can be won without resort to physical strength? Who better than we should know all the power that resides in noncooperation? The House Un-American Activities Committee has reason to believe that we have an instinct for that. (The idea born on the second day of the hearings, of running up to each witness with a large bouquet as she took the stand, was an inspired example of the art of nonviolent defiance, and its force was noted by the press. So was the force of the laughter which rocked that room.) In a statement issued after the first participants had been subpoenaed, WISP declared: "We do not ask any oath of loyalty to any set of beliefs. Instead we ask loyalty to the race of man.... The human ingenuity that can split the atom must be used to keep the human race alive." Don't we call here precisely for the ingenuity to extend the experiment which Gandhi began? Is any form of struggle other than nonviolent struggle consistent with a profession of "loyalty to the race of man?" Margaret Halsey wrote, in support of WISP: "Theirs is one of the most valuable movements of our time. Perhaps it is even the forerunner of a new day, when women will emerge as a tempering influence in a new kind of politics and social action more generous than anything we have been able to invent so far." Women strikers are exerting themselves to become experts on radiation, on the history of disarmament negotiations, on the economics of disarmament. Shouldn't they also take as a field of serious study the history of this "more generous" form of social action—which is precisely a definition of nonviolent action—and the possibilities of further invention here? There will be resistance to the idea, for as David Riesman has pointed out, the American male is haunted by the concept of virility, and nonviolence is still mistakenly identified by many with passivity. But as a matter of fact even in Hollywood lore, the figure of the man who has the power and the skill to hurt, but on occasion leaves his gun behind and walks out unarmed to confront his adversary, is not unknown. Shouldn't it be our role to insist that this more daring way, which disdains physical force, can open up the future to us; that our good hope lies here and not in resort to violence, which is the way of hopelessness? Might not our strength increase if we were to accept this difficult role, so consistent with all our declarations?

Love is the falling rain,
Love is the following flood,
And love is the ark
With two of a kind aboard,
Love is the sequence of long days
At sea, without relief,
And love is the improbable
Return of the dove
Carrying in its beak
The green leaf.

1959

Section 3: The Mid Sixties

Another world still catches at me. I live both here and there—until the two worlds can become one.

—from "Notes After Birmingham"

Give us this day
Our daily breath
Deliver us from
Our daily death

Amen

1959

In the Birmingham Jail

Published in The Nation, *May 25, 1963.*

The day I went to jail in Birmingham for joining a group of Negro demonstrators—children, most of them—who were petitioning, "without a license," for the right to be treated like human beings ("that's what it boils down to, that's all we ask"), I experienced more sharply than I ever had before the tragic nature of segregation, that breakdown of communication between human and human which segregation means and is.

The steps which took me from the Negro church in which I spent the early part of that day, May 6, sitting among the children as they were carefully briefed and finally, in small groups, one after another, marched, holding hands and singing, into the streets—"marching toward freedom land"—the steps which placed me swiftly then in the white women's ward of the city jail provided a jolt for the mind that can still, recalling it, astonish me.

The comedian Dick Gregory describes his experience of a similar shock the day he arrived here to join the struggle—describes alighting from the plane and buying a newspaper. Not a word on the front page of the events that were shaking all of Birmingham. He had been afraid for a moment that the plane had put him down in the wrong city. Locked in my jail cell, surrounded by new companions now, I, too, could ask myself: Am I in the right city? The events of the day were acknowledged as news here; the presence of hundreds of children crowding the cells below us was the chief topic of the white women; but the break with reality was quite as abrupt as though no word about them had been spoken.

The children were no longer children now, the frail boys and girls I had seen singing and clapping their hands and sometimes dancing for a moment in the aisles of the church to find their courage—the amazing courage to walk out and face fire hoses, police dogs, jail sentences; these were now "juveniles"—a word spoken in horror, as though their youth made them particularly dangerous and untrustworthy. These were "niggers" now, "Shit, goddam, they must be fighting among themselves already!" "That's right!" "Goddam, you know it!" "Niggers are wild animals! You know it!" "Yes!

113

That's right!" "Better keep the door here locked tight." The voices would rise in a frenzied chorus—statement and refrain; then hush in awe; then, a little later, break out again. One prisoner would hurry in from her post at a particular window in an adjoining cell, from which a bit of the front yard could be glimpsed, and report that she had seen police dogs out there. Perhaps they would all be safe, then, against these devils in the same building. "All you have to say to one of them dogs is 'Git'm!' Just 'Git'm!'" But perhaps even the dogs were not protection enough. "They ought to throw a bomb in there and blow them all up," one woman cried in torment.

Now and then, when the wind was right, I could hear the children's voices from their cells, high and clear—"Ain't gonna let nobody turn me round, turn me round, turn me round. . . . Woke up this morning with my mind set on freedom!"—the singing bold and joyful still; and with that sound I was blessedly in their real presence again. I strained to hear it, to bolster my own courage. For now I was a devil too, of course—I was a "nigger lover." The warden had introduced me to my cell mates, in shrill outrage, and encouraged them to "cut me down" as they chose. They soon informed me that one of the guards had recommended that they beat me up. No one had moved to do it yet, but the glances of some of them were fierce enough to promise it. "What have you got against southern people?"

I was not an enemy of the southern people, I answered as calmly as I could. I happened to believe that we really were intended to try to love every person we met as we love ourselves. That would obviously include any southern white person I met. For me it simply also obviously included any Negro. They stared at me, bewildered, and I didn't try to say any more. I lay down on my bunk and tried to remove myself from their attention and to control my fears of them.

The unreal drama continued throughout the six days I remained in jail. Three times a day we left our cell block to go downstairs for meals, shepherded by the warden. Occasionally, on these trips, a group of the Negro children would have to pass us in the halls. "Huddle back there in the corner!" the warden would cry out to us sharply—"up against the wall!" The women would cower back like schoolgirls, while the terrifying people God had cursed—as the warden regularly informed us—filed past, harmless, and some of them even still joyful.

As the days passed, I stopped fearing my cell mates and made friends with them. After a little while this wasn't hard to do. Every woman in there was sick and in trouble. I had only to express the simplest human sympathy, which it would have been difficult not to feel, to establish the beginning of a friendly bond. Most of the women had been jailed for drunkenness, disorderly conduct, or prostitution. That is to say, they had been jailed because they were poor and had been drunk or disorderly or had prostituted themselves.

Needless to say, I met no well-to-do people there, guilty of these universal misdemeanors. A few of the women had been jailed not because they really had been "guilty" once again this particular time, but because they were by now familiar figures to the cops; one beer, the smell of it on her breath, would suffice for an arrest if a cop caught sight of one of them. The briefest conversations with these women reveal the misfortunes that had driven them to drink: family problems, the sudden death of a husband, grave illness. All conspicuously needed help,not punishment—needed, first and foremost, medical help. The majority of them needed very special medical attention, and many while in jail were deprived of some medicine on which they depended. One woman was a "bleeder" and was supposed to receive a blood transfusion once a month, but it was many days overdue. Each one of them would leave sicker, more desperate than she had entered; poorer, unless she had chosen to work out her fine. One woman told me that the city had collected $300 in fines from her since January. From those who have not shall be taken.

One day, in jest, one of the women cried to the rest of us when the jail authorities had kept here waiting endlessly before allowing her the phone call that was her due: "I ought to march with the Freedom Riders!" I thought to myself: you are grasping at the truth in this jest. Toward the end of my stay I began to be able to speak such thoughts aloud to a few of them—to tell them that they did, in truth, belong out in the streets with the Negroes, petitioning those in power for the right to be treated like human beings.*
I began to be able to question their wild fears and to report to them the words I had heard spoken by the Negro leaders as they carefully prepared their followers for the demonstrations—words counseling over and over not for the vengeance they imagined so feverishly ("They all have knives and guns! You know it!") but forbearance and common sense; not violence but nonviolence; I stressed for them the words of the integration movement's hymn: "Deep in my heart I do believe we shall live in peace some day—black and white together." One after another would listen to me in a strange, hushed astonishment, staring at me, half beginning to believe. By the time I was bailed out with the other demonstrators, on May 11, there was a dream in my head: if the words the Negroes in the nonviolent movement are speaking and are enacting ever begin to reach these others who have yet to know real freedom, what might that movement not become? But I was by then perhaps a little stir crazy.

---

* see Introduction, page 6.

Notes After Birmingham

Published in Liberation, *Summer 1963.*

Home .

Home. A world calm and beautiful. Everything is familiar, yet I have the sensation of staring at an illusion which I cannot quite bring into focus. Another world still catches at me. I live both here and there—until the two worlds can be one.

Part of Me Now Lives in That Other World.

Part of me now lives in the stark undecorated room at the Negro Y.W.C.A. in Memphis where I stayed on my way home. A CORE* fieldworker has been living there—Mary Hamilton, who took me under her wing in Birmingham. Typed field reports spread on the spare cot. A room for a while, but not home. Her few things tucked away at random. Now she is on another mission, and will live in Chattanooga; a minister has opened his house to her and to several other "soldiers." The night I stayed there, two or was it three people shared a couch-bed; others, curled in blankets or in sleeping bags—long, restive cocoons—scattered themselves about the dining room and living room floors.

Part of me lives in the bombed house of A.D. King, in Birmingham. His wife sits staring into the next room which had collapsed like a tent the moment after she had run from it—toward her children's room—at a strange sound. Her eyes shining, she tells their neighbors who have gathered, "He led me out of that room. I'll praise Him and serve Him, praise Him and serve Him, all the rest of my life!" Two police officials wander through the shambles. A Negro minister asks them, "What are you looking for? It was you who

* Congress of Racial Equality(JM)

116

did this.'' ''It wasn't us!'' one of the cops answers quickly. ''Well, it was your boss.'' A tall Negro sings out, ''That's right. Speak the truth, Reverend!'' The cop's eyes, meeting mine for a moment, turn away.

And I live in my room at the Gaston Motel—headquarters for the movement. The motel, too, has been bombed now. King's eleven-year-old daughter sits up most of the night there, waiting for her father. He is going about the streets, with others, trying to calm the Negroes of the district who have begun to riot against the police. We can hear his voice, at intervals, raised above the garbled voices of the rioters. They, too, suspect the police of having been involved in the bombings. I urge the little girl to lie down and rest, like the other woman who has taken shelter with us. But she insists that she'd rather sit in the big chair by the door. She seems very calm, her hands quiet in her lap. I beg her one further time to lie down on the bed, and then she tells me softly: ''I don't want to lie down because I might fall asleep, and then I might dream about the bombing.''

Toward dawn, her father picks her up. Mary Hamilton comes in from the streets to get a little rest. I've gone to sleep on the soft carpet on the floor, so that others, more tired than I, can use my bed. I wake. Some noise in the courtyard has drawn Mary to the window again. She stands, holding the curtains, peering out—her whole body arched, tense, her head, thrust forward, turning quickly to the left, the right.

Having Entered This World That Is Theirs, I Live In It Too Now. But I am Able to Leave.

What a queer feeling to be able to travel in a few minutes from this world into quite another world—as they cannot. The day I leave Birmingham, I simply drive out of it, in a taxicab.

Most of the day I spend in hiding. Who knows whether or not it is necessary? The violence of a few Negroes the night before has provided the police with an excuse to be even more violent themselves. The state police, in particular—rushed in by the governor—roam the district, clubbing people at random. I walk down to the motel's office to use the telephone there and have just lifted the receiver when I see several white men moving into the drive. I leave the phone and duck into what remains of the room behind the office. I stand in the corner of the wrecked room, waiting—letting the dust of fallen plaster settle on me there—when, through the jagged opening torn by the bomb in the wall across from me, I see the figure of another white man, stooping to examine something. I hurry out of that room into a bathroom around the corner, and sit on the tiled floor for almost an hour, until I figure that the way is clear. Then I stay in my room. "You're learning to be smart," Mary Hamilton tells me.

I have begun, even before this day, to feel a sudden unpleasant catch in my stomach every time I step out onto the street and see a white man. What is he going to do? So now I know what it is like. Now I am a Negro. Except that I can drive away from it.

The cab drives round the last police guard set up at an intersection, and rolls smoothly through the streets—eerily—on out toward the airport. At the airport, a traveler holds the door open for me with a little bow. The building is hung with gracious signs: "It's nice to have you in Birmingham." The clerk at the counter where I buy a pencil and a newspaper tells me the price of the pencil in gentle murmuring tones, and as she hands me my change grants me a honeyed smile. Wait, I am moved to say to them, you don't intend those smiles for me. I am not the person you think; or rather, you do not think me a person. You taught me this my first day in Birmingham. Nigger-lover, nigger.

The First Day. Scene in the Park.

The city authorities are turning the high-pressure hoses on a group of demonstrators who have marched peacefully, two by two, out of the Pilgrim Baptist Church—driving them into the park nearby. The playing hoses make a sound like machine gun fire. The water pressure can be turned up to over two hundred pounds. By the end of the day, bark has been stripped from many of the trees in the park, and the clothes have been stripped from some of the people. A small crowd of onlookers, white people, screams with glee as the water knocks the demonstrators to the ground, tumbling them like objects. Yes, they are not people but dark objects which the water can drive this way and that! Hurrah! Soon there is a high wailing of sirens and several police cars drive up and the big dogs are led out on leashes. The onlookers give a cheer. Bull Connor* is directing the scene, a cigar in his mouth, a sweaty gray straw hat on his head. He doesn't put the dogs into action for a while. He lets them squat in the corner of the park, as a promise. Their masters lean over and pat them now and then, with boyish smiles—good fellowship between them. Bull Connor keeps trying to keep the onlookers—including newsmen—out of the park itself. He explains himself, finally, in a loud voice: "I don't want anybody here to get hurt."

* Chief of Police in Birmingham (JM)

The Demonstrators Give the Lie to Bull Connor's Words.

They are not bodies. They are dark objects which the water tumbles at will. But as one's heart leaps, the demonstrators prove this to be a lie. Some of the young boys and girls manage to leap high in the air above the spurting water—holding up their limp but still recognizable signs: "Freedom!" And they manage to stand. They do it by clasping hands, by holding one to another. More run to join them against the water's force. Two young girls, glancing at each other, find their courage, take hands and run to join the rest. They manage to stand.

In the Church.

And in the church that evening they shatter his lie. Many people have gathered, after the arduous day; they pack the church to bursting. The leaders review for them what has taken place: they're not to think that the demonstration in which they took part has been the only demonstration this day; many different groups of them have kept the city officials busy. Plans for the next day are revealed. And everybody sings. Again they join strength to strength—they join their voices; and the song swells and shakes the walls. It shakes the ground under my feet. Sitting in the midst of this rush of sound, I know myself—with awe—to be at the wellspring of that which is human—which insists that it is, which at long last is sure that it is, and affirms it: "Freedom! Freedom! Freedom! Freedom!" One woman, a newcomer, looks about her, dazzled, eyes wide. Has she not thought freedom possible? It exists, within these walls, here and now.

The Newsmen Stand Across the Street.

Each day the people gather in the churches—before the demonstrations and after them. The newsmen stand across the street. Bull Connor doesn't like to see them going into the meetings—though he has his own "reporters" there—so they stand on the curb. "No sense asking for trouble," one explodes to me, when I question this. "A reporter's job is to get his copy in, not to wave any fucking banners." (Not even the banner: freedom of the press.) "Connor must wish he could keep us away altogether," says one reporter. "Without this publicity, the demonstrations would stop." At the distance he keeps, how little he understands the demonstrations. Their purpose: to assert a certain truth and to hold to it. If the newspapers didn't report them, the force of that truth would be diminished—but would remain. The truth is also for the Negroes themselves.

One part of the truth which they are grasping: We have no right to be ashamed of anything. "Our hair is not like white folks'? What's wrong with kinky hair? Let's talk about that. For too long the white man has told us that our hair is bad because it's kinky, and our noses are bad because they're thick, and our lips are bad, they're blubbery, and we've giggled; and it's time we stopped this. We've got to change all the values. Hear me." It's James Forman talking.

Another part of the truth: the Negro has helped to bring this city and this nation into being. "Once Birmingham was nothing but wilderness. Who cut the trees, dug the ditches and laid the streets, built the skyscrapers?...We don't want to take over, either. We just want to live as brothers....But we're not going to go back to Africa until the Englishman goes back to England, the Italian goes back to Italy, the German goes back to Germany, and the white man gives this country back to the Indians." (Delighted laughter. "Talk to us, Ralph!") Reverend Ralph Abernathy is talking.

And Reverend James Bevel is talking: "I want everybody to listen to me. Everybody listen." He's talking to the children, telling them not to go back to school—to march off to jail instead. "You get an education in jail, too. In the schools you've been going to, they haven't taught you to be proud of yourselves and they haven't taught you good history—they haven't taught you the price of freedom....The white man has brainwashed us, tricked us; but Mr. Charlie's brainwashing is washing off now....And the most important thing in the struggle is all to stay together. This is why we've been enslaved all these years: our parents didn't have enough love for one another to suffer for one another. We've got to start learning to love one another enough to say: as long as one Negro kid is in jail, we all want to be in jail. If everybody in town would be arrested, everybody would be free, wouldn't they?"

Forman is talking again: "This is a great day, people. Let's talk about it. Let's try to understand what's going on." There is the noise of sirens outside, and uproar of the crowd. Some of the children run to the windows. "Now this is the thing that can cause confusion," he says. "Let's be orderly. Let's not worry about what's going on outside. The important thing that's happening is happening right in here."

This is so. The words in one of their songs run: "The truth shall make us free." Within these walls, the truth they affirm is making them free. The same truth that will carry them out into the streets.

And now Martin Luther King is speaking: "They can handle violence; but we have a weapon that they can't handle. They don't know what to do with us when we are nonviolent; they are confused. You don't need to strike them in return, or curse them in return. Just keep going. Just keep presenting your body as a witness to the truth as you see it. Don't get tired. Don't get bitter. Are you tired?'' The answer comes in a great shout: "NO!"

One Part of the Truth is Out.

The reporters stand across the street, assigned to report the truth—though they stand rather far away from it. The cops and the firemen stand there assigned to break it up, to douse it. For it doesn't match the official truth. This truth has been expressed to me by the soft-voiced lady in the white piqué dress who sat next to me on the plane: "Most of them are quite content, quite content. When my mother died last spring, two Negro women called me at once. 'We've heard about Muddy. We're coming to take care of you this week.'... They wouldn't take a penny.'' The other part of her truth, oddly enough: "My friends are putting floodlights in their backyards—afraid. They're ready enough to murder us in our sleep, you know.''

The demonstrators have taken out of their pockets anything that could possibly be called a weapon—"even a nail file, even a spoon.'' They march out of the church, two by two, holding up their signs: WE WANT FREEDOM! The firemen maneuver the heavy hoses into position. "It's a strange thing,'' one of the leaders has said, back in the church, "They have the idea that water can put out all fire. They don't seem to know that there's a certain type of fire water can't get to.''

A group of children has emerged now from a side door of the church. Firemen drag a length of hose in their direction. The children are singing bravely but their voices waver a bit. Mary Hamilton hurries over to join them. She dances in front of them, clapping her hands to their song with fierce gaiety. The song gains spirit. Moving from foot to foot, she stamps the off-beat of the tune, on the beat striking her hands together with the motion of cymbals. Sometimes she faces the children and sometimes she faces the sweating fireman. The fireman is hypnotized by her; aims the hose but can't quite seem to get the water turned on. Then all of a sudden the children vanish back into the side door—will-o'-the-wisp. They'll be out another door a little later on.

All through the city the firemen drag their hoses, trying to douse this fire. But the demonstrators spring up first in one place and then in another—WE WANT FREEDOM!—then in another, then in another—WE WANT FREEDOM!—assembling, then spreading out from half a dozen churches across the town. Sometimes they picket, sometimes they march, sometimes they sit-in. The water doesn't quench their truth, so the cops begin to try to put it away. They stuff the demonstrators into paddy wagons and rush them off to jail. The cars go rocketing through the streets of the city, from every direction—hands waving through the bars, the Negroes calling at the top of their voices: WE WANT FREEDOM! WE WANT FREEDOM! WE WANT FREEDOM! The city couldn't have provided them with a better public address system. The citizens of Birmingham stand on the sidewalks, eyes opening wide.

Another Part of the Truth.

The demonstrators sing gaily as they ride off to jail: *"Everybody* wants freedom! Bull Connor wants freedom! Our mayor wants freedom! The driver wants freedom!" They like to announce in church: "Now we'll all pray for Bull Connor." They are being playful. But they are also serious. At the meetings they make it plain: "We're struggling not to save ourselves alone....This fight is for the freedom of the white man also—to free him from fear and from hate....We're going to have to teach him."

The press—standing across the street—misses these words. The demonstrators come marching out of the church; the hoses are turned against them, and the water drives them this way and that; they are mingled with onlookers from the neighborhood. Some of the onlookers lose their heads, and the bottles and the stones begin to fly. A riot is reported. It's not made clear that the demonstrators themselves have remained nonviolent throughout. ("Negroes have been throwing bottles and cussing for the last hundred years and it hasn't ended segregation. We're going to *peacefully* protest, and we're going to break it down this way.") WE WANT FREEDOM!—that part of the truth is out. But another part of the truth has been blurred: THIS FIGHT IS FOR THE FREEDOM OF THE WHITE MAN ALSO.

The Freedom of the White Man Also.

I recall the contorted faces of whites in the crowds. I recall the puckered face of the lady on the plane. "Martin Luther King? A dreadful man!" She draws away from me; her chin is trembling.

I recall my own distress—own sharp sense of a distance between black and white hard to travel.

On my way to Birmingham, S.N.C.C.* has arranged hospitality for me at the house of an old Negro lady. I arrive rather late at night along with

* Student Non-violent Coordinating Committee

one of their field workers, Ruby Doris Smith. The old lady, in her nightgown, opens the door to us, and stares and stares at me; fetches herself a glass of milk with bits of bread in it and, spooning it slowly into her mouth, stares again, trying to believe what she sees. What have we done that she must stare like that—unable to believe that I am there?

Dick Gregory's mournful words return to me: "Whitey has made so many mistakes. Oh yes."

I stand on the lawn of A.D. King's bombed house and suddenly notice another old lady, close by, staring at me—not in amazement, this time, but in dread. Her finger is pointed at me. Too aghast to be able to speak, she just stares and points. Am I not one of them, the enemy—"whitey"? I put my hand on her shoulder: "I am a friend, a friend." Her look stays with me.

I stand in the church. The congregation has risen to sing "We shall overcome some day." They have linked hands. Have I the right to reach out and to take hands, too? I am not sure. I stand self-conscious.

They Sing: "The Truth Shall Make Us Free Some Day. . . Black and White Together, We Shall Live in Peace."

The truth is that the distance between us is unreal. I have always known it. But the distance nevertheless has been there.

The evening that I arrive in Birmingham, at a mass meeting, I decide that I want to join the demonstration the next day. There *is* no distance between us; I know it; and I wish to affirm the fact. Then on the way back to the motel afterwards I suddenly lose my nerve. First, the recognition jumps at me that the jail will be segregated. I won't go marching off to it black and white together; I'll be marched, quite by myself, into a cell with other whites who may well feel like beating me up.

I struggle with this fear. I manage to come to terms with it for a moment. Other fears leap up in me, to reinforce it. Even if I get through the days in jail—what will happen to me when I come out? I won't be welcome in this city. Will anyone be there to set me on my way home? Or will I be forgotten by my fellow demonstrators—on my own? A sense of stark abandonment enters my soul. I give up the plan.

Then, over the next days, the people I move among give me their courage. There is a contagion to it, and I catch it; it is simple as that. I catch it through closeness. They make me one of them.

The afternoon of my second full day there I enter one of the churches for a meeting. I go in through a side door, and I'm no sooner inside than word is passed that Guy Carawan, the folk singer, has been arrested for trying to enter; Bull Connor has decided to allow no white people in the meeting. So I keep in the wings, wondering what is going to happen now. A.D. King is headed up to the podium, to speak, and as he passes the place where I'm standing he comes toward me and takes my hand in his, with extraordinary gentleness. We've never met before. "I'm A.D. King," he says very softly. "Happy to see you, but I thought you might be interested to know that they've just arrested Guy Carawan." His voice is altogether calm, and the calm enters me from him, as the warmth of his hand passes to my hand. Some of the people standing there gather closely round me and move me, hidden in their midst, up into the balcony where Connor's spies are unlikely to come. Then at the end of the meeting they gather round me and move me to a back door. One of the students, "Meatball," will bring a car up to the door and smuggle me out. But when I reach the door, he has not yet been able to maneuver the car there, through the thick of other cars. And suddenly someone calls out in a whisper: "Bull Connor is just outside!" A tall, thin man, a stranger to me, hurries close, assuming a comic falsetto: "Don't you worry, honey! We'll get you out! Won't let Bull Connor get you! Bull Connor out there!" His piping voice imitates a childish panic—so charmingly that my panic evaporates. "Here, we'll wrap you up, honey." Someone has borrowed a thin black cape from someone else. They wrap it round me. "Here, push your hair up under—Here!" and the tall man claps a man's straw hat on my head. The car has drawn close at last. They gather round me, chattering, and lead me out—I am an old man—and thrust me down onto the floor of the car. Several of them jump in, chattering, laughing, and we head for somebody's house. After we've driven for a while, "Here, you can sit up now, but put my hat on you," a woman called Jimmie tells me. I pull a large purple velvet cloche down to just over my eyes. We enter the district where a friend of hers lives. "Now you're safe as a rabbit in a briar patch."

They have wrapped me in their own clothes; they have smuggled me into their briar patch. They have wrapped me in their gaiety and their courage. I am not any longer the same.

It is my third morning in Birmingham. Almost a thousand children have gathered in the church—bringing their toothbrushes and their rubbers, ready to go to jail. James Forman is talking to them. He tells them, "The reason they were able to defeat your parents is that they'd take one out, they'd pick on one, and all the rest would just stand and look. We have to learn to stay together." He looks about and sees several white faces. Joan Baez is there, to sing with the children for a few minutes; and another young white woman is present, a friend of hers; and I am sitting there. Forman tells them, "If they come in here today and try to arrest any of our white friends, tell them at that moment, 'Take all of us!' Don't hesitate. We'll stand and say, 'Take all of us!' " His words touch me like a blessing. I know I am one of them, and because of that, I know I have the strength finally to go off to jail—even by myself. After a few groups have lined up and marched out onto the street, I stand up to join the next one. I stand next to one of the few mothers who have come that day—a large gentle woman who has brought her three-year-old son. I put my hand on her shoulder. I'm trembling a little bit. "Don't be afraid," she tells me. I tell her I won't be. Then each of us takes one of the little boy's hands. The children begin to sing. And it's time to walk out onto the street.

Prison Notes

From Prison Notes *(Beacon Press, 1966), chapters one, two, three, and seven.* Prison Notes *is Barbara's account of the month she spent in the Albany, Georgia, city jail early in 1964. Barbara was arrested in Albany while participating in the Quebec-Washington-Guantanamo Walk for Peace.* (JM)

Chapter One

January 27, 1964

Albany city jail, Georgia. The cop locks the door on us and walks off. Now we're out of mischief. The barred steel door has banged shut; the big key has made a lot of noise; they have "put us away." People still believe there is some magic in the turning of a key.

He walks past some other cages, running his night stick, clattering, along the bars; and then we hear him make a curious little clucking noise to the prisoners—as though human speech were not quite appropriate to cross the distance between us. Magically, now, we are no longer quite of the same species.

As he goes, he glances down at his boots, and he puts his hand—as if to be sure of something—upon his wide belt with its creaking tooled-leather holster.

"Sonofabitch cop!" a prisoner rages, and grasps the bars and rattles them. "Oh goddam motherfucking sonofabitch! Wait till I get out of here tomorrow!"

I am reminded of a fairy tale I once heard about a miser and his old slippers. One day they cause him embarrassment and he tries to throw them away. He isn't able to. He throws them out the window, he buries them in the garden, he tries to burn them, he travels to a distant country and drops them in a pond; but each time fate returns them to him, and each time in a way that causes him mischief. They are too much a part of him. If the miser could not get rid of his old slippers. . . . But people persist in believing that they can put other people from them.

Yes, they manage to sound very reasonable to themselves as they talk of deterring others from crime; but the act of putting a man in jail remains essentially the act of trying to wish that man out of existence. From the moment of arrest one begins to feel against one's flesh the operation of this crude attempt at sorcery.

I remember suddenly the first time I was ever arrested, in New York City, 1962. As I begin to write about time I have served in Albany's jail, my earliest impressions of the world of jail crowd upon me.

A bitter March morning. The United States has just announced resumption of nuclear testing, and in protest I have sat down with a group of pacifists in front of the A.E.C. building on Hudson Street. A small group of us sit, expecting arrest; a larger group circles there, immune from arrest, in a simple picket line. The arrests are swift. Before we have time to shiver on the cold sidewalk, we are picked up and dumped into a paddy wagon waiting at the curb. We are dumped into the back, but we crowd that section, and one of the cops tells three or four of us to crawl over into the space up front in the wide cab. Up there we can stare out the open door at our friends walking past, almost within our reach. And they could look in at us easily, exchange a few friendly glances. But not one of them does, though we sit there for quite a long while before we are driven away, and they circle past us, circle past us again. With our arrest, we have become invisible, even to them. My friends are being dignified, of course; but there is more to it than that. When people are arrested, a kind of primitive awe can take hold of everybody involved. They are caught up in spite of themselves in the ritual act of denying our existence.

I remember the woman guard sitting outside the detention cell in which some of us were held before being taken to the Women's House of Detention—remember her uneasiness every time she noted in us signs of life.

She spies dangling from my lapel the lettered white ribbon we have all worn that morning: NO TESTS EAST OR WEST. She snatches for it. "No banners in here!" A little later she says that she can make one telephone call for each of us. One young woman in the group writes out a message to her sweetheart. She makes it, carefully, very brief, but her feeling for him is clear in it—it flies this banner. The guard gives a little start as she reads it, takes a pencil, swiftly edits. Nothing of the young woman's self now remains in the message.

Nobody has to print in a manual for guards that the prisoner must be wished out of existence for society's sake; this magic principle is grasped as if by instinct. Prison routine varies from place to place, but the one blind effort shapes it everywhere. Here is part of the routine of our "admission" that day:

A policewoman takes us into a small room in the building where we are arraigned. She searches our handbags for sharp objects; we take off most of our clothing for her, unfasten the rest as she peers at us. The guard outside the temporary detention cell examines our bags for a second time, removes a few more possessions. At the House of Detention, a third guard empties the bags, keeps every remaining article. We have packed a few things with which to keep ourselves decent; comb, toothbrush, deodorant, a change of underclothes. She take them all—even, in my case, some pieces of Kleenex. And if I have to blow my nose? "Find something else to blow it on," she tells me cheerfully. She explains then: I might be smuggling in dope this way. I am led into a large shower room and told to strip. Another guard shakes out each piece of clothing. Hands on her hips, she watches me closely as I take my shower, and I struggle hard now for self-possession. Her stand reminds me a little of that of an animal trainer. Now she asks me to hold my arms wide for a moment, turn my back and squat. I ask the reason. She, too, is searching for dope—or for concealed weapons. One of my companions has been led in by another woman and has stripped and is sitting on the toilet there. Her face is anguished. She explains her predicament to the guard: she is menstruating, but her extra sanitary napkins have been taken from her. "Just don't think about it," the woman tells her. I don't know how to help her; catch her eye and look away. I am given a very short hospital gown and led now into a small medical-examination room. Another of my companions is just leaving the room and smiles at me wanly. I climb up on the table. I assume that the examination performed is to check for venereal disease. The woman in the white smock grins at me and then at her assistant, who grins back. No, this too is a search for concealed dope or dangerous weapons.

I hear myself laugh weakly. Can they frisk us any further now? As a matter of fact, if their search is really for dope, they have neglected to look in my ears, or up my nose, or between my toes. They wouldn't be able to admit it to themselves, but their search, of course, is for something else and is efficient: their search is for our pride. And I think with a sinking heart: again and again, it must be, they find it and take it.

Sometimes, all of a sudden, one of them will give it back. People are everywhere, happily, unpredictable. I am told to dress again before going to my cell, but I'm not allowed to wear my tights (because I might hang myself with them?) or my fleece-lined English snowboots (these are labeled "masculine attire," forbidden). A young Negro guard tells me to find some shoes for myself in an open locker she points out. I stare at the heap of old shoes and tell her wearily, "It's hopeless. Most of these have heels and I can't wear heels. Also, my feet are very big."

She looks at me and smiles. She says, "If you thought anything was hopeless, you wouldn't have been sitting on that sidewalk this morning!"

I smile at her, astonished, and feel my spirits return. I tell her, "Thank you. You're right. I'll find a pair."

Before I can, she kneels, herself, and fishes out some floppy slippers that will do.

But more often the guards are caught up altogether in the crude rite of exorcism. I remember the ride to jail in Macon, Georgia, this past November.

We are peace and freedom walkers this time. A number of us who will go to jail again in Albany have been arrested for the crime of handing out leaflets.

The guard who drives the paddy wagon begins to chatter like an excited boy to the second guard as soon as we are locked in, seated in back on the lengthwise metal benches against the sides of the cab. He suddenly lurches the car forward, then, with a gnashing of gears, backward, then forward again, swerving the wheel. Knocked against the metal walls, we link arms quickly; brace our feet, not to be tumbled to the floor. Later we'll meet prisoners who are black and blue from such falls. "Something seems to be the matter with the gear shift!" he shouts, delighting in the pretense. There are railroad tracks to be crossed; he manages some good jolts here by zigzagging, then takes the car on two wheels round a curve. "Yes, something seems to be the matter with this car!" As the drive ends, and he jerks us again in the prison yard, forward, backward, forward, backward, forward, we put out our hands instinctively to touch one another: you are still there. But the exulting excitement in the driver's voice betrays his opposite conviction: we cannot be people any more. He has shaken that out of us.

Now it is Albany, Georgia. This is the city where the police chief, Laurie Pritchett, likes to boast that he has defeated Martin Luther King nonviolently. When we are arrested for walking peacefully down the sidewalk with our signs, and in protest we sit down, conspicuous respect is shown for our persons: we are carried to the paddy wagon on stretchers. But the familiar instinct persists, for all this show. Ralph has been dumped into the wagon gently enough, and I have, and Kit and Tony and Michele. They are bringing John-i-thin. One cop looks at another. Suddenly they tip the stretcher up, the wrong way round, standing John-i-thin on his head.

Magic: Shake it out of them—the fact that they are people. Or tip it out of them. Or frisk them of it. And put them away. Has the relation with them been a difficult one? Now they don't exist.

Our cage in Albany is seven by seven by seven. Three bolted steel walls, a steel ceiling, a cement floor. For bunks, four metal shelves slung by chains—two on one wall, double-decker, two on the wall opposite. Thin filthy mattresses. No sheets, no blankets, but, very recently, muslin mattress covers have been added. The chief expects publicity, perhaps. Against the third wall, a tiny washbasin. Cold water. Next to it, a toilet without a lid.

The mattress of the lower bunk rests against the toilet. The upper bunk is so close above the lower that one can only sit up on the lower bunk with a curved spine. The floor space allows one to pace one short step—if there are not too many inhabitants. We are six at the moment, but we'll be more. Other cells are more crowded. It is not by stretching out that the prisoner here will recover himself.

The fourth wall is made of bars and a thick barred door, centered in it. In the corridor outside, guards and plainclothesmen come and go, day or night. If one is sleeping, a sudden knock at the bars: "Hey!" Or a little tug at the hair of the sleeper's head: "What's this one?" No corner of privacy in which to gather oneself together again.

The dirty windows in the corridor look out upon an alley and a brick wall. (They are very dirty. A prisoner long ago has flung a plate of spaghetti against one of them. Shriveled tatters of it still hang there. On the window next to it a shrunken condom hangs.) A little weak sunlight filters through to us at certain hours, but there is no real day.

And no real night. Our only other lighting is a naked bulb hanging in the corridor out of reach, and this burns round the clock.

Not enough space. No real time.

From the cage behind us, around the corridor, a man calls to his wife in the cage next to us: "Are you still there?" She grunts for an answer. He calls to her: "I'm still here!"

Laboriously scratched in the metallic gray with which our walls and ceiling have been painted are name after name. RUFUS WAS HERE—was "still here." THE MELTON BROTERS (sic) WAS HERE. BOB WIMBERLY. JACKIE TURLEY. "SUPER" NORMON. Was here, was still here. HAWK, to remind himself, has uttered his name seven times, has flown from wall to wall to ceiling to wall.

The cops read the names with irritation. It is cheating for the prisoners to assert in this way that they do exist. "We hardly get it painted fresh when it's covered over again." FREEDOM! LULAMAE. The names appear where they oughtn't, as cries might issue from under the earth.

We have scratched our names, too: QUEBEC-WASHINGTON-GUANTANAMO WALK FOR PEACE AND FREEDOM. EDIE, YVONNE, KIT, MICHELE, ERICA, BARBARA. Later, CANDY AND MARY will appear.

The man calls to his wife again. She doesn't answer. He calls again. She doesn't answer. He calls again.

"Yeah."

"Do you love me?"

Very low, very tired, "No. You're no good."

I remember suddenly the first prison cell I ever entered—twenty-six years ago. I entered that day out of curiosity an abandoned New England small-town jail, attached to the old courthouse friends and I were turning into a summer theater. The few cells were like low caves, windowless; the walls were whitewashed rock. In one, I noticed on the uneven plaster of the ceiling, scrawled in candle smoke—or cigarette smoke—the declaration I AM A JOLLY GOOD FELLOW. I tried, that day, imagining myself the prisoner—tried and failed. But the words have recurred to me over the years. Today I think of them again.

Hard work, in here, to feel like a jolly good fellow; and so pride almost requires a man to feel he is the very opposite.

From one cell to another an old man calls to a pair of teen-age boys, just arrived. We have heard a detective talking with them; they're in for breaking into a store. "Who are you?" the old man calls. His voice is slurred with drink.

"I know who I am!" one of the youths shouts.

"I'll show you who you ain't," the old man teases.

"You want me to come over there and whip your ass?" one of them asks.

"I bet you're tough," says the old man.

"You're goddam right."

"You think you're bad, don't you?"

"*Bad, bad!*" assets the boy.

A little later, "What are you in for?" the old man calls.

There is a pause.

"*Murder!*" one of them suddenly shouts.

"What are your names?"

One of them starts to answer and the other cuts in: "The Sizemores," he decides. (Later we'll find that name scratched on the wall of their cell—dated months earlier.) "We're the Sizemores. Ed and my brother Dan and my brother Richard. He's not here. Ed is. I mean I am. And Dan. Don't you know the Sizemores? The Sizemores, man—the meanest motherfuckers in town!" He elaborates upon the theme.

The old man is full of words, half incoherent. Somebody yells at him, "Shut up, Pop, shut up!"

The two boys take it up: "Shut up, Pop!" He begins to beat against the bars.

"Only baboons beat on the bars," one of them yells. "And queers. He's a queer, ain't he?"

And now they launch into an endless obscene tirade against him. Pop returns the compliments. The voices rise in hysterical crescendo. "Talk to my ass awhile; my head hurts."

Both sides tire; there is a lull. I hear the two boys tossing on their mattresses. One of them groans to himself, "Oh God, oh God."

Then it begins again. "I'm the motherfucking superior of you!" the old man suddenly insists. "I'm here because I want to be!" He begins to beat again upon the bars.

They taunt him: "Keep a-beatin', keep a-beatin', beat on, beat on!" The voices swell again, in flood.

Silence. They have tired again. I doze a little; wake. They are calling again. My companions are awake, too, and we stare at one another. The voices are quieter now and contain a different note.

The old man is asking, "Did you mean those names you called me?"
"I did at the time," one of the boys replies.
A pause. "Give me some reason not to and I'll withdraw them."
Pop relapses. "You're a no-good sonofabitch."
Silence.
And then we hear the young man call out again in a voice suddenly as
frail as a child's: "You want to be friends? Heh—you want to be friends?"
"I'd rather be friends than enemies," the old man mumbles—then abruptly
declares, "I'm friends with everybody."

Another night: We hear the familiar scuffling, cursing, the slam of the
metal door. A drunken officer from the nearby air base has been brought
in. "Don't put me in here with that goddam drunk!" he commands. "Get
me out of here! Cop, come here! Open this door! Open this door!" A fellow
prisoner makes a comment. The officer yells, "Shut that goddam sonofabitch
up or he's dead!" His voice shifts to a growl: "I'm going to kick the
everloving shit out of you." He screams, "Open the door!" Then suddenly,
"Leave it locked, you sonofabitches! Shut up, you're dead." He begins to sob. Then again; "Anybody who moves is dead!" His voice
mounts in hysteria.
Somebody calls, "I know you're tough-assed, but take it easy."
The officer breaks into quavering song, to the tune of "Bye bye Blackbird":

> *"You can kiss my ass, ya ya!*
> *"You can kiss my ass, la la!"*

Somebody calls to him, "How long have you been in service?"
"Thirteen everloving goddam years."
"What are you in—I mean, besides jail? The goddam air force?"
"The Peace Corps," he growls. "Shut up, you're dead!" He resumes,
"Open the door, open the door!" Then very very quietly, "Open the door!"
Then in a yell.
And then suddenly, almost eerily—we stare at one another again—there
issues out of the midst of all this clamor that other voice we have heard,
frail, childlike: "Heh friend, heh friend," the officer calls. "You think they'll
let us out of here tomorrow?"

It is another night—scuffling of feet again, the clanging to of the steel
door. Curses. Groans. More curses. A fellow prisoner calls out, "You're
a bad-ass, aren't you?" "Yes, I'm a bad-ass," the new man confirms loudly.
The familiar exchange of obscenities begins. The voices mount in the familiar
rhythm. But in the very midst of it—we have learned now to expect it—the
voice alters; he calls: "Say—we're friends now, okay?"

We hear the heavy steel doors of the cages clang open, we hear them clang to, as the cops lock the prisoners in or let them out. These arrivals and departures mark the time for us now—a time which stretches, contracts, no longer tidily divided as it was outside jail. I am always surprised, when I glance at my watch, to learn the hour it is. The rhythm of night, day has been broken, as the light burns round the clock, and round the clock, too, the cops come and go, the prisoners yell at them and at one another; so that we sleep, when we do, simply in those stretches, whatever the clock says, when the yelling subsides enough to allow it. Mealtimes no longer subdivide a day; we have broken this rhythm ourselves, for my companions are fasting and I take only a part of one of the two meals the jail provides—a meal that is brought not at the beginning or the middle or the end of the day but at four in the afternoon. We count the separate days as they pass, but as we have not yet been tried and sentenced, we cannot yet count: one day less to serve. Time has its own peculiar quality in here, and, marked as it is by these clamorous arrivals and departures, it takes on a quality more peculiar still as we begin to hear prisoners who have been released being brought back into the cells again. Time, it seems, runs nowhere. We are in Hell.

I remember my first experience of this, in Birmingham's city jail, May 1963. This was my first imprisonment of any duration—six days; I had been in jail in New York less than twenty-four hours. My crime in Birmingham was walking half a block, a sign around my neck: "All Men Are Brothers." I had taken part in one of the Negro demonstrations. (The sentence was six months, but the case was appealed, and after six days we were all bailed out.) I was separated, of course, from my companions and put on the top floor of the jail; Negro prisoners were held on a floor below.

A large airy room, in this case. Still a cage in fact, but room to pace. (My friends below have less room—very much less of everything.) And we are even let out of the room at certain times—herded downstairs at mealtimes (three times a day here), very occasionally called down to the visiting room. The matron comes to the door and yells for one of us or all. And sometimes she yells a very particular phrase, calls the name of the prisoner and then adds, "All the way!" This means that the prisoner is being released. Festive phrase! The prisoner hurries to gather up her few belongings; she straightens out her skirt, pats quickly at her hair, grinning, shouts a quick goodbye. I remember Ruth saying goodbye, I remember Flo. I remember. . . . It is the middle of the next night. There is a sudden racket on the stairs, the heavy door is swung open, and I sit up on my top bunk to see who will come in. I have been asleep, and for the first moment I feel that I am having a senseless dream. She is wearing a different dress now, but that is Ruth who stands there. Her dress is soiled, she is barefoot, one of her eyes is swollen and she is cursing, her face contorted. "You know what that bitch of a matron did? She slapped me! She slapped me!"

It is two nights later. Racket on the stairs again. The door swings open, and Flo staggers in again. She gives me a funny little sideways smile as she passes—sly and despairing. She wanders distracted for a few minutes in the long aisle between the double-decker bunks, then sinks down on the bunk below me. I fall asleep again, then wake to the sound of splashing water. Flo is squatting in the aisle, her skirts lifted. She suddenly passes out and falls forward, sprawled in the puddle she has made. A section of thin glass is set into the floor at that spot, and the feeble greenish light that glows through it from below outlines her there, helpless, her red curls unraveled, her dress twisted, her frilled petticoat showing.

Now in the Albany city jail we hear derisive shouts, welcoming back a man who has been released three days before. He begins at once to curse at someone: "If your brains were made of cotton, there wouldn't be enough to make Kotex for a red-eyed beetle!"

The cop who has brought him in, on his way out, strolls back past our cell, hitching his pants. The look on his face asserts: A job well done; our city is safer now. He slaps his hand against his pistol holster, as if to reassure himself: Yes, there is power in me; I am a member of the force.

No wonder you touch yourself for reassurance.

I think of the heavy doors shutting, the heavy doors opening. First the rite of casting them out of existence. It is time they serve, no eternity, so then the rite of returning them to society. "All the way! All the way!" A cry in a dream. Punishment can almost convince a man that he doesn't exist; rite of casting them out of existence. It is time they serve, not eternity, so then the rite of returning them to society. "All the way! All the way!" A cry in a dream. Punishment can almost convince a man that he doesn't exist; it cannot make him feel, Now I am one of you. If society was embarrassed by them before, will it be less embarrassed by them now?

Chapter Two

We are not let out of our cage, day or night. There is no mess hall in this jail; my one meal is shoved to me in a tin plate along the floor under the door's lowest bar. (Usually bologna, which I leave; grits; black-eyed peas; a slightly bitter diced vegetable which I suppose is turnips.) Our toilet is there in the cell. (If a guard comes by while one of us is sitting on it, we hold up a coat for a screen.) There is no prison yard. We get our only exercise climbing up and down from the top bunks. (And Erica, with determination, once a day, stands in the narrow space between the bunks and brings up her knees to her chin a few times.) Here we are. We sit on our bunks or we lie on our bunks.

We sit and listen to the life about us in the jail. We can see from our cage only the corridor outside and, through the row of dirty windows, the alley, the brick wall. But to our ears the prison, all on one floor, lies open—except for one distant room, "the hole." Acoustics play strange tricks, and it's hard to locate exactly from where it is the voices come, but we can shout back and forth to the men in our group—even to Ray and Ronnie and Tyrone, in a segregated cell because they are Negroes. We don't shout very often, because it takes a lot of energy. But Ray, several times a day, sings out to us: "Oh-oh freedom! Oh-oh freedom!" Sometimes we join in, sometimes we just let his single voice roll down the corridors, around the various corners, into all the cells.

Now and then the other prisoners call to us. Most often they call to Yvonne. Something in her voice intrigues them.

"Eevon!"

"What?"

"Do you have any cigarettes?"

"No—I'm sorry."

"All right."

When Candy arrives, they call as often to her—intrigued by her name, of course, and by her youth: she is only seventeen.

"Candy, you there? You all right, baby?"

"Yes, I'm fine. Thank you."

"All right."

But mostly they call back and forth to one another—teasing, cursing, or appealing. Or they talk or groan to themselves.

We talk among ourselves, too, but for long stretches we sit in silence, listening. I look at my friends and see their faces marked by a kind of awe. I recognize it. I remember suddenly the night I left jail after my first brief imprisonment in New York—bailed out, to my surprise, in the middle of the night. I remember walking away, up Greenwich Avenue, turning and turning to look back at the high gloomy building there, my feet, in spite of me, dragging, drawn to retrace my steps and at least touch the walls of the prison; turning to touch it with my eyes, and wondering as I lingered at the strength of my feeling that I was walking away from something of which I was deeply a part.

We sit and listen to the cries, the groans, the curses. Who has not at some time uttered that groan, uttered essentially that curse, of one estranged from others and from his own groped-for life? Those who have thrown us in here wanted to dispose of us; but instead of throwing us out of society, as they would have liked, they have admitted us, by their act, into its inmost room. Here are men and women at their weakest; here, too, society confesses itself at a loss. These are people with whom it has been unable to cope, whom it has been unable to sustain.

A cop unlocks the heavy door of our cell and pushes in with us a pretty curly-haired young woman who has been arrested for drunkenness. She presses her body against the bars as he retreats, shrieking after him. She pulls off one of her pretty white cowgirl boots and begins to bang at the bars with it in a tantrum. The paper drinking cups we have lined up there spill to the floor and roll. Our underclothes, which we have washed and hung there to dry, are scattered too. A button goes flying off her boot into the corridor.

We try to calm her, ask her questions about herself. She quiets down for a moment but then begins to rage again: "I'll kill them all, kill them all!" She takes a bobby pin from her hair and, reaching around the door, begins frantically to try to pick its lock. We point out that it's hopeless, laugh at her gently, and she finally begins to laugh too, her tantrum dissolving— though she picks away for a little while still.

Leaning against one of the bunks, then, she tells us about herself: "I was married at fourteen....Seven miserable years with him....I'm nothing but a whore, I suppose....I called my mother the other day; she sounded just like my enemy." Turning her eyes on us, lost, shining: "I never had any kind of life."

In the cell next to us for a while is a young traveling salesman, member of a fly-by-night company that has been doing something illegal in town. After he has told us with good humor that if our peace walk came through his town and "started a ruckus" he'd just as soon shoot us "as anyone" ("A kid I won't shoot, but if it's a grownup I don't care if it's a man or a woman"), he goes on to describe his manner of life to us a little, to tell us of the good times he and the others in his company have, as they move in a group from one motel to another: "We don't know till we jump where we go....We have a ball"—lying in bed and ordering chicken dinners and watching television, each with a girl on call. "The boss keeps our money for us. Saturday night he doles it out. We shower up and go to the honkytonk. Everybody gets drunk." The recitation of his joys is almost as sad as the young woman's recitation of her sorrows; he is so hectically eager to have us believe in them.

One night two cops unlock our door and steer into the cell a drunken weeping woman, huge as a sow, with pendulous belly, pendulous chins. Tears run from the corners of her eyes and black rivulets of snuff from the corners of her mouth. She stands blindly in the small space between the bunks, staring at us, confused; then sinks, like a mountain sinking into the sea, onto a lower bunk we have quickly cleared. We take off her shoes for her. She suddenly reaches out her hand toward me and I take it and she begins to tell us about herself: "I am so old....My husband...doesn't love me....My grandchildren...ashamed of me....I'd like to be pretty like all of you....I am so old." We ask her how old she is. Fifty. We tell her that isn't old. One of us asks why she doesn't see a doctor if it bothers her to be fat. She has been to see a doctor. "He laughed at me." Have we anything to eat? Have we any snuff?

In the distance a Negro woman begins to cry: "Oh, my baby! Let me go home to my baby! Oh, help!"

The fat woman grips my hand more tightly. What are we in for? We tell her about our Walk. "You didn't walk with niggers, did you?" she asks, frightened. "They have more than whites do, you know it—better schools, better everything. I have a cook, she's a nigger, and she says she wouldn't want things different." Her eyes implore us. Suddenly she falls asleep.

She wakes, turning in bed, groaning. "Have you really walked all this way?" And then, in a voice that is almost a whisper, "Girls, I want to ask you something. Did you ever do anything you were so ashamed of you didn't know what to do?"

Yvonne tells her, "No, I believe you do things because you can't help it."

She whispers to us, "Do you think it's very wrong to go with a young boy? My husband doesn't love me. One day I just couldn't stand it anymore....The boy was only twenty-one. I got him to drive into the country. We went into the back room of a church." She ends, her voice flat: "He couldn't do anything." The tears begin to run from her eyes again.

We stare at one another, helpless; and I stare again at all the names scratched on these walls: Bobby. Linda. Jimmy. David. Rufus. Over the toilet someone has scratched an arrow and This Way out. High up in the corner of the wall next which the woman lies, in letters slanting down, someone has scratched: For God So Loved The World....

I remember suddenly a woman in the Macon jail—Evelyn, in and out constantly for drinking. A handsome, restless woman, she moves to and fro about the room (in Macon's jail there is space in which to move), conversing with herself when not with us, to keep up her spirits, making a kind of bitter fun of herself and of her plight. A plane passes close overhead, and we all stop what we are doing to listen to it. Evelyn raises her arms—marked with dark bruises where the cops have been rough with her—and cries out: "Mr. Pilot! Mr. Pilot! Here I am! Help me! Take me away!" The plane passes on, high overhead, the humming of its motor growing fainter. "Mr. Pilot!"

she cries. "Oh, come back, come back, don't leave me! Come back and get me, Mr. Pilot!" She throws herself upon her cot—"Mr. Pilot, Mr. Pilot!"—half laughing, half weeping loudly. "Oh, why are you abandoning me?" We laugh too, we almost weep too. Her comic cry is the cry of almost all in here, a cry everybody knows, the cry in uttering which Jesus took on the flesh of every person born: "My God, my God, why hast thou forsaken me?"

I remember again the first hours I ever spent in jail—in the New York Women's House of Detention. We have been questioned, fingerprinted, photographed, and searched one two three four five times. The elevator doors open and we step out into the ward to which we have been assigned. The doors open and the scene explodes upon us, explodes within us. The clamor of bedlam bursts in our ears—wild giggles, shrieks of rage, distracted pratings. The motions of bedlam meet our eye. It is the hour just after dinner; the women have not yet been locked in twos in their cramped cells for the night. They wander in the halls like lost spirits, some of them dejected, heads hanging, others running here and there, others clinging together, amorous—timid about this, some of them, some of them eager to be noticed. They roll their eyes in our direction to see who we are. "Where did they pick *them* up? Look, look." And there also bursts upon us the strong smell of the place—disinfectant, bad cooking, sweat, urine, and something more than this: that special distillation of the flesh of those who are miserable, the smell, simply, of human desperation.

We have missed the dinner hour but are given a hasty meal by ourselves in the mess hall, while a prisoner sloshes a mop about the place. On each tin plate a very sticky mass of macaroni and a large turd which we decide is a fishball. The stuff is hard to swallow; we dump most of it into the garbage pail which stands in the hall.

Then it is time for all to be locked in their cells. I am given a cell with one of my fellow pacifists. Two cots, side by side, a toilet (an empty bottle floats in it), a tiny basin with cold water and no stopper. During the day the one cot can be pushed under the other; when they are side by side, no floor space remains. We talk a little, then try to settle down. This jail provides sheets, but they are the size of crib sheets and don't stretch the length of the mattresses. I feel in spite of myself that I share the bed with prisoner after prisoner who has slept here before me, sweated on this mattress, wept on it, exhaled her despair, been sick, been incontinent. I have undressed and put on the knee-length prison nightgown that has been given to me, but I decide now to put my underclothes and my skirt back on. And I try to curl up so that no part of me touches the mattress itself. And as my flesh shrinks from the touch of certain things here, my spirit shrinks from contact with the life about me. The prisoners are calling out to one another from their row of cells. Much of the language is unfamiliar slang, but the cries sound to me lewd and abandoned . I think with despair: See to what a hardly human condition the human being can be reduced. In a delirium of depression, I begin to laugh. My companion has turned her face to the wall. A guard yells at the women to stop their racket—there is supposed to be no talking after a certain hour. The place hushes for a moment. Then some giggling begins.

Suddenly there is a shriek: "What's this in my goddam bed? Matron, turn on the light, turn on the light!"

"It's probably Mickey the mouse," someone calls. "Old Mickey never fails."

There is more giggling, and a great deal of commotion in that cell. Then another hush.

Then suddenly from the cell across from me a woman imitates the plaintive, rather delicate miaowing of a cat. A pause. "Moo! Moo!"—sad and low. And from another dark cell, staccato: "Oink! Oink!" "Baa! Baa!" trembles the length of the corridor. And then a rooster's voice bursts the air in prolonged fireworks: "Cockadoodle doodle doodle doodle doodle doo!"

My depression is scattered. I feel all at once light of heart and no longer set apart in spirit from these others, able to feel for them only pity and distaste.

Someone calls, "Good night, Joan," and someone, "Good night, Lola."

"Good night, Doris!" "Good night, Cookie!"

"Good night, Toots!"

My cellmate is sitting bolt upright, smiling, and I guess from her look that her feelings now are something like mine. She is a young college girl, very bright and very grave, with heavy glasses, a somewhat peaked look. We nod at each other mutely and she lies down again in bed.

I sit there, leaning my head against the wall, listening. From the small window over the toilet, sounds of traffic far below enter our cell—very clear. Down the corridor I hear the small sounds of prisoners turning in bed or stirring, sighing. I sit there a long time, a peculiar joy rising in me, my sense of distance from all the others here more and more dissolving, a sense of kinship with them waking in me more and more. I reach out and grasp one of the bars of the cage with my hand. I have only to remember that gesture...I feel a queer stirring in me, and it is as though my heart first bursts the bars that are my ribs, then bursts the bars of this cell, and then travels with great lightness and freedom down the corridor and into each stinking cell, acknowledging: Yes, we are all of us one flesh. This motion of my heart seems, in fact, so very physical that when I hear my companion turn in her bed, I decide abruptly: this disturbance in the air may frighten her. I call it back into its cage and sit trembling.

I hear a little sound from her. Is she weeping? I whisper, "Are you all right?"

She whispers, "Oh yes, oh yes! You?"

I whisper, "Yes."

I lie now in this cage in Albany, Georgia. There are eight of us, and four bunks. Candy and Mary have been arrested too, and are with us. We have asked for two extra mattresses and been given them and they are on the floor. Three people lie there, closely side by side, legs under one bunk, heads half under another. The third person has her coat over her head because she lies right next to the toilet. I lie alone on a lower bunk tonight; it is my turn to stretch out. From the bunk above me, Edie's thin foot dangles in the air, and in the crack between that bunk and the wall, Erica's square hand is visible. I am not always so sure which limb belongs to whom.

We lie and listen to the cries, the groans, the curses. We are all of us wakeful tonight, but heavy-headed too. No window has been opened for a long time, and the air is thick. A cop has just taken a bottle of corn liquor off someone he has brought in and poured the stuff out in the corridor. The fumes of this spread, too. The man who has been brought in is screaming, "Oh get me out of here, get me out of here!"

I remember suddenly the legend of the Harrowing of Hell. After Jesus, dying on the Cross, cried out that he felt abandoned, the rocky foundations of hell are supposed to have been tumbled out of place; and before he ascended into heaven he is said to have gone down into hell to gather all those spirits who wanted to be gathered.

I think: Let the foundations of every jail that exists be tumbled out of place—let these hells be harrowed, let them be emptied. I think of all the men and women cast, for a time, into this damnation, and marked by it. I think of their troublesome return to society. I think of the senseless attempt to build heaven more securely by creating hell. The one region can never be shut off from the other. I remember Debs' statement: "While there is a criminal element, I am of it; while there is a soul in prison, I am not free"— not a sentimental statement but a simple statement of fact. I think: The only way to build anything resembling heaven, the only way to build "the beloved community," is to seek again and again not how to cast out but how to gather, is to attempt to imitate Jesus' action. I remember Evelyn again, whom we met in Macon's jail. "We need more company," she had said at one point: "I'm going to ride the broom." A battered broom stood leaning against the wall in a corner, and she straddled it and trotted energetically back and forth the length of the room. This was supposed to be a kind of magic to bring more company in. I think: Yes, ride the broom, ride the broom! Ride it until you have ridden *all* in who are outside! For if any live in hell, then all do. "We are members one of another." Let them all know this place. When they know it, let them cry out. Then let the walls fall!

Chapter Three

There is a jail within a jail here, hell within hell. The men and women behind these bars are not supposed to exist, but some are supposed to exist even less than others.

A prisoner who has just been brought in screams in panic. An old-timer calls to him from a cage around the corner: "Take it easy!"

"You goddam black sonofabitch," cries the newcomer, "you kiss my ass!"

Silence. Then, "How you know what color I is?" the Negro asks softly.

"Fuck you, chocolate drop, I know you're black. Don't talk shit to me; I'm white, I'm the aristocrat. My God, you wish you could change white, don't you?" His voice speeds up. "All you goddam niggers wish you were white! You don't show me shit, you black bastard. You ain't even a son of God, you son of the Devil!" He erupts in what is supposed to be an imitation of the other man's speech: "Blah blah blah blah blah blah blah—"

The Negro answers him wearily, "I don't give a damn if you *blue*; you in jail."

"I'm in jail and I'm blue," the white man suddenly states blankly—for a moment confronting the facts. Then he begins to rattle the bars in another fit. He yells, "Let my ass out of here, you bastards!" He screams again. And again he turns his attention to the other prisoner, for relief. "Where's Martin Luther King at tonight? He going to get you out of jail? Where's old Martin Luther at?" He offers a few obscene suggestions as to where King might be. "You goddam gob of spit," he suddenly cries. "You would like to be white, you Martin Luther King! *Least* I don't run round wanting to be black and segregating with you sons of bitches. *Least* I don't run round sitting on my knees praying up to heaven: 'Turn me white, turn me white!' Nigger!" he screams; and then with all his breath, "Niggggggaaaaaaaaaaa!"

The cry is like the cry of a man dropping through space. Save me somehow! Save me! I am nothing! It is an invocation shrieked: Damn, damn your soul, be less than I, and I am something! Nigger, nigger, naught, naught, *help*!

The man cries, "Tell that woman in the cell over there she's a nigger, too!" And then he screams again.

None of us can speak. We are at the bottom of the world.

141

I lean against the cold steel wall, arrange my cramped limbs in a new position, and try to think, try to struggle to the surface again after that cry.

I stare at the wall across from me. A former prisoner has scratched in wide letters: FUCK THE COPS! It should really be UNFUCK THE COPS, one peacewalker has suggested; unlove them is what is meant. But a man who feels violent can imagine the act of love as an act of murder. I consider how many of the threats hurled back and forth in here take the form of coarse invitations to make love. These cries waver sometimes, in weird fashion, between the note of abuse and the note of actual flirtation, the distance between the two notes surprisingly slight. It occurs to me that I shouldn't be surprised. In each case the cry is really the same. It is: Give me your life! I hear again in my head the segregationist's hideous scream, and I think: Yes, at the heart of most violence is this delusion—that one's existence can be made more abundant by it. Just as the act of love can be imagined as murder, murder, or what amounts to it, can be imagined as an act that gives one life. It is a delusion which tantalizes us all, in one extremity or another.

Yes, the easiest way to free ourselves does always seem to be to put certain other people from us. Real or imaginary murder can be swift and apparently simple. For the moment it *is* magic, *can* set one free. It is only in time that the magic fails. In time it is proved that our lives are bound together, whether we like it or not.

I think again of this jail. The man who is cast in here—out of society— remains a member of society and in time returns, more trouble to others and to himself than he was before. The Negro, cast more violently still out of the world of people, remains a person, and the truth of this returns to trouble those who wish him a "nigger" merely, meant for service. I recall how, ironically, for those who try to believe him less than a man, this no-man tends to loom, finally, larger than life. I recall a conversation with one of the cops who has stopped in his rounds to talk with us.

We have got onto the subject of Negroes' being denied their rights. He argues for a while that their rights are not denied. "They have some advantages over us!" he suddenly asserts. "You put a prisoner who won't work into a sweat box. If he's a white man, he'll go to work after three days. A nigger can stay in there as many as thirty days!" He eyes us. "Cut a nigger and maybe he'll bleed just a little, right after you've cut, but then it'll stop. Cut a white man like that, he'll bleed to death!" He shakes his head again. "And syphilis won't drive a nigger crazy! So they have advantages *we* haven't got!" He grins. "I'm going to write to Bobby Kennedy!" I think: Your words are wild, but you are right to say that you, too, live at a disadvantage—for you are haunted. I hear again a young Negro leader addressing a mass meeting in Birmingham: "We're going to win our freedom, and as we do it, we're also going to set our white brothers free."

I remember another person who is haunted, hear again the trembling voice of a white woman two of us met while visiting influential Albany families to try to talk with them about the peace walk. She is a middle-aged woman with a face that is still pretty, but anxieties have creased and crumpled it. "We love our colored people, we love them!" she exclaims, her hand on my arm, urgent, her face peering into mine with such an entreaty that I can't help reassuring her, "Of course you do. I know." Her hand is on my arm again. "They are happy here, with things just as they are! Happy, I know it!" She begs us to leave town. "I can see that you are dedicated people, you mean well, but oh dear, you'll just do harm, you don't understand!" I ask her as gently as I can, "But if they really are happy, how can our coming make any difference?" She stares at me, confused, then just begins to shake her head.

My thoughts of her are interrupted. A cop has come into the room that opens onto the cell blocks, and the man who was yelling before begins again: "Officer! Officer!"

"What?"

"I want to talk with you!"

"What do you want? Some service?"

The man yells, "I want to get out of here!" and the cop yells back, "We all do. We're in jail, too." He gives a snort of laughter and walks off. A door slams.

The prisoner gives a great roar of frustration: "Arrrr! It's the stinkiest dirtiest cell I was ever in!" And he lifts his steel bunk on the chain by which it is slung from the wall, then drops it, lifts it, drops it, lifts it, drops it, *clang, clang, clang.*

The Negro he has been taunting calls out, "I'm just as drunk as you are and I'm not making all that racket!"

The white man cries, "Fuck you, black bastard, I ain't fucking with you! Your ancestors were goddam slaves!" But he stops.

I think myself back into the house of the pleading woman. Sunlight pours through tall windows into the room where we sit—plays on the polished furniture, on the silky rosy-patterned rugs. She offers us, in a graceful glass dish, caramels she has made herself. Her husband is particularly fond of them, she confides; she loves to make them for him, and also to arrange the flowers. She smiles a little girl's smile. I listen for the step of servants in the large house, but hear no sound. They exist, of course; the house and the encircling garden are beautifully cared for. At the mill her husband runs, they exist too, these people whose ancestors were her ancestors' slaves, and whom, without thinking, she still calls "ours"—without thinking, but her face, as she speaks the word, dented by anxieties.

I remember the term so often used against us: We are "outside agitators."
Her face before my eyes, I think: Yes, agitators, but it is above all your own
doubts about your lives which we agitate; when you insist that we are
outsiders, it is because, in fact, we come too close to you.

I remember the cry with which she has met the two of us at her door. At
her first vague, inquiring look, we have introduced ourselves as members
of the peace walk. "Oh, I'm so distressed!" she exclaims, staring at us, and
her cry and her staring look draw us in an instant surprisingly near. I feel
almost as though we have been recognized as relatives from out of town,
appearing at a time of troubles. She leads us quickly into the house, seats
us beside her on a sofa, scanning our faces. Then almost before we can begin
to speak, the words leap out: "We love our colored people, love them!"

She clearly needs to have us believe it and to be able to believe it herself.
She has a soft heart, has to see herself as a loving person. But clearly, too,
she loves with a love that pleads: Don't make it uncomfortable for me to
love you. Please don't insist on showing me all that you are, all that you
feel. Let me continue to love you as my happy servants.

There pass again in my imagination Negro faces met on the road in our
walk, faces of two kinds. A car approaches, goes slowly by us. A Negro
family. No glance meets ours. The eyes of all are carefully veiled as they
pass. On no face are feelings legible; each countenance has been drained of
them as by a blow. Only a seemingly endless patience can be read there. A
second car approaches. A young Negro woman is alone at the wheel. At the
sight of us, black and white, and the sight of our signs, her eyes open wide,
and then her whole face leaps into life, feelings written upon it like skywriting.
She flings up her arms, calls out, "Well, all right then!"

The noisy prisoner is shouting again: "Shut your big black mouth. Shut
your big black mouth!"

I think: The lady who offered us her caramels would turn in horror from
this yelling man. And she would turn in horror from these cages which hold
us; she would weep, and mean it, if she could see us in here. And yet the
man yells, actually, her own desperate wish, which she cannot bear to
acknowledge; and it is the daydream she dreams that holds us between these
steel walls. The charge against us could be said to be that we refused to make
it easier for her to live with herself.

Why are we here? We are charged with refusing to take through Albany
the one route Police Chief Laurie Pritchett told us he would allow—
Oglethorpe Avenue. We have attempted to take a route that varied from his
for five blocks and would have brought us into the business area, where more
people could read our signs. We are here for trying this twice. Some of us
tried on December 23 and served twenty-four days for it; more of us tried
again on January 27 and sit here now. After that first arrest, the city attorney

argued in court that the issue was whether outsiders could come into Albany and tell the police chief how to run his department. Attorney C.B. King, who defended a few of us (others defended themselves), argued that the issue was whether "one Laurie Pritchett" could "pit himself against the highest law of the land" and claim the right to deprive us of freedom of speech. King, a local Negro, has experience of Pritchett's claims to power, for Albany has seen wave after wave of peaceful Negro demonstrations—or rather has not been allowed to see them. The Chief has always swiftly and tidily jailed the demonstrators; when the city jail has run out of space, he has farmed them out to the counties. At issue now—King knows, everybody knows—is not what a handful of peacewalkers is going to do (we would take a little more than half an hour to pass through and be on our way, if not arrested); it is really what nearly half the inhabitants of Albany are going to be allowed to do. Pritchett has been frank about it finally in his discussions with us. Oglethorpe Avenue marks a rough division between the city's black community and its white community. "While I'm here, nobody is ever going to demonstrate north of Oglethorpe." He is not even going to let us walk down the north side of that street. "If I let you, there'd be others." So the charge against us is really that we challenge his right to "shut the big black mouths" of those who want to demonstrate that they are not happy here. The city's more tenderhearted white citizens like to dream that Negro discontent does not exist, and they have delegated to Pritchett, and to the court, the power to enforce that dream.

I think of the courtroom during those early trials. I have stayed out this first time to help maintain contact between the prisoners and the outside world, and I sit there as a spectator. What childish rites are acted out as the dream is ruled to be reality! The prosecuting attorney is speaking. The court listens. Now one of my friends is speaking. It is very simple: the court stops listening. The various cops who sit up there in a line next to the judge turn to one another and begin to whisper and to laugh; the Chief and the city attorney whisper together; the Chief gets up and goes to whisper to the judge. Carl has some questions to ask the Chief. Carl is a Negro, so the Chief pretends not to be able to understand what he is saying. As Carl persists, the Chief shifts his chair so that his back is nearly turned to him. All the cops shift their chairs and laugh and yawn. Now another peacewalker is making a statement. The city attorney decides to stroll out of the room for a while. A friend of the Chief's wanders down the aisle for a brief visit with him, then wanders away again with a wave of the hand. The judge sits up there playing with the pages of a large book. If the defense rises to object to any statement by the prosecution, he swiftly overrules the objection. If the prosecution rises to object to any statement by the defense, he as swiftly honors that objection. At the conclusion of the "trial," Pritchett hands around copies of the verdict, which has been typed up in advance.

Can the truth really be manipulated as simply as this? The actors themselves appear a little self-conscious. The cops seem almost to be playing at cops. During recess, a reporter steps up to one of them to congratulate him on a promotion and the officer blushes, laughs, points at his shiny black boots: "Yes, I'm the big Gestapo now!" While the trial is in process, they sit sometimes, hands on billysticks, chins jutting—pictures of "the law." Then all at once they abandon this posture to give one another boyish punches in the stomach or to set each other's caps wrong side forward over their eyes. I half expect everyone to break out suddenly into loud guffaws and cry, "All right, all right, now let's be serious. Order in this courtroom!"

No one cries out any such thing. The absurd drama plays itself out. The absurd verdict is rendered. The prisoners are marched down to their cells, to the reality of steel walls, hard bunks, foul air, groans, curses.

Here we sit. The prisoner is yelling, "Are you in jail, are you, you black bastard? Oh, I'm glad I'm not one of you fucking niggers!"

Someone yells, "What are you in for?"

"I'm in for the hell of it!" he yells back.

Here we sit, and here I persist in thinking: The truth cannot be manipulated as simply as that. The power we have seen displayed is based on lies, and so we can prevail against it if we are stubborn. This hope has brought us here a second time. We sit and hope; we sit and stare at the steel walls and shift our cramped limbs.

Chapter Seven

It is a little later. Footsteps. A brisk knock on the wall beyond our cells. "C.B.!" everyone cries, sitting up. It is C.B. King on his daily visit to bring us our mail. Sometimes his associate, Attorney Thomas Jackson, is with him too—tall and shy, a little smile twisting the neat line of his narrow mustache. Today he is by himself. "And how are the ladies today?" He opens his briefcase and begins to sort the bundles of letters. Some are for us, some for the men in the cell block around the corner, some for the men in the "hole," some for Bradford in the county jail across the street.

Edie reaches out her hands: "Oh hurry, C.B.!"

He tells her, "I expect from all of you a saintly patience." He looks at me. "How is Miss Deming today?"

He teases me with the formal address, though he calls the others by their first names. I tell him that I am really out of trouble now, but that Yvonne fainted yesterday.* A shadow passes across his face. Then he begins to hand out the mail.

The time of this daily visit, too, is a time when the bars of our cell seem for a moment to melt. It is not only that he brings us letters and takes ours safely out. As Yvonne and Edie begin to banter with him now—"You're wearing a beautiful sweater today, C.B." (it is a soft lavender), "My sweater meets with your approval?" (deadpan)—I think of the distance we have traveled toward each other.

When the Walk entered Albany, a good many of us had entertained naive hopes about the welcome we would receive from people in the Albany Movement. We took it for granted that if we engaged in a struggle with the authorities here, Movement people would welcome the opportunity to renew their own battle in coordination with ours. Instead we found them wary of making any move at all. We were invited to a number of their leadership meetings, and at these meetings one man, Reverend Samuel Wells, kept suggesting demonstrations in our support—"If people are fasting, we should be moving quickly; that's not a play toy." (He has fasted himself in jail here.) But the Movement's president, Slater King (C.B.'s brother), and its secretary, Marion Page, and C.B. himself had always urged that they think about it a while longer. "We need more than faith," C.B. had commented to Wells.

We might, really, have anticipated this caution, because we had first met most of these people—a few weeks before, in Macon—when we attended some sessions of the trials which the federal government was conducting against them. They had submitted to Washington any number of complaints about abuses they had suffered from the Albany authorities, and no action had been taken; but when a local white merchant filed a complaint against *them,* in connection with the boycott they had started, the federal government had decided to prosecute—"a bone thrown to the segregationists," as one civil-rights lawyer put it. It was little wonder that their present mood was one of discouragement.

But it wasn't only that they were discouraged. They were obviously skeptical about us, too. We learned with shock that some of them even believed the rumor the white community had spread that we were Communists. C.B. never took that rumor seriously, but his attitude toward us was one of great reserve.

*At this point, Barbara's friends have been fasting for 15 days. (JM)

I remember a long talk I had with him back in December, the day before our group first walked into Albany. I didn't walk with them that day, because I was called to appear in court in Macon—having volunteered to appeal the constitutionality of our earlier arrest there. C.B. was my lawyer and drove me up. Ron Moose came along as a witness. As we drove through the sad countryside, past the unpainted shacks with collapsing porches where Negroes lived—hard to decide, often, which shacks were abandoned and which still lived in—I remember talking eagerly about my hopes that the struggle for civil rights and the struggle for disarmament would become one. C.B. listened courteously. On the subject of disarmament he posed the usual questions about whether one could abandon all national defense, then listened quietly as I argued the necessity of adopting nonviolent defense now that we lived in the nuclear age. Yes, he could see that men should take this new step; but would they? And then he confided that he had not, for himself, given the subject much thought. When you were a Negro—when you were down in a ditch and the white man had his foot on your throat—you didn't often look beyond the ditch and the struggle there.

I was to see him that day in the Macon courtroom and later in the courtroom at Albany, waging his own hard combat, which is brilliant, impeccable, and again and again frustrated. Albany: the cops slouch in their chairs, their caps set on their heads askew as they joke with one another; the prosecutor, in his loose suit rumpled as an elephant's skin, dreams with his feet up, enjoying his cigar. C.B. enters. His face is alert and his back straight; the crease in his trousers is a careful one. As the arguments begin, his words, too, are careful, and they are full of style, in contrast to the drawled and grunted statements of most of those who speak for the prosecution. Out of language he has made for himself a precise sword and a polished shield, and he moves in close to his opponents; he plays a daring game—again and again moves up to the very boundary of open contempt for them. The argument he presents is always clear and carefully reasoned; everyone in the court can follow it; but he delights, too, in using certain words here and there with which his opponents are probably unfamiliar—as he delights in repeating, deadpan, with a question mark attached, a word one of them has misused or a phrase that is ungrammatical. They pretend, all of them, that none of this is happening—pretend that this is just old C.B., Albany nigger, doing a little ungainly dance and shuffle for them. They yawn and turn away.

"Now, C.B.," drawls the Chief.

"Yes, Laurie," says C.B. quietly.

The judge raps sharply with his gavel, and the Chief turns to him: "I don't want him to address me by that name."

C.B.: "I am no more appreciative of his addressing me as C.B."

The judge: "We're going to proceed in an orderly manner. His official title is Chief Pritchett."

C.B.: "I say respectfully that my official title is Attorney King."

The judge: "We're going to proceed."

Whether C.B. is arguing for one of us or for some local Negro client, the ruling is against him, invariably. He has not been known to win one case in this courtroom. But week after week he reappears, a bitter but persistent figure; outmatches them all again, and again is judged the loser.

I remember the trip up to Macon with him, and I remember the trip back. At my trial that day the court dismissed the charge against me, saying that Macon's city council intended to revoke the ordinance against passing out leaflets that had been cited in our arrest there. C.B. asked to be allowed to argue the case, for what if the ordinance were *not* revoked? That would be the end of our challenge to its constitutionality. But his request was denied. We were not to question the council's good faith.

C.B. then took me and Ron to report the outcome to a local Negro who had just started his own small newspaper. The man wanted to use a picture of me and asked an assistant to drive me to a photographer's near by where I could have one taken very quickly. Afterward the assistant asked me whether we wanted him to drive us anywhere else. Ron mentioned an errand at the other end of town he wished we had time for, but agreed with me that we didn't have the time—as C.B. would have to wait for us. The assistant misunderstood and drove us there; so C.B. did wait. On our return, he made no complaint. I apologized clumsily, feeling my words inadequate. I couldn't help thinking that *he* would be thinking: she wouldn't have kept a white attorney waiting. Ron had been involved, of course, and he was a Negro too, but I was the older and so responsible.

In the course of the drive home I began to see that the delay had meant more than C.B.'s having to wait for us. It meant that it was dark before we got home, and a Negro man was driving through the dark seated next to a white woman. C.B. was driving fast, to make up the time a little, and the result, ironically, was that he took a wrong turn and lost his route. He had to stop several times to ask directions. He never stopped in any of the places we would have stopped if this had been the North—at a gas station or in the middle of a town at an intersection where a policeman stood: he slowed down only on the outskirts of towns when he could spot in his headlights a Negro walking by the side of the road, and no white man in sight. Glancing at him at he sat next to me at the wheel, concentrated on this trip through the dark—conversing courteously still but his face a mask, composed with obvious discipline—I thought of my eager words to him that morning and the words he had spoken in reply; and I felt in every particle of my being his distance from me.

I was to feel it again, as sharply, on another day. My friends had been in jail about two weeks and were awaiting trial. Brad sent a message out that he needed certain papers to prepare his defense; would I ask C.B. to bring them in to him? Someone else had called to suggest a number of questions I should ask C.B. before the trial. This was Sunday; the trial was set for Tuesday; C.B. could sometimes vanish for a day to appear at court in another town. Afraid of missing him if I waited to call him at his office the next morning, I called him at his home. In a voice that was quiet and courteous and cool, he told me that he did like to reserve Sunday as a day to spend with his family. Again I felt with a pang that perhaps he thought: She wouldn't have disturbed a white attorney. This time I wrote him a note of apology.

I lie now thinking of the constraint there has been between us and of how it has at last dissolved. I think of yesterday, another Sunday. The day before yesterday when C.B. visited, I still felt quite sick, and frightened about myself. Yesterday I woke, feeling better, took a little breakfast, then drowsed off again, and then woke to see C.B. standing there. He was dressed as I had never seen him, in the slacks and loose shirt and slippers he wore about the house. We all sat up in surprise. "I've come to see how Princess Barbara is," he said. I stared at him, not able to find anything to say except that I was better and that it was very good of him to come on Sunday morning—but for once I didn't care if I was awkward. All the panic I had felt in the past about what he might think, feel, doubt, subsided as he stood there. His words were as usual lightly teasing, but his look put no distance between us. I thought: At last you don't mind our seeing you without a mask. I stared at his face as though I had never seen it before. It seemed suddenly rounder than I had thought it to be, and softer in outline. I thought: Now I dare look at you, too.

Now I sit thinking of how his face flinched when I told him that Yvonne fainted. And the fact that he has shown fear for us suddenly makes the fear that I feel for us myself very much easier to control.

"Am I a God at hand?"—Jeremiah

Pray for us.
One and true, God is
Each new day a new
God, abides with us
But hides from us who it is He is.
Pray for us.
He awaits us in unheard of places
With His despaired of graces.

1952

Section 4: The Late Sixties

Surely all of us are nerved by one another, catch courage from one another.

—From "We Are All Part of One Another"

VARIATION

Locked in winter, summer lies.
Gather your bones together. Arise.
Day puts forth its leaves upon night's stalk.
Stand. Walk.

This poem is a variation of the poem on page 100   1960

The Temptations of Power—
Report of a Visit to North Vietnam

*Talk given, on speaking tour, in winter and spring of 1967, after visiting
North Vietnam for eleven days in December and January 1966-67.* (BD)

At the turn of the year I visited North Vietnam for eleven days with three
other American women—Diane Nash Bevel, Grace Mora Newman, and Pat
Griffith.

I want to talk about what we saw in North Vietnam. And I want to talk
about what it has been like to try to report on what we saw, back here at
home. Both are painful subjects.

The first thing we asked to be shown were the sections of Hanoi which
had been bombed by our planes. We were taken to all four quarters of Hanoi
which had been bombed; and there *are* only four quarters of Hanoi. Then
we asked to be taken to a number of other bombed towns and villages outside
of Hanoi, and we were taken first to a little Catholic country village not far
from Hanoi which had been leveled by our planes and then rebuilt—Phu
Sa. And then we were taken on two longer trips, on one day south of Hanoi,
first to Phu Ly and then even further south to Nam Dinh, which is the third
largest city in the North. It's about seventy miles south of Hanoi. On another
day we were taken north to Vinh Yen, which is a provincial center.

In each of these places we saw very much the same thing. We stood among
the wreckage of schools and nurseries and children's playgrounds, and the
wreckage of hospitals, of Buddhist pagodas and Catholic churches, of cultural
centers, and the wreckage of the houses simply of workers and peasants. We
stood, for example, in Phu Ly, which is a town that used to have a population
of about eight thousand, and today it has a population of nobody; because
the planes came in April, in July, in August, three times in October and finally
the night before Christmas, and there is hardly a building in that town—if
there is one; I didn't see one building—that has been left intact.

The pattern of our visits to these places was always pretty much the same.
First we would be greeted by the officials of that town or village, who would
tell us something about its history. Then we would walk at length through
the ruins caused by our bombings. In most of these places that have been

hit they would have built—after the bombings—museums containing exhibits from the bombings and photographs taken before and after. We would see exhibits like, for example, the school blackboard with the pellets of a bomb we have invented called the Lazy Dog bomb—I have one here—imbedded in it; or we would see a pile of school books perforated by these same pellets. And they would always have a number of samples of the weapons that had been used against them; because some—like this one—would not have exploded. Or they would have the fragments of them. Or they would have the metal casings in which they came down. Then we would meet a group of the people of that place who had suffered most; and they would tell us in detail about the day, or the days, when the planes came. And then we would visit the hospital, where the wounded lay. Many of these were always children. And most of those hurt had always been hurt by the Lazy Dog bomb.

As soon as we had returned from Vietnam and started giving our reports, we were told at a press conference that the War Department was saying—to discredit the four of us—that the weapon these four foolish women were calling a Lazy Dog bomb was not a Lazy Dog bomb at all. Well, that is the name by which the Vietnamese called it, and I have seen it given that name in a number of American publications, but perhaps the War Department is correct and the bomb in question is actually the same bomb by another name. I don't really care what its name is. I will describe it to you. It comes down in a long metal container. We saw a number of these containers in the museums I have spoken of—and yes, with American markings on them. Each container carries three hundred of these little bombs. Each bomb, as you can see, is about the size of a baseball. It contains explosive and when it explodes, it explodes out of the casing in which they have been imbedded hundreds of little steel pellets. You can see them afterwards, if you want. They look very much like ball bearings. They explode with great force over a large area, apparently the length of several football fields, and any people standing in the open in this area will get these things in them.

Now I trust that it occurs to you, as I describe this weapon, that it has little to do with hitting the "steel and concrete" which our government persists in saying is the only target we are interested in in the North. These little pellets can imbed themselves in steel or concrete—and we saw many examples of this—but they cannot knock anything of the sort down. They are very specifically and very ingeniously designed for the flesh. When we visited hospitals, the doctors explained to us—showing us many X rays and showing us also the long incisions in the bodies of patients—that it is terribly hard to locate these pellets in the body and terribly hard to extract them. A good many of the people we saw in the hospitals will never regain their health. For example, many of the children will always be paralyzed.

At this point I should remind you—as we kept reminding ourselves in Vietnam—that what we were seeing there in the North is really *nothing* compared to what we could see if we were to visit the hospitals of the South. Perhaps some of you have read a long article by Dr. Pepper in the January, 1967, issue of *Ramparts,* about what we are doing to the children of South Vietnam; or an article by Dr.Perry in the January *Redbook*, or an article by Martha Gellhorn in the January *Ladies Home Journal*—all three about what we are doing simply to the children of Vietnam. In the South we are doing it above all by napalm. Dr. Pepper estimates that for every guerilla we kill, we kill six civilians, and that four of these six civilians are children. He estimates that, to date, we have killed about a quarter of a million children, and that we have maimed—often unspeakably, with napalm—about three-quarters of a million children. And there are thousands and thousands of children we have left homeless, and orphaned, who are now wandering about that countryside or through the city streets, just trying to fend for themselves. This is just to mention the children.

We saw two napalm victims in Hanoi. I'll describe just one to you, a boy of about fourteen called Dan. He was a mild case, or he wouldn't have been able to make the hard trip from the South to the North for treatment. But he had had large areas of his arms and hands and legs and neck burned. He had been under treatment for about a year and the doctors had been able to give him a certain amount of help. They had been able to free the use of his limbs for him. Because when a person is burned by napalm his limbs can be literally melted together. By operations they had freed his arms from his side, and they had freed his fingers, which had melted together. He could now hold a pen in his hand, though clumsily. They didn't think, though, that they'd be able to do much to relieve the burning aching he still felt in those parts of his body which had been burned. And they didn't think they would be able to do much about the terrible itching of those areas—whenever there was the slightest motion of air.

We also saw in Hanoi a victim of the chemical spraying we do so much of in the South—which our government says is strictly for the purpose of removing the leaves from the trees so that our pilots can see better what they are doing, but which is also gravely affecting many people—and also of course animals, birds, fish. This was a doctor—who had been treating many people suffering very much from this spraying, and who had finally been affected himself after a particular raid. He, too, had been treated in the North for many months, and had been helped considerably, but his eyesight was very nearly gone, and his digestive system was permanently wrecked.

This is just, as I say, to remind you that in the South things are very, very much worse than what we are reporting about the North.

But from the North itself we came back with the painful conviction that our government is not simply bombing military targets, "steel and concrete," as it insists, but that it is waging a war of terror against the civilian population, in an attempt to force them to surrender—or, as our government would put it, to bring them to the peace table.

Two images of that trip I find particularly hard to forget. They haunt me especially for some reason as images of how little quarter we give in this war. One is of a little baby we saw in one of the hospitals in Hanoi. His name is Ngoc Lau. A pale, feeble little boy whose mother had been living in a country village not far from Hanoi until the day when the planes came and, as usual, dropped fragmentation bombs. One of the fragments from the bomb struck this woman in the hip. She was in her last month of pregnancy and when she was hit she collapsed and was rushed to the hospital. After about an hour she gave birth to the little boy whom we saw; and when the doctor lifted up the newborn baby in his hands, he saw to his surprise that there was a large bloodstain on his temple. A fragment from the bomb had pierced through even into this woman's womb and wounded her baby even in this shelter. The doctor was able to save the baby's life, but he is very frail and nervous and probably will not develop normally.

The other thing that I find it hardest to forget is one of the few things I will tell you about that I didn't actually see with my own eyes. But I saw photographs of it and even a long section of motion picture about it; and the doctor who told us the story, if he was not telling the truth, is one of the most consummate actors I have ever met. This is the story of a leper sanatorium—at Quynh Lap. It was too far from Hanoi for us to visit. It was by its very nature of course in an isolated spot, and furthermore the roads leading to it were narrow country roads—nothing that heavy military equipment could be moved over. And it was clearly marked on its roofs by red crosses. It was also an internationally known hospital, which cared for thousands of lepers. The Vietnamese were particularly proud of it. They had had many cures there. We were told that our planes hit the hospital, in a succession of different days, thirty-nine times in all—wrecking every one of its 160 large and small buildings. The doctors and nurses moved those lepers who had not been killed to nearby caves, and improvised temporary structures around those caves. And then, we were told, our planes returned and bombed and strafed the caves.

By then we had already hit a number of other hospitals, including a large TB hospital. The minister of health protested the bombing of the leper hospital, after the first raids, and you would think that if there was any misunderstanding on the part of our government as to what this place really was, it could have checked. If there is anyone in this audience who can persuade me that all this was a misunderstanding, I will be very grateful. I have not been able to persuade myself.

So we are waging war in Vietnam even against children; and we are waging war even against the sick and utterly helpless—against lepers. WHAT ARE WE DOING? It seems to me that Americans must begin to take a very hard look at themselves, and at the role we are playing in the world today.

I noticed some days ago among letters to the editors of *The New York Times,* a letter from one man among the many who are protesting our bombings of Vietnam. He quoted the *Columbia Encyclopaedia* about Guernica—which is, as most of you will remember, the Spanish city which was the first in which Franco's planes bombed civilians during the Civil War. The Encyclopaedia says of it that it became "the very symbol of Fascist brutality." Americans had better begin to ask themselves: What will our actions in Vietnam symbolize to future generations? What do they symbolize right now to people around the world?

Of course our government keeps assuring us that we are acting with restraint. And it is perfectly accurate in saying so, because we now have literally the capacity to kill off every single person in the world. So you can still say that we are acting with restraint in Vietnam. But we have already left Guernica far behind. We had better take a very hard look at what we have done to the people of Vietnam, in our restrained way. We had better take a hard look at what we are still capable of doing.

I want to talk a little about what it's been like to try to report on what I saw in Vietnam when I got back home. I'll start by quoting a few words from an editorial written about me in a Cape Cod newspaper (I live on Cape Cod)—and this is typical of many other things that have been written and said. The writer asked: "...How can Miss Deming be so ready to believe the worst about Americans?...We find it difficult to believe that Americans would conduct wholesale bombings against civilians, that American pilots with families at home would drop Lazy Dog bombs in a program of sheer terror. We just cannot believe American guys would do that."

I could remind the man who wrote that, of course, that it is much easier to do certain things at a distance—from the air. I have certainly yet to meet an American guy who would pick up a child in his hands and thrust that child into a fire and watch that child burning alive. But the frightening thing is that it is so very much easier to push a button, up in a plane, that releases napalm that literally does just that—burns children alive. I'll also have to say that I sympathize with the man who wrote those words. There were many times in Vietnam, seeing the things we saw, when everything in me wanted to cry out: this is not so! But there it was, in front of my eyes, and day after day, for eleven days.

One of the questions that I have been asked again and again is: "But did you actually see any American planes in the sky? And did you actually see any bombs falling?" We saw no American planes in the sky—though we saw one pilotless plane immediately after it had been shot down; and I can assure you that when the bombs were actually falling we were always in a bomb shelter. But when I gave this answer, a sharp gleam would enter the eye of my questioner and he would nod to himself emphatically—the implication being that if we had not actually seen the bombs falling through the air, then all that we had seen, all the wrecked schools and playgrounds and hospitals and churches and houses, all the samples of the bombs themselves, all the grieving people with their stories of the day the planes came, all the wounded in the hospitals—all this was simply a very elaborate Hollywood production fabricated by these cunning Orientals to dupe the four foolish American women.

As soon as we got home our government began to make a whole series of statements to discredit us. For example, one of the things it began to say was that all the damage to civilian areas we described could be explained in terms of damage caused by the Vietnamese's own antiaircraft—which could miss and then fall back. So we are supposed to believe, apparently, about a place like Phu Ly—which I described to you—that these same people who on the one hand could be infinitely cunning could on the other hand be infinitely stupid—clearly an inferior race—because they could day after day fire off antiaircraft which would miss and fall back, damaging their own buildings, and they could persist in this clumsily, day after day, until finally they had leveled an entire large town around themselves.

Well, especially after Harrison Salisbury—who was there at the time that we were—reported seeing deep bomb craters that could hardly be explained as the result of antiaircraft fire, the line from our government began to change. And whereas originally when they claimed that we bombed only "steel and concrete," they claimed that we we were able to do this with great accuracy, suddenly they were saying that it just wasn't that easy to hit a target. Misses, accidents, were almost bound to happen.

But I ask my government: Is it, then, by accident that again and again and again, in place after place after place, the Lazy Dog bomb is dropped—which is ineffectual against steel and concrete, but deadly effective against human flesh?

Everywhere I go, I find so many American people ready to accept without question our government's statements, and unwilling to believe our reports about what we are doing to the people of Vietnam. They refuse to believe that American guys would resort to terror, that our government would play the part of the bully. And I find this unwillingness to believe that we could be playing the bully very frightening. I am frightened that we Americans are on our way to becoming the *world's* bullies, all the while the majority of us confident in our hearts that we are a well-intentioned people and therefore incapable of atrocities. And I find this unwillingness to look at what we are doing particularly frightening because I find it again and again in conjunction with another mental block. That is the refusal to believe that we could possibly withdraw from this war. I am sure that you have all talked to people who say, "You're right, we never should have gone into Vietnam, but now that we are there, how could the powerful United States possibly withdraw?" So look what you have: in one and the same person you have the refusal to believe that we could be playing the part of the bully, and the refusal to believe that—given our tremendous power—we shouldn't really be able to expect to have our way. These two visions of ourselves, of course, are deeply contradictory—and in conjunction, I would say, particularly frightening—but few Americans are able to recognize the contradiction. And I beg Americans at this point to begin to try to look at themselves, to know themselves.

I think we stand at a very crucial moment in our history. We hold in our hands this unprecedented power—literally the power to destroy all life on this planet. And the temptations of great power are classic. The temptation to abuse it. Or the temptation to persist in its use even when we have lost all control of it. One man in the audience the other night made a point in this connection which I though very telling. That audience had been particularly troubled by my story about the leper sanitorium—unable to believe that this bombing had been intentional. The man made the point that even if one decided that certain terrible acts like this were unintended, were accidental—we were still responsible. We have to face the fact that he is entirely right. And Americans are now confronted by a very large question: Have we the spiritual strength to resist the temptation to abuse our power—or, if you will, to resist the temptation to persist in using it even when we are unable to control it? Or one could put the question in another way—and this is the way in which I would put it: Have the American people the spiritual strength to wrestle peacefully with their government, to wrestle with their leaders, if these leaders—as I certainly feel—are unable to resist such temptations?... [*Several pages of the essay have been cut here*]

For those of us who don't want to wage war on children, and don't want to wage war for the right—hardly an inalienable right—to determine for people thousands of miles from our country what kind of a society they are not going to build even if they want to, there are ways, as I've suggested, of struggling peacefully with our government about this: ways in the tradition of Gandhi, ways of noncooperation, or if you will, of the strike. We can say to our government, "Wage this war without us," knowing that if enough of us say that and act upon it, this war cannot be waged.

It cannot be waged without the money we pay our government in taxes, and we can refuse to pay these taxes. Hundreds and hundreds of Americans are beginning to refuse, and even more hundreds are now beginning to refuse at least to pay the 10 per cent tax added to the telephone bill which goes straight to pay for this war. We can, of course, refuse to buy government bonds, and if you have any you can turn them in. And of course this war cannot be waged without the materials of war, and we can refuse to work in the places that make the Lazy Dog bombs, and the helicopters, and the napalm; and we can boycott companies like Dow Chemical that make napalm and also make products like Saran Wrap. And certainly our scientists and engineers can refuse to invent these things and to "improve" upon them, as it is called—making, for example, stickier napalm. And I saw, just the other day, a sheet asking for signatures which says, "I promise not to buy a new car until this war is over, since General Motors and the other companies have so many war contracts."

Above all, this war cannot be waged without the young men whom our government orders to go over there to fight it, and those of us who are not young men can give much more support than we have even begun to give to those young men—and there are more and more of them—who hesitate to fight in Vietnam but who hesitate to *refuse* to fight because it is still a very lonely act to take. But the rest of us could give them the kind of support that would make it no longer a lonely act. In North Vietnam we learned of a group of women called Soldiers' Mothers. When there are soldiers in any town or village away from their homes, all women over fifty take it upon themselves to play the part of these soldiers' mothers. It seems to me that in this country we should have War Resisters' Mothers, or War Resisters' Families. The real families of war resisters are often embarrassed or ashamed and abandon these young men. We could become their families. We should make ourselves visible all over the country as groups ready to give every kind of support to these young men—all the way from writing them letters to attending their trials, to picketing for them, to offering to care for their dependents.

Don't forget the power of the strike. We literally could end this war.

I know that there are always people, when I make suggestions as drastic as this, who ask very sincerely if such actions wouldn't be disloyal. Well, I think they are profoundly the opposite. Because if you really feel your leaders are taking you down a road that is both ignoble and utterly reckless—which could even take us into the third and final world war—surely the role of loyalty is to try to prevent this. I would also ask you if our loyalty is not due primarily to the people of our country, and don't we owe loyalty to government only in so far as it serves the interests of the people? How does this war serve the interests of the American people? I feel very deeply that in waging it, our leaders are waging war not simply against the Vietnamese people but against the American people as well. It is wasting our resources over there—all the money that should be doing something about our cities, doing something about poverty, doing something about the pollution of our air and water. Above all, of course, it is sending to their death more and more of our young men—particularly from the poor and exploited among us. I would also ask you: Don't we owe loyalty not only to the people of our country but to people everywhere, and isn't this loyalty actually implicit in our Declaration of Independence—which doesn't say: "All Americans have certain rights"; it says very clearly, "All men are endowed with certain inalienable rights." Among these it happens to mention life. It seems to me that Americans these days stand in much too much awe of government, and much too little awe of that inalienable right of all men to their lives.

I ask you to consider whether we really even can still call our government a government by and for the people. I know it has never been completely that—it has never been government by and for the Negro people of this country, for example—but it seems to me that lately it has become government by and for fewer and fewer of us. The war, for example, is in the interest only of those few against whose unwarranted influence in government, President Eisenhower, surprisingly enough, warned us just before he retired—calling them the Military Industrial Complex. The crucial decisions in our lives—like the decisions about this war—are more and more made by these few men. The rest of us are simply blindly carrying out their will.* And I suggest that it is time—and long past time—that we began to *balk* at doing this. If we would balk—and begin to carry out a nonviolent campaign of noncooperation—we could not only literally end this war, but in the process we could begin to return this government to the hands of the people—where it is supposed to belong.

*See Editor's Note, page ix.

We Are All Part of
One Another

Published in Liberation, *May-June 1967.*

In other years when other individuals were singled out to receive this award*, it never seemed strange to me. But this year when I learned that I was being singled out, it suddenly did seem very strange to me. I asked myself why. It's not that I have any less ego than the next person. But knowing myself a little, I am very conscious that the actions I have taken for which, I assume, I am given this award, were all taken not only with other people but because of them. It seems strange to be standing here without them.

I think, for example, of the trip I took to Saigon last April—along with A.J. Muste and Brad Lyttle and Bill Davidon and Karl Meyer and Sherry Thurber. I remember very clearly the day on which the Call to volunteer for that project arrived in the mail. I had heard about the project for some months, and it had always seemed to me a particularly right and necessary project—to protest the war on the very spot where it was being waged. But it had never occurred to me for a moment to volunteer to be one of those to go. I remember the day the Call arrived. I read it and thought: "Wonderful! It's really going to happen, then!" (because there were a lot of people who had volunteered already). But I still didn't even pose the question to myself: Would I volunteer? The answer was so plain to me: I was much too scared to. But I wanted to be present at the meetings at which the project was discussed. I turned up at the first meeting and there was Mary Christiansen, who was one of the first to volunteer: and I went up to her and told her that I thought it was wonderful, that she had. And I asked her, "You're not frightened?" She said, "I hadn't really thought about that yet." I thought: That is really the correct order of priorities to give things—to think first about an action that is right to take, and to think later about coping with one's fears. And the moment she said what she did, by a familiar but mysterious process, everything was a little different for me, and for the first moment it occurred to me that I might be able to cope with my own fears.

*The Annual Peace Award of the War Resisters League

Then we sat down to the meeting. I particularly remember A.J.* at that meeting—with that extraordinary concentration he had on a particular situation and a particular action proposed to speak to the situation. Sitting next to him, I felt my own concentration on such an action sharpen, and my fears did begin to fall into second place. By the end of the meeting I said tentatively, not to put me down as a volunteer but to put me down as a possible volunteer.

I could tell very much the same kind of story about any of the other actions I have taken. I make a point of this not to be humble but because I think it touches us all. I know there are those among us who are more capable than others of acting on their own; but surely none of us acts quite alone— of and by himself. Surely all of us are nerved by one another, catch courage from one another. As I.F. Stone quoted at the Memorial for A.J., "We are all part of one another."

So I would like to talk a little more about some of the fears I experienced on that trip to Saigon. Because my fears didn't end, of course, when I found myself able to volunteer. And in each case these fears taught me again to recognize our interdependence.

Perhaps the most oppressive fears I felt were in the several days before we left this country. I remember being so hypnotized by the fear of being killed over there that, sitting talking with friends and family, I would realize again and again with a shock that I was hearing the sound of their voices but not hearing the words they were speaking. Then the evening we were to set off arrived and I met the rest of the group at the airline terminal—and the moment I walked up to them I suddenly didn't feel any more fear; I felt a very peculiar kind of joy. And we all seemed to be feeling it. We were all smiling at each other almost foolishly. Of course we could all be happy that we were finally acting, not brooding about it. And of course we all believed in what we were doing—which is a happy feeling. But there was something about setting out together—at least for me—that made it very much easier to feel the joy and not the fear of acting. One smiled at the next person with a kind of tentative happiness in acting, and when that person smiled back, the happiness was no longer tentative. This giving and taking of spirit—one *from* another and *to* another—involves a wonderful kind of mathematics. There are situations in which, as E.E. Cummings noted, 2 and 2 "is 5"—at least. Given this exchange, we are all of us more than ourselves.

Now I would like to talk about one other experience of fear. It is the experience, I think, through which I learned the most on that trip—with the exception of conversations with some of the Vietnamese we were fortunate enough to meet.

When we first arrived in Saigon I was uneasy in a way that was unfamiliar to me on such projects. Every project in which I had taken part before had

* A.J. Muste was a leading spirit in the radical pacifist movement. (BD)

been completely open—that is, our purposes had been frankly announced. In this project there was of necessity an element of secrecy: unless we postponed an announcement of our presence and our purpose until the end of our week there, we would have little chance of taking the action we wanted to take, and little chance of making first the many contacts with Vietnamese which might allow us to speak for them as well as for ourselves. But this meant that we would have to be guarded in encounters with strangers; and it was this that made me uncertain of myself. Because I had learned to rely above all in situations of danger on creating an atmosphere of friendliness about us. One could hardly count on this to prevent violence as if by magic, but it was the best deterrence we had, and sometimes a remarkable one. It is difficult to create an atmosphere of friendliness when one has to be secretive. So having learned to trust in myself by learning to open myself to the most direct human contact with others that was possible, I found it difficult now to summon up the right spirit on which to rely.

Some of the others on the project clearly had a similar problem. And everyone met the problem in a different way. There were those who still put the greatest emphasis on being friendly to everybody, and who were in the process somewhat indiscreet—for example, about revealing to strangers our attitude toward the war. There were others who put the emphasis on discretion and were in the process stiff with curious strangers—even to the point of making them angry. And what began to happen was that one team member would become alarmed at the first kind of action and another would become alarmed at the second. It was too easy for all of us in that situation to imagine encounters that would suddenly endanger us all. In short, we began in those first days to scare *each other*. What followed, of course, was that some began to wish that this person or that person had never come on the project. I could see this happening in other people and I could feel it in myself. As one pictured in imagination some encounter in which he or she would do just the thing that would be fatal, and one began to tremble, the simplest resolution was always to imagine the person who—supposedly—would do the wrong thing, just magically not there.

I remember at a certain point recognizing with a shock that *nothing* put us in such danger as precisely this relation to each other which I have been describing. If any of these imagined situations were to occur, to be concentrated on the futile wish that one or the other of my companions were not there, would hardly enable me to cope with it imaginatively. And if any of my companions sensed my fear of them, it would hardly help *them*. Instead of finding new spirit now, when we looked at each other, we would lose it, we would paralyze each other. I had learned on earlier projects to beware, when confronted by an *antagonist*, of letting myself panic. And I think one can define the state of panic precisely as that in which one tries to wish that other not there—instead of trying, persisting in trying to establish some kind of human contact with him, which could possibly, in the case of an antagonist, disarm him—and in the case of a companion, it occurred to me slowly now, help him to recover himself if he has made an error. It slowly occurred to me that while we were here, all of us were sure to make mistakes of one kind or another (and this would certainly include me) and the way to ensure that these mistakes would be fatal was to freeze toward one another.

Why have I talked at such length about this particular experience? I might add, before I answer my own question, that by the time we did announce our presence in Saigon and attempt to stage our protest, we were all again at relative ease with one another and again able, in the various moments of strain which followed, to borrow the extra courage from one another that we sometimes needed. But why have I talked so much about this particular experience of fear? It is because I feel very strongly that in the days ahead of us, unless a very great many of us move from words to acts—from words of dissent to acts of disobedience—we are going to have no effect at all upon our government's policy, no effect in halting the terrible momentum of this war. If we do become more bold, and therefore more effective, I think it is fair to predict that our government will, in turn, move more boldly to discourage us. And then if we do not all stand together, helping always *whomever* is singled out for punishment, our effectiveness will end. To stand together is going to be hard. Our movement is composed of all kinds of groups and all kinds of individuals. It is certain that many of us will make all kinds of mistakes. It will become very tempting to wish that this group or that group, this individual or that individual, were simply not among us. My particular plea is that we not surrender to this temptation. We must certainly be frank with each other when we disagree, but my plea is that we not begin to be afraid of any of us and, in a panic, try to wish any of us out of the picture. We will need every one of us. We are all part of one another.

It is, finally, on behalf of all those who are some part of me—and they are too many to name—that I accept this award.

On Revolution and Equilibrium

Published in Liberation, *February 1968.*

"What we want to do is to go forward all the time...in the company of all men."
"But can we escape becoming dizzy?"
Frantz Fanon in The Wretched of the Earth

"Do you want to remain pure? Is that it?" a black man asked me, during an argument about nonviolence. It is not possible to act at all and to remain pure; and that is not what I want, when I commit myself to the nonviolent discipline. There are people who are struggling to change conditions that they find intolerable, trying to find new lives; in the words of Frantz Fanon in *The Wretched of the Earth,* they want to "set afoot a new man." That is what I want, too; and I have no wish to be assigned, as it were, separate quarters from those who are struggling in a way different from mine—segregated from my companions rather as, several years ago in Birmingham at the end of a demonstration, I found myself segregated in the very much cleaner and airier white section of the jail. I stand with all who say of present conditions that they do not allow men to be fully human and so they must be changed—all who not only say this but are ready to act.

At a recent conference about the directions the American Left should take, a socialist challenged me: "Can you call degrading the violence used by the oppressed to throw off oppression?" When one is confronted with what Russell Johnson calls accurately "The violence of the *status quo*"—conditions which are damaging, even murderous, to very many who must live within them—it is degrading for all to allow such conditions to persist. And if the individuals who can find the courage to bring about change see no way in which it can be done without employing violence on their part—a very much lesser violence, they feel, than the violence to which they will put an end—I do not feel that I can judge them. The judgments I make are not judgments upon men but upon the means open to us—upon the promise these means of action hold or withhold. The living question is: What are the best means for changing our lives—for really changing them?

The very men who speak of the necessity of violence, if change is to be accomplished, are the first, often, to acknowledge the toll it exacts among those who use it—as well as those it is used against. Frantz Fanon has a chapter in *The Wretched of the Earth* entitled "Colonial War and Mental Disorders" and in it he writes, "We are forever pursued by our actions." After describing, among other painful disorders, those suffered by an Algerian terrorist—who made friends among the French after the war and then wondered with anguish whether any of the men he had killed had been men like these—he comments, "It was what might be called an attack of vertigo." Then he asks a poignant question: "But can we escape becoming dizzy? And who can affirm that vertigo does not haunt the whole of existence?"

"Vertigo"—here is a word, I think, much more relevant to the subject of revolutionary action than the word "purity." No, it is not that I want to remain pure; it is that I want to escape becoming dizzy. And here is exactly the argument of my essay: we can escape it. Not absolutely, of course; but we can escape vertigo in the drastic sense. It is my stubborn faith that if, as revolutionaries, we will wage battle without violence, we can remain very much more in control—of our own selves, of the responses to us which our adversaries make, of the battle as it proceeds, and of the future we hope will issue from it.

The future—by whom will it be built? By all those whom the struggle has touched and marked. And so the question of how it marks them is not irrelevant. The future will be built even, in part, by those who have fought on the losing side. If it is a colonial struggle, of course, a good many of the adversaries can be expected to leave at the end of a successful revolution; but if it is a civil struggle, those who have been defeated, too, will at least help to make the new society what it is. How will the struggle have touched them? How will it have touched the victors?

Carl Oglesby, in *Containment and Change,* quotes a Brazilian guerilla: "We are in dead earnest. At stake is the humanity of man." Then he asks, "How can ordinary men be at once warm enough to want what revolutionaries say they want [humanity], cold enough to do without remorse what they are capable of doing [cutting throats], and poised enough in the turbulence of their lives to keep the aspiration and the act both integrated and distinct? How is it that one of these passions does not invade and devour the other?" Yes—the question is one of equilibrium. How does one manage to keep it?

Oglesby would seem to answer that, generally speaking, one cannot expect the rebel to have the poise he describes. "He is an irresponsible man whose irresponsibility has been decreed by others. . . . He has no real views about the future. . . is not by *type* a Lenin, a Mao, a Castro. . . . His motivating vision of change is at root a vision of something absent—not of something that *will* be there...a missing landlord, a missing mine owner, a missing sheriff...." Ultimately, says Oglesby, he must *become* responsible. But how? It is in the midst of the struggle that he must at least begin to be, isn't it? And so the very means by which we struggle, and their tendency either to give us poise or to leave us dizzy, is surely, again, relevant.

I think of the words with which Fanon opens the final chapter of *The Wretched of the Earth:* "Come then, comrades; it would be as well to decide at once to change our ways." I quote Fanon often—because he is eloquent, but also because he is quoted repeatedly these days by those who plead the need for violence. It is my conviction that he can be quoted as well to plead for nonviolence. It is true that he declares: "From birth it is clear...that this narrow world, strewn with prohibitions, can only be called in question by absolute violence." But I ask all those who are readers of Fanon to make an experiment: Every time you find the word "violence" in his pages, substitute for it the phrase "radical and uncompromising action." I contend that with the exception of a very few passages this substitution can be made, and that the action he calls for could just as well be nonviolent action.

He writes, for example: "Violence alone, violence committed by the people, violence organized and educated by its leaders, makes it possible for the masses to understand social truths and gives the key to them. Without that struggle, without that knowledge of the practice of action, there's nothing but a fancy-dress parade...a few reforms at the top...and down there at the bottom an undivided mass...endlessly marking time." "Knowledge of the practice of action"—*that* is what Fanon sees to be absolutely necessary, to develop in the masses of people an understanding of social truths, accomplish that "work of clarification," "demystification," "enlightening of consciousness" which is the recurring and the deepest theme of his book. This action could be nonviolent action; it could very much better be nonviolent action—if only that action is bold enough.

Here is Fanon as he argues the necessity for "mere rebellion"—which Oglesby has described—to become true revolution: "Racialism and hatred and resentment—'a legitimate desire for revenge'—cannot sustain a war of liberation. Those lightning flashes of consciousness which fling the body into stormy paths or which throw it into an almost pathological trance where the face of the other beckons me on to giddiness, where my blood calls for the blood of the other...that intense emotion of the first few hours falls to pieces if it is left to feed on its own substance.... You'll never overthrow the terrible enemy machine, and you won't change human beings if you forget to raise the standard of consciousness of the rank-and-file."

The task involves the enlightening of consciousness. But violence "beckons me on to giddiness." I repeat Fanon's words: "It would be as well to decide

at once to change our ways." Another man with whom I was arguing the
other day declared to me, "You can't turn the clock back now to
nonviolence!" Turn the clock back? The clock has been turned to violence
all down through history. Resort to violence hardly marks a move forward.
It is nonviolence which is in the process of invention, if only people would
not stop short in that experiment. Fanon again: "If we want humanity to
advance a step further, if we want to bring it up to a different level than
that which Europe has shown it, then we must invent and we must make
discoveries." It is for that spirit of invention that I plead. And again I would
like to ask something of all readers of Fanon. Turn to that last chapter of
The Wretched of the Earth and read it again. Is he not groping here visibly
for a way that departs from violence?

He writes, "We today can do everything, so long as we do not imitate
Europe." And earlier in the book he has reported, "The argument the native
chooses has been furnished by the settler. . . . The native now affirms that
the colonialist understands nothing but force." He writes, "We must leave
our dreams. . . ." And earlier he has written, "The native is an oppressed
person whose permanent dream is to become the persecutor." He writes,
"Leave this Europe where they are never done talking of man, yet murder
men everywhere they find them, at the corner of every one of their own streets,
in all the corners of the globe. . . . Europe has . . . set her face against all
solicitude and all tenderness. . . . So, my brother, how is it that we do not
understand that we have better things to do than to follow that same
Europe. . . When I search for Man in the technique and the style of Europe,
I see only a succession of negations of man, and an avalanche of
murders. . . . Let us combine our muscles and our brains in a new direction.
Let us try to create the whole man, whom Europe has been incapable of
bringing to triumphant birth. All the elements of a solution. . . have, at
different times, existed in European thought. But the action of European
men has not carried out the mission which fell to them. We must try to set
afoot a new man." And he writes, "It is simply a very concrete question
of not dragging men toward mutilation. . . . The pretext of catching up must
not be used to push men around, to tear him away from himself or from
his privacy, to break and kill him. No, we do not want to catch up with
anyone. What we want to do is to go forward all the time, night and day,
in the company of Man, in the company of all men."

But how in the company of all men if we are willing to kill? In the passages
I have quoted does Fanon not warn us again and again against murder, warn
us that murder cannot possibly bring to birth the new man—that it was
precisely Europe's propensity for murder that kept her from carrying out
the mission we now inherit? What really but radical nonviolence is he here
straining to be able to imagine? We must "vomit up" the values of Europe,

he has written. Is it not above all the value that Europe and America have put upon violence that we must vomit up? He writes, "It is simply a very concrete question of not dragging men toward mutilation." Yes, very concrete, I urge, because it comes down to the means by which we struggle, comes down to a choice of *which* "practice of action" we are going to study.

At this point suddenly I can hear in my head many voices interrupting me. They all say: "Who among us likes violence? But nonviolence has been tried." It has *not* been tried. We have hardly begun to try it. The people who dismiss it now as irrelevant do not understand what it could be. And, again, they especially do not understand the very much greater control over events that they could find if they would put this "practice of action," rather than violence, to a real test.

What most people are saying just now of course is that nonviolence gives us no control at all over events. "After years of this," says Stokely Carmichael, "we are at almost the same point." Floyd McKissick expresses the same disillusion: all the nonviolent campaigns have accomplished essentially nothing for black people. They have served to integrate a token few into American society. Even those few cannot be said to have been absorbed into the mainstream; they still are not allowed to forget the color of their skins. And the great majority of black people are actually worse off than before. He declares, with reason, "We are concerned about the aspirations of the 90 per cent down there"—those of whom Fanon spoke, the many "endlessly marking time."

I won't try to pretend that progress has been made that has not been made. Though I would add to the picture these two men and others paint that there is one sense in which things hardly can be said to be at the same point still. If one speaks of psychological forces that will make a difference—the determination of black people not to accept their situation any longer, the determination of some white people not to accept it either, and a consciousness on the part of other white people that changes are bound to come now, doubts about their ability to prevent them—in these terms all has been in constant motion. And these terms—Fanon for one would stress—are hardly unimportant. Literally, yes, one can speak of gains that seem to mock those who have nearly exhausted themselves in the struggle for them. But I think one has to ask certain questions. Have gains been slight because nonviolent tactics were the wrong tactics to employ—or did many of those leading the battle underestimate the difficulties of the terrain before them? Did they lack at the start a sufficiently radical vision? Can those who have now turned from reliance upon nonviolence say surely that resort to violence over those same years would have brought greater gains?

There are those who are implying this now. One observer who implies it strongly is Andrew Kopkind, writing in the *The New York Review of Books* in August about the uprisings in the ghettos. He writes, "Martin Luther King and the 'leaders' who appealed for nonviolence, CORE, the black politicians, the old S.N.C.C. *are all* beside the point. Where the point is is in the streets....The insurrections of July have done what everyone in America for thirty years has thought impossible; mass action has convulsed the society and brought smooth government to a halt." He itemizes with awe: they caused tanks to rumble through the heart of the nation's biggest cities, brought out soldiers by the thousands, destroyed billions of dollars worth of property. This violence (or as Dave Dellinger better names it, this counterviolence of the victimized) certainly called out the troops. One thing violence can be counted on to do is bring the antagonist forth in battle dress. The question that hasn't been answered yet is: Did this gain the rebels an advantage? It gained them many casualties. The powers-that-be paid their price, too, as Kopkind points out. But it is one thing to be able to state the price the antagonist paid, another to be able to count your own real gains. Kopkind gives us the heady sense of an encounter really joined at last, of battle lines drawn. But in the days of Birmingham, too, people had the excited sense of an engagement entered. Kopkind himself grants, "It is at once obvious that the period of greatest danger is just beginning."

I have slighted, however, one point that he is making, and a very central point: "Poor blacks," he writes, "have stolen the center stage from the liberal elites...their actions indict the very legitimacy of [the] government." Yes, this is a fact not to overlook: the people of the ghettos have thrown down a challenge to government that is radical. But Kopkind is writing about two things: the offering of radical challenge and resort to violence. And he writes clearly as though he assumes that such a challenge can only be offered violently. It is with this assumption that I argue.

It is an assumption many share. Carl Oglesby seems to share it. In *Containment and Change* he criticizes "the politics of the appeal to higher power...the same thing as prayer...a main assumption of which is that [the higher power] is not bad, only misinformed." He appears to see all nonviolent action as covered by this definition. "This way of thinking brought the peasants and priests to their massacre at Kremlin Square in 1905....It rationalized the 1963 March on Washington for Jobs and Freedom. The Freedom Rides, the nonviolent sit-ins, and the various Deep South marches were rooted in the same belief: that there was indeed a higher power which was responsive and decent....The Vietnam war demonstrations are no different....The main idea has always been to persuade higher authority...to do something. Far from calling higher authority into question, these demonstrations actually dramatize and even exaggerate its power."

He goes on then to describe how the "whimsical" hopes that are entertained about the powerful evaporate: "Sometimes mass-based secular prayer has resulted in change. But more often it has only shown the victim-petitioner that the problem is graver and change harder to get than [he] had imagined....It turns out that the powerful know perfectly well who their victims are...and that they have no intention of changing anything. This recognition is momentous, no doubt the spiritual low point of the emergent revolutionary's education. He finds that the enemy is not a few men but a whole system whose agents saturate the society....He is diverted by a most realistic despair. But this despair contains within itself the omen of that final reconstitution of the spirit which will prepare [him]...for the shift to insurgency, rebellion, revolution....At the heart of his despair lies the new certainty that there will be no change which he does not produce by himself.''

With this description I do not argue at all. It is a very accurate description of the education those protesting in this country have been receiving. May more and more read the lesson. I argue with the contention that nonviolent action can only be prayerful action—must by its nature remain naive. Too often in the past it has confined itself to petition, but there is no need for it to do so—especially now that so many have learned "change [is] harder to get than they had imagined." As Kopkind writes, "All that has come until now is prologue." But this does not mean that our alternatives have suddenly been reduced. There have always been those in the nonviolent movement who called for radical action. The pressure that nonviolent moves could put upon those who are opposing change, the power that could be exerted this way, has yet to be tested.

I have introduced the word "power" deliberately. When the slogan "Black Power" was first taken up, the statements immediately issued, both for and against it, all seemed to imply that "power" was a word inconsistent with a faith in nonviolence. This was of course the position taken by Stokely Carmichael: "We had to work for power because this country does not function by morality, love and nonviolence, but by power. For too many years, black Americans marched and had their heads broken and got shot. They were saying to the country, 'Look, you guys are supposed to be nice guys and we are only going to do what we are supposed to do. Why...don't you give us what we ask?'...We demonstrated from a position of weakness. We cannot be expected any longer to march and have our heads broken in order to say to whites: Come on, you're nice guys. For you are not nice guys. We have found you out."

Carmichael gives us the humble appeal to conscience on the one hand, the resort to power on the other. If the choice were really this, anyone who wanted change would certainly have to abandon nonviolent action. For as Bradford Lyttle comments in a paper on Black Power, no, most people are not nice guys. "It isn't necessary to be hit over the head to learn this....Some Christians call the un-niceness of people 'original sin.' It's Freud's 'ego.'

Naturalist Konrad Lorenz studies it as aggressiveness and argues convincingly that it's instinctive with men. Whatever the un-niceness may be, it is part of all of us, and our job is to minimize it.''

The trouble is that advocates of nonviolence themselves often write in terms that seem to corroborate the picture Carmichael paints. When they actually engage in direct action, they pay great attention to other than moral pressures that can be and have to be placed on those with whom they are struggling. But on paper they tend again and again to stress only the appeal that can be made to conscience. Bradford, in his paper on Black Power, notes: "Carmichael's vision isn't limited to Negroes. Machiavelli had it:...'A man who wishes to make a profession of goodness in everything must necessarily come to grief among so many who are not good. Therefore it is necessary...to learn how not to be good.' '' Then he pleads that to put one's faith in coercive power is tragic, and his argument is "Throughout history, those who have most deeply touched the hearts of hardened men have been the ones who chose not to defend themselves with violence.'' He, too, seems here to pose a narrow choice: resort to power (learning how not to be good) or appeal to conscience (learning, Carmichael would put it, to do only what we are supposed to do).

But the choice is very much wider than this (as Bradford of course knows); and the distinctions that seem to have been set up here are unreal. To resort to power one need not be violent,* and to speak to conscience one need not be meek. The most effective action *both* resorts to power *and* engages conscience. Nonviolent action does not have to beg others to "be nice." It can in effect force them to consult their consciences—or to pretend to have them. Nor does it have to petition those in power to do something about a situation. It can face the authorities with a new fact and say: Accept this new situation which *we* have created.

If people doubt that there is power in nonviolence, I am afraid that it is due in part to the fact that those of us who believe in it have yet to find for ourselves an adequate vocabulary. The leaflets we pass out tend to speak too easily about love and truth—and suggest that we hope to move men solely by being loving and truthful. The words do describe our method in a kind of shorthand. But who can read the shorthand? It is easy enough to recommend "love." How many, even among those who like to use the word, can literally feel love for a harsh opponent—not merely pretending to while concealing from themselves their own deepest feelings? What *is* possible is

---

* Although those in the Movement who issued critical statements against use of the slogan "Black Power" seemed almost always to imply that "power" was an improper word, I couldn't help noticing that just that word had a way of slipping into their own publicity releases—an S.C.L.C. release, for example, repudiating the slogan but speaking the next moment of the "political power" they sought through pushing voter registration. (BD)

to act toward another human being on the assumption that all men's lives are of value, that there is something about any man to be loved, whether one can *feel* love for him or not.* It happens that, if one does act on this assumption, it gives one much greater poise in the situation. It is easy enough to speak about truth; but we had better spell out how, in battle, we rely upon the truth. It is not simply that we pay our antagonist the human courtesy of not lying to him. We insist upon telling him truths he doesn't want to hear—telling what seems to us the truth about the injustice he commits. Words are not enough here. Gandhi's term for nonviolent action was "satyagraha"—which can be translated as "clinging to the truth." What is needed is this—to *cling* to the truth as one sees it. And one has to cling with one's entire weight. One doesn't simply say, "I have a right to sit here," but acts out that truth—and sits here. One doesn't just say, "If we are customers in this store, it's wrong that we're never hired here," but refuses to be a customer any longer. One doesn't just say, "I don't believe in this war," but refuses to put on a uniform. One doesn't just say, "The use of napalm is atrocious," but refuses to pay for it by refusing to pay one's taxes. And so on and so on. One brings what economic weight one has to bear, what political, social, psychological, what physical weight. There is a good deal more involved here than a moral appeal. It should be acknowledged both by those who argue against nonviolence and those who argue for it that we, too, rely upon force.

If greater gains have not been won by nonviolent action it is because most of those trying it have, quite as Oglesby charges, expected too much from "the powerful"; and so, I would add, they have stopped short of really exercising their peculiar powers—those powers one discovers when one refuses any longer simply to do another's will. They have stopped far too short not only of widespread nonviolent disruption but of that form of noncooperation which is assertive, constructive—that confronts those who are "running everything" with independent activity, particularly independent economic activity. There is leverage for change here that has scarcely begun to be applied.

To refuse one's cooperation is to exert force. One can, in fact, exert so very much force in this way that many people will always be quick to call noncooperators violent. How, then, does one distinguish nonviolent from violent action? It is not that it abstains from force, to rely simply upon moral pressure. It resorts even to what can only be called physical force—when, for example, we sit down and refuse to move, and we force others to cope

*Sometimes, if one disciplines oneself to act upon this assumption, the feeling itself of love for one's enemy enters one, taking one by surprise—a kind of grace. Some readers may ask: Why should one want to feel love for one's enemy? But I note that Fanon in *Black Skin, White Masks* writes, "I, the man of color, want only this:...That it may be possible for me to discover and to love man, wherever he may be." (BD) somehow with all these bodies. The distinction to make is simply that those committed to a nonviolent discipline refuse to injure the antagonist. Of course if nonviolent action is as bold as it must be in any real battle for change, some at least of those resisting the change are bound to *feel* that injury has been done them. For they feel it as injury to be shaken out of the accustomed pattern of their lives. The distinction remains a real one. Perhaps there is another way it could be put. The man who acts violently forces another to do *his* will—in Fanon's words, he tears the other away from himself, pushes him around, often willing to break him, kill him. The man who acts nonviolently insists upon acting out his *own* will, refuses to act another's— but in this way, only, exerts force upon the other, not tearing him away from himself but tearing from him only that which is not properly his own, the strength which has been loaned to him by all those who have been giving him obedience.

But the distinction I have just made is a little too neat. In almost any serious nonviolent struggle, one has to resort to obstructive action. When we block access to buildings, block traffic, block shipments, it can be charged that we go a little further than refusing obedience and impose upon the freedom of action of others. There is some justice to the charge. I nevertheless think it appropriate to speak of nonviolent obstruction, and I would revert to my original description as the definitive one: the person committed to nonviolent action refuses to injure the antagonist. It is quite possible to frustrate another's action without doing him injury.* And some freedoms are basic freedoms, some are not. To impose upon another man's freedom to kill, or his freedom to help to kill, to recruit to kill, is not to violate his person in a fundamental way.

But I can imagine the impatience of some of my readers with these various scruples. What, they might say, has this to do with fighting battles—battles which are in dead earnest? How can we hope to put any real pressure upon an adversary for whom we show such concern?

This is the heart of my argument: We can put *more* pressure on the antagonist for whom we show human concern. It is precisely solicitude for his person *in combination with* a stubborn interference with his actions that can give us a very special degree of control (precisely in our acting both with love, if you will—in the sense that we respect his human rights—and truthfulness, in the sense that we act our fully our objections to his violating *our* rights). We put upon him two pressures—the pressure of our defiance

---

* It is possible, but not always simple. When we stage an act of massive obstruction in a city, for example, there is always the risk that we will prevent some emergency call from being answered—prevent a doctor's car from getting through, perhaps. One has obviously to anticipate such situations and be ready to improvise answers to the human problems raised. (BD)

of him and the pressure of our respect for his life—and it happens that in combination these two pressures are uniquely effective.

One effect gained is to "raise the level of consciousness" for those engaged in the struggle—those on both sides. Because the human rights of the adversary are respected, though his actions, his official policies are not, the focus of attention becomes those actions, those policies, and their true nature. The issue cannot be avoided. The antagonist cannot take the interference with his actions personally, because his person is not threatened, and he is forced to begin to acknowledge the reality of the grievance against him. And those in rebellion—committed to the discipline of respect for all men's lives, and enabled by this discipline to avoid that "trance" Fanon describes, "where the face of the other beckons me on to giddiness," are enabled to see more and more clearly that (as Oglesby says) "the enemy is not a few men but a whole system," and to study that system.

The more the real issues are dramatized, and the struggle raised above the personal, the more control those in nonviolent rebellion begin to gain over their adversary. For they are able at one and the same time to disrupt everything for him, making it impossible for him to operate within the system as usual, and to temper his response to this, making it impossible for him simply to strike back without thought and with all his strength. They have as it were two hands upon him—the one calming him, making him ask questions, as the other makes him move.

In any violent struggle one can expect the violence to escalate. It does so automatically, neither side being really able to regulate the process at will. The classic acknowledgment of this fact was made by President Kennedy when he saluted Premier Khrushchev for withdrawing nuclear missiles from Cuba. "I welcome this message," he said, because "developments were approaching a point where events could have become unmanageable." In nonviolent struggle, the violence used against one may mount for a while (indeed, if one is bold in one's rebellion, it is bound to do so), but the escalation is no longer automatic; with the refusal of one side to retaliate, the mainspring of the automaton has been snapped and one can count on reaching a point where de-escalation begins. One can count, that is, in the long run, on receiving far fewer casualties.

Nothing is more certain than this and yet, curiously, nothing is less obvious. A very common view is that nonviolent struggle is suicidal. This is, for example, Andrew Kopkind's view: "Turn-the-other-cheek was always a personal standard, not a general rule: people can commit suicide but peoples cannot. Morality, like politics, starts at the barrel of a gun." (A surprising sentence, but by morality he means, no doubt, the assertion of one's rights.) The contention that nonviolent struggle is suicidal hardly stands up under examination. Which rebels suffered more casualties—those who, under Gandhi, managed to throw the British out of India or the so-called Mau Mau who struggled by violence to throw the British out of Kenya? The British were certainly not "nice guys" in their response to the Gandhians. They, and the Indian troops who obeyed their orders, beat thousands of unarmed people, shot and killed hundreds. In the Amritsar Massacre, for example, they fired into an unarmed crowd that was trapped in a spot where no one could escape and killed 379 people, wounding many more. There was a limit, nevertheless, to the violence they could justify to themselves—or felt they could justify to the world. Watching any nonviolent struggle, it is always startling to learn how long it can take the antagonist to set such limits; but he finally does feel constrained to set them—especially if his actions are well publicized. In Kenya, where the British could cite as provocation the violence used against them, they hardly felt constrained to set any limits at all on their actions, and they adopted tactics very similar to those the Americans are using today against the Vietnamese. In the struggle for independence, many thousands of Africans fighting in the forest and many thousands of their supporters and sympathizers in the reserves were killed. Many were also tortured.*

One can, as I say, be certain if one adopts the discipline of non-violence that in the long run one will receive fewer casualties. And yet very few people are able to see that this is so. It is worth examining the reasons why the obvious remains unacknowledged. Several things, I think, blind people to the plain truth.

First, something seems wrong to most people engaged in struggle when they see more people hurt on their own side than on the other side. They are used to reading this as an indication of defeat, and a complete mental readjustment is required of them. Within the new terms of struggle, victory has nothing to do with their being able to give more punishment than they take (quite the reverse); it has to do simple with being able, finally, to make the other move. Again, the real issue is kept in focus. Vengeance is not the point; change is. But the trouble is that in most men's minds the thought of victory and the thought of punishing the enemy coincide. If they are suffering casualties and the enemy is not, they fail to recognize that they are suffering *fewer* casualties than they would be if they turned to violence.

Actually, something seems wrong to many people, I think, when—in non-violent struggle—they receive any casualties at all. They feel that they are not hurting anybody, then they shouldn't get hurt themselves. (They shouldn't. But it is not only in nonviolent battle that the innocent suffer.) It is an intriguing psychological fact that when the ghetto uprisings provoked the government into bringing out troops and tanks—and killing many black people, most of them onlookers—observers like Kopkind decided that the action had been remarkably effective, citing as proof precisely the violence of the govern-

* see *Mau Mau from Within* by Barnett and Njama. (BD)

ment's response. But when James Meredith* was shot, just for example, any number of observers editorialized: "See, nonviolence doesn't work." Those who have this reaction overlook the fact that nonviolent battle is still battle, and in battle of whatever kind, people do get hurt. If personal safety had been Meredith's main concern, he could, as the saying goes, have stayed at home.

Battle of any kind provokes a violent response—because those who have power are not going to give it up voluntarily. But there is simply no question that—in any long run—violent battle provokes a more violent response and brings greater casualties. Men tend not to think in long-run terms, of course; they tend to think in terms of isolated moments. There will always be such moments that one can cite, in which a particular man might have been safer if he had been armed. If Meredith had been carrying a loaded pistol, he might well have shot his assailant before the man shot him. (He might also well have been ambushed by still more men.) Whatever one can say about overall statistics, some men will always *feel* safer when armed—each able to imagine himself the one among many who would always shoot first.

To recognize that men have greater, not less control in the situation when they have committed themselves to nonviolence requires a drastic readjustment of vision. And this means taking both a long-range view of the field and a very much cooler, more objective one. Nonviolence can inhibit the ability of the antagonist to hit back. (If the genius of guerilla warfare is to make it impossible for the other side really to exploit its superior brute force, nonviolence can be said to carry this even further.) And there is another sense in which it gives one greater leverage—enabling one both to put pressure upon the antagonist and to modulate his response to that pressure. In violent battle the effort is to demoralize the enemy, to so frighten him that he will surrender. The risk is that desperation and resentment will make him go on resisting when it is no longer even in his own interest. He has been driven beyond reason. In nonviolent struggle the effort is of quite a different nature. One doesn't try to frighten the other. One tries to undo him—tries, in the current idiom, to "blow his mind"—only in the sense that one tries to shake him out of former attitudes and force him to appraise the situation now in a way that takes into consideration your needs as well as his. One is able to do this—able in a real sense to change his mind (rather than to drive him out of it)—precisely because one reassures him about his personal safety all the time that one keeps disrupting the order of things that he has known to date. When—under your constant pressure—it becomes to his own interest to adapt himself to change, he is able to do so. Fear for himself does not prevent him. In this sense a liberation movement that is nonviolent sets the oppressor free as well as the oppressed.

* First Black student at University of Mississippi (1962); in 1966, began a 200-mile voter registration walk from Memphis to Jackson, was ambushed and shot in the back. (JM)

The most common charge leveled against nonviolence is that it counts upon touching the heart of an adversary—who is more than likely to be stony of heart. His heart, his conscience need not be touched. His mind has been. The point is that you prevent him from reacting out of fear—in mindless reflex action. You also prevent him from being able to justify to others certain kinds of actions that he would like to take against you—and may for a while attempt to take. Here one can speak of still another sense in which nonviolence gives one greater control. If the antagonist *is* unjustifiably harsh in his countermeasures, and continues to be, one will slowly win away from him allies and supporters—some of them having consciences more active than his perhaps; or perhaps all of them simply caring about presenting a certain image, caring for one reason or another about public relations. An adversary might seem to be immovable. One could nevertheless move him finally by taking away from him the props of his power—those men upon whose support he depends. The special genius of nonviolence is that it can draw to our side not only natural allies—who are enabled gradually to recognize that they are allies because in confrontation with us their minds are not blurred by fear but challenged (and they begin to refuse orders, as several soldiers did in October at the Pentagon).* Even beyond this, it can move to act on our behalf elements in society who have no such natural inclination. When the Quebec to Guantanamo walkers were fasting in jail in Albany, Georgia, the men who finally put most pressure upon the authorities to release them and let them walk through town were clergymen not at all sympathetic either to the walkers as individuals or to the message on their signs and leaflets. Nonviolent tactics can move into action on our behalf men not naturally inclined to act for us; whereas violent tactics draw into actions that do us harm men for whom it is not at all natural to act against us. A painful example of this was Martin Luther King's act of declaring that the authorities were right in calling out troops to deal with the ghetto uprisings. John Gerassi provided another example in a talk I heard him give about revolutionary prospects in Latin America. He told how a plan on the part of a rebel group to gain support among the people by assassinating policemen backfired—because every slain policeman in that society of very large families had so many relatives, all unable to see the death as a political act that might help them, able to see it only as a personal loss. Violence makes men "dizzy"; it disturbs the vision, makes them see only their own immediate losses and fear of losses. Any widespread resort to violence in this country by those seeking change could produce such vertigo among the population at large that the authorities would be sure to be given more and more liberty to take repressive measures—in the name of "Order."

* refers to a major demonstration against the war in Vietnam. (JM)

Some readers might comment that such a development would be educational, for the underlying nature of the society would then stand revealed; and it is necessary to know the enemy. But it is necessary, too, to know that one has a certain power to affect those who stand against us. It would be easy enough to know the worst about them—by acting in a way that allowed them to behave toward us in the worst way that they could. It is more practical, even if it is more difficult, to act in a way that prevents this. If it is important not to be naive about their capacity for doing us harm, it is just as important not to be blind to our own capacity for moderating their action. In histories of the Chinese and Cuban revolutions, there are many accounts of generosity shown by the rebels toward enemy troops— resulting in widespread recruitment from among those troops. It proved very practical to act on the assumption that not all among them need be labeled permanently "enemy." Those engaged in nonviolent battle simply act on this assumption in the boldest degree. They declare, in the words of the Vietnamese Buddhist Thich Nhat Hanh—words that are startling and sound at first naive: "No men are our enemies." By this we do not mean that we think no men will try to destroy us; or that we overlook the fact that men from certain sections of the society are above all likely to try it. We mean, first, of course, that we are committed to try not to destroy them; but we mean furthermore that there is a working chance—if we do refuse to threaten them personally as we struggle with them—that in certain instances at least some of them may be willing to accommodate themselves to the pressure we put on them to change, and so both they and we may be liberated from the state of enmity. We mean that we refuse to cut ourselves off from them in any ultimate human sense—counting it as both decent and practical to do so.

I have been reading William Hinton's *Fanshen: A Documentary of Revolution in a Chinese Village,* and I have been struck by how many times in the course of his story he reports a decision taken by the revolutionary leaders that greater humanity shown this group or that group will advance the revolution. There is, for example, a decision at one point to be more lenient toward counterrevolutionary suspects among Catholic peasants. "They could never be won if they were isolated and discriminated against. They had to be drawn into full participation." In one dramatic instance it is decided that the attack on middle peasants has been overdone—that the land of many of these families has been wrongly expropriated, and that they must be reclassified as friends rather than enemies of the revolution. "We must make clear to them that they have their...rights." Because of this decision, too, things improved, the revolution gained momentum. The decisions which he reports are for the most part taken "to enlarge the united front of the people and to isolate as popular enemies only those diehard elements who could not possibly be mobilized to support a 'land-to-the-tiller' policy." One of the leaders explains, "In proposing any basic social change. . .revolutionaries had to decide who should be brought together and who isolated, who should be called a friend and who an enemy." Experience seemed always to be showing that the more people who were called friends, the better things went. I noted that as time went on leniency began to be advised even toward the gentry and the landlords; it was decided that here, too, the attacks had been at first overdone. "Families cannot be driven from house and home forever." As one leader put it: "We have to show everyone a way out."

This is of course just what nonviolence teaches—not to be naive about the fact that some men more than others will see it as in their interest to try to destroy us, and will often persist and persist in trying to; but to recognize that they never can see it in their interest finally to accommodate themselves to the changes we are forcing unless we give them the liberty to do so. And they will only believe that we offer this liberty, only be able to imagine new lives for themselves, if we have refused to threaten them with any personal injury.*

I have had conversations with a Marxist who argues that it is absurd to claim we can avoid personal injury to others in any serious social struggle; for "men are reduced to functional elements": to threaten to deprive a man of his accustomed position in society is to threaten his very person. It will certainly be felt in many instances as just such a threat. But no man is ever reduced quite in his entire being to a functional element in society. And precisely because the rebel who is nonviolent distinguishes, as he struggles with another, between the man himself to whom he offers a certain basic respect (simply *as* another man) and the role that man has been playing, which he refuses to respect, it becomes more possible for the other, too, to begin to make the distinction. It may indeed at first be literally impossible for him to see himself, if he tries to imagine himself functioning in any way but the way that he has been. But the fact that others seem to be able to, makes it easier—especially if so much pressure is put on him that it becomes impossible for him to see himself functioning comfortably any longer in the old way. It is necessary to remember—as Oglesby says—that "the enemy is not a few men but a whole system," to remember that when the men with whom we struggle confront us it is as functional elements in this system that they do so, behaving in a certain sense automatically. It is necessary to know this well. But it is precisely if we refuse to treat them as nothing more than this—if we insist on treating them not as parts of a machine but as men, capable of thought and of change—that we gain a very much greater control in the situation. It is practical, in short, always to be *talking* with the enemy.

---

* There is a cliché often applied to the enemy: "All he can understand is force." But men "understand" brute force in the most narrow sense only: They understand that they are being hurt, or may be hurt by it—and so that they had better either surrender or manage to hurt the other side even more. Brute force cannot make the other understand that in a new world he could find a new life for himself. (BD)

Oglesby describes the rebel as one who is quite unwilling to talk. "The rebel is an incorrigible absolutist who has replaced ... all 'solutions' with the single irreducible demand that ... those who now have all power shall no longer have any, and that those who now have none—the people, the victimized—shall have all ... 'What do you want?' asks the worried, perhaps intimidated master. 'What can I give you?' ... But the rebel ... answers, 'I cannot be purchased.' The answer is meant mainly to break off the conference." One reason the rebel wants to break it off, Oglesby explains, is that he has as yet no really clear vision of "the revolutionized, good society," and would be embarrassed to have to confess this. He is not yet a responsible man. Then Oglesby adds: Ultimately he must become so. I am not quite sure *how*—as Oglesby sees it—he is to become responsible. My own suggestion is, of course, that nonviolent battle in itself teaches one to be.

It is a more difficult way. It does, for example, complicate the process of defining for ourselves and others who can be expected to act as our allies and who can be expected to resist us as harshly as they dare when, of the latter, we have always to be making two points at the same time: (1) here are men toward whom we have to be on our guard and (2) here are men for whom we have to show human concern. It can be done, though, and in very few words. I remember James Bevel addressing a church audience in Birmingham: "We love our white brothers"—pause—"but we don't trust them."

The trouble is that people tend to *feel* that they are taking bolder action when they disdain all conversations with the adversary. We had experience of this often on the Quebec to Guantanamo walk while we were in the South. There were any number of times when, at the edge of a town, we would find ourselves confronted by police who would inform us that we weren't going to be allowed to walk through. We had a constitutional right to walk through, and a few people in the group were always in favor of simply saying, "Try to stop us!" or saying nothing at all—and marching forward. What we actually did, always, was to stop the walk for an hour or two, drive into town, and discuss the matter with the chief of police. We would talk very quietly and always show him courtesy, and respect for his *proper* authority (for example, where traffic control was concerned), but in the course of the talk we would let it become clear to him that he would save himself a lot of trouble by letting us walk through; we knew what our rights were and had been to jail before for them and weren't afraid of going again. Time and again, after a certain amount of bluster on the chief's part, we would be allowed to walk. A few people in the group were always dissatisfied with this way. For it *felt like* deferring to the authorities. If we had simply marched forward, of course, feeling very bold, we would not have made our way through the town—we would have made our way right into jail, the authorities doing with us what they liked. The action that felt less bold won us our way.

All this is relevant, I think, to discussions going on now in the Movement about how to pass from protest to resistance, from merely "symbolic" actions to "practical" ones. To define clearly which actions are symbolic—and which more than that—one has often to look twice. A bold foray that is absolutely certain to be stopped is, surely, symbolic action. For example, those who rushed up the steps into the Pentagon on October 21st—to be thrown back at once by the troops, and quite predictably—were surely engaging in symbolic action; whereas those who tried to communicate with the troops confronting them, and were able to cause at least two defections from those troops, were surely engaging in action that was more than symbolic. The whole subject is infinitely complex. I am hardly saying that bold forays are never in order; but I am saying that dialogue with the other side is deeply practical.

Again I can imagine certain readers interrupting—to remark that I am over-looking, in this essay, one fundamental point. It is all very well to talk of the advantages of nonviolence, they might say, but how many are going to answer the call to such battle? A certain form of struggle can hardly be called practical if one cannot recruit very many men to try it; and to get most men to fight, one has to offer certain things which nonviolent struggle does not offer. I have heard people state, for example, that men from the ghettos would never turn to nonviolence because it does not allow them to speak out the full measure of their hatred for the white man. I have heard others say that few people would turn to it because it does not offer them the chance to feel, for once, like men. How a certain action makes one *feel* is not irrelevant.

But if nonviolent action is boldly taken it does allow men to speak out their deepest feelings; and if it is boldly taken, it does allow them to feel that they are standing up to others like men. It may not permit them to act out their hatred for others by taking revenge; but it allows—it requires—them to act out all the truth they feel about what the other has done, is doing to them, and to act out their determination to change this state of things. In this very process, one's hatred of the other can be forgotten, because it is beside the point; the point is to change one's life. The point is not to give some vent to the emotions that have been destroying one; the point is so to act that one can master them now.

What is it to assert one's manhood—one's human rights? Let me quote Fanon again. He writes in *Black Skin, White Masks:* "I have only one solution: to rise above this absurd drama that others have staged round me." "I have one right alone: that of demanding human behavior from the other." This is, to me, a very accurate description of nonviolent struggle. He writes, "I will impose my whole weight as a man on [the other's] life and show him that I am not that. . . [which] he persists in imagining." "What is needed is to hold oneself, like a sliver, to the heart of the world, to interrupt if necessary the rhythm of the world, to upset, if necessary, the chain of command, but. . .to stand up to the world." "Man is human only to the extent to which he tries to impose his existence on another man in order to be recognized by him." He immediately adds, "If I close the circuit, if I prevent the accomplishment of movement in two directions, I keep the other within himself." He writes, "I do battle for the creation of a human world—that is, a world of reciprocal recognition." The battle for this world, I would plead, is one that *can* only be waged nonviolently.

It is true enough, however, that one of the chief difficulties those who believe in nonviolence must face is how to recruit others to trust themselves to this way. My own conviction is that one can recruit to this form of battle only by setting the very boldest kind of example. Those of us who believe in nonviolent action should listen closely to the words of those who mock it. For if the portrait the latter draws of it is a caricature, and reveals their own ignorance of what such action can be, it reveals, too, a great deal about our own failure to carry experiments with it far enough. We had better look hard at what it is men seek when they turn away from us.

The cry for Black Power, for example, was taken up with swiftness. Why? Because too many—though certainly not all—of the nonviolent actions taken to that date *had* been, as charged, essentially acts of petition; and the necessity of self-assertion was felt very deeply. The gestures of the slave had clearly once and for all to be put from them by black people. And the nonviolent actions in which they had taken part had too often seemed but to repeat those ancient gestures of submission—quite as Carmichael put it: Look, master, we are only going to do what we are supposed to do; we may be on the streets, but see, we're still your good niggers; won't you help us? In this context, the assertion of love for the other seemed too much an echo of the old defensive hypocrisy toward the master: Look, we are your loving servants—who love you, respect you, more than we love, respect our own lives. Only nonviolent actions daring enough to quite shatter that pattern could possibly release either side from the bondage of the old relation.

It is not only black people in our society who are suffering now from the sense that their lives are out of their control, and who are going to be satisfied only to take actions that give them some sense of beginning to assert such control. At this point in our history, nonviolent action had better be taken boldly or one need hardly bother to take it at all, for one will be taking it alone.

Those who believe in nonviolence face a sharp challenge. They must decide whether or not we really are engaged in a struggle that is "in dead earnest." If we are, certain consequences follow. One of them is that we must act boldly; another is that we can expect to be hurt. Those who commit themselves to violent struggle take this for granted—which gives them a certain advantage. In the very act of entering battle, they prepare themselves for this—knowing it, very simply, to be the nature of battle. We had better learn, too, to accept that it is. They can claim one other advantage: they are less apt to lose recruits. Fanon writes in *The Wretched of the Earth,* "You could be sure of a new recruit when he could no longer go back into the colonial system—because he had assumed 'the responsibility for violence' and committed some act that made him a hunted man."* It is easier to retreat from nonviolent battle. We face the challenge of persisting in spite of this.

Yes, the challenge to those who believe in nonviolent struggle is to learn to be aggressive enough. Nonviolence has for too long been connected in men's minds with the notion of passivity. "Aggressive" is an ambiguous word, of course, and my statement needs qualifying. In this connection I recommend to all the book *On Aggression* by the Austrian naturalist, Konrad Lorenz. I have quoted Bradford Lyttle's reference to it: "Lorenz studies [the un-niceness of people] as aggressiveness and argues convincingly that it's instinctive with men." Actually, though Lorenz does argue that aggressiveness is instinctive—in men as in animals—he challenges the view that there is anything basically "un-nice" about that instinct. The correct translation of his original title, *Das Sogennante Bose,* would be *The So-Called Evil Instinct.* He argues that this instinct plays a very positive, life-*promoting* role among animals. Just to give one example: the instinct of each member of a species to fight for its own bit of territory "gives an ideal solution to the problem of the distribution of animals"—so that they don't all crowd into one place and eat up all the food available there and then starve. "The environment is divided between the members of the species in such a way that, within the potentialities offered, everyone can exist." "What a peaceful issue of the evil principle." Aggressiveness may "function in the wrong way" sometimes, by accident, he writes, and cause destruction, but "we have never found that the aim of aggression was the extermination of fellow members of the species." He writes of another, a very special instinct that has been developed in the process of evolution "to oppose aggression . . . and inhibit those of its actions that *could* be injurious to the survival of the species." He describes various ritualized "appeasing" gestures that are made by the weaker animal of the species at a certain point in any conflict, and describes how the stronger animal is then automatically restrained from taking advantage of the other and inflicting real injury upon him. He points out the "strangely moving paradox that the most bloodthirsty predators, particularly the Wolf . . . are among the animals with the most reliable killing inhibitions" (toward their own species, that is). For this "built-in safety device" was developed specifically in those creatures who were born heavily armed. And he points out the special dilemma of Man. He is born "harmless," and so "no selection

---

* I wrote earlier that one could substitute the phrase "radical uncompromising action" for the word "violence" in Fanon's text with the exception of a very few passages. This is one of those passages. (BD)

pressure arose in the prehistory of mankind to breed inhibitory mechanisms preventing the killing of his" fellows—and then he invented artificial weapons! Fortunately, Lorenz comments, "Inventions and responsibility are both the achievements of the same specifically human faculty of asking questions." Clearly the questions he has asked have, to date, resulted in a more rapid development of invention than of self-discipline, but Lorenz remains optimistic about Man, and sees him as still capable of evolving. "I assert," he writes, "that the long-sought missing link between animals and the really humane being is ourselves"—a hypothesis that I find persuasive.

What has very clearly worked, in the evolution of animals, to preserve and advance the life of each species, has been a particular *balance* of two instincts. The one, as it were, asserts the individual's right to exist. This is the so-called evil instinct. Lorenz names it "aggression." But just as I would substitute another word for Fanon's "violence," I would substitute another word here—and rename "aggression" "self-assertion." The second instinct restrains the first when it endangers *another's* right to exist. In human terms, the first amounts to respecting one's own person, the second to respecting the person of the other. Lorenz points out, by the way, that the only animals capable of love are those that are "aggressive." One can, it seems, *only* love another "as one loves oneself."

This life-saving balance—this equilibrium between self-assertion and respect for others—has evolved among animals on the physiological plane. In human beings it can be gained only on the plane of consciousness. And the plea this essay makes is precisely that we make the disciplined effort to gain it—all those of us who hope really to change men's lives, who, in Fanon's words, "want humanity to advance a step further," want to "set afoot a new man." My plea is that the key to a revolution that would "go forward all the time...in the company of Man, in the company of all men," lies in discovering within ourselves this poise. But it calls equally for the strengthening of *two* impulses—calls both for assertion (for speaking, for acting out "aggressively" the truth, as we see it, of what our rights are) and for restraint toward others (for the acting out of love for them, which is to say of respect for their human rights). May those who say that they believe in nonviolence learn to challenge more boldly those institutions of violence that constrict and cripple our humanity. And may those who have questioned nonviolence come to see that one's rights to life and happiness can only be claimed as inalienable if one grants, in action, that they belong to all men.

Mud City

Published in Liberation, *September 1968.*

Resurrection City was created in Washington, D.C., by poor people of all colors during the summer of 1968 under the leadership of SCLC (the Southern Christian Leadership Conference). Planning for the Poor People''s Campaign, leading up to and including Resurrection City, had begun under the SCLC leadership of Dr. Martin Luther King, Jr.; Dr. King was assassinated on April 4, 1968. (JM)

"Mud is fertile—" (Painted on the wall of one of the shacks in Resurrection City)

I have been reading some of the press accounts of what Resurrection City is supposed to have been like. I lived there for almost three weeks and grant that most of the facts cited are indeed facts. The streets were mud—often thick enough to pull off your shoes. (It rained, it seems, twenty-two out of the forty-three days of the city's life.) Garbage was not collected often enough and it got flung about on the mud. The only water supply was a few drinking fountains or outdoor running taps placed at rare intervals throughout the fifteen-acre camp, so it was hard for people to keep clean. The food was poor. Cornflakes and milk for breakfast. For lunch—day after day—baloney sandwiches. And there was a great deal of chaos in the camp and a great deal of friction. People stole from each other; some beat each other up or beat up visitors. Or threw things at passing cars—and then the police felt justified in shooting in "tear gas" to "disperse the troublemakers." (Here the stories become less factual. The police shot in not tear gas but Mace, and rather more than enough to disperse a few individuals. On the night of June 22nd, two days before the government occupied the city, they shot in enough to blind and choke most of its occupants—many of them children and old people as they knew; enough to choke some into unconsciousness and leave many suffering for days after from troubled vision, burns, and difficulties in breathing.)

189

Anyone who lived there in the mud could, if he wanted, add to the list of discomforts, or present any one of them in stronger terms. The news accounts, for example, make little of how noisy the place was. Not only did big planes roar over constantly but our own public address system babbled almost without stopping—bits of random information, instructions, emergency calls, greetings, music—like some kind of madman in our midst. When a workshop was in session, or the Poor People's University, special pleas were often made for the system to be turned off, but these pleas were almost always in vain. So that just as walking through the city had to be specially paced—as you put your feet down in the muck, trying not to slip, or placed them carefully along the dilapidated and also slippery sections of boardwalk that crossed some of it—talking had to be specially paced, too: the speaker had to spend as much time pausing, until he could be heard again, as speaking. As for the violent encounters among ourselves ("the menace in our hearts against one another," one woman put it) any one of us could write in stronger terms of these, too.

There remains the mysterious gap between the final impression of the city any newspaper account managed to give and the actual experience of being one of its citizens. When the government's permit expired and it was announced in a meeting that we were going to be evicted (though the Indians still gave us permission to stay, and this was the only permission we had asked), one old woman rose and declared: "We have this choice. We can stay here and live or go back home and die. I'm going to stay here and live oh Lord oh Lord!" What, then, was that "life" to which she referred—and which could never be guessed at from the press reports (or even from reports in presumably sympathetic magazines like *The Progressive* or the *New Republic*)? One man who lived there tells of driving another old woman past the site, after the government had dismantled the city. (He was driving her to the warehouse where the government had dumped all the belongings people had had no time to gather up. Police had smashed or torn or stolen a good many of the things, it turned out.) As she saw the bare ground where the city once had been, he said she gave a great cry of anguish. "I'll never forget it. It was torn out of the very depths of her." What, then, was the life that she—and so many others—felt had been taken from her?

A terrible truth is, of course, that some of the people who lived in the leaky plywood shelters of Resurrection City could say that they were sleeping in better houses, eating better food, enjoying better circumstances generally than they ever had. What a judgment upon this country. Many of them had built the shacks themselves, too, and could say: I never had my own house before. The painted lettering on the walls of many shelters seemed a spontaneous expression of this feeling, for almost every one bore its own signature:

NASSER AND POPCORN LIVES HERE.
NEW KENYA—JAMES THE PIMP AND JESUS.
THIS IS SIX FANG J. DOG.
THE SOUL MAN, "POPPA," WILM. DEL.
MR. AND MRS. EZRA HAMPTON, HATTIESBURG, MISS.
SOULSVILLE, THE PENGUIN.
DEEP DEEP SOUL.
WALTERS WABBITS, SOUL CITY, SOUL POWER.

But when people spoke of the life in that city they meant more than living in their own houses—paying no rent and no taxes.

I, too, keep rehearing that old woman's cry—though I first heard it only in imagination. And I keep remembering my own feelings when I returned to the field from which the city had vanished. For what I experienced is still mysterious to me. As I started to walk over the ground—which was dry now and leveled off by bulldozers, just occasional scraps of clothing or of tin cans or paper plates sticking up through the packed soil—as I began to try to trace by certain landmarks (electric poles, trees, and shrubs which had become familiar) where the dining tent, the "many-races culture" tent, the training tent, and the shelter of various friends had stood, I felt, with every step I took, a strong trembling. But my own body was not trembling. The motion seemed to be both inside of me and outside of me. Recalling it later, I was reminded of one of these moments in a Shakespeare play when there is suddenly "music in the air and under the ground." I found the cinder blocks that had made the foundation of an outdoor fireplace in the neighborhood where I had stayed. Further along, in a little grove, I found the blackboard James Bevel had used in his workshops on nonviolence—still standing upright. I looked around to see whether the chalk was still there, too, for I was moved to write on the blackboard: WE ARE STILL HERE. But there was no chalk and I suddenly felt the gesture to be unnecessary anyway. What was the trembling I experienced if not a kind of presence there, still, of that tumultuous city, a kind of memory of shared life so intense that it took this curious physical form?

It was a memory perhaps above all of the voices joined there, of the great Babel of sound that was so often raised—at the front gate or in the dining tent or outside the two-room shack named City Hall where we went for mail or went to try to get information.

I first listened with awe to that mixture of voices on my way up from the South with the campaign. I had gone down to Memphis early in May for the start of it at the Lorraine Motel where Dr. King had been murdered, and on to Marks ("where he wept the tears," as one woman told it; King had visited the houses there that stood in festering swampy water), and on up through Nashville and Knoxville and Danville, recruiting more people as we went. Our nights, on the road, we spent most often in huge municipal gymnasiums—where the several hundred voices of the campaigners sounded and resounded against the walls. The clamor kept up always until two or three o'clock in the morning, and began to gather again as early as five o'clock. The first two nights—with the encouragement of several mothers of small children—I made vain gestures of pleading for quiet after midnight. There was never any hope for quiet, of course. Here were lots of people away from home for the first time in their lives, and here were people only recently released by this movement from resignation about their lives, on their way to give battle ("Socksoul! Socksoul!"), and keyed high by all their hopes about that and fears about that. How could they sleep? By the third night, I had given up trying to sleep, myself, and learned to lie back and simply listen to the noise objectively, as one might listen to some clamorous piece of music. It was worth listening to in that way. For here, in the form of sound—here in the air for one to study—were all the elements of the gathering struggle.

Some of the musical elements I could lie and disentangle in my mind. I could recall the peculiar high pitch in the voice of a small boy in Marks, marching, singing, back to town, in a line of others, down the highway from the field where a mass rally had been held—as we passed a state trooper at an intersection, the child's arm outflung, his finger pointing out the man and his voice rising again for the words, *"no more po-lice over me, over me!"* so physically possessed by the courage he had learned that night that now and then he had to leave the line of march and turn somersaults in somebody's patch of roadside lawn. I could recall the voice of the young man of twelve ("boy" would be the wrong word for him), a very gifted gospel singer—his voice more sober, but trembling, breaking now and then with feeling, as he told me how we must pray for more force, more strength, and doors would open if we did. "God moves in very mysterious ways." Or the voice of the talkative young man sitting up front on the bus as we finally entered Washington—suddenly quavering out, solo, "We are not afraid! Oh yes, we are!" We passed some buildings where members of the National Guard were training, and a little girl of eight, sitting between me and her brother of five, turned to me and whispered, "Carl says we are going to die here."

These notes and a thousand more are in the tumult to which I listen. Voices of the young women dancing down the sidewalks: *Soul Power, Soul Power, ooh! ahh!*—the sounds "ooh! ahh!" thrown off like sparks. *You better do right, white man, do right!*—the key shifting. *Everybody has a right to live!* Every feeling that has drawn these people into this adventure, every feeling that agitates them now that they are on their way, takes the form of sound. And here the sounds have rolled in upon each other: they mix, they collide, mount, tremble, and roll into one great wheel of sound—a not quite perfectly rounded wheel, one that staggers somewhat as it moves. The peculiar music of this gathering struggle.

What I was listening to, of course, was above all the sound of many people who had never met before, encountering each other. And if this was so on the road up from the South, it was so above all in Resurrection City. Along the way up from Memphis, it was above all black people who were recruited, though a few white radicals were gathered up, too—usually arriving, as I did, from a distance. But in Resurrection City of course poor black people and poor white people and Mexican-Americans and Indians and Puerto Ricans met—which had been the central idea of the campaign from the beginning, the idea that in such a coming together they might find a new kind of power, "poor people's power."

They came together and, just as all the papers reported, they began to fight. This was so much a fact that a good many of the Mexican-Americans and Indians and Puerto Ricans never even made the complete move into the city, but slept and ate at the Hawthorne School where they were supposed to have stayed simply until enough shacks were built for everybody.

Of course they fought. It is one thing to say the words, "If all the poor unite, they will be strong." (A poor white woman from Chicago describes a hush during the first meeting of leaders from the different groups that Dr. King had called in Atlanta. "Do you know what we have here?" someone had asked, and there was a long moment of silence as they sat there, each one thinking about it.) But it is quite another thing to be able to live out the idea.

This is what Resurrection City was: people trying to live with that idea. This is what the clamor I have described was: the beginning of this effort in common, the blurred beginning—a great staggering wheel, unable yet to go very far forward, blundering in circles still for the most part, but turning and turning, trying to round itself out.

It was easy enough for a reporter to step into the city and find casualties of this life—to interview this person or that who was on his way home, sick of it all. I met many more people who had tried to leave the place and found that they couldn't do it. I met several who had actually gotten onto a bus and started home and, once home or sometimes halfway home, gotten onto a return bus and come right back. They had decided that it was foolish to stay, given all the unpleasantness there was to face and all the obvious mistakes the leadership was making, for they hadn't been able to see clearly anything significant that was being accomplished. But when they actually made the motion of leaving, some deeper, more accurate sense of things had told them that too much really was happening for them to be able to leave.

The very collisions with other people that were painful were the reason to remain. One young woman who was always saying goodbye to her friends but never actually left, tried to explain to me one day why she was still there: "I've never learned so much about myself or about other people in such a short time. Here you can't run away from confrontations and what your responses to people really are; you have finally to look at them."

These confrontations were unending. One night after another I would lie on my cot, the oilcloth flap at the front of the shelter open a little for air, and listen to some new sequence of them. The outdoor fireplace in our neighborhood drew people to it. I would hear someone singing quietly or a couple of people talking in level tones, and I would doze. Then I would wake to some sharp exchange of words; a scuffle—everything in a crescendo. The explosion would almost always be followed by more talk, those involved firing questions at each other now: "What's the matter with you? Why when I said this did you say that?" I would doze off again. Then wake. One of the skinny black cats of our part of the camp would be lapping a drink from the plastic bucket of water I kept by my bed. And outside the voices would still be persisting: "Brother, you don't seem to understand—." Suddenly more shouting. As it rained so much, a canvas canopy had been improvised over the fireplace. Often the commotion of rain upon the canvas mixed with the commotion of voices. The incessant rains began to seem only natural here—part of the one elemental process of bringing us all together, mixing us all in. The rain and the mud. "Nobody has as much mud on their shoes as we do, do they?" a little boy ran around shouting on day.

How much coming together was there, then? How much unity did we achieve—beyond that of being able to show mud on our shoes? How can one measure such a thing? I can only say that I kept being surprised at the degree of unity many people took for granted. I remember, for example, the day that I.F. Stone came to talk about the war in Vietnam—for the Poor People's University. Very few people were waiting to hear him when he arrived, though once he began to talk, as always, more people gathered, and he was upset to find that more than half of those sitting there at the start were people like myself who couldn't be classified as poor—peace workers, student activists. "Intellectuals," Stone tagged us. Most of us had "just come to report about the place," he decided; and he asked could we let the people of the city do all the talking. It was one of the men whom he counted as a proper citizen of the place who immediately objected to the distinction being made, and said that everybody present should be allowed to speak. A little later in the discussion, a white man in an exchange with a black man used the words "you people," and the black challenged him at once: "What do you mean 'you people'? We're united here. This is a factuality."

It was an uneasy "factuality" perhaps, but there it was for a lot of people. "We all feel better toward each other," as one woman put it. And the new feeling included even those of us from the middle class who had chosen to come and live in the mud. (Revolutionary people are not identified by race or by social place, James Bevel taught in one of his workshops on nonviolence; they are identified by perception. "A revolution grows out of expanding the minds of people. . . . Perception determines whether you are in the revolution or not. . . . A man may be starving and not understand why. . . . My father is poor and he just sleeps. . . .")

At one session of the Poor People's University, a teacher, a white man, was talking about economics. A young black man had just wandered up. "You come out here to lecture us," he began. "I live with you, man," the speaker answered him. "Don't come to lecture us out of any motherfucking book," the man persisted; "I didn't learn what I know from any motherfucking book!" And again another black man interrupted him: "This is a table of brotherhood. We've come here to get together." "You're sounding good," still another black man called out.

Bevel taught: "There is power in human spirits coming together . . . When the spirits of men meet and blend, then you get power." "Tell it, Truth!" people in the audience sometimes encouraged him.

I heard one young woman saying to another: "All of us are aching to be part of something that doesn't exist. . . . What we have to do is learn to trust one another, so that I can represent your poverty and you can represent mine. But our minds aren't ready yet." That is what was happening at Resurrection City. People were trying to get their minds ready.

"Resurrection City is the university," Bevel taught. I heard an old man one day refer to the Reflecting Pool by mistake as the Illuminating Pool. His slip of the tongue was significant.

"This is our first action," Bevel would say—"clearing up our minds." Some might say that he chose to stress this because the demonstrations there in Washington were turning out to be less bold than many had hoped they would be. But whether or not it was in part an excuse that he was making, he spoke the truth, I believe. This was the action in which the great majority of those in the city were engaged; and it was in itself a radical action. What is sad about the Poor People's Campaign is that the leadership as a whole seems to have overlooked the fact of just how significant an action it was. Julius Lester in *The Guardian* noted it, and he blames radicals for not involving themselves in the campaign in greater numbers. He says too—rightly I think—that if they had, they might have been able to bring about the confrontation with the government that never really happened.

One major confrontation should have taken place, I feel (and others, too, feel it), on the day the government closed the city down. The people of the city certainly wanted it. But instead of calling for nonviolent resistance that morning, and instead of issuing a general call for supporters to come and stand with them, the leadership negotiated with the government to make the eviction as quiet and uneventful as possible. They arranged to have only a token few people there on the site when the troops arrived; the rest were marched off with Reverend Abernathy to a demonstration at the Department of Agriculture. A certain number of people disobeyed instructions and stayed behind at the city, raising the token number from the requested fifteen or twenty to almost a hundred, but the gesture of resistance remained an insignificant one.

By this time the leadership of the Poor People's Campaign meant, in effect, S.C.L.C. leadership. Originally a steering committee had been set up that included representatives of each of the various ethnic groups, but leaders of the other groups felt that, despite this apparent structure, they were given too little voice in how things went, and by this time, I gather, the committee had been dissolved. So it was S.C.L.C. officials alone who managed the negotiations about the closing of the city. But as far as I know, no leader in any of the other groups spoke up, either, in favor of making a stand there.

A demonstration that could have had deep meaning never occurred. And the ending of this story is more disappointing even than that. In public statements made at the time several S.C.L.C. leaders actually welcomed the government's action. Andrew Young declared, "We got bogged down in Resurrection City and wasted a lot of energy here. In one sense whoever it was who ran us out of there did us a real favor." By statements like this, the very meaning of what had happened in the city was belittled for the public—and for all those who had lived there.

It is easy to understand all the ways in which Resurrection City was a strain on the S.C.L.C., both financial and administrative. ("A millstone round our necks," Hosea Williams put it.) The whole campaign—both the building of the city and the bringing together of all those different groups—was an immense venture to undertake, especially so soon after the assassination of Dr. King had stunned them all. In their most recent fund-raising letter, Dr. Abernathy writes: "We honestly conccde that we stumbled under fatigue, sorrow and strain." And little wonder. For a group of leaders so used to working as a close-knit team to try suddenly to work in coalition with other strong leaders was a particular strain, of course. They are used to staging in their own way the living theatre in which they believe. Their way has often been inspired, but they have also faltered when they have because it is a way that does not often involve consulting the actors in the drama, even when they are their own people. Here was a situation that called above all for everyone to be listening to the thoughts of others. S.C.L.C. leaders were both too exhausted to do so and too used to being the ones to be listened to rather than to listen. If this had not been so, I think that the people there in the city could have suggested to them how to stage a demonstration that would not have been quickly forgotten by this country.

The people in the city repeated many times on those last days that Resurrection City, if it were dismantled, should be built again (as its very name recommends)—in other parts of the country. There should be Resurrection Cities "set up everywhere." Those who want change in this country should not disregard that call, I think. It is my own belief that only if more and more people try living in that city—try, that is, in one form or another, living out the experience that was to be found there—will the revolution be made.

On the Necessity to Liberate Minds

Talk given in Palo Alto, California, June 12, 1970.

Some months ago when I heard Cathy Melville tell the story of the DC 9's raid on the Dow Chemical office in Washington, one moment that she described struck me with the force of symbolism. She told me how they had trouble getting in through the door and finally broke into the office through a glass wall. As they were going about their work in there, scattering files, pouring blood, a stranger appeared in the hall, looked in through the large break in the glass wall and asked, "Is anything wrong?" Cathy told him, "No, everything's all right" and he went away, apparently reassured that everything *was* all right.

As of course it was—for a change—up in that office. Here was a corporation that had been making and selling the stuff with which babies are burned alive. Some people were trying to make it harder for them to do this. To most of us, I assume, that would very clearly be all right.

The difficulty is of course—the tremendous difficulty—that to a great many Americans the act of those nine people who scattered Dow files was a much more questionable, much more disturbing act than the act of Dow in making and selling napalm. So that the incident Cathy reported was like a war resister's dream: you are engaged in an act of interfering with the military-industrial machine—a death machine—and a member of the public asks you: Should I be alarmed by what you are doing? And you tell him no—and he accepts your reassurance.

Yes, like a dream. Because in actuality, as we confront a social apparatus that seems to us flagrantly irrational, out of control, in its blind quest for wealth dealing out death both home and abroad—dealing it out even to children, both abroad and at home, killing its own children now, clearly a machine that must be stopped—.

But I'll interrupt myself because the imagery that I just used is inadequate. If it were just that we had to stop a death-dealing machine in its tracks, this would be relatively simple to accomplish—although we could count on being hurt in the attempt. In a society like this one—so dependent upon

198

technology—sabotage is terribly easy. A relatively small number of people can cause a tremendous amount of damage, can throw everything into confusion. But our task is not to wreck. Our task is to transform a society that deals out death into a society that makes life more possible for all. To build such a new society, very many people are needed. So as we strike at the machinery of death, we have to do so in a way that the general population understands, that encourages more and more people to join us.

This is surely the great challenge to the movement: How to make the public understand that it's "all right" to attack the death machine—that it is necessary? How to free their minds to see this and to join us?

And here is the preposterous difficulty. We are all living now in a society so deranged that it confronts us not only with the fact that we are committing abominable crimes against others—crimes we shouldn't be able to live with; it confronts us also with threats to our own existence that no people in history have ever had to live with before. And confronts every single member of society with these threats—even the most privileged, even those in control of things, or rather, out of control of them. Confronts us, in the name of "defense," with the threat of nuclear annihilation. Confronts us, in the name of "national profit," with the threat that our environment may be completely destroyed. The society is this insanely deranged. And yet—we have to face the strange fact that most people are very much less terrified of having things continue as they are than of having people like us trying to change things radically.

For most Americans are in deep awe of things-as-they-are. Even with everything this obviously out of control, they still tell themselves that those in authority must know what they are doing, and must be describing our condition to us as it really is; they still take it for granted that somehow what *is,* what is *done,* must make sense, can't really be insane. These assumptions exercise a tyranny over their minds. Those of us committed to try to bring about change have above all to reckon with this tyranny, have above all to try to find out how to relieve men of it.

I read this past winter of a specially painful example of it, read in the *Times* the story of Michael Bernhardt, who was the young soldier who was the first to talk about the massacre at Songmy. He had volunteered for service in Vietnam—full of faith in the words he had heard from his leaders about what this country was trying to do over there. He found himself almost immediately in the action at Songmy. He didn't take part in the killing. As his comrades began to shoot old people, women, babies—the reporter quotes him: "I just looked around and said, *'This is all screwed up.'* " But after the action it took him quite a while to come forward and talk about it. Because he very quickly experienced the eerie feeling that neither those in command of the war nor most Americans would agree with him. There is an almost unbearable passage in the story where he is quoted as saying, "Maybe this was the way wars really were. . . . I felt like I was left out, like maybe they forgot to tell me something, that this was the way we fought wars, and everybody knew but me." The reporter writes then that the clash between this experience he had at Songmy and his convictions about his country is something he still cannot resolve. "It became almost a question of sanity." But, he writes, "if he were forced to pick, he would choose his convictions over his experiences." He quotes him as insisting, "We hold out a hope, you know."

A terrible story, and one worth being very attentive to. Here is a young man who was exceptional. He did not take part. He saw the action for what it was: all screwed up. And yet—*he did not know how to cope afterwards with this vision. It just made him feel left out.* Because he suffered from the bondage I speak of—the awe of what *is,* of what is *done.* He suffered from the anxious sense that if one isn't part of it, *whatever* it is, one is then nowhere. And so in effect he dismisses the insight he had. Or does his best to. He chooses to accept not the truth of his own experience but something he has been told is truth: that our country "holds out a hope."

The question is: How do we cure men of this bondage? And of course how do we cure our own selves more completely? How do we set all of us free to trust our own experiences of the truth that everything is all screwed up?

The tantalizing thought is that there can hardly be an American living who has not had *some* glimpse of this truth. This must be so even of those who are most favored by the present system of things. (Even they, for example, must often now try to breathe an air that is unbreathable.) Some among us who want change talk much of the need to "know your enemy." It is of course very necessary to identify those in the society who are going to try the hardest to hold to things as they are. But it is certainly not appropriate to think of oppressed and oppressor as though the distinction between them were absolute. For the first time in history one can say that we are really *all* the oppressed—though some are certainly very much more thoroughly oppressed than others; we are all the threatened—as long as things stay as they are.

How can we release the minds of more and more men to be able to see this? See it not just as a nightmare suffered that one tries to put out of mind; see it as meaning that we have to act to change things altogether. How do we give people the courage to trust that if they name things-as-they-are insane, they will not in doing so simply find themselves set adrift?

Much too briefly: I think that those of us who act must always be saying with the actions that we take two things—*and always saying these two things at the same time.*

We have to be saying very strongly—and not just with words of course: Things are not going to stay as they are. The machinery of things-as-they-are is a machinery of death, and we are going to so disrupt it that it will not be able to continue functioning as it has been. To waken men's minds, *to keep them from postponing and postponing all real thought about our condition,* we have first to give them this necessary shock.

But even as we give that shock, we must be communicating something else, too—again not merely with words but above all by our actions. We must be saying: Don't be afraid of *us.* It is the system we are attacking that you need to fear—that all of us need to fear. For it is reckless with lives. *But we are not.* Don't fear us. What we seek is precisely a new community of men in which we are all careful of each other—and of the natural world around us. And look, we are beginning to build that new world right now—in our relations with each other, in our relations even with you. *Don't be afraid of us. We are trying to release men from fear.*

I think that we have to find more and more ways of making this second point, of acting it out. It is going to be very tempting to take the road of striking at the military machine quite blindly, to think: Can't we be more and more effective by being more and more destructive? Especially tempting because, as I have said, in this society a very few people could cause a very great deal of destruction. But again: a very few people could not find a new world among the ruins. This new world can only be built in the company of a great many people.

And so our acts of disruption should be taken in the most careful spirit. The actions through which it is easiest to communicate that spirit of carefulness are actions simply of noncooperation, actions by which we declare to the state: Not with my life!—you'll not commit murder by my hand, or commit it by spending my money, or by applying my wits or my labor. And of course if enough people would declare this by their acts—if enough young men would refuse to fight, and enough of the rest of us support them in that stand, so that more and more would find courage; if enough of us would refuse our taxes; if enough scientists would refuse to loan the state their minds, and enough workers would refuse to work in war industries; if there were enough ready people to launch a general strike—escalating from the recent refusal of students simply to continue their studies as usual—we could end the war by these means alone, and we could also initiate profound changes in the social order.

The trouble is that there are not yet enough people willing to make the changes in their lives that this would involve. And so unless the number of those who are willing grows very rapidly now, there will have to be more of the more aggressive acts taken—such as the blocking and occupation of buildings; and more of the still more aggressive acts such as those taken by the Catonsville Nine,* the DC 9 and others. There is such a terrible urgency about halting the machinery of death that is still unimpeded. *For our actions even to be effective as symbolic actions—as actions that speak the truth of our condition*—they must communicate this urgency. They must communicate the utter necessity to stop a machinery so careless of lives.

But when we take actions of this sort, it does become immediately more difficult to communicate at the same time our desire for a new spirit among men, a spirit of respect for one another—more difficult to act out that respect right now. May the men and women who take such actions feel the same responsibility to communicate this spirit felt by the Catonsville Nine, the DC 9, the others in that tradition.

May they be careful above all not to harm any person. And careful, too, to make clear that they never would be willing to. May they also be scrupulously careful not to destroy the kind of property that has a valid life meaning for people. Some activists tend to speak of private property as though none of it has ever had such meaning. But some property of course is like the very extension of a man's life—or the extension of many men's lives. May people take patient care to know what they are doing here, make the most sober distinctions—willing to destroy only property that is by its nature deathly or exploitative, and unambiguously so. May they repeat and repeat to themselves the question: Can we by these acts release the minds of more and more people—who should be on our side but who have been paralyzed—so that they will feel free to face the truth of our condition, free to join us?

Postscript

I have suggested that we must always be saying with the actions that we take two things, and always saying these two things at the same time. But I might better have said: at the same time or in close time sequence. For it could not always be possible to make both statements literally at one and the same time, in one and the very same action.

It would often be necessary either to "stand" for the action after it has been taken—finding, inventing occasions to interpret to the public the felt need for that act and the careful spirit in which it was taken—or to build up to it beforehand with a series of more conventional challenges that in retrospect make its true nature clear.

Unless you can be sure of finding ways in which to speak a necessary reassurance even as you provide a necessary mental shock, I would say

* A group which destroyed files taken from a Selective Service office, in an attempt to interfere with the conscription of men to kill and die in Vietnam. (JM)

bluntly: Better not to take the action at all. Just as I would say—with even greater emphasis: Do not take the action, interrupt it at any point, unless you can feel sure that it will cause no serious injury to another.

A final word, about "standing." More and more activists feel that to stand and wait to be arrested is inappropriate—seems to say that they respect the authority of those who will seek to punish them—when actually part of the message they are trying to communicate is, precisely, that the so-called "authorities" should not be respected as such. I agree very much with this reasoning. The problem remains: how to manage nevertheless to stand in frankness before the *public*—acknowledging their act and seeking to clarify it. Different activists have already solved this problem in a number of different ways—"surfacing" not to surrender themselves but at public rallies or at a continuous series of smaller gatherings; or through privately taped interviews or films later made public—on these occasions either exerting themselves to elude capture or not bothering to (depending on whether they could see themselves as more hampered in their lives as revolutionaries by serving time in jail or by having to live from then on secretively). There is obviously no one correct way in which to act here. There is only the persistent question to try to answer: How best to speak by one's actions—and continue able to speak—in ways that open the minds of others to radical insights about our present condition, and to the courage to trust this new vision and to act upon it themselves.

Behind her the sea the sea hisses—
A serpent in a new skin.
Each altering moment it sloughs from it an old
and glistens in another skin again.
And she and she—
Dances to its many-throated
Its never-for-a-minute silent song ("Listen, listen!")
And sings, herself: Here
I mean to dance away my fear.
It binds me like a jacket I have worn too long.
(Yes, I hear your song.)
I'll slip it from me
As you slip your watery coats
And dare be naked, known
As whatever self I am
Or I become.
And grimaces (for a moment doubting this?)
But dances on.

1971

Section 5: The Seventies

So much has been taken from us.
But we will take it back....

Woman woman.

We take it back.

—from "Poem to Barbara Smith"

I lie at the bottom of my spirit's well
And try to still my breath
And still my heart
That staggers in my side
Like an uneven wheel.

Above me, agitation of the waters.
Some of this motion is life,
Some is death.
Each is mistaken for the other,
In panic, often, that turns to wrath.
I see that wrath cut back
Everything new, green, that we try to begin.

And will life or will death prevail?
My fear is asking the question
And the answer to fear, of course, is: Death.

I lie at the bottom of my spirit's well.
If I lie quiet here
Can I elude my fear?

1969

On Anger

A talk written for delivery at the War Resisters' League national conference in Athens, Georgia, September 4-6, 1971. (Read by a friend, because I was in an automobile accident on the way there.) Published in Liberation, *November 1971. (BD)*

I have been asked to talk about the relation between war resistance and resistance to injustice.

There are many points to be made that I need hardly belabor. I don't have to argue with any of you at this conference that if we resist war we must look to the causes of war; try to end *them*. And that one finds the causes of war in any society that encourages not fellowship but domination of one person by another. *We must resist whatever gives encouragement to the will to dominate.*

I don't think any of you would object to my stating the relationship between the two struggles in another way (restating it, for it has been often said): Bullets and bombs are not the only means by which people are killed. If a society denies to certain of its members food or medical attention, or a political voice, the sense of their own worth, the freedom to exercise their talents—this, too, is waging war of a kind.

No, I can't imagine a very lively debate here about whether or not the two struggles are one struggle. I can remember well enough when this question *was* debated among us, but it isn't any longer.

Now, I think, another question troubles our minds and divides us among ourselves: What should our relation be to the very many people we find struggling alongside us against social injustice and against a particular war—comrades who are not committed, as we are, to nonviolence. That's what I am going to try to talk about.

I think it relevant to go back for a moment and talk about the time when we *were* still arguing over whether or not the two struggles were one.

I remember the first Peacemaker conference I ever attended—in 1960. (This was my introduction to the nonviolent movement in this country.) At the time, you'll remember, there were very few activists in the field, but almost all of them professed a faith in nonviolence. The Reverend Fred Shuttlesworth attended the conference and talked about his experience of the nonviolent discipline, struggling in Birmingham for integration. And the question as to whether or not pacifists should take part in civil-rights actions began to be discussed. Many pacifists who were present said that we shouldn't. Because there were so few of us and disarmament was such a pressing priority, they were afraid that we would dissipate our energies. I remember one man making the point: "If we all blow up, it's not going to matter whether we blow up integrated or segregated." That fight was for later. Many disagreed, of course.

I remember, too, all the discussion we had before setting out on the first peace walk through the South—the Nashville to Washington Walk, in 1962. A walk, again, speaking to disarmament. We had endless discussions about whether or not to talk about race relations, too, as we went. One black man, Bob Gore, was walking with us, so the subject was sure to come up. Should we pursue it, or should we try to get the talk quickly back to disarmament? Almost everyone who advised us—including James Farmer, then head of CORE*—advised us not to try to mix the two issues. It was hard enough to talk about either; it would be harder if we linked them. And we wouldn't be helping black people by associating ourselves with their struggle—we would just be dumping on them the added burden of that association.

Most of us who were actually on the walk felt very uncomfortable about the advice given us and felt in our bones that the two issues had to be joined. And what happened is that in the course of the walk itself, we just naturally, inevitably, did join forces with the civil-rights people.

But no—it wasn't inevitable, and we almost spoiled it. The very first day, walking out of Nashville, we walked right past a Simple Simon's where several black students were sitting in. Walked dutifully past—feeling that it was wrong to do. It felt wrong enough so that we talked about it at Scarritt College there—and learned that the students felt it made no sense either. A dialogue between us had begun. And blacks began walking with us for certain stretches, near their home towns—turning it by that act into a walk for integration as well as disarmament. We began to stay at black churches. And our causes were joined. Our encounters with each other added strength and insight. I think we learned more from them than they from us; but it worked both ways.

As I look back now at the discussions before the walk started, I find them a little hard to believe. And I imagine that some of you must, too. Here we were, two groups, pitifully small in numbers, both committed to nonviolence, and we were wondering whether we should link forces. It hardly seems real. But I think it is very important to look back and remind ourselves that it was real indeed. The obvious did not seem obvious to us at the time. So it may not now.

* Congress of Racial Equality (JM)

What did seem obvious to a lot of pacifists then was that a black man who professed belief in nonviolence was inconsistent in his thought, was fooling himself that he was nonviolent unless he came out against war. I remember at that 1960 Peacemaker conference one young pacifist flinging that challenge at Shuttlesworth—who had been risking his life daily, remaining nonviolent under the most extreme provocation: "The key to whether you have really adopted nonviolence or not is: How many of your men refuse to go into the army?" But it *wasn't* obvious to a lot of pacifists that *they* were inconsistent in their nonviolence if they didn't act against racism. I remember an editorial of Dellinger's* in *Liberation,* entitled "Are Pacifists Willing to Be Negroes?"

Well the problem back then seems simple to us now—the problem of how we were going to relate to others who professed the same nonviolent faith. The question now seems much more complex: How are we going to relate to those who don't profess that faith?

But I submit that the answer is basically the same. We are in one struggle. There is a sense, even, in which we can say that we *do* share the same faith. When we define the kind of world that we want to bring into being, our vision and theirs too is of a world in which no person exploits another, abuses, dominates another—in short, a nonviolent world. We differ about how to bring this world into being; and that's a very real difference. But we *are* in the same struggle and we need each other. We need to take strength from each other, and we need to learn from each other.

I think it very important that we not be too sure that they have all the learning to do, and we all the teaching. It seems obvious to us right now that the methods they are sometimes willing to use are inconsistent with the vision we both hold of a new world. It is just possible—as we pursue that vision—that *we* are in some way inconsistent, too. For we have been in the past.

The question I want to try to discuss is: What kind of thinking on our part is likely to result in our learning the most that we can from them and their learning the most that they can from us?

I'm going to talk particularly about our relation to anger, because I think that lies at the heart of the question. A lot of people next to whom we find ourselves struggling are very angry people. Black people are angry. Welfare mothers are angry. Women are furious, as one of the buttons claims. Gay people—in spite of that name—are angry. Veterans, GI's, prisoners are angry. How do we relate to their anger? And how do we relate to anger when we feel it in ourselves? Because that has a lot to do with how we relate to them.

* Dave Dellinger: long-time nonviolent activist and writer. (JM)

I started thinking about this most especially after a recent experience I had with a friend, a sister—a young woman who has been very deeply touched and changed by the women's liberation movement. When I first met her she was much involved in the antiwar movement and committed to nonviolence. Now she has concentrated above all on resistance to her own oppression and that of her sisters; and she was no longer sure that she was committed to nonviolence. Though in the past she had remained nonviolent in the most extreme situations—taken jailings, taken beatings, she told me that she could now all too easily imagine killing a man.

We had a long talk. I spoke to what seems to me the deep, deep need for the women's movement to be a nonviolent movement—if we want to make the changes that we need swiftly and surely as we can, and if we want to see the fewest possible people hurt in the struggle. For I can more and more see this struggle becoming a very bloody one.

I spoke of the need I see for us to reassure men continually as we take from them the privileges they have had so long, take from them the luxury of not having to be weaned from their mothers' care, because they can count on wives, mistresses to play mother to them still; spoke of the need to convince them that this loss will not be as grievous as they fear, that the pleasures of relating to others as equals may really prove greater than the pleasure of relating to others as merely shadows of themselves, second selves. I spoke of the inevitability of panic on most men's part; they are so used to the present state of things. And so, the need to reassure them at the same time that we stubbornly refuse them the old relationships.

Well, it was a long talk. I wasn't at all sure how persuasive I was being. And, as it happened, some time later a mutual friend reported to me that my sister felt estranged from me. And here is how she summed it up. *She didn't feel that I sufficiently respected her anger.*

This took me by surprise. For I feel that I do indeed respect it. I have often enough felt very deep anger myself, about the roles in which women and men are cast.

I told myself, at first, that someone who was giving up a faith in nonviolence must feel, in spite of herself, jealous of the person who still holds it. And I think there is some truth in this. But I began to think, too, that I shouldn't be sure that this was the whole answer. I had better question my relation to her anger more deeply—meaning, really, my relation to my kindred anger.

Perhaps I had withheld from her a full description of that anger, because it was painful to me to describe it and to look at it. I think that I could not kill anyone. But when I study myself I have to acknowledge that in many moments of anger I have, in effect, wished a man dead—wished him not there for me to cope with. So I should have acknowledged precisely this to her, during our talk.

I think of a chapter in Erik Erikson's book, *Gandhi's Truth,* in which he writes a letter to Gandhi as though he were still alive, and offers certain criticisms of him—in the light of insights introduced by psychoanalysis. He writes, of certain things Gandhi wrote, "I seemed to sense the presence of...something unclean, when all the words spelled out *an unreal purity.*"

He charges Gandhi with seeming to be unaware of —*wanting to wish or pray away*—a coexistence of love and hate, an ambivalence, which, he says "must become conscious in those who work for peace." He found this especially when Gandhi wrote of very close relationships.

He says, "If, in order to fathom the truth, we must hold on to the potential of love in all hate, so must we become aware of the hate which is in all love." He submits that only if we accept the presence of ambivalence in the most loving encounters does truth become just what Gandhi means by it—that which supports evolving human nature in the midst of antagonisms, because these antagonisms call for conscious insight rather than for moralistic repression. (Erikson says that of course Gandhi could not possibly have known of the power of ambivalence. But contemporary Gandhians do know of it, or should.)

I think that this is a chapter all pacifists should read and muse about. Because I believe that the response he describes is a response to *us* experienced by many of our comrades. They sense in us an unreal purity. It is a response that puts a fatal distance between us, and makes them feel that they have nothing to learn from us. They feel—too often—that they can't learn from us and can't count on us, because *we don't really know ourselves,* don't *dare* know ourselves.

There is a terrible irony here. Because we want above all to be able to persuade people that truth is a powerful weapon—*the* most powerful weapon if, to use Gandhi's phrase, one *clings* to the truth—not only speaks it out, that is, but acts it out, and stubbornly. (The truth, above all, that every human being deserves respect. We assert the respect due ourselves, when it is denied, through noncooperation; we assert the respect due all others, through our refusal to be violent.) But how can we communicate the power there is in acting out truth, if we give the impression of not daring to be truthful to ourselves—about our own deep feelings; not daring to respect *them?*

Let me quote from a letter from quite another sister, in response to a pacifist mailing. She ascribes to middle-class hangups what she, too, clearly feels to be unreal purity on our part: "It's a rotten shame that middle-class people get so uptight, uneasy about so-called violence. Y'all, in fact, seem not to understand that often the most healthy, beautiful thing to happen is for people to have a knockdown, dragout fight. It's just another form of communication for ghetto folk....All I hear is peace, peace, love, love, Barbara, that is not what I want. I want friction, confusion, confrontation—

violent or not, it doesn't matter. People grow when they are agitated, put up against the wall, at war. All the peace talk is merely a cover-up for weakness, or unwillingness to wage total struggle.... This I have learned from experience.''

Well, it's easy enough to point out that she fails to make certain distinctions. She's right that for people to grow there has to be confrontation, agitation—disturbance of the peace, the charge often is. Whether it's violent or nonviolent, it's almost always *called* violent. But no, she doesn't distinguish clearly between the so-called violence of many such confrontations (including, I for one would grant her, certain knockdown fights) and the very real violence of those that actually harm or kill. If someone ends up dead, then the confrontation hasn't been just a form of communication, and certainly can't be said to have been healthy for that person.

So it may seem easy to put the letter from us. But I think we shouldn't. I think we should pay close attention to the evidence in this letter and other statements like it that many people feel that we fear *so-called* violence quite as much as violence itself. That we fear any stark confrontation or communication; fear telling-it-like-it-is. And fear the emotions roused in us at such moments—don't want to have to look at them.

I recall a letter from still another sister. I had written her about feeling a lot of anger in myself and written that I had found that anger exhausting. She wrote back: "Good healthy anger at the appropriate target is...just as pure and justified as feelings of love, joy, etc....Your reason for not accepting it may be similar to what mine was; being brainwashed all my life into thinking that such emotions were wrong." (This is another sister, by the way, who is turning from nonviolence.)

There is the word "healthy" again. Many radicals feel that we are not quite healthy. They feel that there is health in anger. In the women's movement, a song has been written that sums up their positive feelings about it: "Our anger is changing our faces, Our anger is changing our lives."

They see anger as a necessary emotion if there is to be change.

I think there is some truth in this. I think there is clearly a kind of anger that is healthy. It is the concentration of one's whole being in the determination: this must change.

This kind of anger is not in itself violent—even when it raises its voice (which it sometimes does); and brings about agitation, confrontation (which it always does). It contains both respect for oneself and respect for the other. To oneself it says: "I must change—for I have been playing the part of the slave." To the other it says: "You must change—for you have been playing the part of the tyrant." It contains the conviction that change is possible—for both sides; and it is capable of transmitting this conviction to others, touching them with the energy of it—even one's antagonist. This is the anger the sister who wrote me that first letter speaks of: It communicates.

I think, by the way, that it is accurate to say that A.J. Muste was often in states of anger. And they were healthy states indeed—did change faces, change lives. I can remember a number of meetings about one project or another, in which everything had started to fall apart, because of differences about tactics, because of differences about whether or not the action was feasible at all. And A.J. would begin to describe the existing situation the project was a response to—all that was outrageous about it, demanding our resistance. And our differences would begin to seem unimportant, we would be energized anew, unified by his anger. I think one has to call it that.

It strikes me, though, that when I talked about A.J. at a memorial service after his death, I talked about just such moments and it never occurred to me to use that word.

Why do we who believe in nonviolence shy away from the word?

Well, because there is another kind of anger, very familiar to us, that is not healthy, that is an *affliction,* which, by the way, is the first synonym for anger that is given in the big Webster's International Dictionary.

This anger asserts to another not: "you must change and you can change"—but: "your very existence is a threat to my very existence." It speaks not hope but fear. The fear is: you can't change—and I can't change if you are still there. It asserts not: change! but: drop dead!

The one anger is healthy, concentrates all one's energies; the other leaves one trembling, because it is murderous. Because we dream of a new society in which murder has no place; and it disturbs that dream.

Our task of course, is to transmute the anger that is affliction into the anger that is determination to bring about change. I think, in fact, that one could give that as a definition of revolution.

It is crucial to the task to distinguish between the two kinds of anger. And I think it is very much our task. But I think we are not as capable as we should be of teaching the distinction. To become more capable, I think that we have to face the anger that afflicts us more honestly than we sometimes have. One cannot transmute anger that one represses, but only anger that one faces honestly in its raw state. And it is awkward to try to teach others to do what we haven't done ourselves.

It is particularly hard on us as pacifists, of course, to face our own anger. It is particularly painful for us—hard on our pride, too—to have to discover in ourselves murderers.

I remember suddenly the beautiful frankness of Thomas: "Lord, I believe! Help thou my unbelief!" We have to be as frank: Lord, I love my neighbor. Help me to stop wishing him dead!

I should remark, parenthetically, that there are, of course, radicals who would assert that it is quite possible to kill without hating—kill simply out of that determination to bring about change I have called healthy, kill with a sense of tragic necessity. I think that we should acknowledge that it is possible to kill in this spirit—as Che Guevara surely did, as many North Vietnamese surely do. I don't have to argue here, of course, that if one kills—even in this spirit—one blurs in spite of oneself the vision of a society in which all have the right to life.

But I was talking about the difficulty, for us, of confronting the anger that is affliction. Clearly the anger that is most frightening, because least in our control, almost impossible to try to look at without its rising up to overwhelm us, at least for a time, is anger about our own particular personal oppression.

I think again of the sister who was nonviolent under great provocation while resisting war—but now is resisting her own oppression as a woman and is not sure that she can be nonviolent.

It is not, I know, that she did not feel the war as an oppression of her own being—the war against the Vietnamese and also the possibility of nuclear war; the one a threat to our moral well-being, the other a threat to our very right to be. But to one who is a woman—or black, or chicano, or gay—there is of course an oppression that is more personal than this. It calls into question one's right to be oneself, fully oneself. It touches one's pride in the deepest sense.

Now anger at this has to exist—for it is pride in one's own fundamental worth, is the affirmation of it. But when this anger—this pride—is under the duress of oppression, and when it feels alone, helpless to work the change its nature demands, it can exist only in hiding. And there it becomes *less than itself.*

It does sometimes find ways of keeping itself in relative health. In *To Be a Slave* Julius Lester describes how slaves on plantations would meet in secret in the woods and there hold meetings, dances—in which they could be themselves. He quotes from a song from the time: "Got one mind for the boss to see, Got another mind for what I know is me." In secret, they would be themselves—keep those selves precariously intact.

Black people have done better in this regard perhaps than women—for they did *jointly* acknowledge their oppression, which was more obvious, and jointly acknowledge that they had other selves than the selves presented to the master. Women have had, for the most part, to try to keep alive their pride in isolation from one another. And they have all too often hidden their anger even from themselves. Black people have done this, too, of course. But women have done it more.

A friend of mine had an eloquent dream about this. She is divorced from the man she lived with for many years. She dreamed that she was living with him again and in the dream he had killed a young girl—by accident—and was asking her to help him conceal the fact; and she was doing so. Before she woke from the dream, she asked herself: Why am I living like this? Why am I helping to conceal this murder? I asked her: "Who do you think the young girl in the dream is?"—making my own guess. And she answered, as I would have, that the young girl was her Self.

A dream that speaks a classic truth. For when we are oppressed but see no way out of that oppression, we often actually conspire to suppress the truth about the damage being done to us—and our anger about it.

Just because our anger is in great part hidden—from others and even from ourselves—and when it is finally allowed to emerge into the open—this pride—it is shaking, unsure of itself, and so quick to be violent. For now it believes and yet it doesn't quite dare to believe that it can claim its rights at last.

I think of the severely suppressed anger of the Chinese peasants William Hinton writes of in *Fanshen* when, during the revolution, the property they had always been denied began at last to be divided among them; and they were encouraged, after a lifetime of oppression by the landlords, to speak out what they felt to be due to them from those men—speak out their anger. As they began to speak it, it would overwhelm them and they would often beat the landlords to death on the spot—in a passion, a passion, in part, of uncertainty that their new rights were really theirs.

It is, of course, precisely when some real hope is born at last, when a movement for change begins to gain momentum, that anger pushes up—and has to be contended with.

I have experienced this in the context of the women's movement in a way that took me very much by surprise—because I thought my own anger as a woman was quite known to me. I thought I had noted the situation women are born to, disapproved it, and found my own way to face it. I had, for example, long ago made an instinctive decision not to marry. Given the obvious power relationship between the two sexes, I was afraid that my life would never be my own if I lived with a man—as his would be his own. I recall James Bevel at Birmingham talking about the relation of blacks in that movement to whites: "We love our white brothers; but we don't *trust* them." I didn't dare trust even a man who loved me to let me be myself—not merely his second self. Was afraid that I wouldn't be able to live in comradeship with a man—as a woman can live with a woman.

And so, as I say, I thought I knew my anger. I didn't think of it as suppressed anger—as it had to be in the cases of women who led married lives. And yet—as the women's movement began to gain some momentum, I found that expressions of the male will to dominate began to rouse in me anger in a new degree—anger rising from my toes with a force that startled me at first. Even when the man would be a very young man and obviously under great pressure to act as he thought a man must—and I would know this and with part of myself forgive him. Part of me couldn't forgive him. It was very painful for me to look at this new anger; and it is only gradually that I am learning to transmute it—into determination. For a while I felt helpless in its grip.

Now one way, of course, that we avoid looking at the anger that most afflicts us, one way we find of affirming our pride *without* facing its anger (which we sense can overwhelm us) is by resisting the oppression of that pride, as it were by analogy.

I remember some years ago being asked why I walked through the South; and I questioned myself and decided that perhaps the deepest explanation was my relation to a black woman who worked for my family for many years, and my growing painful awareness that she led too little of her own life, too much simply of ours. I think my love for her certainly had something to do with my walking through the South, but I think now that the more fundamental explanation is that I was protesting that there is any such classification as second-class citizen—and protesting it in my own name.

I am sure this is true for many of you who are white and who joined the struggle against racism. You didn't do it out of altruism; you did it because you knew in your souls something of what it is to be a nigger. If you were gay, and known to be, you even knew what it was to receive the hate stare.

And as pacifists it was much easier for you to control the anger that was in you, to transmute it, to be nonviolent, in *this* struggle—where you could deal with that anger by analogy.

Some of us are perhaps tempted to continue to deal with it always by analogy; and I guess one of the main recommendations I would make at this conference is that we all resist that temptation.

I am not suggesting that we abandon any of the struggles that we have been taking part in. I am suggesting that if we will take upon ourselves the further struggle of confronting our own most particular, own personal oppression, we will find ourselves better able to wage those struggles too—because in more conscious solidarity. Confronting our oppression, I mean, in the company of others—for what seems deeply personal is in truth deeply political.

I find myself very much in agreement with Shulamith Firestone when she writes, in *The Dialectic of Sex,* that the sexual class system is the model for all other systems of oppression, and that until we resist *this,* until we eliminate *this,* we will never succeed in truly eliminating any of the others.

For those of us who are women—or gay—it is probably clear enough what anger I mean should be faced. Though it is often hard enough to admit to, even so. But I would very much include, among those who have a personal anger to confront, the men among you. For if women are oppressed by men, and cannot fully be themselves, men in succumbing to all the pressures put upon them from an early age to dominate, lose the chance to be freely themselves, too—to follow all kinds of contrary impulses. And I cannot believe that there is not in men a deep, buried anger about *this*.

I had written this in my notes for this talk, and I opened the latest *WIN** and there were two articles about just this, written by men. Apparently there are now men's liberation groups springing up. I had been going to suggest that, as WRL has played an important role in counseling men who are unwilling to commit aggression in wars, it might consider playing a comparable role in counseling men who would like to know how to resist committing aggression at home—against women. I do still recommend this.

I could entitle this talk, perhaps: "Are Pacifists Willing to Be Angry?"

I suggest that if we are willing to confront our own most seemingly personal angers, in their raw state, and take upon ourselves the task of translating this raw anger into the disciplined anger of the search for change, we will find ourselves in a position to speak much more persuasively to comrades about the need to root out from all anger the spirit of murder.

---

* A national magazine focusing on nonviolence; ceased publication in 1983.

A SONG FOR GORGONS

Gorgons, unruly gorgons,
With eyes that start, with curls that hiss—

Once
I listened to the father's lies,
Took their false advice:
I mustn't look at you, I'd turn to
Stone.

But now I meet your clear furious stare and
It is my natural self that I become.
Yes, as I dare to name your fury
Mine.
Long asleep,
It writhes awake.

Ssisters, ssisters—of course they dread us.
Theirs is the kingdom
But it is built upon lies and more lies.
The truth-hissing wide-open-eyed rude
Glare of our faces—
If there were enough of us—
Could show their powers and their glories
To be what they merely are and
Bring their death-dealing kingdom
Down.

This is a song for gorgons—
Whose dreaded glances in fact can bless.
The men who would be gods we turn
Not to stone but to mortal flesh and blood and bone.
If we could stare them into accepting this,
The world could live at peace.

I sing this song for those with eyes that start,
With curls that hiss.
Our slandered wrath is our truth, and—
If we honor this—
Can deal not death but healing.

I sing: This *will be done!*

I sing: Their kingdom wane!

(With thanks to Grace Shinell—in *Heresies*—for this spelling of "ssister".)   *1979*

Two Perspectives on Women's Struggle

A talk given at the Catholic Worker March 30, 1973. Published in Liberation, *June 1973.*(BD)

1

> I cannot live without my life!
> —Emily Bronte, *Wuthering Heights*

I want to talk about women's struggle from two different perspectives—first, from the eye of the storm, as it were; next, from off at an angle.

I have just reread many of the novels by women that I felt had meant the most to me: Jane Austen's *Pride and Prejudice,* Charlotte Brontë's *Jane Eyre* and Emily Brontë's *Wuthering Heights,* George Eliot's *Middlemarch;* and from this century, Colette's *The Vagabond,* Willa Cather's *The Professor's House,* and some others I'll mention later. As I reread them I asked myself whether there was anything all these books had in common. They had been written by women very, very different from one another. Virginia Woolf (in *A Room of One's Own*) says of the first four of them that four more incongruous characters could hardly be found. She points out that Charlotte Brontë failed entirely to understand Jane Austen. She might have added that Charlotte wrote of her sister Emily's novel, "Whether it is right or advisable to create beings like Heathcliff, I do not know; I scarcely think it is." However different from each other they may have been, the more I brooded over their four novels, the more I found that is in common—and that could not, I think, be found in novels written by men. To put it in the briefest possible way: All four dramatize the danger in which the Self within one stands if one is a woman—the danger that it will be blighted, because of the authority of men.

Yes, how different *Pride and Prejudice* is from *Jane Eyre.* Yet in each there is a similar drama. In each a man proposes to the heroine with the assurance on *his* part that it is a rich gift he offers; but the heroine at first rejects him. At which he is amazed. Furious, too. She rejects him because she feels her own autonomy threatened.

220

In Colette's *The Vagabond,* too, the heroine rejects a man's proposal—
although she loves him. And because this heroine is particularly articulate
on the subject, let me quote a number of things she says. I think she speaks
for the other women, too. She says (to herself, for she feels she cannot speak
the whole truth to him), "I have met you before and I recognize you. Are
you not he who, thinking he is giving, takes for himself?" She speaks of
his "superb authority, which disposes of me, my future, and the whole of
my little life.... That's all very well, but...what do I become in all that?"
She says, "He is a thief, who steals me from myself." She says, "Instead
of saying, Take me...I ask...What are you giving me? Another myself?
There *is* no other myself."

I might quote the heroine of *Middlemarch* here, too. This heroine,
Dorothea, unfortunately has not rejected Mr. Casaubon's offer. But after
her marriage she speaks to herself comparable words, recognizing now that
she has "shut her best soul in prison, paying it only hidden visits, that she
might be petty enough to please him"

In *The Vagabond* the heroine rejects the man definitely—even though she
loves him; and chooses to remain a vagabond—an actress and a writer. In
Middlemarch the husband (no longer loved) fortunately dies. But *Pride and
Prejudice* and *Jane Eyre* both end with the heroines finally accepting their
suitors, because they can feel at last that there will be equity in the
relationship. Jane can say, "I am my husband's life as fully as he is mine."
And Elizabeth can have the same happy sense of things. The work of both
these books has been to bring this equitable situation about. But it *takes* a
lot of work.

It is harder work in *Jane Eyre* than in *Pride and Prejudice.* Charlotte Brontë
has to resort to something approaching melodrama—have the man's great
house burned to the ground by his mad first wife, and have him badly crippled
in that fire—before the heroine can feel that she can live with him as an equal.
In *Pride and Prejudice* the hero's pride is moderated by less drastic means.
And the crisis has not been as deeply felt by the author to begin with. At
issue actually, as the title implies, is not only his pride but her prejudice.
Jane Eyre, on the other hand, when she refuses Rochester, sees him clearly
enough. The issue for Charlotte Brontë is solely his too masterful behavior.

Those of you who remember *Jane Eyre* may be objecting at this point that
I am reporting the book inaccurately, objecting that Jane rejects Rochester
not because of his attitude toward her but simply because she finds he has
a wife already (who's insane) and she doesn't want to be anybody's mistress.
My suggestion is, however, that you try rereading the book and taking it
less literally. Charlotte Brontë, writing about her sister, says something that
is very true about *herself:* "This I know: the writer who possesses the creative
gift owns something of which he is not always master—something that, at

times, strangely wills and works for itself.'' Much of the material of this book is the author's conscious observation of life, but much, too, I think, is material thrown up out of her unconscious, which she makes what she can of, but never quite controls—as Jane Austen does control her material. Though I think, with Virginia Woolf, that she is the deeper genius.

Here is my suggestion: Read Jane's refusal of Rochester as though the mad wife did not literally exist as a separate character, as though she existed only for Jane, as a nightmare image of her own possible future state if she should marry him. In the scene in which she sees this woman in her room trying on her wedding clothes, then rending the veil and trampling upon it, it is not irrelevant, I think, that she doesn't see her directly; she sees her in a long mirror. Robin Morgan says somewhere that every woman wears around her neck the amulet of madness. I think Charlotte Brontë had this vision of women, too. The scene I have just described follows a series of other scenes after Jane has first said "yes" to Rochester and he then, in "boastful triumph," has taken her out shopping, to buy her new clothes, and has behaved so like a sultan that she has suffered "annoyance and degradation"—and spoken up rebelliously. I would try reading the book as though she refused soon after this not to be *literally* his mistress but to enter a marriage in which she would *feel* like a mistress—feel, in her words, like "a slave who has been bought."

I would also recommend that you try a similar experiment while reading *Wuthering Heights* (a book utterly in the author's control, and yet this book, too, very much born from the unconscious). I suggest that you read it as though Heathcliff were not literally a separate person but were simply—as Cathy herself speaks of him—*herself*. "Nelly, I *am* Heathcliff," she says. She speaks of him as "my own being." Study her marriage—which she, too, hesitates to enter—as though Heathcliff were a Self within her which, when she marries, she abandons for a while. She married Edgar to raise herself out of degradation. (It is true for all these heroines that they can enter a more spacious life only through attaching themselves to a man. In Charlotte Brontë's *Villette,* there is a sequence in which the heroine, an unmarried schoolteacher, has to stay by herself within the walls of the school taking care of a cretin—while everyone else is off on vacation. Again I think one can see this cretin as a dream image of her own condition. Here is the woman's dilemma in these novels: Remain unmarried and undeveloped [the cretin] or marry—and become lost to herself in another sense, the maddened slave.) By marrying Edgar, Cathy improves her condition. She has wanted to marry him partly to be able to pay for the education of the one she calls her "own being." But this being feels utterly abandoned when she does marry. After she has been married for a while, this abandoned Self returns, and her husband—who has been content with her behavior up to now—objects. He tells her, in almost these words: "It is impossible for you to be *my* friend and [to be the friend of this original Self of yours] at the same time, and I absolutely require to know which you choose."

This is the threat the heroine of each of these four novels has to consider. In *Middlemarch,* for example, Dorothea's husband dismisses in "a matter of fact way" "stirring thoughts" that rise in her. Dorothea and Cathy react to this suppression in very different ways. In Dorothea "the resolved submission [does] come." Cathy becomes so rebelliously distraught that she sickens and dies. As Heathcliff cries out after her death, "I cannot live without my life! I cannot live without my soul!"

Perhaps for some of you I labor my reading of *Wuthering Heights.* I suggest then that you study Willa Cather's novel *The Professor's House.* The main character here is a man, but I think it is significant that she chooses to tell the very same story of a Self that is lost in the course of marriage. And it is interesting, too, that toward the end of this book, in the attempt to fully communicate the feeling of loss of Self, she uses consciously this very device I have been suggesting that Emily Brontë uses unconsciously (though with mastery)—the device of imagining that lost Self as a separate character: here a young boy who is left behind, but who, late in the hero's life, reappears to him in visions. "This boy and he had meant back in those faraway days to live some sort of life together." But it had not happened that way. He feels now quite "indifferent" to this life he has actually led, and it seems to him "like the life of another person."

A Self that has been lost, or that stands in danger of being lost. That is again and again the subject of women novelists. It is often the subject of women poets, too. I have just reread many of Emily Dickinson's poems. Here is a passage from a poem about specters of different kinds:

> *Our self behind ourself concealed*
> *Should startle most,*
> *Assassin hid in our apartment*
> *Be horror's least.*

And what is the women's movement all about? Women are now determined to bring this Self out from concealment—a Self still in pain, at this point, still grimacing strangely, as Heathcliff grimaces, still crying out as he cries out.

Emily Dickinson, by the way, calls her poems "nosegays for captives." They are very much that. For again and again she sings, precisely, of "a soul admitted to itself"—"Itself its sovereign, of itself/The soul should stand in awe."

"I cannot live without my life! I cannot live without my soul!" is Heathcliff's cry. Probably all of you who have read the book find him a very haunting figure. Well, he is a figure created out of the very depths of a woman's being. Here is how the narrator describes him as he utters that cry: "He dashed his head against the knotted trunk; and lifting up his eyes howled, not like a man, but like a savage beast getting goaded to death with knives and spears. I observed several splashes of blood about the bark of the trees, and his hands and forehead were both stained. . . . It appalled me."

It is going to appall a lot of people, I am afraid, but in one mode or another, some more subdued than this, some not, that is what women now are going to keep on crying: "I cannot live without my life! I cannot live without my soul!"

As a matter of fact, I don't think the world can well survive without the release of that Self. But here is still another subject.

Let me quote again from *The Vagabond* (which was Colette's favorite among her books, by the way). That heroine cries out: "Whence come I and on what wings that it should take me so long, humiliated and exiled, to accept that I am myself?"

I have been talking about women's struggle from the eye of the storm. Whether you are a woman or a man, I urge you if you haven't done so to enter in imagination that storm center, and listen for Heathcliff's cry—in something written by a woman, or something said by her; or you may be a woman saying it to yourself, not quite audibly yet: "I cannot live without my life!" A lot of women still feel uneasy about uttering that cry aloud.

A fascinating book in *that* respect is Mary McCarthy's *A Charmed Life*. It's a book whose central drama is precisely the drama I have talked about in other novels. The heroine still lives under the shadow of her former husband. Her rational self does not concede him authority over her, but in one dramatic episode after another, she grants him that authority in spite of herself. She struggles against it, and by the end of the book she has struggled free. But it's the very end of the book I want to talk about. The heroine is driving along in her car, alone, and talking to herself about this victory she has just recognized: ". . . She could trust herself. For the first time in years, since the summer she had married Miles, she could say this aloud. She said it and her wonder grew. She had changed; she was no longer afraid of herself." In almost the next sentence she sees the headlights of a car coming round a curve—on the wrong side of the road—and realizes that she has been crashed into, and killed.

I took part with Mary McCarthy in a three-day panel discussion of Women in Literature held recently at Washington and Lee University. (This was the occasion of my rereading the novels I have been talking about.) And I asked her: Isn't it as though you were saying here, unconsciously: if a woman dares to say aloud to herself that her life is her own, Heaven will strike her dead? She answered that she hadn't intended such a reading and explained the ending in terms of a certain comic theme, about mortality, she had been working with throughout the book. But she is a wonderfully honest woman and she added: Who ever knows, of course, what one's unconscious is doing? I persist in believing that her unconscious was making the dramatic point: Better perhaps not to speak aloud—even to ourselves—of our struggle to possess our own souls. Better perhaps to wage that struggle secretly.

The other evening I went to a reading at the Manhattan Theatre Club of a group of poems Louise Bernikow has been collecting for an anthology— the kind of poems by women that never have been chosen for anthologies in the past because the editors and publishers have always been men. The first poem read was a poem by Muriel Rukeyser about Käthe Kollwitz which begins: "What would happen if one woman told the truth about her life? The world would split open." Many women, I think, still hesitate to wage our struggle aloud because they fear just that—fear that in one way or another the world would split open.

But I think one could answer the poet's question in another way: What would happen if one woman told the truth about her life? She would reveal the truth that for a long time now, for too long a time, the world *has* been split open. It is about this split that I want to talk next. Here is the other perspective on our struggle that I'll attempt.

2

Perhaps the sexes are more related than we think.
—Rainer Maria Rilke, *Letters to a Young Poet*

I think the world has been split in half for much too long—between masculine and feminine. Or rather, between what is said to be masculine and said to be feminine. *"Vive la différence!"* has been a popular saying—everybody pretending that it was something to be celebrated. Something to be forgotten at one's peril, too. There is an obvious physical difference between us that serves to re-create the race. (Though it has served us rather too well.) But psychic as well as physical differences have been meant. And I would like to argue that perhaps our most crucial task at this point of history—a task for women *and* men—is not to celebrate these so-called differences between our natures but to question boldly, by word and act, whether they properly exist at all, or whether they do not violently distort us, whether they do not split our common humanity.

In *Jane Eyre,* by the way, when Rochester proposes to Jane under a great chestnut tree, a storm brews. As he begins to exult at her answer, the author suddenly asks: "What ailed the chestnut tree? It writhed and groaned." That night she has the tree split in two, its life blighted.

I think the tree of all our lives has been split in two between the so-called masculine and the so-called feminine. Manliness has been defined as assertion of the self. Womanliness has been defined as the nurturing of selves other than our own—even if we quite lose our own in the process. (Women are supposed to find in this loss their true fulfillment.) But every individual person is born *both* to assert herself or himself *and* to act out a sympathy for others trying to find themselves—in Christian terms, meant to love one's self *as* one loves others, the two motions of the spirit not really divisible if one assumes that there is that-of-God in each of us. Jesus never taught that we should split up that commandment—assigning "love yourself" to men, "love others" to women. But society has tried to. And its assignment of assertion and sympathy to separate sexes has had fatal consequences.

Fatal in the first place to all of us as individuals—distorting our natures whether we are women *or* men. Women lost to themselves in one way—their selves merged in the selves of others; men lost, one can well say, in another way: Coming to feel that the energies of others belong to them by right of their sex, and no need for mutuality here; coming to regard themselves as nature's lords, and expected by the world to be just that, they have lost the sense of what their human natures really are. This has been hard on them, I am quite sure—though it has been intoxicating, too. Virginia Woolf writes in *A Room of One's Own:* "Women have served all these centuries as looking glasses possessing the magic and delicious power of reflecting the figure of man at twice its natural size." Men have had to carry around these selves twice their natural size. A burden, because a lie. It is the truth that frees us.

I keep harking back to Charlotte Brontë, but I find her an almost inexhaustible source of images that enlighten this subject. So let me describe now two passages from her novel *Villette* that to me speak very clearly of the need in which we stand. They are very much flights of her unconscious mind. She hasn't introduced them for any reasons that are evident. They are in no way necessary to background or to plot. She was just—moved to put them in; her spirit, I would say, trying to dream some cure for the disorder she describes again and again in her books: a deep disorder in the relations between men and women.

In the first passage, the heroine, who is a teacher at a girls' school, is persuaded to substitute in the school play for a student who is sick. When she is handed a man's costume to put on, she refuses, but then suddenly decides to wear *half* of it: She puts on a man's vest, jacket, tie *over* her dress. She finds, then, that a mysterious energy fills her; she plays her part with great zest. On another occasion, she and the young doctor whom she loves attend an event at which prizes are given out. She wins a cigar case, the doctor a woman's headpiece with a veil. He wants to swap with her but she refuses; she keeps the cigar case, and his mother, who has accompanied them, takes home the headpiece. Later in the book, the doctor sits dozing at home in an armchair, and the mother, seeing him sleeping there, tiptoes off to fetch the filmy headpiece, sets it upon his head, then wraps him in her shawl, and stands gazing at him—finding in this a mysterious satisfaction.

During the third evening of discussions at Washington and Lee, I spoke of these passages and said that they seemed to me to dream the saving answer for all of us, women and men. I presented the argument that I am making now to you—that the task for all of us is to erase the so-called differences between the sexes, bring out the woman in all men, the man in all women. And I expected a great deal of resistance to this idea. But to my astonishment the young men in the audience were no more alarmed than the young women. One of the other writers present, Caroline Kizer, told me that I should get a book that is just out, *Toward a Recognition of Androgyny* by Carolyn G. Heilbrun. I've now read it and recommend it to all of you. (It's published by Knopf.) Here I found the very thesis I had struggled toward on my own. And who knows how many other people, unkown to each other, are arriving at this answer—because necessity is the mother of invention. Carolyn Heilbrun writes: "I believe that our future salvation lies in a movement away from sexual polarization and the prison of gender toward a world in which individual roles and the modes of personal behavior can be freely chosen. The ideal toward which I believe we should move is best described by the term 'androgyny.' "

She makes the point, by the way, that the androgynous ideal persists in all the dreams of mysticism. She quotes Norman O. Brown: "In the West, cabalistic mysticism has interpreted Genesis 1:27—'God created man in his own image...male and female created he them'—as implying the androgynous nature of God and of human perfection before the Fall. From cabalism this notion passed into the Christian mysticism of Boehme, where it is fused with the Pauline mysticism of Galatians 3:28—'There can be no male and female; for ye are all one man in Christ Jesus.' " (One human, he might better have said.) And Brown quotes Berdyaev: "According to God's conception of him, man is a complete, masculinely feminine being....Original sin is connected...with division into two sexes and the Fall of the androgyne, i.e. of man as a complete being." That vision holds great truth for me.

This Fall, one can add, has resulted not only in the distortion of both our natures, but in general violence. By splitting human natures into the so-called masculine and the so-called feminine we have got: lost women nurturing men who become the exploiters of others, and of Nature itself. A man is taught violence at his mother's knee, as he watches her let her Self be taken from her. Another novel I reread before going to the conference at Washington and Lee was Virginia Woolf's *To the Lighthouse,* and in it there is a wonderful passage that dramatizes just such a moment. Mrs. Ramsey is reading a fairytale to her small son, when her husband appears, wanting sympathy. He has been feeling depressed about his work. The little boy is annoyed and tries to hold the mother's attention. "But no, nothing would make Mr. Ramsey move on. There he stood, demanding sympathy. . . . Mrs. Ramsey, who had been sitting loosely, folding her son in her arm, braced herself, and half turning, seemed to raise herself with an effort, and at once to pour erect into the air a rain of energy, a column of spray, looking at the same time animated and alive. . . quietly though she sat . . . and into this delicious fecundity, this fountain and spray of life, the fatal sterility of the male plunged itself, like a beak of brass, barren and bare. He wanted sympathy. He was a failure, he said." She reassures him. A man named Charles Tansley thinks him the greatest metaphysician of the time, she tells him. "But he must have more than that. It was sympathy he wanted, to be assured of his genius, first of all, and then to be taken within the circle of life, warmed and soothed, to have his senses restored to him, his barrenness made fertile, and all the rooms of the house made full of life." She reassures him again. "But he must have more than that. . . . He must be assured that he too lived in the heart of life; was needed; not here only, but all over the world. . . . Standing between her knees, very stiff, James felt all her strength flaring up to be drunk and quenched by the beak of brass, the arid scimitar of the male, which smote mercilessly, again and again, demanding sympathy. . . . He was a failure, he repeated." She reassures him still again. "If he put implicit faith in her, nothing should hurt him. . . not for a second should he find himself without her. So boasting of her capacity to surround and protect, there was scarcely a shell of herself left for her to know herself by; all was so lavished and spent." He is finally satisfied and leaves. And the child notes that his mother seems to fold herself together in exhaustion.

Perhaps some of you have read Shulamith Firestone's *The Dialectic of Sex.* If you haven't, there is a chapter in which she reinterprets Freud's concept of the Oedipus complex. I find it very persuasive. And here is another look at the lesson the mother allows the child to receive. The writer submits that "the only way that the Oedipus complex can make full sense is in terms of power." Though both parents have power over the child, she points out, the child "has a bond with [the mother] in oppression" because she, too, is oppressed by the father. Deep down the child has a certain contempt for the father, with all his power, and sympathizes with the mother. But at a certain point the boy is expected to begin to identify with the father. He resists this, but the father makes it clear to him that he is the one who can show him the road into the world. So he finally represses his deep attachment to his mother, represses his contempt for his father, and emerges into the honorable state of manhood. She writes, "No wonder that such a transition leaves...a complex. The male child, in order to save his own hide, has had to abandon and betray his mother and join ranks with her oppressor." And, she stresses: here is "an all too beautiful transition into power over others." I agree. Here within the home is the primary imperialism. Not primary in the sense of the most cruel; primary in the sense that it is the first learned; here the habit is formed. And no wonder, too, that this child grows up willing to despoil the earth itself, that has mothered us. For this is not the way in which a child should come into manhood.

In the original story of Oedipus, you may recall, the way in which Oedipus has come to worldly power has produced at last a plague upon the land. And it is necessary for him to search back into the past and recognize the moment at which he committed violence against Nature—the act that led to his taking his father's place. There is certainly a plague upon our world today; and perhaps we, too, have above all to search back to that moment in every man's life when he commits a crime against Nature, so that he can take his father's place in the world. And where mothers, one had better add, commit the crime of letting him do it.

In the original story who is it who is able to see from the start what the crime has been? The seer, Tiresias, who, it happens, has been both man and woman in his life. Carolyn Heilbrun writes at some length about the Oedipus story, and I disagree in certain ways with her reading of it. But I agree very much that at the end of the story, when Oedipus puts out his eyes, this should be read not simply as the act of a man mutilating himself in grief and horror at what he has done, but as an act in which he tries to make himself like the seer Tiresias, who is literally blind, but has an inner vision that Oedipus has lacked. I think that we all have to seek the vision of Tiresias now—of the one who is both man and woman.

If we do seek this vision—seek to return to a state of androgyny which we have lost—we will have to redefine many relationships. First, the relation of mothers to children. Fathers will become mothers, too, of course. And motherliness will be subtly redefined. Let it no longer mean giving one's very life for the father, then the son, to feed upon. Let the mother teach her son: yes, we must give of ourselves, "we are members one of another," but this is not to be read to mean simply: *we* (women) are members of *you* (men). Let her teach both son and daughter equity, mutuality. Which is to say, nonviolence.

(It has occurred to me lately, by the way, that nonviolent actions are by their nature androgynous. In them the two impulses that have long been treated as distinct, "masculine" and "feminine," the impuse of self-assertion and the impulse of sympathy, are clearly joined; the very genius of nonviolence, in fact, is that it demonstrates them to be indivisble, and so restores human community: One asserts one's rights as a human being, but asserts them with consideration for the other, asserts them, that is, precisely *as* rights belonging to any person—mine and therefore yours, yours and therefore mine.)

The relations between parents and children will be redefined. So, of course, will the relations between men and women. There are many men and women who very much fear still what any such change will bring about—such as the critic who reviewed Carolyn Heilbrun's book for *The New York Times*—who fears, in the absence of polarization between the sexes, an alarming falling-off of sexual desire. My own conviction is that there is sufficient difference between any two individuals born (if only they will allow themselves to be individuals) to create polarity enough for desire to flourish. I believe there is deep eroticism in comradeship.

Perhaps, though, the deepest fear among both women and men now is one that is rarely acknowledged. Here let me read one of the poems I heard the other night at the Manhattan Theatre that I found most remarkable. It is a poem by Elizabeth Barrett Browning:

> I thought once how Theocritus had sung
> Of the sweet years, the dear and wished-for years,
> Who each one in a gracious hand appeared
> To bear a gift for mortals, old or young:
> And, as I mused it in his antique tongue,
> I saw, in gradual vision through my tears,
> The sweet, sad years, the melancholy years,
> Those of my own life, who by turns had flung
> A shadow across me. Straightway I was 'ware,
> So weeping, how a mystic Shape did move
> Behind me, and drew me backward by the hair;
> And a voice said in mastery, while I strove,—
> "Guess now who holds thee?"—"Death," I said. But, there,
> The silver answer rang—"Not Death, but Love."

What an acutely painful vision. A vision that all too many women would confront if they dared look deeply into themselves: a vision of love—that force which is meant to create and to sustain—instead drawing her backward by the hair; love acting upon her in such a way that she can mistake it for death. I think the truth is that many women fear at this moment to acknowledge even to themelves their own struggle, because they fear, if they look too closely, to find love wears this very aspect for them. And they fear that they may see the choice before them as one of renouncing love altogether. And men fear, too, that they will make this choice.

But of course it is not love itself that wears this aspect, but the distortion of love: a love that is supposed to move a woman in one way, a man in quite another—causing the woman to cleave to the man, the man to cherish her as his so-called better self, but as just that, merely that: a portion of his self.

With this ideal of love held for so long, no wonder that we have been taught to think of homosexual love as sick. For if such *is* the ideal, the example of two people living together simply in loving comradeship is of course very threatening. I could almost say that I think homosexual love should be the model for love between men and women. I cannot quite say it because homosexuals have for so long been half-persuaded to think of *themselves* as ill, that they—that we—rarely enough serve as such models. Still I do think that as men and women struggle now to work out new relationships, marked by equity, it will be helpful for them to ask themselves, at difficult moments: How would we decide this if we were simply two men living together, or two women?

Let me end with a passage from Rilke. For as Carolyn Heilbrun documents, poets as well as mystics long ago dreamed what others are now beginning at last to speak about. He writes in *Letters to a Young Poet:*

> And perhaps the sexes are more related than we think, and the great renewal of the world will perhaps consist in this, that man and maid, freed from all false feeling and aversion, will seek each other not as opposites, but as brother and sister, as neighbors, and will come together as human beings.

Yes, if men and women—and women and women, and men and men—should finally learn to come together simply as human beings, *no more* and *no less,* then love would no longer draw women backward by the hair, away from themselves; and it would no longer drive men to seek themselves where they will never find themselves, in despoiling others, and in despoiling the earth itself.

Confronting
One's Own Oppression:
An Exchange of Letters

These letters are excerpted from a 1971-72 correspondence between Barbara and Ray Robinson, whom Barbara has described as "a black comrade with whom I walked through the south in 1963-64 on the Québec to Guantanamo Walk for Peace and Freedom." During that walk, Barbara and Ray both served time in the Albany, Georgia, city jail (an experience described in Barbara's book Prison Notes*). Barbara also corresponded with Ray's wife, Cheryl Buswell-Robinson, who is white. All the letters have been edited and many have been omitted altogether. Ray and Cheryl lived at the Peoples Farm they had established near Selma, Alabama—working to produce food to fuel the revolution and to provide a radical consciousness raising center. Introducing this correspondence in her book* We Cannot Live Without Our Lives, *Barbara noted: "Most of the people who have found their way to the farm have been white college students. Ray complained to me in earlier letters of their staying too briefly. Then in one letter he exclaimed, 'Really they don't have anything.' I wrote back, 'Do you judge them too harshly? Could that be why no more of them stay?' " The first letter below is Ray's response to that question.* (JM)

Letter from Ray Robinson, *sent January 14, 1971*

Barbara my sister—the silence on my part have been because I'm very calm and at ease. We now have the use of a machine that will gather our harvest— Now we are only waiting for a nice day to go to the fields with the tractor. . . . I said I feel relaxed and at ease because I remember your asking me "about me judging" too harsh! This I will try to drive home again to you. I have been the victim of these over pampered naive thrill seeking people who now have learned to use their index finger with a sign saying peace. . . . I cannot tell these people that what is being done to the oppress people have full bearing on them. I cannot tell them that they are the enemy—yes they are the enemy of my people. The onliest way that they'll not is for them to "prove" that they have given up their class priviledges. Now I'm telling it like it is. . . . I'm tired of seeing my two children and all the rest in my community suffering from rickets of the bones while these over fed fun seeking "revolutionaries" comes thru here. I'm tired of this. I tired of hearing on the radio that my brothers in struggle is being cut down like dogs in the street, while these young over fed rich kids run in here and start giving me all this shit about "I'm being too hard on them." I'm getting very much up tight with these people who are so hung up on themselves, knowing not nothing about the people around them—which happens to be my people....Then it hit me hard Barbara, what are you doing now? What? Do you know that this is happening? Maybe this is why we cannot communicate? I'm getting so God damn tired of people telling me that I'm too hard on people. This is a laugh. I'm tired of people relaxing. I have given myself to Revolution and I can only communicate with fellow revolutionaries. I'm tired of hearing people talk about their little hang-ups. Their escapes. On on on and on stories....Barbara I often think of what you said about me—"I really wish I could understand Ray." Well if you have never been to the bottom, complete bottom, no you cannot understand me. I can never forget the struggle. I am deeply involved in it. Just like the day you left Albany. I could not leave. The entire country, world is Albany to me. There could be no rest. I am forever involved. Why cannot you see this. Then if you could why would you say such things as "maybe I could be a little hard on the people here— as far as judging goes." ....I know that these people know nothing at all. But they want to have a good thing and don't want nobody to tread upon their freedoms. Why cannot a revolutionary understand, their duty is to serve....Why can't these people understand that they are servants to the Struggle. *But maybe this is that they can't see themselves servant to black people.* This may be the reason. But I say I will shake the dust out and keep on keeping on. I know poor people. I am one.

From Cheryl Buswell-Robinson:

Barbara—I feel like a burden has been lifted from me by Ray writing this letter. I've been accused of hating white people (another way of saying I hate myself) because I keep hitting at white skin privilege and class privilege. Very few white persons have come here who could understand the black experience in depth, they can't communicate with free, strong black males and then blame it on Ray for their lack of humanity. But I feel good, every bit of scorn tests us to make us stronger. Oh, *live the revolution!*

Cheryl

Letter to Ray Robinson and Cheryl Buswell-Robinson,

dated January 15, 1971

Ray, dear brother

Cheryl, dear sister—

Thank you both for writing as you did. Yes, it lifts a burden—on both sides—to have the truth spoken out.

I do, I do understand your anger.

I haven't of course, Ray, been to the bottom, complete bottom, that you have touched. Have been there, perhaps, for moments—like the moment when the doctor walked away from me in the Albany jail.* But to be there for moments isn't at *all* like being there day in day out, and I know that well. Yes, I could leave Albany for home—which would be altogether unlike Albany. As you say, the entire country is Albany to you. I could leave and did leave. And you, Ray, went on walking. And I recognize what that means about the difference between us. True, I went home to write about it, and feeling that that work was the work I could do best. But that's just part of the truth. You write, "I'm tired of people relaxing." I enter the struggle, then rest, enter it, then rest. You never rest.

And yet the terrible thing that I have to face in myself is: even so, I seem to be worn out now. I try and try to find my energies again, so that I can take more part. But I feel like a tired old woman. I can't believe that this will last forever. But it does last and last.

Now in part, in part, I think, this is because—for the past two years in particular—I have been at another kind of bottom. Not the bottom you know, but a bottom nevertheless. And knowing the anger of being powerless— others having a power over me that no one should have over another. Having to live with this day in day out as you live with *your* oppression. Which is why I can say, I think, very truly: I do understand your anger.

And perhaps it is anger which has taken my strength. Of which I never had enough. Because I haven't known well enough how to turn it into revolution. (Yes, Cheryl, "live the revolution!") And as I write this, the tears begin to gush from my eyes, and I know that I'm writing the truth of it.

The bottom I write about of course is the bottom of being a homosexual. Facing always the threat of being despised for that. Facing these past two years the threat of more than that—the threat that a man without scruples (X's former husband) would exploit the fact that society turns its face against us to take her children from her or, by threatening this, keep the power of dictating how she shall live. I think that threat has waned. Our paying what

---

* A moment I describe in *Prison Notes*. Exhausted by fasting in the Albany City jail, I felt at one point very sick and was scared. The jail doctor was near, and my cell mates called to him to come and look at me. But because of his hostility to us he refused. (BD)

amounted to ransom for the children quieted him. (But how it hurt to have to resolve things that way—not daring an open struggle, because the children were hostages.) And—the fear of what he might do is still in me. And the knowledge that society would willingly aid and abet him. And the anger about this....

Letter to Ray Robinson, *February 18, 1971*

Ray, dear brother—

Thank you for your letter. And thank you for the love in it.

You write as though the local authorities were really out at this point to jail you all. Tell me what they figure out to charge you with.

But about my "problem."

Ah, but no—not *my* problem, any more than "the Negro problem" is *your* problem. The racist and the sexist are the problem. We are the sufferers. Well, they are too in their way. But we must be the healers—if we can find our strength to be, our pride. If we have a problem, this is what it is: to find that strength and that pride.

Which you have done. And how it thrills me to know that you have. And which I have not yet done. But am determined to do. Oh I've begun. Began many years ago. And even, actually, thought that I had completed the job— had my full pride. I have been astonished to find that it is not so.

And so this is my most immediate task now—to find that pride in its fullness.

You write me, Ray, that you have been trying to call me "to duty" for over two years now. But you see—I think that *this* is my present duty. I think that until I manage to complete this task, I will be a very poor revolutionary on any other front.

You write me that you told Beth* the problem she talked about was only part of the struggle, just like a spoke in a wheel. "Every spoke counts," you wrote. But I wonder a little—do you really entirely believe that this spoke counts? That this pride counts as black pride counts? "One cannot just deal with it as though it everything," you write. Of course, of course. It is a spoke in the wheel. But it *is* a spoke. You write me, "Get involved with the total Revolution. Then you see that what is called your problem will be solved— mainly because the over-all prize is so big, so great and beautiful, that what you think is a big, big problem is just a mild steppingstone." But, Ray— well, two things.

---

* a lesbian woman who had been staying with Ray and Cheryl. Beth became able to talk with Ray about her sexual identity only after he shared with her Barbara's letter of Jan. 15, 1971. (JM)

What do you think I have been doing over the past ten years, if not get myself involved in other parts of the Revolution as deeply as I was able?— pluck up my courage to walk through the South, to march on the Pentagon, to go twice to Vietnam? But this did *not* solve my "problem."

Now the fact that I have this "problem" (or rather that sexists have it) is probably one reason that I did walk through the South, did go to Vietnam. I am not black but because I am homosexual I know in my deepest being what it feels like to be despised—so I didn't walk out of some sense that it would be nice of me to help the downtrodden; I walked because I am a nigger too. And no one should be a nigger. My soul protested it for all of us. And I went to Vietnam because you and I are gooks too. No one should be a gook.

Yes, there it is in the Bible: There could be no more revolutionary statement: "Love your neighbor as your self." Acknowledge his, her, right-to-be as equal to your own. This is the wheel of which you speak, surely—of which all the spokes are a part. A wheel of love for one another, respect for one another. Or rather, the turning wheel of our insistence that this respect be born. I joined myself to that wheel.

But then a strange thing happened. No, not strange at all, I guess. I could find the courage to walk through the South or to go to Vietnam because I was a nigger too, and because I had in part, in part, and yet in a very real way, already found my pride—enough to want to assert it with all my being: *no* person is a nigger. I was actually building up more and more courage, though I would often be exhausted, have to take time out for my strength to return, because I am not a fearless person by temperament. I'm scared of water, I'm scared of high places. I'm scared of being hurt— But I was gaining more and more courage, nevertheless. Courage to meet the bully— and stand up to him. But then— I had this new encounter with a bully, with a series of bullies. New because I wasn't called a nigger-lover this time, or an un-American traitor; I was called a degenerate. Called that (just to describe one instant in the struggle)—called that to my face by the lawyer of my adversary, and our own lawyer not rebuking him or contradicting him, clearly enough assuming that what he'd called us was undeniable. One person after another lining up next the original bully (X's former husband) as ally to deny X and me any human rights because of our "degeneracy." In short, my pride was for the first time, perhaps, assaulted *in its depth*. One's sexuality—well, it is so at the heart, the heart, the heart of one. And just as one fears physical hurt to that part of one's body, feels its vulnerability, so one fears the psychic assault—and of course, yes, precisely because it is most deeply joined to what is spiritual in us, what allows us to lose the cramped sense of being only single selves.

I don't yet entirely understand it, and must seek to understand it better, but: this particular confrontation (given especially the very real threats poised of damage not simply to me and to X but to X's children)—exhausted my courage, as it had not been exhausted by any of the other confrontations, even those in which I literally risked my life. And I have found, to my dismay, that I now lack the courage I had once even for *other* kinds of encounters. When I went out to the trial of the Chicago 7 last winter, and began to be hassled by the marshals there—in the old days I would have found my poise much more readily to deal with this. But I felt a helpless trembling somewhere inside me that I didn't know how to dispel. Or a while ago when the Income Tax people summoned me to their office to demand that I pay the taxes I refuse, and I still refused and they threatened to seize my car, marched me out to it with a great martial show (then were thwarted, comically, because it was not registered in my name)—there too I was dismayed to find myself much more affected by their bullying bluster (though I hope I concealed it) than I would have been in the old days. It must be that any bully or group of bullies now recalls to me those other bullies who touched my pride where I could not bear to have it touched.

And so, and so—what I am trying to say is that it would be wrong—it would be useless—for me to throw myself again into the larger struggle (wholeheartedly, I mean; I still do take a certain part) before I find how to quiet this trembling in myself. I could not be effectual. I have now to face squarely *my own particular oppression*—never never forgetting—of course—but how could I?—that others are oppressed in other ways—and all of us linked. But do you remember when Brad told C.B. that he should not think merely about his own problem as a Black man but should be out at the military base protesting war as well as racism? And C.B. told him that while the white man had his foot on his throat, his efforts had first of all to be to get that foot off—I am in that position now. Well—who knows when the foot (sexism) will be removed? Not soon. My efforts have to be, first of all, to find my proper pride for this struggle. Once I have it—I will be so much stronger a spoke in the larger wheel. And so much more able to bear a little weight for others—whether like me or unlike me in their oppression.

Which brings me back to the question I started to ask earlier: Do you really entirely believe that this spoke counts—that this pride counts as Black pride counts? You, too, once thought that we were sick people, didn't you? Needing to be shown the true womanly path? I remember your speaking to me in that way—most gently and lovingly, but clearly assuming that what I needed was not to find my pride in my sexual nature but to find a cure for it. Have you completely changed your mind about that? Or do you still somewhere, in the depths of you, think—as some people think: He's a Jew, *but* a wonderful fellow; or he's a Black man *but*...she's homosexual *but* I love her? You see, when you say that it's not really such a big problem—well, there are millions and millions of us. Have been billions of us down through history. We're not as visible as Black people. Which makes it in a lot of ways easier for us, in some ways more difficult—because we can lead divided lives, and this does peculiar things to the psyche.

Very very much love.

And may your child be born safely.

. . . .

. . . .

. . . .

On September 2, 1971, on my way to a War Resisters League conference in Athens, Georgia (at which I expected to give the talk "On Anger" included in this book) I was in an automobile accident. This left me disabled and bedridden for almost a year. (BD)

Letter to Ray Robinson, *June 28, 1972*

Ray, my brother—

Your letter chides me again—"I must see actions now coming from you."

I am barely on my feet again, after almost a year of being a complete invalid....In the days when I had my health (such as it ever was) did I not act? And at my own bidding.

It is cruel of you to write as you do, Ray—though I know you don't mean to be cruel. Don't you think that it gives me pain—not to be in the struggle?

If I were able to be in it now, it would be in the women's movement especially that I would be active....You would probably still be calling to me to take *different* actions. But we have to find our own bearings, don't we? You yourself have done this, in a wonderful way....

You write in your letter, "Come aboard....Trust our judgment." But Ray, no, no. You don't really mean that, do you? We have always to judge for ourselves, as best we can—don't you really believe?—though always questioning our judgements, trying to deepen them. You know, in a letter some time ago which I think I never answered, you rebuked me for leaving Resurrection City for New York on the day the troops closed it down. Yes, it was the *wrong* direction to head. I know it well. I knew it then. And do you know why I headed in that wrong direction? (As I walked down the boardwalk, someone—whom I didn't know—remarked, "Hey, you're walking in the wrong direction." And I can remember still everything in me crying: Oh, yes, oh yes, I know I am, oh dammit dammit dammit! But still I went in the wrong direction.) Why? Because I listened meekly to a call from someone else, instead of the call in my own heart, which said: stay, stay,

stay right here. (And if I had stayed, I wouldn't have marched off to any Department of Agriculture building, or wherever it was that Abernathy marched everybody. Almost everybody. I would have stayed, as you did, there at the *city,* which is yes where every one of us should have stayed that day.) But Dave Dellinger had asked me to be at a meeting in New York that night to talk about actions in Chicago at the time of the Convention. And he had said that he needed me there. I made no contribution at all at the New York meeting—because all I could think of was: what is happening at Resurrection City? and why am I not *there?* And the joke is, too, that Dave himself, if he had been in my position, would have known that he should stay. I learned that day—I hope—always to trust my own deep sense of what I should do, and not just obediently trust the judgment of others—even others better than I am. I can't just come where you call me, Ray. I have to find my own bearings. When I have the strength. I have to continue to analyze and to face up to my own oppression. As you have done to yours. *This* will make us true comrades—not my running off meekly to jump aboard a ship you're captain of.

LOVE SONG

I want to try to tell you what I feel
When you and I lie naked together:
                              The walls

Of this house fall—
We embrace in the wide air.
Near branches (lilac), clouds in streamers,
The glimmering stars,
Become one seamless garment that we wear.
Voices of crickets take small stitches in it;
The pattern of their airy cries is pricked
Upon our flesh.
Wind turns the leaves of the lilac upon their stems
And this rush of leaves is our breath—
Taken between kisses.
As day and dark and no and yes are shaken together, we
Rock each other awake.
                              With her quick
Quiet leap, our cat comes to the bed.
She likes the way we smell now in our heat,
Stares at us, then lies down at our feet
To hum an elated song.
Does she, too, dream as she hums
That all life is one?

1977

Section 6: Full Circle

I must undress down to the bone, take all the
pictures off the wall
and remember who I am.

—from a poem written in 1939-40

FOR BARBARA SMITH

Your first words to me—"We've
Been in the same struggles"—
Generous words
For I steal time-out that you cannot.
But yes, our lives join.
I keep dreaming a poem to you
Which rejoices in this.

My voice shakes, though.
In place of words
I find tears in my throat.
They have been locked in me
But now burst.
So much has been taken from us.

But we will take it back.
I sit next to you again—
My hands in yours.
They took this: our right to touch.
Black, white
Woman, woman.
We take it back
We take it back.

1981

The Purpose of Sexuality

Bradford Lyttle and I were comrades during the 1960's in a number of actions against war and against racism which the Committee for Nonviolent Action organized. And as members of the C.N.V.A. executive committee we also sat through innumerable meetings together. He was the coordinator of many of the actions in which I took some part (and he was often the one who had dreamed them up)....

In the summer of 1974 Brad visited me one afternoon and we fell into a discussion of homosexuality. I had come out publicly as a lesbian the year before. He said he thought it wrong to deny homosexuals their civil rights, but felt that homosexual relationships were "substitute relationships" formed by people who could not seem to form "satisfactory" heterosexual relationships and, soon after, we exchanged several letters. The one included here was printed in WIN *magazine, October 10, 1974. (BD)*

8-12-74

Dear Brad—

Yes, I really do want to discuss "these matters" with you—sexuality.

You write: "If human animals possess a genital differentiation, obviously for purposes of sexual reproduction, it seems reasonable to expect them to have a corresponding and appropriate emotional differentiation. Heterosexuality would seem the appropriate biological attitude." I don't follow you here. Would you try to put into words for me what you feel to be the appropriate emotional differentiation? How should a man feel toward a woman, a woman toward a man? My own strong conviction is that this very belief that we *should* feel differently toward one another lies at the root of all our difficulties. Yes, the genital differentiation is for purposes of reproduction, obviously. But what purposes would you say that the emotional differentiation serves? *I* would say that down through history the claim that there must be such a differentiation has served the purposes of male domination.

243

Actually, later in your letter you yourself write in a way that plays down those so-called differences between us. Writing of Reich, you say, "[His] notion about a generalized sexual energy leads to a corollary that Reich didn't seem to see the significance of, that is that the energy doesn't necessarily have a male or female character." And you write: "what this means in regard to the question of gayness is that the male or female psychological aspects of a person's personality are superficial in comparison to the person's deeper sexuality." I very much agree. And here is a question for you: Does this energy not have a biological source? I ask this because you write earlier in your letter, "Gayness seems to have no reasonable biological origin. Why should nature frustrate the mechanisms of procreation?" I'll answer your question with another question: *Shouldn't* these mechanisms be frustrated rather more often than they are? Isn't overprocreation a problem? And I'll answer it with a deeper question: Is the only reason for sexuality procreation? That's not Reich's view, is it? (You say that you find yourself "in almost complete agreement" with him.) I've not yet read Reich, so let me speak simply for myself. I would say myself that our sexuality is given us so that we can commune with one another—and with our universe. It "cracks our single selves", I say in a poem I'll enclose. And for me this reason for its being given us is quite as primary as that of procreation. Without sexuality we would be impossibly isolated within our individualities. We could not experience community, could not experience in our flesh the truth that we are, all of us, "members one of another", and of all that is. The sense of this is very lacking in the modern world—because our sexuality is, yes, very damaged. Damaged, I would say, *by* the attempt to split it into the so-called male and the so-called female—the one sex supposedly by nature dominant, the other supposedly happy in surrender—all possibilities of communion weakened by this lie. For dominance and submission can produce only distortions of communion.

If we can free ourselves of the will to dominate (or the willingness to submit), our sexuality allows us, I very much believe, to commune not only with other people but with the whole world of nature. You write that "Reich's discoveries about sexual dynamics led him to believe in a generalized sexual energy, which, if fully released in orgasms led to mental health, but if dammed up led to neurosis." I would express the same belief—except that I would leave out the words "in orgasms." The language of genital sexuality is a wonderful language for communion, but not the only language. There have been periods in my life when I have been, literally speaking, celibate and yet in such communion with others that I felt no sexual frustration at all. (This was very much so for the months I was on the walk to Cuba, for example.) I know that others have had comparable experiences. I have just been looking through some of Rilke's letters and here is a sentence from one of them: "And I really believe I sometimes get so far as to express the whole impulse of my heart, without loss and fatality, in gently laying my hand on a shoulder."

Let me quote a passage, too, from a kind of journal in which he describes a communion with the natural world which I would call sexual in a profound sense. (He is writing of himself in the third person):

It could have been little more than a year ago, when, in the castle garden which sloped down fairly steeply towards the sea, something strange encountered him. Walking up and down with a book, as was his custom, he had happened to recline into the more or less shoulder-high fork of a shrublike tree, and in this position immediately felt himself so agreeably supported and so amply reposed, that he remained as he was, without reading, completely received into nature, in an almost unconscious contemplation. Little by little his attention awoke to a feeling he had never known: it was as though almost imperceptible vibrations were passing into him from the interior of the tree....It seemed to him that he had never been filled with more gentle motions, his body was being somehow treated like a soul, and put in a state to receive a degree of influence which, given the normal apparentness of one's physical conditions, really could not have been felt at all....Nevertheless, concerned as he always was to account to himself for precisely the most delicate impressions, he insistently asked himself what was happening to him then, and almost at once found an expression that satisfied him, saying to himself, that he had got to the other side of Nature....Later, he thought he could recall certain moments in which the power of this one was already contained, as in a seed. He remembered the hour in that other southern garden (Capri), when, both outside and within him the cry of a bird was correspondingly present, did not, so to speak, break upon the barriers of his body, but gathered inner and outer together into one uninterrupted space, in which, mysteriously protected, only one single spot of purest, deepest consciousness remained. That time he had shut his eyes, so as not to be confused in so generous an experience by the contour of his body, and the infinite passed into him so intimately from every side, that he could believe he felt the light reposing of the already appearing stars within his breast.

Our sexuality, I would say, makes possible experiences like this—which I have known, too, and assume that you have known. Would you not agree that we lack fullest mental health if we are not capable of *this?*

Sexuality can dissolve the boundaries of our individual selves; it makes possible a deep relation with the rest of the world. Reason enough for being placed within us. That the act which can result in the birth of new life results itself from this urge to touch other life than our own is as it should be. But the creation of children is not the only reason for our sexuality.

You write that "the biological inclination" is to be heterosexual. I would say that the biological inclination is simply to be sexual. You write: "A social origin for gayness seems. . .likely." I would say that a social attempt to force us to be heterosexual is obvious. If society did not try to make us all heterosexuals—and if patriarchy were dispelled and, with it, the power inequities that make most heterosexual relationships so distorting—my guess is that we would find ourselves quite naturally attracted to either sex. It would be a matter simply of which individual person awakened love in us.

Love—
Barbara

Spirit of love
That blows against our flesh
Sets it trembling
Moves across it as across grass
Erasing every boundary that we accept
And swings the doors of our lives wide—
This is a prayer I sing:
Save our perishing earth!

Spirit that cracks our single selves—
Eyes fall down eyes,
Hearts escape through the bars of our ribs
To dart into other bodies—
Save this earth!
The earth is perishing.
This is a prayer I sing.

Spirit that hears each one of us,
Hears all that is—
Listens, listens, hears us out—
Inspire us now!
Our own pulse beats in every stranger's throat,
And also there within the flowered ground beneath our feet,
And—teach us to listen!—
We can hear it in water, in wood, and even in stone.
We are earth of this earth, and we are bone of its bone.
This is a prayer I sing, for we have forgotten this and so
The earth is perishing.

1973

Love Has Been
Exploited Labor

In the early seventies Arthur Kinoy, a lawyer involved in the defense of civil rights and anti-war activists, proposed the formation of a People's Party. Barbara wrote a response to his proposal, addressing her thoughts especially to the women involved in trying to make the Party a reality. "As it turned out," she noted later, "Kinoy himself was the first to take my words seriously." The original paper and Barbara's response were published in Liberation. *Subsequently, Kinoy responded to Barbara (his response is included in her book* Remembering Who We Are). *The following letter/essay was Barbara's response to his response.* (JM) *Published in the pamphlet* Women and Revolution: A Dialogue, *issued by the National Interim Committee for a Mass Party of the People, April 1975.*

Dear Arthur—

It was good to have your letter in reponse to mine. Now we have discussed it face to face; and you have sugggested that we try to put down on paper the substance of our dialogue—so that we can share it with others.

The spirit in which you talk with me moves me very much. You enter territory that is strange for a man. It is hard, you admit, for male radicals to think of themselves as beginners. But you are willing to think of yourself in that way. You hesitated before writing your letter—aware that you would have to try to speak of what you had never directly experienced; and yet, you say, you no longer believe that it is written in stone that a man can never feel what a woman feels—though he must struggle with himself for a long time before he can. I agree. I remember that many weeks ago I quoted to you Adrienne Rich who speaks of "the ghostly woman in all men", and her phrase affected you strongly. You acknowledged that ghost in your own self—in childhood, you said, no ghost but a living part of you, which you had felt impelled to kill. I asked you whether you ever missed that part of yourself and you said you did, and would like to be able to call it back to life. Yes, the day may indeed arrive when a man can feel as a woman; or rather—if we struggle for it—the day may arrive when every one of us can freely feel neither as "woman" or "man" but as the complex individual

248

person each really is—the very arbitrary sexual categories that now constrict us, and that now divide us from one another, at last shucked.

Into what new territory can it lead a Marxist if he begins to open himself to feminist insights? That is what we are both asking, isn't it? For a while all the thinking about this that you do on your own may disappoint you—because you will keep discovering that women have had such thoughts before you, and taken them further than you have been able to. After your letter came, I sent you the pamphlet *Women and the Subversion of the Community* by Mariarosa Dalla Costa and Selma James, and you said then that you were tempted to give up your own study of the subject. These two women had said all that you say in your letter, and more. But I was happy when you decided not to be discouraged by this. We would all be the losers if you did.

For a while, let me hazard, your ventures of thought may above all make it more and more possible for you to really hear when feminists themselves speak. Don't flinch when I say this. For a man to learn to hear women—to really hear them—well, as Marx says in a passage Rowbotham quotes in *Women, Resistance and Revolution,* "A personal consciousness of the opposite sex is an historical achievement". By the opposite sex he clearly means of course woman. *The* sex is for Marx, himself, still man. Nevertheless he was able to say that when man could succeed in "perceiving the woman as another human being with a distinct consciousness" he would take a next step in the creation of his own nature.

There are men who would interrupt me here to ask: And when do women intend to perceive *men* as human beings? But I don't think you would ask that. I think you would agree that the very difficult next step that *women* are now taking—and so making history (and so, too, making possible a next step by men—and then, let us hope, a step by all of us together out of what Carolyn Heilbrun calls "the prison of gender") this step for women is the step of perceiving *themselves* as human beings, each with a consciousness distinct from the consciousness of any man. The act of perceiving women in a new way, which Marx could see as an historical necessity, women themselves are very naturally the first to take. Though Marx, as you note, was unable to see that *this* would have to be so—to see women as history's agents (unable himself, that is, quite to see us as equally human). Or to see that our action would be in the nature of a work strike. For woman's work, to date, has been precisely the work of helping not herself but man to become what he feels he must become. That is really—isn't it?—what both the Dalla Costa pamphlet and your letter to me are all about: the fact that this form of production—the production of men by women—has been overlooked by Marxists. Dalla Costs puts it, "A woman's first job is to reproduce other people's labor power". "Previously", Selma James writes, "so-called Marxists could not see that women in the home produced.... The commodity [women in the home] produce...is the living human being—the laborer himself.''

You point out in your letter (and Dalla Costa in her pamphlet) that without reproduction of this commodity, living labor, the system itself could not function. In your words, it is "the creating source of surplus value." And as you say, an extraordinary fraud has been perpetrated here, because this commodity women produce in the home has been expropriated virtually without a payment. (Woman, the slave of a wage slave, as Dalla Costa puts it, is really the slave of the boss. Her man's wage commands a much larger amount of labor than has ever been acknowledged in factory bargaining.) Most incredible of all, you say, "the workers, the women, who produce this most essential of all commodities for the capitalist, living labor, are not even recognized...as a class of workers producing a critical commodity!"

Yes, incredible. But we had better believe it. And we had better analyze closely what has prevented recognition of the obvious.

I think a necessary first question to ask is: what is the *precise nature* of the production which Marxists have overlooked for so very long?

In your letter to me you re-examine Marx's concept of surplus value—that profit which is accumulated into capital. Marx defined it, you remind me, as the difference between the exchange value of the commodity produced by workers (those he recognized as workers) and the value put on their labor—that is, the wages paid them. He goes on to say that the value put on any worker's labor is determined, just as the value of any other commodity is, "by the labor time necessary for [its] production and consequently [its] reproduction." But then, you say, a curious thing happens: Marx seems to forget the second half of what he has just written. His "definition of the value of living labor revolves almost exclusively around the *maintenance* of the labor. Discussion of the value to be attributed to the *reproduction* of living labor never develops." This lapse, you think, is the origin of the subsequent inability of Marxists to see women as essential producers and therefore as potential agents of revolutionary change.

I wish I had thought to ask you while we were talking the other day: what, exactly, then, do you mean by the maintenance of living labor and what, exactly, do you mean by its reproduction? By its reproduction you mean, for one thing, I suppose, the bearing and rearing of children who will be a new generation of workers. But this isn't—is it?—the only work that women do that you think Marxists have omitted in their analyses? It *is* acknowleged, both by Marxists and capitalists, that the worker has to be able to feed and clothe and house not just himself but a family—or there will be no next generation of workers. In terms of the price of food, rent, etc. etc., the value to be attributed to labor's reproduction *is* dealt with. It is simply not dealt with in terms of any price that should be set upon a mother's labor. That labor is taken for granted—by both capitalist and Marxist.

But so is the labor of the wife—the labor of serving not children but husband. Isn't there much more to the *maintenance* of living labor than Marx acknowledges, for all his discussion of "the necessity for the production of the means of subsistence?" By maintenance he seems to mean only that the worker has to be able to pay for food that has been grown and clothes that have been manufactured, etc. etc. I am not well-read in Marx, as you know, but I gather that he fails to acknowledge that the food the laborer eats must not only be grown but shopped for, cooked and served, and cleaned up after; the clothes that he wears not only manufactured but washed and mended (if they are not actually made in the home), etc. etc. As Dalla Costa remarks, men often "do not even know that they have been waited on (by women), so natural it is to them for mothers and sisters and daughters to serve 'their' men". And this would seem to have been so even in the case of Marx.

But what is more—*what is very much more:* when Marx writes about the "means of subsistence" he refers only to material means—doesn't he? I would call *this* his most serious oversight. Selma James says of the commodity, living labor, "This is a strange commodity, for it is not a thing". How true. The boss—reckoning how to make a profit—chooses of course to regard it as a thing. But the Marxist can hardly afford to forget that it is not that. The plain fact is: the man who labors does not subsist simply on food and drink.

Selma James herself sometimes writes almost as though he did. Speaking of that strange commodity, living labor, she says, "The ability to labor resides only in a human being whose life is consumed in the process of producing. First it must be nine months in the womb, must be fed, clothed and trained; then when it works its bed must be made, its floors swept, its lunchbox prepared, its sexuality not gratified but quietened, its dinner ready when it gets home...This is how labor power is produced and reproduced when it is daily consumed in the factory or the office". I think this describes its production and reproduction too narrowly. Unless by "sexuality" she means everything that term could possibly mean.

Dalla Costa's vision is wider.* She writes, "The woman's role in the family is not only that of hidden supplier of social services who does not receive a wage...[Her] function is essentially that of receptacle for other people's emotional expression... *This passivity of the woman in the family is itself 'productive'.*... It makes her the outlet for all the oppressions that men suffer in the world outside the home and at the same time the object on whom the man can exercise a hunger for power that the domination of the capitalist organization of work implants....She acts as a safety valve".

Men hungered for power before the capitalist era. But Dalla Costa is certainly describing with accuracy here a form of maintenance that Marxists

---

* I have learned that Selma James and Mariarosa Dalla Costa wrote Dalla Costa's piece together, so it is inappropriate to make the distinction between them that I do here. (BD)

have overlooked. The wife makes it possible for the laboring man—no matter how exploited he is at work, no matter how alienated he feels there—to feel in relation to *her,* once home, that he is Somebody, is still "a man". And yes, this service is certainly productive—productive for capitalism: it is an essential service to that system in which the capitalist gets away with theft (the theft of surplus value). For if the wife did not play the role that she plays, the laborer would surely see that theft takes place—would see that he gives very much too much away, almost gives away in fact his very self. The wife (if she is what is known as "a real woman") is able to provide him with the illusion that he has *not* lost that self.

I agree with you. Woman is "the creating source of surplus value." When she is not the laborer herself she is reproducing the laborer and she is maintaining the laborer.

She is reproducing and maintaining, of course, both laborer and boss. Women of all classes are reproducing and maintaining men of all classes. Maintaining, above all, men's pride in themselves (or false pride).

I think this is important to note: this commodity for men—pride in themselves as "real men"—can be produced by women who perform little or no housework. A lady of leisure, who has servants to keep the house for her, can produce this commodity. She is sometimes, even, better able to produce it. Her "uselessness" can make the man feel even more "useful" himself. This so-called "useless" woman is in fact used.

You should look for a book by Andrea Dworkin, published by Dutton— *Woman-Hating.* (That is a title the publishers gave it, not the title she wanted; she wanted to call it *Freedom or Death.*) She has a relevant chapter on Chinese foot binding—that hideous custom which for centuries forced women to do the work of binding the feet of their daughters—the work of crippling them— to produce for men the luxurious sense that, in contrast to women, they were heroic, powerful. (She tells how in "love" play, the little shriveled foot was always fondled. The fetish of this foot "became the primary content of sexual experience for an entire culture for 1,000 years".) The richer a man, the more crippled a wife he could afford to keep—since he could also afford servants to do the work she was disabled from doing.

Yes, the more helpless a woman allowed herself to be made, the more pride in himself (the more "virility") she produced for the husband who could afford her. This was so clearly the case in ancient China that it makes it easier to see that it is the case in our own culture too—that here, too, "useless" women are productive. And that working women are asked to produce a good deal more than Marxists have ever taken into account. I had never realized that even peasant women in the old China had their feet bound. They were bound very much more loosely, because these women had, after all, to perform heavy labor. But bound they were (the toes turned painfully under). A distinction between the two sexes had always to be made in this way. To be manufactured. As Andrea notes, "footbinding did not formalize existing differences between men and women—it created them. One sex became male by virtue of having made the other sex...something other...called female." Something maimed, dependent. Maimed—this is precisely Freud's image of us, isn't it? The violence of mindbinding imposed upon us this time. Woman, with a body able to bear and nurture children (with the brief assistance of a man), is supposed to think of that body as a mutilated version of a man's! Through this mental contortion producing, again: Man, the Proud. That is the labor we are invariably assigned: to produce men who are proud of themselves. That is the labor we are assigned, whatever our class. And this demands of us always that we consent to seeing ourselves as less than men—dependent on them for our lives.

More and more men, these days, are eager to show how little is asked of women. Just the other day, for example, a man writing for the Op Ed page of *The New York Times* wrote of how he had clocked the time it took him to do the housework one week when his wife was ill. Hardly any time at all. Of course he didn't have the care of small children; nor, as I recall, did he refer to women who hold down jobs in factory or office and come home to do the housework too. But the real point is: it's not just time that women have been robbed of. The theft of a woman's sense of herself as a complete person—autonomous, self-sufficient—produces for the husband his *surplus* sense of himself.

In your letter to me you suggest that a recognition of woman's real role calls for the making of radical demands. Among these demands, you think, should be the sweeping demand that all women involved in the production of the "commodity" living labor be paid a wage commensurate with the most skilled workers (a wage to be financed directly from the profits of industry). But how radical is this demand, actually? If a woman's very Self is being stolen from her, what wage can compensate her for the theft? Isn't the only demand that could be radical enough the smashing of the role, itself, that women have been assigned? And this is what Dalla Costa demands: "The role of housewife...must be destroyed.... Women must completely discover their own possibilities". I agree. This is the only truly radical demand.... *

When we talk about the exploitation of women, we are not talking simply about an unfair division of labor. We are talking about an unfair *division of be-ing*. Woman is supposed to want to produce not her own self but man's self. She is supposed to think this the only possibility there *is* for her—to produce her husband, to produce her son. (Here I think again Freud. Do

* The demand for a wage for housework can be a useful first step in smashing the role of housewife, of course. For it makes the role more visible. Dalla Costa says that she has come more and more to see it as useful in just these terms. (BD)

you recall that in Freud's vision of us, we, poor women, consumed by penis-envy, are able to be relieved of that envy, to feel completed, only when we give birth to children who do possess the penis—give birth to man-children? What a debasement of the role of mother, it suddenly hits me. Not mother as one who mysteriously gives birth to a life distinct from hers—to *new* life. Mother as one who gives birth to a life in which she must then seek to find her own—for she is naught until she does. Yes, a kind of devouring of one's own children is demanded, in fact. And then bad-mouthed, of course. Think of Philip Wylie's tirades against mom-ism.)

The woman is asked to produce not her own self but man's self—to find her own self in that labor. The name given this surrender of autonomy is of course "Love". And this is of course why women's labors have for so long been invisible. It is time to give the term "labor of love" a new reading. Love has been exploited labor.

When I started going to women's conferences, I was struck by the fact that one phrase was spoken over and over again by the women attending: "I don't want to give my energies to men any longer!". "I don't want to give them my energies!", "And I don't want to give my energy to any woman who will just take it and use it for men!" One day it suddenly occurred to me: What they are talking about here is what Marxists mean by surplus value. Too much has been stolen from us. Do you remember what Mary Woolstone-craft cried? "I cannot live without loving, but loving leads to madness."

Yes, too much has been stolen from us. And again let me note: It has been stolen from all women. From women of all classes. Doesn't this mean, perhaps, that women of all classes are potential subversives? I think, myself, that they are just that.

Dalla Costa never makes this point. And yet she writes: "domestic work...is essential to the production of surplus value. *This is true of the entire female role.*" (Emphasis mine.)

Yes, do tell me your reponse to this suggestion: that *all* women (a little more than half the population) should be thought of as potential radicals.

I appreciate that for a Marxist (male or female) to entertain any such thought must be peculiarly difficult. For it jolts the whole assumption that class struggle alone will bring about the just society. I received a letter from Andrea Dworkin the other day, in which she talked about how hard it is to find adequate words to describe (to those who are not feminists) the kinds of profound structural changes that we believe must take place. She wrote, "It's like some kind of shift in the earth." It is just that. And (whether or not one is a Marxist) the mind itself must accomplish a great shift to be able to think of it.

But, as I say, for Marxists perhaps it is especially hard. Did you notice the very honest acknowledgement that Selma James makes: "...history...is not simple. We have to note that some of the most incisive discoveries of the [women's] movement and in fact its autonomy have come from women who began by basing themselves on a repudiation of class and class struggle." She goes on to say, "The task of the movement now is to develop a political strategy on the foundations of these discoveries and on the basis of this autonomy," and she salutes Mariarosa Dalla Costa for her analysis which, she says, rejects on the one hand feminism subordinated to class but on the other hand class subordinated to feminism.

Here, though, is a question I have—with which I may startle you: Do not Marx and Engels themselves—without quite realizing that they are doing so—subordinate class to feminism? Here is how Selma James herself puts it: "For Marx...the family, even before class society, had the subordinated woman as its pivot; class society itself was an extension of the relations between men on the one hand and women and children on the other, an extension, that is, of the man's command over the labor of his woman and his children."

And here is Engels in *The Origin of the Family, Private Property and the State:*

> In an old unpublished manuscript, the work of Marx and myself in 1846, I find the following: 'The first division of labor is that between man and woman for child breeding.' And today I can add: The first class antagonism which appears in history coincides with the development of the antagonism between man and woman in monogamian marriage, and the first class oppression with that of the female sex by the male. Monogamy was a great historical advance, but at the same time it inaugurated, along with slavery and private wealth, that epoch, lasting until today, in which every advance is likewise a relative regression, in which the well-being and development of the one group are attained by the misery and repression of the other. It is the cellular form of civilized society, in which we can already study the nature of the antagonisms and contradictions which develop fully in the latter.

If class society is an extension of man's command over the labor of "his" woman and "his" children, then why does it not clearly follow that to attain a classless society we must destroy man's command over woman and children (eliminate that possessive pronoun)? Which is of course the feminist goal.

Here is a passage from an essay by Andrea Dworkin in the November 23, 1973 *American Report*. Tell me whether you can agree with it—as I do.

> Patriarchy is a system of ownership wherein women and children are owned. Patriarchy is the original authoritarian model, the molecular totalitarian model, and every tyrannical form is derived from it. The

destruction of the master-slave political scenario, however we describe it (capitalists-worker, whites-blacks, rich-poor, etc.) requires the destruction of the source of that scenario—patriarchy. The destruction of the psychologies and behaviors which we call dominant (master, male) and submissive (slave, female) or aggressor-victim, demands the destruction of the source of those mental sets and behaviors—patriarchy...Violence is interwoven into the social fabric because it is the substance of sexuality as we know it....To transform the world we must transform the very substance of our erotic sensibilities.

Andrea titled her essay *Marx and Gandhi Were Liberals—Feminism and the "Radical" Left*. She wrote in it, "To the extent that the Left is not consciously and conscientiously feminist, that is, to a very great extent, it cannot help but perpetuate the same forms of dominance and submission that it purports in other areas to oppose." She names Marx "liberal". But does not all that she is saying follow from what he was saying?

"Patriarchy is the original authoritarian model." Or as you have put it, "Women are the creating source of surplus value." Now Marx saw this and now he didn't. But don't you agree that he saw it? Don't you agree that feminists are now looking at the very truth he was looking at—simply staring at it steadily? Women are of course more able to do this. It is hard for man whose pride is produced by woman to look steadily at the truth that women should halt this production.

Here is a passage from Susan Sontag's essay published in *Partisan Review* (volume 2, 1973)—*The Third World of Women*. Tell me if you agree with her—as I do. Sontag was replying to a series of questions, and the question just asked her had been: "What is the relationship between the struggle for women's liberation and the class struggle? Do you believe the first must be subordinated to the second?" She wrote:

The structures built around the existence of two sexes...are irreducible to structures built around the existence of social classes....The oppression of women constitutes the most fundamental type of repression in organized societies. That is, it is the most *ancient* form of oppression, predating all oppression based on class, caste and race. It is the most primitive form of hierarchy....Because this is so, I do not see how 'patriarchal oppression' (your term) can be considered as any kind of contradiction....On the contrary, the structure of this society is precisely based on patriarchal oppression, the undoing of which will modify the most deeply rooted habits of friendship and love, the conceptions of work, the ability to wage war (which is profoundly nourished by sexist anxieties), and the mechanisms of power. The very nature of power in organized societies is founded on sexist models of conduct....The task is not so much to exploit a contradiction as to dislodge this most profoundly rooted of structures. The women's movement must lead to a critical assault on the very nature of the state—the millenial tyranny of patriarchal rule being the low-keyed model of the peculiarly modern tyranny of the fascist state.

Marx's dream was of course the withering away of the state. Feminists are now asking: how can a growth wither away whose roots are still hardy?

Yes, the task of the women's movement is to "dislodge this most profoundly rooted of structures," which itself roots all other oppressive structures: patriarchy, man's command of the labor of "his" woman (and "his" children)—the labor most especially of producing for him his pride in himself.

I think it would be tragic if the new party you want to help found should fail to commit itself to this same task—the task of ending sexual division of labor and division of be-ing. This has been named a feminist task. It should be named as well a humanist task.

How did patriarchy come into being? It is intriguing to look at Engels' answer to this question. "That woman was the slave of man at the commencement of society," he writes, "is one of the most absurd notions that have come down to us from the period of Enlightenment of the 18th Century. Woman occupied not only a free but also a highly respected position among all savages and all barbarians of the lowest and middle stages and partly even of the upper stage." He describes the early "communistic household, in which most of the women or even all the women belong to one or the same gens, while the men come from various other gentes." (Bachofen is his source.) This household, he says, "is the material foundation of that predominancy of women which generally obtained in primitive times." In those times, he agrees with Bachofen, there was group marriage. And there was mother right. Descent was reckoned solely through the female line.

He next describes the transition from group marriage to the pairing family. He agrees with Bachofen that women must have been responsible for this "advance." Here is his reasoning: "The more the old traditional sexual relations lost their naive, primitive jungle character, as a result of the economic conditions of life, that is, with the undermining of the old communism and the growing density of the population, the more degrading and oppressive must they have appeared to the women; the more fervently must they have longed for the right to chastity, to temporary or permanent marriage with one man only, as a deliverance. This advance could not have originated from the man, if only for the reason that they have never—not even to the present day—dreamed of renouncing the pleasures of actual group marriage." Engels, as an historian, does seem to get ahead of himself here. If the relationship between the two sexes was not yet one in which the man was master, why should it have been any more oppressive to the woman to mate—at will—with several men than to mate with one man? On the other hand, if man was already master and could *force* his attentions upon her, how did marriage to one man gain her "the right to chastity?"

He next raises the question of how the transition came about from the pairing family—easily dissolved—to strict monogamy ("for the women only, of course." Of course.) He asks what "new social driving forces had come into operation." And here is his answer: Up until this time, fixed wealth had consisted almost entirely of the house, clothing, crude ornaments and the implements for procuring and preparing food. Food had to be won anew day by day. But now the domestication of animals and the breeding of herds that with the most elementary care increased in numbers and provided rich sources of food introduced an entirely new kind of wealth. "According to the division of labor then prevailing...the procuring of food and the implements necessary thereto, and therefore also the ownership of the latter, fell to the man; he took them with him in case of separation, just as the women retained the household goods. Thus, according to the custom of society at that time, the man was also the owner of the new sources of foodstuffs—the cattle...According to the custom of the same society, however, his children could not inherit from him...The property had to remain within the gens....Thus, as wealth increased, it, on the one hand, gave the man a more important status in the family than the woman and, on the other hand, created stimulus to utilize this strengthened position in order to overthrow the traditional order of inheritance in favor of his children. But this was impossible as long as descent according to mother right prevailed. This had, therefore, to be overthrown, and it was overthrown...."

A number of thoughts come to me. He speaks of the father wanting to overthrow the traditional order of inheritance "in favor of his children." He might more accurately have written "in favor of his sons," for he really means sons here. But he might more accurately still have written "in his own favor." It strikes me that the father was very probably less interested in his sons *having* property than in his sons *being* property—*his*.

For one thing, he must have wanted their willing labor in caring for his new wealth in cattle. If at his death the cattle were to pass into hands other than theirs, the sons would have much less interest in helping him to care for them. Engels points out that, with the herds, for the first time in history it was useful to have other people working for you. When food was still won anew day to day, human labor power "yielded no noticeable surplus...over the cost of its maintenance." But now it did yield surplus. So "slavery...was invented." Vanquished foes began to be used as slaves, he tells us. In fact they constituted part of the new wealth, along with the cattle. Clearly, too— though in the passage I've just quoted Engels does not put it in any such words—it was now in the father's interest to hold the *sons* in a kind of bondage. And of course it was in his interest to hold the wife—as an obedient breeder of "his" sons. Before pairing marriage it had not been possible for a father to say: These children belong to me. But now it was. "Pairing marriage," Engels notes, "had introduced a new element into the family. By the side of the natural mother it had placed the authenticated natural father."

The man had, of course, an interest in claiming his sons as "his" that predated his need for their labor with the herds. And Engels fails to take this fully into account when he decides that Bachofen was "absolutely right" in saying that pairing marriage "was brought about essentially by the women." The woman's interest in achieving through this new living arrangement a supposed "right to chastity" would seem a good deal less real than the man's interest in authenticating his paternity. For if the prehistoric woman held a highly respected position, why was it, after all? It was because maternity needs no authentication. In the Preface to the 4th edition of *The Origin of the Family* Engels notes precisely this: the "original position of the mother as the sole certain parent of her children assured her, and thus women in general, a higher social status than they have ever enjoyed since." Yes, the woman was from the beginning recognized and respected as a giver of life. Before it was realized that the man played a part in reproduction too, she must have been regarded by man with some awe. And clearly was. The earliest divinities were female. Engels knew from Bachofen that this was so. He still slights in his analysis the question of the very real wealth this once gave women—which is to say the self possession. One must count among possessions possession of one's self. And Marx and Engels do sometimes speak in just these terms—in terms not only of the production of things but of the production of one's own nature. Early man must have been very jealous of woman's nature.

The overthrow of mother right, Engels notes with reason, "was the world historic defeat of the female sex." But he doesn't look steadily at the reason. He doesn't think to speak in terms of this particular kind of wealth the woman had once held—the wealth of self-possession; and he doesn't think to speak in terms of theft of that wealth.

There is one passage in his essay that I cannot read without bitter laughter. He comments that it was not so difficult to overthrow mother right as it appears to us now. "For this revolution—one of the most decisive ever experienced by mankind [sic]—need not have disturbed one single living member of a gens. *All the members could remain what they were previously.* [Emphasis mine]. The simple decision sufficed that in future the descendants of the male members should remain in the gens, but that those of the females were to be excluded from the gens and transferred to that of the father."

All the members could remain what they were previously, indeed! The pairing marriage, Engels notes, placed by the side of the natural mother the authenticated father. But he fails to note that the overthrow of mother right amounted to the natural mother's *disauthentication*.

He does (in the Preface to the 4th edition) refer to Bachofen's "absolutely correct" reading of Aeschylus' *Eumenides* as proof of the historic overthrow of mother right by father right. When that play has Apollo and Athena acquit Orestes of the murder of his mother—excusing him because his mother killed his father (she killed him, let me interject, because he had sacrificed one of their daughters)—this judgement, Engels agrees, reflects the overthrow of mother right. But he doesn't quote the passage that is most relevant here. He quotes the furies who argue that the mother should be excused because she was not related in blood to the man she slew, and Orestes should be found guilty because he has killed his closest blood relative. But he doesn't quote the argument with which Apollo clears Orestes. Listen to it:

> *The mother is no parent of that which is called her child, but only nurse of the new-planted seed that grows. The parent is he who mounts.*

Father right was not just a matter of affirming paternity. It was a matter of denying maternity.

This fact is reflected in the subsequent change in religious practise. It is not that from now on new divinities are worshipped who are both female and male. God, the Creator of all that is, is now supposed to be seen as simply Father. Once we have struggled free of this superstition, it can be seen as comical, grotesque—"a kind of cosmic joke" as Mary Daly puts it (in *Beyond God the Father)*. But of course for long centuries it was, for women, no joke at all. For as Mary Daly comments, "If God is male, then the male is God." And he has expected to be regarded as such. If man in prehistory felt inferior in nature to woman, if he suffered from his awe of her, he gained with the victory of father right not an equal right to self-respect, but revenge.

Engels does really say as much: "The overthrow of mother right was the world-historic defeat of the female sex....The woman was degraded, enthralled, the slave of the man's lust, a mere instrument for breeding children." In effect, he says it: the woman's very possession of her own nature was stolen from her. And yet he seems unable to look steadily at all this implies in terms of the source of men's wealth—their wealth in goods and their wealth also in pride.

He cannot look steadily at it because he is a man himself, and so still shares in the spoils of the ancient theft. Note that he speaks of the father's wanting to "overthrow the traditional order of inheritance in favor of his children". He could have written "the children" or "their children", but never thought to. "His".

He declares flatly: "Mother right had to be overthrown." But did the problem as he presents it really have to be resolved in just that way? At random; Couldn't the herds have been said to belong to both father *and* mother—to be divided between the two parties, in case of separation; to be inherited at the death of the parents by both sons and daughters?

Engels quite skips over the question of an inheritance for the daughters, doesn't he? One sentence in the passage I have quoted makes it oddly clear that he means by the man's children his sons only. He refers to the sons and to the daughters, respectively, as "the descendents of the male members" and "those of the female"—rather as though sons were created by fathers and daughters by mothers. Did you note this? (The real act of creation being the creation of the male?)

"Mother right had to be overthrown," he says. Because the sons mustn't labor without reward? But what of the daughters' labors? One could ask: Did it have to be sons and not daughters who tended the herds?* But even assuming that sons tend the herds and daughters do the work connected with the home: would the fathers and sons be *free* to work with the herds if the equally hard work at home were not being done by the mothers and daughters? The herds demanded very little work, Engels admits— demanded "most elementary care". "Inheritance in favor of his children"— he uses the phrase with too little thought. Favor to the sons was no favor to the daughters.

One can ask, too: if ownership were thought of as communal, not private, except for very personal possessions—if the real wealth belonged not to man or woman but to the gens, where would the problem be? Where would there be need of revolution? The complicating element is private property, isn't it? And then the question has to be asked: What was the origin of private property?

Engels suggests a certain progression: first the early communism was eroded (he doesn't really spell out how), then pairing marriage evolved, and then mother right was overthrown and strict monogamy introduced. My own guess would be that communism was eroded and private property created *by* the move to overthrow mother right. Doesn't father right make private property a necessity? For how can paternity be authenticated unless woman herself is held as property? Yes, didn't the lust for property *begin* with man's lust to own "his" children by owning their mother?

Engels looks for the social driving force that brought about the overthrow of mother right, looks for that sense of lack that impelled men to attempt such a "revolution". I think he makes a very serious mistake by concentrating

---

* I have now read Bachofen for myself and he writes: "In those early times when the men were engaged exclusively in warfare which carried them far away from home...the women remained at home, taking care of the children and the cattle." Hmmmmm. (BD)

on the issue of those herds (of horses camels donkeys oxen sheep goats and pigs) and who was to inherit them. Animals which had been domesticated by women in the first place, by the way, according to Elizabeth Gould Davis in *The First Sex*.

The social driving force that brought about that change which Engels calls one of the most decisive revolutions ever was surely the felt need not for possessions as such but for a new sense of themselves to rival women's rich sense of themselves. If they had not been driven by *this* urgency, surely adjustments to ensure fair inheritance could easily enough have been made within mother right. Men wanted to overcome their awe of women. It was *self*-possession that they craved. And, disastrously, instead of reaching for it fairly, they reached for it by theft—the theft of woman's selfhood; reached for it by a lie. Instead of asserting: I am a parent too, a life-giver too, though at first not known to be, man tried to claim: I am *the* parent, *the* life-giver, life is my seed, and woman is only a wife in whom I plant that seed, only nutrient ground for us. Yes, he tried to produce himself by theft, by making woman *his,* no longer a person in her own right but in Engels' words "a mere instrument for breeding children"—children he could claim as "his".

This act of violence took place of course not in one historic moment. It became a long struggle—which is described in *The First Sex*.

The overthrow of mother right, says Engels, spelled the defeat of the female sex. I think it spelled a great defeat for humankind. Engels writes of it— writes of monogamy under father right—that it was a great historical advance. But he adds, recall: "at the same time it inaugurated, along with slavery and private wealth, that epoch, lasting until today, in which every advance is likewise a relative regression, in which the well-being and development of the one group are attained by the misery and repression of the other." Quite a qualification to make about a great advance. I would call the overthrow of mother right not a revolution but a travesty of a revolution—which must be undone, to allow the human race at last truly to advance.

Do you notice, by the way, that in the particular passage I have just quoted Engels seems to agree that private wealth began with mother right's overthrow? Yes, the first private wealth that was claimed was surely woman herself and children—title to *them*. The only reason that private property in things is wrong is—isn't it?—because it involves this owning of other people—owning their labor, their lives (or *depriving* them of life sustenance or the chance to labor as they choose). Property in other peoples' lives is the basic, is the original wrong, isn't it? We desire a society in which nobody owns another person. Didn't mother right make such a society possible, and didn't father right then make it impossible? Yes, wasn't the possibility of true communism aborted by the so-called revolution of father right? Doesn't

Engels almost glimpse this, but fail to see the full truth because for a man to look straight at it is not quite possible?

Let me acknowledge again that I am not well read in Marxism, but my impression is that in their studies of history Marxists have concentrated much too much upon the ownership and upon the production of *things* as "the means of subsistence" and have scanted a study of the ways in which people try to subsist upon one another. I more and more realize that this is why I never was able to become a Marxist myself. The realities that Marxists scanted were the realities with which I was most concerned.

Do you remember this passage in Rowbotham's book? "Women's liberation implies that if the revolutionary movement is to involve women, not as supporters or attendants only, but as equals, then the scope of production must be seen in a wider sense and cover also the production of self through sexuality. That is, in fact, a reassertion of Marx's concern to study how human beings reproduce their lives in a total way."

Yes, *the scope of production must be seen in a very much wider sense.* Let Marxists begin to study the ways in which, throughout history, men have produced themselves at woman's expense, and tried to remake woman into a mere means of man's subsistence. More and more feminists are making this their study.

I have sent you a copy of Jeanne Gallick's essay, *Phallic Technology and the Construction of Women* (published in the lesbian feminist journal *Amazon Quarterly*). She writes on the subject: the "logic of male creation is founded in a negation." Man, she says, jealous of the woman's power of creation, wanting to assert *his* power "to mold and control life", felt the need to deny woman's power. (Not the need to match it, note, but the need to deny that it existed—so that he could feel superior to her.) "Once denied her ancient identity, woman had to be reconstructed. She became man's first artificial product, the first matter (from mater or mother) that could be technologically reconstructed...according to his dream. Man created woman his Mother into his Wife...an empty vessel in need of activation, at which time an 'automatic' process begins which results in birth. Passive reproduction, machine production, is her defining function in life, which she neither initiates nor controls. Like all machines she is conceived as an extension of man's powers...."

Man extended his powers at the expense of woman. And once he had made of woman The Other—though she is of the very same flesh and blood—he had formed the habit of treating any life at all as quite Other than his life (though *all* life is really one), treating it (in Gallick's words) as a mere means of producing those things that he desires.

The remaking of woman, Gallick writes, the overthrow of the Mother and her recreation into the submissive wife, "set the model of making that has guided the progress of our civilization." It "was the primal technological act."

And technology has now of course led us to a moment of history in which all life on earth is threatened. It seems to me that Marxists would do well to examine this crisis with the perspective Gallick suggests: "the abstraction of man from the earth...is grounded...in his relation to woman"—his jealous denial of her own being, his wish to see her simply as that which can give something to *him*.

Yes, it is not just that Marxists have concentrated too much upon the ownership and upon the production of *things* as "the means of subsistence" and have scanted a study of the ways in which people try to subsist upon one another. They have scanted the truth that our attitude toward the use of natural resources to produce things that we "need" is *affected by* our attitude toward other people, by whether or not we see *them* simply as our resources.

In your paper you rejoice in the fact that "the material forces of production" in this country are "more than sufficiently developed to provide for an economy of plenty" and so "the objective conditions may exist for the first experience in human history of the 'withering away' of the repressive form of the state....A fantastic fact." But isn't it a fact that is fantastic in the sense of threatening to dissolve even as we grasp for it? You do mention the ecology crisis but I think you belittle it. Man's "productivity", for all its promises, now also sets all of life in jeopardy.

In *Beyond God the Father,* Mary Daly makes the same connections that Jeanne Gallick does, and calls for "a great refusal of rapism". She writes: When technical knowledge is cut off from other forms of knowing and so strips that which it perceives of subjectivity, it "degrades its object and dehumanizes the knowing subject. Because it reduces both to less than their true reality, at a certain point it even ceases to be knowledge in any authentic sense." But she writes, too, of where hope lies: "Widening of experience so pathologically reduced can come through encounter with another subject, an I who refuses to be an It." Women can make that refusal—are making it. And "the contagion of this refusal of objectification" extends outward, "toward male liberation", clearly means, too, "refusal to rape earth, air, fire, water....We will look upon the earth and her sister planets as being *with* us, not *for* us."

Yes, let Marxists begin to study (for life depends upon such study) the ways in which man has tried to produce himself through making of woman and of the earth itself a mere means of *his* subsistence—has tried, in short, not to become fully human but to deify himself. Mary Daly quotes a startling remark of Sartre's: "man fundamentally *is* the desire to be God." Yes, man *has* been that desire—for all too long a time,. Women had better help him now to recover from it. For—to state the obvious—it is not a practical desire.

One can guess at its origins in prehistory. Then, as I've written, man must have stood in painful awe of woman and of nature—since they could give birth and he could not. His sense of himself as lesser must have been bitter and his late discovery that he, too, played a part in the drama of birth must have been too heady for him. He then wanted that role that he played to mean more than it did—mean everything. He wasn't content to find that he, like woman, was an active part of nature. He must be woman's lord and nature's lord—to really savor pride.

Of course his attempt to make himself Lord has kept him, in fact, a child.

Look more closely at his attempt to produce himself through woman. He has named her, as Jeanne Gallick aptly puts it, "submissive and evil". Yes, submissive—his wife, simply, a mere extension of his own being. But also evil. There is a curious contradiction here. Why evil? Gallick, with other feminists, points out the transformation of ancient myths under patriarchy. "Eve, who is called Mother and whose name literally means life" is made over into the mischievous figure in the Old Testament. Why? Pandora, too, "was originally the Earth Mother." Her name, meaning "all gifts" or "all giving", refers to "the Mother as the source of the blessings of life." She, too, is made over into the source of evil. Jeanne Gallick remarks, "Like all neurotic symptoms that are grounded in denial, the 'feminine' woman is aimed at man's destruction." But one can say something further. Man's dual message to woman exposes what he truly wants. He wants to be Lord, but he wants to be Lord without ever taking life into his own hands. He wants woman to be responsible for him. He says to her in effect: You have been called The Mother, the birth-giver. All right. Then keep on giving birth to man for the whole of his life. That is to be *your* life, woman's life. And you are to blame for anything that goes wrong. Which is to say, he refuses adulthood. At the very same time that he asks to be treated as a God, he asks to be treated as a perpetual child. The thought suddenly flicks into my mind: is this the reason why a favorite subject of painters down through the years has always been the infant God upon his Mother's lap?

Yes, to be both God and Child—-this has been man's dream. But it is time for him to wake.

I live with a cat who likes
To dance
I once set her on my shoulder and began
A slow prance
And now
Each day
She asks
With a small cry
For me to take her up and
Step away

She hums as we go—
Her tail a furry wand that stirs the air
In solemn figure-eights—as though
She'd bring a turnaround to all our lives
And all we think we know

                        Cat, what dance is this?
The Bible raves of Man's dominion over
Everything that moves
Is this a dance to dance an end
To all dominion?
I meet your glance that's shining
In a mirror as we pass
It says: Yes! Yes!

1981

To Fear Jane Alpert
Is To Fear Ourselves —
A Letter To Susan Sherman

Jane Alpert went underground in May 1970, after she had been charged—with Sam Melville, David Hughey and Pat Swinton (Shoshana)—with conspiring to bomb government property. Melville had first confessed to carrying out the anti-war actions by himself.... But she and Hughey were told that if they pleaded guilty to conspiracy, Melville's sentence could be reduced from a probable life sentence to thirteen to eighteen years; she and Hughey would get four to six years. So she and Hughey also pleaded guilty. Shoshana had avoided arrest by going underground. Alpert now jumped bail and went underground too. The men went to prison. Hughey was paroled after two and a half years. Melville died in the September 1971 Attica prison uprising.
a radical feminist and could not wage that struggle freely enough while underground. The New York Times *quoted the government as saying she was "cooperating fully". Alpert herself in an interview published in the March 1975* Big Mama Rag *and in the May-June* Off Our Backs *declared she was giving no information that could endanger anyone. On January 13, 1975 she was sentenced to twenty-seven months. (BD)*

Published in WIN, *May 22, 1975, and in* Off Our Backs, *May-June, 1975. Susan Sherman is a poet and playwright. From 1965-69 she edited* IKON, *a radical magazine of the arts.*

Dear Susan—
Several days ago a sister wrote to tell me that she was signing a statement denouncing Jane Alpert—and throwing her out of the women's movement. Now I have read the statement that you signed, denouncing her, too, and in effect throwing her out of the human race.
I ask and ask myself what deep fear Jane Alpert has stirred in you both to move you to words so harsh and so unrealistic. Is it realistic to throw anyone out of the human race? We are all in it, like it or not. Is it realistic to throw anyone out of the feminist movement? At this point of history, I would say, every one of us is caught up in this movement—whether willingly or unwillingly. And every one of us is being changed by

267

it. Those of us who have *chosen* to be in it are being changed unutterably. The old advice, "judge not", is now especially pertinent. A woman we may judge one day, met a few months later, can be a quite different woman.

This is of course just what Jane Alpert has been saying: I am not the woman I was when you last thought you knew who I was. She has said to the State: I am not the same woman, so please judge me accordingly.

The statement my other sister signed denounced Alpert as an informer. The statement you signed (with Ti-Grace Atkinson, Flo Kennedy, and Joan Hamilton) does not make this charge, and I am glad. Women close to her insist that she has taken scrupulous care to say nothing that could be used against anyone. Other women, who do not charge her *consciously* informing, complain that she has been reckless unwittingly and, by talking as much as she has to government officials, risked giving them information they could use. Here is a question that deserves much discussion: just what does play into government hands? But it is not the question that you raise. You raise questions about the change as a person that she has undergone. You see that change as one that betrays us—betrays feminism. It's about this that I write to you.

Alpert has said in court—and in her *Letter From Underground*—that she is no longer the woman she was in 1970 when she was convicted with Sam Melville and Dave Hughey of conspiracy to bomb government property. She says that she is now her own woman—whereas back then she let herself be pressured by Sam Melville into playing the role that she did—in the group he "half-led half-dragged along with him"—pressured in ways "peculiar and common to male-female relationships."

When the police mass murder of the Attica rebels took Melville's life and his *Letters From Attica* were published, Alpert wrote from underground a profile of him that served as an introduction to the book. She was already a feminist when she wrote it and was amazingly honest about his treatment of her. (She writes, for example, that he indulged in comic fantasies about her being raped.) But it remains an appreciation of him—"the most dynamic human [she'd] ever met." And she mourns him very explicitly. The piece ends, "he died for things in which his belief had never altered, an end to racism and liberation from senseless authoritarianism. I find some solace in knowing" that. She writes, "the lines of an Edna St. Vincent Millay sonnet keep recurring to me:

Say what you will, kings in a tumbrel rarely
Went to their deaths more proud than this one went.

If I could come out of hiding...I would engrave those lines on his stone".

Her *Letter From Underground,* however, ends with the jolting words, "And so, my sisters in Weathermen, *you* fast and organize and demonstrate for Attica. Don't send me news clippings about it, don't tell me how those deaths move you. I will mourn the loss of 42 male supremacists no longer".

The statement you signed is a clear retort to those words. you declare, "We are *more* than what we are as individuals. We are what we identify with. And our identification must be with all oppressed peoples. We do not 'support' or 'not support' the brothers of Attica. We *are* Attica. We are Attica or we are nothing. Not feminists, not women, not human beings."

"Our identification must be with all oppressed peoples"—I think you must know that I say yes to this. And yet—Susan, isn't the complicating truth that confronts us the truth that women for centuries and centuries have been allowed to be *only* what we identified with, acknowledged as human beings (the kind called "real women") *only* in so far as we identified with others (quite specifically, with men)? We have for so long been very much *less* than what we could be as individuals. As Ti-Grace Atkinson puts it in *Amazon Odyssey,* "A woman by definition has no life, no destiny, no identity"; "by class definition, women are not individuals, or free but rather extensions of other human beings." So when you write, "We are what we identify with," when you write, "We are Attica or we are nothing", part of me assents, but I also can't help exclaiming to you: Wait, wait! I fear those words. When I have heard them before, so many times before, they have been used to keep me in my so-called place.

After I had read your statement, I looked on my table for your book of poems *With Anger/With Love* and I turned to the wonderfully beautiful poem "Lilith Of The Wildwood, Of The Fair Places." A poem about Lilith, about her

> *refusing anything but her* own *place*
> *a place apart from any other*
> > > *her own* [my stress].

It begins:

> *And Lilith left Adam and went to seek her own place*
> *and the gates were closed behind her and her name*
> *was stricken from the Book of Life.*

I stared at these words, and stared again at the statement you have signed. Can you really be striking Jane Alpert's name from the Book of Life? You write of Lilith,

> *She is here   inside me*
> *I reach to touch her.*

You write,

> *To fear you   is to fear myself*
> *To hate you   is to hate myself*

And I write to ask you, isn't Jane Alpert, too, there inside you, inside all of us? Can't you reach to touch her? When you fear her, don't you fear yourself? When you hate her, don't you hate yourself?

You ask in the poem, for Lilith, "And how does one begin again?" And yes—how does one begin again? How was Jane Alpert to begin again? She writes in *Letter From Underground,* "I am not asking you...to break all personal and emotional ties with the men who are important to you. I know that those ties are never broken out of a simplistic political decision but only when and if consciousness of oppression makes them so inconsistent with self-respect that they can no longer be borne. Even then it is with enormous pain and grief and in spite of an ever reluctant part of ourselves."

Yes, how was she to begin again? Atkinson writes in *Amazon Odyssey,* "those individuals who are today defined as women must eradicate their own definition. Women must, in a sense, commit suicide....We must create, as no other group in history has been forced to do, from the very beginning." She writes, "The male class is the oppressor class of the female class. Or, in political terms, men oppress women. That means all women. Is that point clear?"; "A woman can unite with a man as long as she is a woman, i.e., subordinate, and no longer. There's no such thing as a 'loving' way out of the feminist dilemma: that it is as a woman that women are oppressed"; "The proof of class consciousness will be when we separate off from men".

And now Jane Alpert—who was asked by the man she loved to share in the hard consequences of his actions, but not asked to share in the decisions as to whether or not those actions should be taken (she tells of this in her profile of Melville)—now Jane Alpert has separated off from men.

Atkinson writes, "The journey from womanhood to a society of individuals is hazardous". She writes, "one must begin by jumping off one cliff after another". Yes, the journey is hazardous. Isn't one of the hazards precisely that we have to make demands of ourselves that are at first glance contradictory? We say, "our identification must be with all oppressed peoples". And we also say, "we must separate off from men". But many oppressed people happen to be men. Which is to say, many oppressed people happen to be our oppressors. So how are we to act? How are we to begin?

As you probably know, I was in an automobile accident several years ago. For almost two years after the accident, until I had an operation that largely corrected it, I suffered from double vision: friends had two heads, four eyes, two noses, etc. etc. It was hard to live with. Feminists, it seems to me, for a certain period of time now must expect to have to live with what amounts to *political* double vision. When we look at any man who would classically be termed oppressed, we are now going to have to see *two* men: one an oppressed person, and so a comrade, but the other a person who oppresses us. More grotesquely still, if we are, as I am, white and from the middle class, we are going to see: one person who oppresses me, another who sees me as *his* oppressor.

This is hard to live with. Double vision produces vertigo. But in this case we should not take it to mean that something is wrong with our eyes. We are now seeing truly at last—seeing patriarchy truly. For it is patriarchy that is wildly askew—splits each one of us, away from each other and away from our true selves. We are daring to look at this now. It is not comfortable to do this.

Atkinson writes, "We are still imprisoned by Marx". I agree. And isn't one of his concepts that imprisons us—makes our new vision *especially* uncomfortable—the concept that we must name "the enemy"? In classical Marxism, if I understand it, the enemy is the enemy—period. One it may be necessary to destroy. The enemy cannot possibly be at the same time a comrade. You say in your statement, "It is the essence of oppression to set us against other oppressed peoples. . . . It is not war that destroys us, but betrayal". But when you think of Jane Alpert as a traitor, don't you assume that in naming the Attica rebels oppressors she does so in the simplistic Marxist sense—names them "the enemy"? She will mourn them no longer, she says. That is hardly to say that she is glad they are dead. She *has* mourned them, after all. She wrote to her sisters in the Weather Underground, "Believe me, I understand your side of it. I've been on that side—I've practically drowned on that side". (Must one call her a traitor because she doesn't want to go down for the third time?)

The feminist vision, I have said, entails a kind of double vision, which produces vertigo. This vertigo I'm afraid will end only when we end patriarchy. Unless we choose to end it by retreating from feminism. I think the only choice that will enable us to hold to our vision without being scared into *wanting* to retreat is one that abandons the concept of naming enemies and adopts a concept familiar to the nonviolent tradition: naming behavior that is oppressive, naming abuse of power, that is held unfairly and must be destroyed, but naming no *person* one whom we are willing to destroy. If we can destroy a man's power to tyrannize, there is no need, of course, to destroy the man himself. And if the same man who behaves in one sense as a tyrant is in another sense our comrade, there is no need to feel that we have lost our political minds (or souls) when we treat him as a person divided from us (and from himself) in just this way.

I should acknowledge quickly that Atkinson in *Amazon Odyssey* does make precisely the distinction I am arguing for. She writes, "I always understood that it was male *behavior* that was the enemy". It is difficult, however—for any of us—to hold with confidence to this distinction—the distinction between male behavior that is the enemy and males themselves—because patriarchy does its best to teach us that no such distinction is possible. It teaches us that if we identify with a man we identify with him—period. Or we are nothing. It teaches us, as Atkinson has said, to think of ourselves as "extensions of other human beings" (men). There is not one of us who has shaken quite free of that teaching yet....

[A large cut has been made here]

I began by addressing this letter to you, Susan, but now I seem to be speaking more and more to Ti-Grace Atkinson as well. I address it to you both. I find *Amazon Odyssey* a book full of deep truths. But there are a few passages in it which bewilder me. One is that in which she says that "Women's identity must be sought in the eyes of the Oppressor". I think that is the one place where we *cannot* find it—as the oppressors cannot bear yet to see us as distinct from them. She says, "To turn to other women for ego support is like trying to catch a reflection of herself in a darkened mirror". I think "darkened mirrors" is a beautiful and accurate description of us in our present condition. But I also think that it is precisely in those mirrors, if we look patiently, waiting for them to lighten, that we will find ourselves.

What we first see there of course will be disturbing. For it will be faces contorted with anger. Anger at men—for treating us as mere extensions of themselves. Anger at ourselves—for allowing them to do this. While we are in the throes of our anger, we will often seem to be beside ourselves. But it is the only way that we can begin again. We have been in the possession of others. This is the only way that we can burst ourselves out of that condition. Jane Alpert has been in those throes. Not everything that she has said has been perfectly balanced. Not everything that any one of us will say will be. If we are afraid of Jane Alpert, aren't we afraid of ourselves?

Don't forget, Susan, what you have written about Lilith—"cursed of God" the Father. You do not name her a betrayer of men. You name her "Mother of us all". Once we have dared to shake from us in anger the lie that we are the *creatures* of men, we and they can be comrades. Once we have dared to remember—and to hold in remembrance—the truth that we were born of the flesh of our mothers; and dared to affirm that we were born (all of us alike) to seek a communion with one another that can be learned (and learned without need of words) from that bond that existed with our mothers—once we have angrily dared all this, we will be able to pass beyond our anger. But not until then. And so in this letter I plead with you...not to be afraid of us, and of yourself, as we try—in the not always "becoming" throes of our anger—to "begin again".

This hugging has unlocked our bodies
We exchange limbs
My mouth now sits on a small branch
Of the starfruit tree outside your window
And sings:
Am I her mouth or mine?
Are these my hands or hers
Among the summer grasses
Fingers tangled?
Is this my tongue that has found the sweet salty
Very center of the earth—
Which as it turns
Flings us akimbo yet together
And also turning
In slow
Rings and rings and rings?

1981

Remembering Who We Are

Delivered as a talk at the Florida State University in Tallahassee on March 4, 1977—sponsored by the Women's Center and the Center for Participant Education. And published in Quest, *Summer 1977, in a condensed version. (BD)*

Dear Susan Saxe—

May I converse with you again? I keep remembering your saying that the feminist movement needs an analytical method, and that leftist women should teach their sisters the method of dialectical materialism. It is "not a male concept", you urge; "it is a tool of liberation"—and would help put our life experiences "into a rational political context". Your suggestion makes me anxious.

I will agree that history can best be understood by examining the changing ways in which we seek the "means of our subsistence"; and best understood as a story always in process, the constant motion of our actions, interactions *as* we seek our lives. I wouldn't name this concept patriarchal. But I do think that those who have used the dialectical method to date have given us a much too limited look at the ways in which we try to find our lives. And I also think that the fact that most of these dialecticians have been men helps to explain why they have overlooked so very much. I sent you once a copy of a letter I wrote to Arthur Kinoy and in it—if you remember—I said that I thought Marxists had concentrated much too much upon the ownership and upon the production of *things* by which we subsist and had scanted a study of the ways in which people try to subsist upon one another. (And I didn't mean upon the labor of others, simply—unless we can call the giving of attention a kind of labor.) Of course if men were to make *this* study, they would have to face the truth that they keep asking *us* to be their subsistence (even men who think they want radical change)—keep taking it for granted that women like and even need to give our deepest attention to *them;* to live, in effect, *their* lives. If they began to study what it is they ask of us, it would raise an uncomfortable question: Do we need our *own* lives? Which is why they look away from the obvious fact that just such a study has to be made;

274

why it took a woman, Kate Millett, to suggest that if we want to understand our history—want to "put our life experiences into a rational political context"—we have to begin to talk not merely about the politics of economics but about "sexual politics".

I have just read Wilhelm Reich's *The Invasion of Compulsory Sex Morality* and was struck by the fact that even this man, whose primary interest is sexuality, when he examines in dialectical fashion the long-ago shift from Mother Right to Father Right, and suggests that "the central mechanism" of this great shift was the ritual of the marriage gift—which became marriage *tribute* rather than gift, and then became bride price ("the first economic *compulsion* of mankind", he names it)—I was struck by the fact that even *he* looks only to economic interests for an explanation of what happened here....Like Engels*, he fails even to suggest the possibility that sexual interests may have been involved. He speaks of the first stirrings of avarice and ownership interest—meaning interest in the ownership of *things*. But he doesn't explain *why* avarice began to stir—though he clearly agrees with others that it did not exist within the communal maternal clan. He notes with Engels that at a certain time a surplus in material goods began to exist. But he doesn't explain why men were moved to claim this surplus for their individual selves rather than for the clan; and why they were moved to begin to exact a price for things, in place of the free exchange of gifts that had been customary. He tells us that the marriage gift became "a preliminary step toward merchandising". *But what, in fact, was the first merchandise?* Clearly enough, by his own account, woman and her children. So why is it not obvious that sexual politics were involved here; were, to use a phrase of Engels' the driving force behind the driving force at which he does look— the greed for *things* which he says began to afflict men at that time born of *another* kind of greed, more primary.

In my letter to Kinoy, if you remember, I suggest that men were moved to force the changes that they did, not because they suffered from the lack of material possessions, but because they suffered from a lack of *self* possession—when they compared themselves with women. They felt a need to produce for themselves a wealth of self regard that could equal—or rather that could more than equal—the rich sense of herself that woman had in those early times, because she was the child bearer. The fact that man had anything to do with the birth of children was for a long time unknown. Each new birth seemed to a man, no doubt, an extension of woman's self. He must have felt himself to be less than she; and he must have resented having to feel that way....

*In *Origin of the Family, Private Property and the State*.

When I wrote as I did to Kinoy, I was unaware of one fact that I learned soon after by reading Evelyn Reed's *Women's Evolution*. (In Reich's *The Invasion of Compulsory Sex Morality* it is made clear, too.) Men moved to claim children as their property *before* they learned that they were their natural biological offspring. Reed writes: "the evidence is unambiguous; before the facts about paternity were known, a man 'begot' a child not through a genetic process but through a property transaction"; he "became the father...by payment in cattle of the bride price and child price".

Though acts of purchase had not existed before this time, it is clear from the evidence she gives that men now managed to insist that such acts had awful power. The property right to children which they purchased could not be dissolved by the woman's remarriage or even by the man's death; it could be dissolved only by the return of those cattle which had been the coin paid. If a woman remarried, but the cattle had not been returned, the children of that second marriage were still "his". If a son were born to the woman years after his death, but the cattle had not been returned, that son could still be claimed by male kin to carry on his "name". When the man did learn that he was a biological father, he then devised very different kinds of laws—to protect his status as "progenitor". But the primary right he demanded was, as before, a property right—property in children and in woman.

Knowing that he first demanded this "right" while in *ignorance* of paternity, I am more convinced than ever that he was seeking compensation for a lack of naturally experienced pride—dissatisfied with the self he felt to be his, hoping to produce a larger self through his purchase of "heirs". *And my own strong guess is that he invented the very concept of purchase to be able to produce his new pride.* A pride tragically abstract. If only he had known earlier that he was by *nature* more than his single self. No need to pretend to be. No need for the theft called "purchase".

Small wonder that money so often obscures what should be natural relationships between people. It appears to have been invented to facilitate a lie. Small wonder, too, that *women* seldom have any real control over money—as Chesler and Goodman make so clear in *Women, Money and Power*. The lie is that we women belong to men and not to ourselves. Money was *invented* to steal from us our independence. It had better be for us, I might add, to dissolve the perverse system.

But to return again to Reich. Why is it that this man, whose particular study was sexuality, who writes in the book I have been citing that sexual needs play a more important part in the formation of character and the development of society than the need for food...why is it that when he examines the acts by which men imposed patriarchy, he himself overlooks sexual interests? He makes certain observations about the sexuality he thinks characterized prehistory that are certainly relevant to the story of the introduction of patriarchy. But then he seems to forget all about them. When he comes to tell that story, he fails to pick up the thread of any one of these speculations.

In the days before patriarchy, as you probably know, the brother of any woman who bore children was the man who shared, with her, responsibility for those children. Reich remarks of the brother in those days that he was "the real husband of the sister except for the genital relationship". He also speaks of legends that refer to a time when brother and sister lived together in incest; and he makes the assumption that at the stage of savagery, people did live in incest—"without being in the least harmed by it". But there began to be restrictions upon genital freedom, he says. The first such restriction was "the prohibition of the sexual embrace within one's own clan, i.e. with all maternal kin". The process of sexual suppression, he suggests, "is older than the 'class conflict' between man and woman and is the cause of this antagonism". Here are a series of observations that one wouldn't suppose he would be likely to forget having made....

If Reich believed that the primary source of antagonism between man and woman was primitive woman's refusal of her brother's embrace, and if he saw the mother's brother during matriarchal times as a kind of husband to her, *except* for this embrace, why didn't it interest him to speculate upon the sexual feelings of the mother's brothers during the time that patriarchy was gaining its victory? As Reed puts it, the victory of patriarchy was "the victory of father right over mother's brother right". The father has to "usurp the long-established primacy of the mother's brother....Only when the mother's brother relinquished all claims to his sister's son could the father acquire it as his 'own' ". Although Reed speaks of "a struggle" here "between two categories of men", every man involved in the struggle of course (or surely almost every man) belonged to both categories—was mother's brother to one woman, mother's mate to another. So what the victory of patriarchy actually meant was that one man after another made a choice: he chose a husband's and a "father's" rights over a brother's rights; he chose the identity of husband and "father" over the identity of brother. As Reed does write, the brother's relinquishing of his claim "required that [he] abandon his sister and sister's children and 'cleave' to his wife and wife's children". I would substitute for the word "cleave", of course, the words "take possession of". (As Reed herself notes, "the root word from which the word for father in all the Aryan languages is derived appears to mean nothing but 'owner', and the same applies to the Semitic ab, abu".)

And why did Reich prefer *not* to speculate upon the sexual interests of the men who chose as they did? I think that the answer is obvious. If he were to look very closely at the act by which prehistoric men sought for themselves a new identity, a new self regard, he would be looking very closely—too closely for comfort—at the very act by which he himself (by which any man) *still* seeks his pride. Reich claimed that Engels was unable to think clearly enough about the part played in history by sexuality because his concept of sexuality considered the function of procreation but left untouched "the function of genital gratification". But I would say that Reich, too, was unable to think about it clearly enough, because he couldn't quite make himself look at the truth that for patriarchal man genital gratification requires the gratification of false pride.

Marxists to date have sought "the ultimate cause and the great moving power of all historical events in the economic development of society". (The words are Engels'.) But we do *not* subsist upon bread alone. I keep remembering a passage in the title essay of Andrea Dworkin's *Our Blood*— an essay subtitled *The Slavery of Women In Amerika*. She writes that black slavery was an outgrowth of that older form of slavery, the slavery of women to men. (I very much agree with her.) And she writes, "The white man perpetuated his view of female inferiority in the institution of black slavery. The value of the black male slave in the market place was double the value of the black female slave; his labor in the field or in the house was calculated to be worth twice hers". You will remember Sojourner Truth's words about working as hard and ably as any man. And slave women gave birth to additional slaves. I'd say that their economic worth to the slave owner was clearly *greater* than that of male slaves. Or rather, it was so, but it was not clear that it was so; it was not allowed to be clear. Man does not subsist upon bread alone; he subsists also upon pride. And he has chosen to construct his pride upon the lie that men and women are very different from one another, and that men are of greater worth.

Shulamith Firestone has dared to propose a concept of dialectical materialism wider than the original Marxist concept—one that incorporates the view that to understand history we have to study economic developments, but names the *primary* moving power behind historic events "the dialectic of sex". Only a woman could have proposed this revision of Marx, I think. And most men will find it difficult to accept. For any scrupulous study of sexual dialectics will confront them again and again with evidence that the pride which sustains them is the product of a series of lies. And these lies are still, tragically, experienced as necessary.

They *live* by the lie that a man has the "right" to think of a child as "his", of a woman as "his". We speak of a shift from "Mother Right" to "Father Right", but women never claimed the "right" to children that men now claim. As Reed and others make clear, a child was once viewed as collectively born to the entire maternal clan. Every nursing mother might participate in suckling a baby. Before patriarchy, no one was thought of as the property of another. But the lie is now that children belong to their fathers—or should not exist, are "illegitimate". And the lie is that those who give birth to men belong to men. Transparent lies. And yet—they have been insisted upon for centuries. And the lie is that men and women are altogether different, one from another. Again, a transparent lie. For how could it be so—when the one is made of the very flesh and blood of the other? But again, it is insisted upon. It is even insisted upon that the male is not *really* born of the mother. The patriarchal church teaches: everything *really* "proceedeth from the Father and the Son". Do not ask how. The lie at the very heart of masculine pride is this: that the mother is not really the mother; the mother is unnecessary.

That we are all born of our mothers is so obviously true that I have to keep reminding myself of how true it also is that we are taught to deny it—and really do deny what our very bodies remember to be undeniably so. "The one unifying, incontrovertible experience shared by all women and men," Adrienne Rich names it in *Of Woman Born*. And yet—this experience that is incontrovertible *is* controverted—stubbornly, continually. Rape is an act by which men violently refuse to remember that the place they batter is the place that gave them birth. Praying to "Our Father who art in Heaven" is an act that more subtly erases memory of the mother. (Try the words, pretending that you believe in them, and see what becomes of that memory.) Under patriarchy, woman is acknowledged as wife, and woman is acknowledged as servant to the child; but we are taught and taught to suppress the memory that she is truly mother—that is, that we are flesh of her flesh and once literally lived within her. Taught to suppress it even though this suppression causes us to live in a state of fear.

A few months ago I was discussing feminism with a young man who had been a companion in the struggles of the sixties. He seemed to me, for various reasons, a man who would be open to feminist thought. But I kept finding in him strong resistance to it. It slowly became clear to me that he shared a fear that affects very many men—the fear that feminists would really like, if they could, to kill off men. It occurred to me to say to him, "There is a lot of anger against men among us, but you don't have to be afraid that we want to eliminate men. Don't forget that women give birth to men." I saw on his face a look of utter astonishment and clear relief. He had, I think, quite forgotten that this is so.

Men have for a long time now tried to live by the lie that "man" is self-made—the mother not really the mother, the source of his life not really the source of his life. (The final image in the movie *Dr. Strangelove* has always seemed to me an inspired image of this false pride: a man straddling a nuclear bomb as it falls from the bomb bay, whooping like a proud cowboy, feeling himself to be altogether "himself" now, altogether *A Man*—as he blows from under him the very earth itself without which he could have no being.) The masculine identity is built upon lies which are sexual lies. And so men will resist studying the dialectic of sex. But as long as this dialectic remains unexamined, the real place of women in history will remain invisible—our oppression obscured, and the means of our release from oppression obscured too. Man will remain master—of a world he is laying waste beneath him.

Firestone writes of Marx and Engels that though they grounded their theory in reality, it was only a partial reality. I deeply agree with her. And I believe it is for women to ground it truly at last. By insisting: We belong in history, too. You have stolen us from ourselves. We do *not* exist for your pride to feed upon. We are who we are.

But suddenly I can hear your voice—raised in an objection. I can hear you saying: "We are who we are, you say. Yet all you keep talking about it how men deny that the mother is really the mother. Women are not all mothers, and women are not simply mothers". No, we are not. I am a woman who has never borne a child and I am, like you, a lesbian. So I really do hear your voice—hear it in imagination. But when men claimed women as their "rightful" property, and in doing so denied, in effect, that they were flesh of their mothers' flesh; when they redefined us as less real than they, real only *as* their property—they of course stole from us much more than our reality as childbearers.

They stole from us, for one thing, our reality as creative *workers*. Because we were considered their property now, all work we did was to be taken for granted; was very often not even *seen* as work. It was service due them. We would of course do what they needed us to do. We would of course want to do it. If we didn't choose to labor in this spirit—labor *for them*—we were not to think of ourselves as true women. In the beginning, Evelyn Reed writes in *Women's Evolution,* women's work was *supremely* creative. In fact, she claims, "it created nothing less than the human species". For social labor distinguishes humans from animals; and in the beginning, she argues persuasively, this labor was largely in the hands of women. We took the lead in inventing agriculture ("primitive men thought we possessed magical powers in the growing of food, akin to our powers in growing children"); we took the lead in domesticating animals; and in developing crafts. It was only later that men took over what women had developed. Reed notes that the term for "mother" in some primitive languages can be translated as "producer-procreatrix". Primitive women "were not simply the procreators of new life, the *biological* mothers. They were the prime producers of the necessities of life: the *social mothers*".

When men, moved by jealousy, laid *claim* to our labor—both the labor of childbirth and that labor which creates us as an evolving species—they stole from us, too, of course, the fullness of our sexual natures. We are not supposed to acknowledge as natural to us any feelings, any actions that are not in men's service. For example, those of us who are mothers and those of us who are lesbians are supposed to feel that we are utterly different from one another. And too often we do feel just as we are expected to—even when one of us happens to be both a mother and a lesbian. But before the time of patriarchy, being a mother did not mean that one belonged to a man— had *better* belong to a man; and for a woman to be both a mother and a lover of other women would have been felt as no contradiction at all. We are who we are—when we don't feel constrained to see ourselves with the eyes of our masters. And surely we once experienced it as quite natural to move toward man *or* woman sexually....Reed, though she is often wonderfully bold about using her own eyes, falters here, not quite able to refuse the patriarchal view that women's sexuality is for men only. Primitive women, she says, segregated themselves after childbirth for very long periods, even for years. She puzzles over this: "How is it to be explained?...it is highly unlikely that savage women...consciously repressed their sexual desires. The terms 'abstinence' or 'continence', so frequently used by anthropologists, are misleading because they imply such suppression". She decides: "The conclusion to be drawn is that savage women felt minimal sexual desires or perhaps none at all during those periods when they segregated themselves". It is not a conclusion that I draw. I conclude—wouldn't you?— that they took other women as their lovers.

Reich, too, resists the thought that we were once this freely sexual. And this leads him, too, to musings I would call fanciful. In one passage in *The Invasion of Compulsory Sex Morality,* he is trying to guess at the origin of the taboo upon the genital embrace between sister and brother. He writes that the primeval hordes were of course nomadic hunters, and often "the young men had to go off hunting and live in abstinence, wandering about for weeks, perhaps for months. When such a horde of hunting men came upon a strange tribe living at peace...the intruders would seize what the peaceful tribe had gathered...and they would steal the women, the men's sisters, in order to embrace them, to which they were especially incited by their abstinence. If they emerged victorious, it was easy to enslave the vanquished men, to prohibit them the genital embrace with their own sister-wives". Engels writes that before patriarchy slavery did not exist, and Reich tends to agree with what Engels writes, so I was surprised to see him take it for granted that the men would be quick to enslave the others. I was surprised, too, to see him assume that they lived in sexual abstinence during their long hunting trips. I assume that they took one another as lovers.

I make my own assumptions, here, you'll notice, and feel very sure of myself in making them. How can I feel so sure, when both Reed and Reich, who would disagree, are learned about prehistory and I am not? I don't think that it requires scholarship to discover that, if we refuse to *suppress* our desires, we are just as inclined to desire those of our own sex as to desire those of the so-called "opposite" sex. Both Reed and Reich do suppose that it was "highly unlikely" that primitive peoples suppressed their sexual desires. There is a saying, "The history of the individual repeats the history of the race". *You* will agree with me, I'm sure, that very many women and men, in telling the stories of their lives, could tell of recognizing at a late date that they had *always* felt desire for those of their own sex, but early in life had learned to refuse to admit it—to refuse to allow themselves to "experience their own experience". (The phrase is Mary Daly's.) Under patriarchy, we are not supposed to belong to ourselves. We are supposed to "know" that we belong to men. (And men who desire other men are supposed to "know" that their "manhood" requires the subjection of women.)

Which brings me full circle in my reponse to the objection I imagined you voicing: the objection that women are not simply mothers. No, we are not simply mothers. But the very act by which men try to take possession of us, and to pretend that our sexuality is there for men only—and so brand lesbians as outlaws; this same act is the act by which they try to pretend that mothers are not really mothers, our sexuality merely passive. I wrote that in the act of rape men refuse to remember that the place they batter is the place that gave them birth. But I could well have added that in the act of "making love" men are supposed to refuse to remember this, too. Ellen Moers in the last chapter of *Literary Women,* noting that all the terms for women's sex have been fabricated by the male mind, comments upon the term "vagina". The word is Latin for sheath or scabbard. The mind that chose it chose to disregard the fact that "as passageway to life for the newborn infant, the canal walls miraculously stretch and expand as no scabbard or sheath can do". The word dictates that we think of that passageway as "a tight receptacle for the male organ, visualized as a sword". The choice of this one word exposes the lie by which the artificial self known as "man" has been produced. A lie that is murderous—as the word's evocation of a sword thrust into a woman's body concedes. A lie that has robbed both women and men of our true sexuality.

Our very earliest sensual feelings are of course feelings that we have as infants toward our mothers. And these are feelings which must contain actual memories—not mental, perhaps, but bodily memories—of dwelling within her body, and at peace with her; aware of our own heart beat but also of hers; aware of the life within us, but aware, too, of life not ours with which we are intimately linked. As a baby suckles, it must drink these memories with its mother's milk. And these are memories that are the same for us whether we are female or male. I have come to believe that, for all of us, women and men, this earliest sense experience is the only *natural* source for later sexual feelings: the experience of remembering, as we touch or are touched, that we are our own self but not this self alone; a single life but also life beyond our life. The bodily memory of this literal fact not rejected but recollected and recollected, and as it were mused upon without words—this is what natural sexuality would be. Not the illusion of proudly "taking", or of being taken by, one who is one's "opposite". A rejoicing in the fact that (whatever our gender; and gender would not divide us), we are kindred, linked to one another and to all of nature. I don't of course mean that the relation of an infant to its mother should be a *model* for an adult relation. For the infant is altogether dependent. I mean very simply that *the child's very body remembers truths which we later repress at our peril. And patriarchy has insisted that we repress them.* Adrienne Rich writes in *Of Woman Born,* "Perhaps all sexual or intimate physical contact brings us back to that first body". Would that it did. Our illness is that we do not allow it. (I don't mean that I think Rich would disagree.)

In the ancient myth in which Persephone is stolen from Demeter, her mother—stolen underground—the result is winter. We have all of us been stolen from our mothers. Patriarchy is our long winter. And perhaps our first task is simply to recover those memories which were rapt from us when we were stolen by the patriarchs, claimed as their possessions. Robin Morgan in her poem *The Network of the Imaginary Mother,* in which she, too, tries to imagine our true natures, asks, "What do you remember? What is it that you long for still?" I think she asks the crucial question. It is a question we must learn to put not simply to our intellects but to our very bodies. I deeply agree with Adrienne Rich when she writes that we must stop trying to think from somewhere *outside* of our bodies, must begin at last to think *through* our bodies. For the lies by which the patriarchs produce themselves—produce themselves as masters (each to be formally addressed as just that—for the dictionary tells me that Mister is but a variant of Master)—these lies are very specifically *lies about our bodies.* The actual physical assaults—the rapes, the batterings which we have had to endure from them—are logical extensions of their attempt to deny in imagination that they are born of our bodies' labor, not of their masterful own selves. The memory that they violently repress—the memory of dwelling within our mothers—teaches us that we are kindred. If our sexuality were allowed to be natural, each movement of desire would stir that memory, reaffirm that truth. The repression of that memory divides us from one another.

Engels writes that class oppression is the result of division of labor. I think it more accurate to say that it is the result of a supposed division of our natures. He writes, with Marx, that the first division of labor was that between man and woman for child breeding. There are very many divisions of labor that have distorted human lives; but that first division of labor happens to be natural. (I am assuming that by the term "child breeding" he means simply that, and not also the *rearing* of children.) Is he naming the man's contribution labor, as well as the woman's—the division being that it is labor of a different kind? Or does he mean that the woman's body alone must *work* to produce a child? I would be intrigued to know. But whatever he means, the "division" that he is writing about here is a natural one. If it were indeed the inevitable source of class oppression, the outlook for an end to oppression would be bleak. I think that Engels does *almost* name the source of our oppression. I think that he looks at it, almost but not quite seeing it. It isn't because the breeding of children involves unequal labor; it's because men once did not know that they played any part in it at all, experienced the difference between us as a division not of labor but of fundamental being—it's because of this, my guess is, that they tried to annex us to themselves, and oppression began here. Because, in their ignorance, they felt themselves to be essentially different—not quite flesh of their mothers' flesh, after all, *less* than us—they tried to distort the "difference" that was a cause of humiliation into a "difference" on which their pride could feed; chose to assert: *"Women* are less than *men;* for they are at our service; they exist only to help us be what we wish to be". The will to negate the selfhood of others, to turn others into slaves, began here. (Engels writes that the first class oppression *coincided* with the oppression of woman by man, in monogomous marriage. I would say that he avoids stating the obvious: that the first class oppression *was* this oppression.)

Divisions of labor can be natural. The "first division of labor" is. And Engels himself says that at certain times, under certain historical conditions, other divisions of labor are natural, in the sense of necessary. He adds that they are always perpetuated by violence and fraud after they have stopped being necessary. This happens, I would say, because men persist in asserting that there is a division of *being* that is natural—the division between "men" and "women"; by which they insist upon meaning: a division between "masters", whose lives are real lives, and those of us whose lives are (supposedly) real only as we help these "masters" to become what they wish to be. Divisions of labor are sometimes natural; but the division of being is never natural. And I would name the attempt to assert that it *is* natural the continuing source of class oppression—and the source of all divisions of labor that do distort our lives. Engels writes that the early communal society, the gens, was burst asunder, *I* would say, by the denial that we are of one nature.

Reed describes how in the maternal gens soon after a child's birth, the women would sit in a circle and the child would be passed around the circle, each woman holding it for a while. The child would then have been born to them all, born into the clan—whether girl child or boy child, one of them now, nobody's possession, but simply kin to all. No, we cannot turn the clockback to matriarchy. And no, I would not want to. Clearly enough there was not the fullness of equity at that time. Men did not sit in that circle; did not know how like they were to women, how *altogether* kin we are. (They felt it perhaps as children, then learned to doubt it.) But I do agree with Morgan (and with Engels) that the truly equitable society would be a revival of that ancient society in a higher form. For the beauty of the maternal gens was that there were no owners, no owned. The lie that one person can possess another person had not yet been fabricated.

What is the revolution that we need? I would say: We need to dissolve the lie that some people have a right to think of other people as their property. And we need at last to form—as welcome to our children—a circle that includes us all, in which all of us are seen as equal. How do we learn to do that?

I think that we have to *begin* by trying to form again a kinship circle that is simply a circle of women and of children. I don't think that we can form that necessary larger circle, which includes men, until we have found our courage to assert with great clarity (and of course with more than words) that we do not *belong* to men. If only the men who felt unequal in that ancient society had known to alter it by insisting, "We, too, should be in the circle that welcomes the newborn". If only they had known that they could insist, "We are not that different from you". But they altered their situation instead by bursting the circle asunder. By teaching each child: "You belong to *me* now". And by forcibly teaching each woman: "You do not belong among your sisters; you belong to *me*". So we have to learn first to assert: "No, we do not belong to you. We are who we are".

And to truly learn who we are, we have to turn to one another again. We do not belong *to* others, but our lives are linked; we belong in a circle of others. We learn best to listen to our own voices if we are listening at the same time to other women—whose stories, for all our differences, turn out, if we listen well, to be our stories too. Their anger, which they begin to acknowledge, we recognize as our anger; the strength which they have doubted, but which that very anger hints at, is our strength too.

In the early days of this second wave of the feminist struggle, very many women who had never before really listened to other women began to—formally and informally, in planned consciousness-raising sessions and spontaneously; to listen to friends, to strangers, to themselves; seeming, often, to hear themselves *as* other women spoke. And talking with one another at last, more and more of us began to dare to believe that we can decide for ourselves who we are; we don't need to look to men to define us, by giving us approval or disapproval. We belong to ourselves—we begin to dare to remember this.

Jung writes that there are memories which belong not to any individual but to the race. And it may be so. Perhaps as we sat together in these new circles of women, remembering together who we were, we began even to remember the long-ago—to remember, with that part of the brain which is nonverbal, not only our individual earliest experience (of drawing life itself from a woman—our flesh knowing well enough that woman's power), but also the earliest experience of the race—an experience, too, of knowing well women's strength.

I don't mean that this kind of remembering was the *subject* of our talk. Our talk was above all about our present slavery. I mean that as we spoke together of our slave state—daring to name it that, daring to trust ourselves to one another as we described our lives—we may well have begun to recover those strengthening memories without even knowing them for what they were.

Whether or not you give any credence to race memories, we did at any rate trust ourselves to one another, and we did begin to feel our strength. It was declared that "sisterhood is powerful". And for a while everyone assented. In the early days of our struggle, when those words were popular, very many women, I think, had for a while the feeling that we couldn't be stopped; tasted, at least, that feeling—that more and more of us were waking up; that we were more than half the human race (the other less-than-half unable to function without us, though they tried to pretend that they could; just let us go on strike!); and now that we had recognized one another *as* sisters, we could communicate with one another so swiftly, almost wordlessly—often upon first meeting—that we couldn't lose our struggle; we might even win it very soon. Carol Hanisch of Redstockings has written (in *Feminist Revolution*), "We thought it would only be a matter of a few years before we would have male supremacy conquered". Very many women, I think, had at least a taste of feeling that.

But then—many women had another experience that followed upon this, painfully. The magic seemed to fail. Communication wasn't that easy. The differences between us began to seem terribly real and to complicate everything. Lesbians began saying that they couldn't talk with "straight" women; "straight" women began saying that they couldn't talk with lesbians. Many women began to feel that class differences divided us. Few of us any longer enjoyed that luxurious feeling that we were sure to win, perhaps even soon. "In retrospect," Hanisch wrote, the idea sounded "a little naive— silly almost".

Naive it was, of course, of all of us—not to anticipate how easily still we could be splintered. But I don't think that the idea was silly. I think that our experience of optimism is one that we should be careful not to forget. If enough of us were able to hold steadily to certain truths, we *could* end male supremacy swiftly. And when we tasted that optimism I think that we were in touch with those truths. But we were in touch with them too simply feelingly. We didn't fully know what it was that we knew. And so we could too easily be frightened into doubting that we knew it.

I think I can hear your voice: "This is precisely why we need the discipline of dialectics—an analytical method". But I have to respond: My anxiety is that if women adopt the method of dialectics as it is now taught, it will not help them to grasp the truths I am talking about. It will distract them from these truths. I think, in fact, that this has already been happening. The method of dialectics, as you know, puts great stress upon the need to identify the contradictions in a situation. I think that under the influence of Marxist thinking, in awe of it, women have sought to name the contradictions in *our* situation, and in this very process have surrendered our strength—calling into question that assumption of commonality among us which we had begun to dare to make, and which is just what was putting us in touch with our strength.

Let me say quickly that I do not mean that I think the theory of contradictions is a useless theory—the idea that "there is internal contradition in every single thing, hence its motion and development" (the words are Mao's); the idea that we should "observe and analyze the movement of opposition in different things and on the basis of such analysis" find the appropriate revolutionary method—a method for *resolving* the contradictions. I think it can be very clarifying to think in these terms. But I also think that when it is the feminist revolution that we are concerned to make, we have to be very very careful to use our own eyes, make our own analysis. In his essay *On Contradiction,* Mao makes the point that we must give especial attention "to the distinction between the principal contradiction and non-principal contradictions. . . .Otherwise we shall make mistakes". In any process, he says, "there is only one principal contradiction that plays the leading role. Once this principal contradiction is grasped, all problems can be readily solved." I have suggested already what seems to me to be the principal contradiction in all our lives. That is the contradiction between the lie men try to live, try to make all of us live—the lie that men and women are of essentially different natures—and the truth that we are of one nature. If we do grasp this as the principal contradiction we have to try to resolve, then what Marxists up til now have spoken of as principal contradictions become non-principal contradictions, and everything shifts.

The Redstockings pamphlet, *Feminist Revolution,* contains in a note a quotation from the 1940 Webster's Collegiate Dictionary: *"Proletary.* L. proletarius, fr proles offspring. In ancient Rome, a citizen of the lowest class, without property and regarded as capable of serving the state only by having children." And then it quotes Catherine Henry, of Red Women's Detachment, who said in 1971: "The word 'proletariat' (from the French) means 'those who breed'. In fact, proletarian women are the proletariat in the proletariat."

But this is what I mean about having to be very careful to use our own eyes. In *fact*—look at the root of the word—*women* are the proletariat; *those who breed are the proletariat.* The proletariat which is women (all women)—

the original proletariat—cannot be said to be contained within the proletariat as Marxists have defined it up until now. The one concept cracks the other concept wide open.

And this is what I mean when I say that I worry about our being in too much awe of Marxist thinking. Catherine Henry looks right at the words "those who breed". But she doesn't trust herself to write "Women are the proletariat". She feels that she *has* to write that *proletarian* women are the proletariat *within* the proletariat. But until we dare to write "Women—all women—are the proletariat", I am afraid that we will remain the underclass that we are. We will remain splintered—divided from one another. And we will fail to make the revolution.

What I have just said, I know, is shocking. To accept this new definition of the proletariat, we would have to look at everything differently. I think that we do have to look at everything differently.

You will ask: Do I think, then, that when Marxists define class struggle as they do they are not describing reality? I think that they are describing reality. But only a partial reality. I would say that they are describing the struggle of *men* who refuse to be the property of others. And they are describing the struggle of women in so far as it coincides with the struggle of men. But I'll repeat: the struggle of women cannot be said to be contained within that struggle. The most oppressed laboring man can go home to "his" woman and show her who's "the man". The most privileged woman can walk down the street and be taught that lesson by a whistle—as we all know. Engels himself, of course, wrote that in the family the wife is the proletariat, the husband the bourgeoisie. But then he forgot that he had said this, seen this. I am daring to say that the class struggle as Marxists have described it is a struggle to resolve a contradiction less fundamental than the contradiction the feminist struggle can resolve. I know this is heresy. It's the man's game that is supposed to matter. There was a piece in the February 6th, 1977, *New York Times* magazine section called "The Clubs Griffin Bell Had To Quit." It reported that in one of these men's clubs wives and children of members are given privileges; but "should a group of men wish to use a tennis court on which women are playing, the men simply step onto the court, say, 'Thank you very much, ladies', and the women depart". I think that most radical men take a very comparable attitude toward women engaged in making revolution. And I think it is time that women refused to get off the court.

I will probably be accused not only of heresy but of introducing impossible confusion. If I say that the class oppression Marxists have defined is a reality, but that the oppression of all women by men must be seen as a reality more fundamental (the reality from which all other oppression derives)—how can one any longer make neat distinctions between oppressors and oppressed? Won't it often happen that we would have to name the very same person both an oppressed person and an oppressor? Yes, it will very often happen. Life is precisely that complicated. And to pretend that it isn't that complicated doesn't help. We need rescue from neat distinctions that are illusions. Patriarchy is founded upon them.

But if we can't distinguish tidily between oppressor and oppressed, how can we possibly wage battle—without destroying comrades as we strike at enemies? I think this is a question that troubles very many women, whether or not they have put it to themselves as a conscious question. And I think the answer that can be given has been obscured, again, by the fact that many of us are hypnotized by the already existing tradition of Marxist struggle. If our struggle against patriarchal oppression were simply to imitate the forms that class struggle has taken so far, the battle scene *would* be a scene of confusion. And I'd suggest that this is one reason so many women still hang back from battle. But Mao has again written something that is relevant. He says, "the methods of resolving contradictions, that is, the forms of struggle, differ according to the difference in the nature of the contradictions". If the fundamental contradiction that has to be resolved is, as I think it is, the contradiction between the lie that men and women are of different natures and the truth that we are of one nature, the truth that no human being should be thought of as The Other, then the appropriate form of struggle is surely that form still largely to be invented: nonviolent struggle. One can't prove a common nature with others by doing violence to them. And again: if the complicated truth is that many of the oppressed are also oppressors and many of the oppressors are also oppressed, nonviolent confrontation is the only form of confrontation that allows us to respond realistically to such complexity. In this kind of struggle we address ourselves always both to that which we refuse to accept from others and to that which we can respect in them, have in common with them—however much or little that may be.

I know that you have declared your belief in armed struggle. And I imagine that, with many others, you see nonviolent struggle as essentially passive—a form of appeal, really, rather than a form of struggle. Just the behavior the patriarchs would like to have us adopt—very lady-like; inspiring; and ineffectual. But the strike is not a passive form of behavior. It has a power that I don't think you will deny. And to struggle nonviolently is to go on strike. If enough women ever really went on strike—refusing the roles that have been assigned to us, insisting on roles of our own choosing—everything, everything would have to change.

To struggle nonviolently is also, of course, to refuse to reply in kind when there is retaliation. This is what is seen as passive. But I would argue that it can be a much more passive, much more desperate act *to* reply in kind—to accept as one's own the oppressor's vision that there is nothing at all to prevent us from trying to destroy one another.

In nonviolent struggle, we seek to hold in mind both contradiction and commonality. We refuse to cooperate with that which is in contradiction to our deep needs; and we speak to that commonality linking us all which, if remembered, can inhibit the impulse to destroy. A nonviolent dialectic— that is the dialectic that I do think accords with feminism and that we must try to invent. We will be called violent, of course. For though I would define our struggle with men as an insistence upon the fact that women and men are alike in nature, ironically, the very attempt to insist upon this will lead again and again to our having to adopt a temporary separatism. If men refuse to relate to us in any but the old ways, our only means of making our point is often to refuse, until they change, to relate to them at all. And there are many men who will interpret this as our wishing them dead. There are many men on the Left who will interpret it in this way. Which complicates our making alliances with them—even when such alliances, if possible, would gain all of us much.

I think we have to beware of naming the alliances more urgent than the feminist struggle. I think—as I started earlier to say—that the most urgent action for us to take is that of forming a strong kinship circle of women. Once enough of us are firm in our refusal to be treated by men as their property, men will begin at last to relate to us in another way. (They'll find that this answers not only to our deep needs but to their own—to relate to us not as masters but simply as kin.) But most of us will only find the courage to refuse the old, the demeaning relation if we have the company of other women. In the old relation, we allow men to define us. And though the definition that they give us grotesquely constricts us, it does give us a place in the world as it is. A narrow place. But we know that place. We have—if we behave ourselves—the security of the beloved house slave. To refuse that place is to step into the unknown. We risk doubting that we live anywhere at all. It has been so many centuries, after all, since we were our own women.

But what I have just written falls short actually of describing women's situation. It is not simply that, like other servants, we are taught to know our place, to pay attention to the wishes of the master and learn to keep our own feelings to ourselves. Other servants lead double lives—the lives of their masters and (though there's little enough time for it) their own. But we are taught from childhood on that a woman's fulfilment is to utterly merge her life with that of the man who chooses her to be his (or with that of the son she bears him; or even with the boss who hires her); taught that we only become our true selves, "true women", when we surrender our selves in this way. If we rebel, it is not only that we risk doubting that we any longer have our place in the world; we risk doubting that we have any identity at all.

This is why I would call the rediscovery of sisterhood our most urgent task. In one another's company we begin to dare to believe that we belong to nobody and can create ourselves. We begin to dare to refuse the lies the masters have expected us to live by, and to listen to the truths our own experience contains. The experience of our sisters confirms ours. We begin to dare to presume to trust our own eyes.

But this trust in ourselves is tentative. To feel it—to feel it sometimes very strongly—is such a new experience for us that we can think it reliable. But it easily fails us. And nothing can more quickly cause it to evaporate than harsh judgements upon us made by other women.

I can remember still my feelings two years ago when I read an editorial in *Off Our Backs* which warned that we had better learn *to* make harsh judgements—warned of our "having to be careful about who we called 'sister' ". I can remember still the constriction in the pit of my stomach as I read those words. The constriction was sudden terror. Terror for the women's movement. And for my self. Within this movement I had begun for the first time in my life to feel that I was allowed to be openly just the person I really was; to decide for myself who I was; and to act upon this. I had felt encouraged to believe that to take this extraordinary freedom—in the company of other women—was in fact to make the revolution. But this freedom was being taken away again. I had to fear again—we all had to fear—being labelled, being found unfit. I think a great many women experienced this shock. I don't mean of course upon reading the editorial in *Off Our Backs*. But each in her own way first experienced sisterhood, and then the sudden fear that she could be told that she was *not* a sister. The fear that she had better stop trying to use her own eyes and instead to try to make sure of saying or doing what a sister "should" say or do. I think as more and more of us received this shock, we began to lose our collective strength.

And as I said earlier, I think that the influence upon us of Marxist thinking had much to do with this—the tradition that says we must be careful to give just the name it deserves to every differing tendency among us. I don't mean to say that there are not very real differences among us. And I don't mean to say that I think we should overlook them. I think it is very very necessary to learn from one another under what varying conditions we live our slave lives. If we don't learn this, we will constantly be hurting one another—failing to imagine the specific difficulties that face us in one condition or another; the specific fears that make it hard to take the actions that can free us. But the longer we listen to one another—with real attention—the more commonality we will find in all our lives. That is, if we are careful to exchange with one another life stories and not simply opinions. If we adopt the mode that is now traditional for consciousness-raising: take turns speaking, speak from experience, don't interrupt, and don't deliver judgements upon one another. This mode of relating can work a kind of magic.

I think of the split between lesbians and heterosexual women. Each group has felt that it was oppressed by the other; felt on many painful occasions that the other would like to exclude it from the revolution. And yet when women from both groups have dared to believe in the possibility that—by listening to one another—they could find much common ground, they have found that ground. I used to especially seek out lesbian groups at women's conferences. Now I often don't bother to. I now know that a woman who is not a lesbian can learn to identify with me not simply by listening to me as I tell of my life, but by listening to her own self as she is telling me of hers. If, say, she is the mother of a daughter, and allows herself to recall freely how she felt toward her daughter as an infant, she may recall that those feelings were clearly sexual; and as she recalls this, may recognize herself in me. I will as often recognize myself in her. If she tells me, say, of feeling like a failed woman upon hearing that her husband has been unfaithful, I who have never had a husband will recognize that I have known the very feeling she reports—every time a man's glance has labelled me one who does not answer to his needs, a "queer". (I have known better than to feel a failed woman at such moments, but—a slave still—have felt it in spite of myself, to my rage.)

Class differences are the differences that have made it most difficult for us to identify with one another. Here we have felt most hypnotized by the Marxist analysis—fearful to commit the act of faith that there is commonality among us; fearful that such an act of faith would be "incorrect", even counter-revolutionary. And yet—it is really only men who belong to the various "classes"; women belong to these classes by belonging to the men. Chesler writes in *Women, Money and Power:* "As many women of the Watergate crisis have shown us, Great Ladies are always one man away from 'the top'—and one man away 'from welfare' ". And Andrea Dworkin writes in her essay *Phallic Imperialism: Why Economic Recovery Will Not Work For Us:* "Everywhere...the female is kept in captivity by the male, denied self-determination so that he can control her reproductive function, fuck her at will, and have his house cleaned. (When the man is rich, his wife does not clean the house; instead she is turned into an ornament, a decoration, and used as a symbol of his wealth....)" She writes, "The phenomenon of the lady is a bizarre variation on a consistently cruel theme". We all really know this. A glance in the street from a man of any class can let a women of any "class" know her true status.

There have been many discussions of class among us, and from them we have learned a great deal about one another. Yet these exchanges have sometimes been so painful that the women involved have then split apart. My guess is that it has most often been indirectly that we have closed this particular distance between us—as we exchanged stories of sexual experience, and came more and more to recognize that these stories show all of us to be servants to men. Their servants or, if we refuse to be their servants, outlaws.

I think that the consciousness-raising session is the basic building block of our revolution. The more we describe our lives to one another, and to ourselves, the more we allow ourselves to acknowledge the real feelings that we have experienced—the more we realize that the condition of all women is essentially the same condition; and that we could act together to refuse that condition.

But it does take a kind of faith to sit together and confide our lives to one another in this way: the faith that we won't find that we have exposed ourselves only to be suddenly rejected. I think that the women's movement needs a kind of Law of Return—like the law that says any Jew anywhere can find a welcome in Israel. I think that any woman who decides she lives in slavery and wants to deliver herself from that slavery should know that she will be welcomed as a sister by other women making the same struggle. If she takes a few steps toward freedom and becomes frightened and retreats, she should know that she will be welcomed back into the struggle whenever she finds her courage again. She is much more likely to find it if she does know this. She should know that she would be welcomed back any number of times, never told "You cannot be one of us".

I am not saying that we can trust all sisters to do us no harm. We begin, all of us, in a state of fear; we begin having been trained to give obedience to men, on fear of punishment. So we have to *learn* to relate to one another as free spirits. The trust that I think we have to dare to give is the trust that we *can* learn, are trying to. There are sure to be many instances in which we do each other injury. When any woman feels that she has been injured she should speak of it. Though I recommend naming the injury received rather than trying to name the motives of those who've injured us. It is also only common sense when undertaking certain kinds of actions to choose as companions women with whom we feel at ease. But—very simply—I think no woman should be judged unfit to be seeking her freedom. We learn to be free as we begin to dare to act not as we have been taught that we "should" but—as the Quakers say—according to the light that is in us. That light may still be faint. It is nevertheless the light by which we have to try to see, if we are going to put off slavery. We shouldn't frighten each other into doubting this. The magic of C-R is that because we don't frighten each other into saying simply what we think we should, we do begin to be able to see by our own light. In fear for ourselves, we have kept this light covered. Now we begin to "let it shine"—to steal a phrase from a '60s black freedom song. Sometimes intellect gives us this light; sometimes our very bodies give it. We begin to pay attention to bodily sensations which are comments upon experience; or comments upon words we start to say but realize that we don't mean. And because we speak without fear of one another, and so begin to speak—to know—what has really been true for us, I have never sat in such a circle in which any woman, no matter how new to the struggle, has not had something to tell from which I have learned.

You have objected to what you call the "line" that "anything a woman does should be supported because she is a woman". That would of course be a ridiculous line to follow. But to support the attempt of all women to learn to see with their own eyes—this, I think, is necessary to our revolution. As we give this support, the lives of other women become almost as real to us as our own lives; and our own lives, because of this, become more known to us—our lives, and the needs which those lives have suppressed, which are also the needs of other women. And without even aiming at it directly, we prepare ourselves to take action together—to change our lives, to meet our needs. Action in which we don't take a leader's orders; actions that come to seem irrepressible. None of us trying to pressure any other sister to join us if she is not yet ready; or if, from her perspective, the project makes little sense. Each of us encouraged to act upon her own sense of the truth. More and more confident that what will seem necessary to one will seem necessary to many.

The very same women who will come to trust one another in this way, and find that they can often act together, if they had sat together and exchanged not experiences but opinions, carefully defining their respective political positions, might well have always felt at odds. In a C-R group which I was part of for several years (would still be a part of if I had not moved to another part of the country), a group in which we developed the deepest kind of loving trust in one another, it occurred to us after a number of months together to ask how we would label ourselves politically. Our answers marked us as in total contradiction with one another—some of us radical, some liberal, some conservative. I remember beginning to laugh. For we had been finding that we had more and more in common, and knew by then that we would continue to draw closer to one another. As more months passed, some of us discovered of course that our true political inclinations were more radical than we had known they were.

It is simply more productive, in the feminist struggle, to try to discover commonality among us than it is to try to find contradictions.

Dialecticians have been for the most part men. And under patriarchy men have sought their very identities in terms of contradiction. A "man" is one who is not a woman; not really flesh of a woman's flesh. And so among revolutionaries contradiction has assumed an importance almost hypnotic. I think we have to awaken from this hypnosis. The truth is that we discover ourselves best as we discover how all our lives are linked.

Engels writes that "without contradiction nothing would exist". But one can also say, "Without commonality nothing would exist". In one piece of writing, Engels himself acknowledges this. There is a beautiful passage in the introduction to his *Dialectics of Nature* in which he imagines the end of our world. "Nothing", he says, "is eternal but eternally changing, eternally moving matter and the laws according to which it moves and changes", and however often suns and earths come into being and go out of being, and with them all the innumerable variations of life, "we have the certainty that *matter remains eternally the same in all its transformations,* that none of its attributes can ever be lost", and so however sure it is to exterminate even the highest forms of life, it is also sure to engender them again.

Reading this passage, it struck me that it bore a surprising resemblance to descriptions I had read of the Great Mother, who is Death Mother and Life Mother, both; who experiences innumerable transformations and who remains eternally the same, able always to engender all things over again. In The Mother, all things exist. The words "matter" and "mater" (mother) are of course very close. Something for materialists to muse about, I think. (In the word "materialist", the two words become the same.)

Beyond all contradiction, female and male are matter and are also mater, flesh of their mother's flesh—the male as a fetus in the beginning female, too; then becoming a variation of the female. Until this truth is accepted, the so-called materialist is not really a materialist.

Rich writes in *Of Woman Born,* "The repossession by women of our bodies will bring far more essential change to human society than the seizing of the means of production by workers". I deeply assent. And as long as the bodies of women are held in contempt by most of those who teach dialectics, dialectical materialism will remain an inadequate "tool of liberation".

In sisterhood—
Barbara

We've battened our house against
A hurricane that's gathering,
Whirls near;
Left one small window open to allow ourselves
This much air to breathe
And now we're inside our one-eyed house
Waiting.

It's later. Night. Lamps out.
I sit up in bed in
The unfamiliar
Tight-fitting dark—
Get to my feet.
Shouldn't we do more than wait?
I call to you:
Shouldn't we gather, too?
Shouldn't we, too, whirl?

These winds birth reveling energies
No one can leash.
Let's dare, then, to feel at one with them—
Turn about, too, in the dark,
Spread out our hands and stir the night air—
Musing, as we do, on all that needs disturbing.
Minds set in deadly rigor,
That can't change a deadly course—
We'll disturb them into
New ways of seeing.
Let's turn about and about and about,
Setting our minds wheeling, too;
Gathering within the gathering storm
Our own force.

1981

More Resources From New Society Publishers

"This is the bravest book I have read since Jonathan Schell's FATE OF THE EARTH."—Dr. Rollo May

DESPAIR AND PERSONAL POWER IN THE NUCLEAR AGE
by Joanna Rogers Macy

Despair and Personal Power in the Nuclear Age is the first major book to examine our psychological responses to planetary perils and to lay the theoretical foundations for an empowering, personally-centered approach to social change. Included are sections on awakening in the nuclear age, relating to children and young people, guided meditations, empowered rituals, and a special section on "Spiritual Exercises for a Time of Apocalypse." As described and excerpted in *New Age Journal* and *Fellowship Magazine*. Recommended for public libraries by *Library Journal*; selected for inclusion in the 1984 Women's Reading Program, General Board of Global Ministries, United Methodist Church.

200 pages. Appendices, resource lists, exercises. 1983.
Hardcover: $19.95
Paperback: $8.95

RAINBOWS NOT RADIATION!
BANANAS NOT BOMBS!
GRAPES NOT GUNS!
XYLOPHONES NOT X-TINCTION!

WATERMELONS NOT WAR! A SUPPORT BOOK FOR PARENTING IN THE NUCLEAR AGE
by Kate Cloud, Ellie Deegan, Alice Evans, Hayat Imam, and Barbara Signer;
Afterword by Dr. Helen Caldicott

Five mothers in the Boston area have been meeting regularly for four years, to give each other support, to demystify nuclear technology—weapons and technology—into terms parents, *and children,* can understand, to find ways of acting which will give their children a future. The result is WATERMELONS NOT WAR! A SUPPORT BOOK FOR PARENTING IN THE NUCLEAR AGE.

—As written up in *Ms. Magazine, Whole Life Times, Sojourner.*

Large format. Beautifully illustrated. Annotated Bibliography. 160 pages. 1984.
Hardcover: $19.95
Paperback: $9.95

REWEAVING THE WEB OF LIFE:
FEMINISM AND NONVIOLENCE
edited by Pam McAllister

". . . happens to be one of the most important books you'll ever read."

—The Village Voice

"Stressing the connection between patriarchy and war, sex and violence, this book makes it clear that nonviolence can be an assertive, positive force. It's provocative reading for anyone interested in surviving and changing the nuclear age."

—Ms. Magazine

More than 50 Contributors – Women's History – Women and the Struggle Against Militarism – Violence and Its Origins – Nonviolence and Women's Self-Defense – Interviews – Songs – Poems – Stories – Provocative Proposals – Photographs – Annotated Bibliography – Index

Voted "Best New Book—1983"—*WIN MAGAZINE ANNUAL BOOK POLL*

448 pages.
Hardcover: $19.95
Paperback: $10.95

A MANUAL ON NONVIOLENCE
AND CHILDREN
compiled and edited by Stephanie Judson;
Foreword by Paula J. Paul,
Educators for Social Responsibility

Includes "For the Fun of It! Selected
Cooperative Games for Children and Adults"

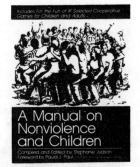

Invaluable resource for creating an atmosphere in which children and adults can resolve problems and conflicts nonviolently. Especially useful for parents and teachers in instilling values today to create the peacemakers of tomorrow!

"Stephanie Judson's excellent manual has helped many parents and teachers with whom we have worked. An essential part of learning nonviolent ways of resolving conflicts is the creation of a trusting, affirming and cooperative environment in the home and classroom. This manual has a wealth of suggestions for creating such an environment. We highly recommend it."

—Jim and Kathy McGinnis,
Parenting for Peace and Justice,
St. Louis, Missouri

Anecdotes, exercises, games, agendas, annotated bibliography.
Illustrated, large format. 160 pages. 1984.
Hardcover: $24.95
Paperback: $9.95

MORE THAN THE TROUBLES: A COMMON SENSE VIEW OF THE NORTHERN IRELAND CONFLICT

by Lynne Shivers and David Bowman, S.J.; foreword by Denis Barritt; afterword by Joseph Fahey, S.J. on "Northern Ireland: Its Relevance for Peace Education".

"No stereotypes about Northern Ireland and its people, its religion, or politics can survive a reading of this carefully constructed account of a packed and eventful history where past and future compete for attention in the present. The juxtaposition of bitter conflict and cooperation makes this story a microcosm of the human condition in this century. The difficult task of documentation is done with loving care. As readers we are at once humbled, sobered, and inspired. . . ."

> —Dr. Elise Boulding, Professor of Sociology, Dartmouth College and the University of Colorado; founder of COPRED (Consortium on Peace Reseach, Education and Development)

Index, appendices, maps, charts, bibliography, photographs. 240 pages. 1984.
Hardcover: $24.95

GANDHI THROUGH WESTERN EYES

by Horace Alexander

"This book stands out as an authoritative guide: clear, simple, and straightforward, both to Gandhi's personality and to his beliefs. As a Quaker, Mr. Alexander found it easy to grasp Gandhi's ideas about nonviolence; the author's prolonged and intimate friendship helped him to know the Mahatma as few men were able to do, and to appreciate that he was something far greater than a national hero of the Indian independence movement—a man, in fact, with a message that is intensely relevant for the world today. Nothing that has so far been published about Gandhi is more illuminating than this careful, perceptive and comprehensive work. It is not only comprehensive—it is convincing."

> —Times Literary Supplement

Letter, Index. 240 pages. 1984.
Hardcover: $24.95
Paperback: $8.95

NO TURNING BACK: LESBIAN AND GAY LIBERATION FOR THE '80S
by Gerre Goodman, George Lakey, Judy Lashof & Erika Thorne;
Foreword by Malcolm Boyd

"No Turning Back fulfills a long felt need for a progressive analysis and pragmatic sourcebook for lesbians, gays and others concerned with replacing patriarchal oppression with a more human alternative. I was quite pleased by the integration of personal statements and experiences into the more theoretical discussion, and by the inclusion of practical and feasible proposals for individual and collective action."

> —Larry Gross, Professor, Annenberg School of Communications, University of Pennsylvania, and Co-Chair, Phila. Lesbian and Gay Task Force

Recommended for public libraries by *Library Journal*.

168 pages.
Hardcover: $16.95
Paperback: $7.95

THE EYE OF THE CHILD
by Ruth Mueller

A brilliant healing myth for a world gone mad!

"Of all the creatures to whom the great mother had given birth all were a part, not apart, but one. Yes all but one flowed as she flowed, born of her womb, dying in her bosom, struggling, true, but never against their own life support. One, only one, capable of standing apart, imagining self above and outside, turning to rend, turning to overpower, to subdue, to conquer the vessel of life itself, creation's own embodiment. Had she not labored for aeons to give birth to a triumph of joy and beauty as fair as dawn, a creature of light to share the glowing consciousness of the whole, one of understanding as deep as her deeps are deep, of laughter as divine as tears and of tears as cleansing as laughter, one who was no alien to mercy, capable of new visions above predation, a familiar to the art of healing, above all a creature of tongues, creation itself no longer mute to express—to express—

"What had gone wrong?"

Ecological speculative fiction of the highest order.

240 pages. 1984.
Paperback: $7.95

WOMEN IN DEVELOPMENT: A RESOURCE GUIDE FOR ORGANIZATION AND ACTION,
by ISIS Women's International Information and Communication Service.

A lavishly illustrated book, with 122 photographs, five years in the making. Women scholars from all over the world contributed to make this one of the most comprehensive and beautiful books of its kind ever published. Sections on women and multinationals, women and rural development, women and health, education, tourism, migration, etc.

Annotated resource lists, bibliographies. 240 pages. 1984.
Hardcover: $39.95
Paperback: $14.95

TWO ESSAYS: ON ANGER and NEW MEN, NEW WOMEN Some Thoughts on Nonviolence

by Barbara Deming

Thought-provoking essays adding new depth to the slogan that 'the personal is political.' Modern classics in the literature of nonviolent struggle, challenging us to recreate ourselves even as we attempt to recreate our world. Originally appeared in Barbara Deming's *We Can Not Live Without Our Lives.*

32 pages 1982. $2.45

RESOURCE MANUAL FOR A LIVING REVOLUTION

by Virginia Coover, Ellen Deacon, Charles Esser and Christopher Moore

The practical tools you need for everything from consciousness raising, working in groups, and developing communities of support to education, training, and organizing skills. Used by women's groups, disarmament and antinuclear activists, and community organizers worldwide. 25,000 copies in print. An activist's dream!

330 pages. Agendas. Exercises. New edition. 1981. $19.95 (hardbound): $7.95 (paperback)

OFF THEIR BACKS . . . AND ON OUR OWN TWO FEET

by Men Against Patriarchy

This pamphlet addressed to men includes three essays: "More Power Than We Want: Masculine Sexuality and Violence," "Understanding and Fighting Sexism," and "Overcoming Masculine Oppression in Mixed Groups."

32 pages. 1983. $2.45

A MODEL FOR NONVIOLENT COMMUNICATION

by Marshall Rosenberg

This groundbreaking work in interpersonal relations helps us more fully open ourselves to give and receive information, share feelings, and overcome blocks to effective communication. It is filled with illuminating examples.

40 pages. 1983. $3.95

To Order: send check or money order to New Society Publishers, 4722 Baltimore Avenue, Philadelphia, PA 19143. For postage and handling: add $1.50 for the first book and 40¢ for each additional book.